Software Engineering and Environment

An Object-Oriented Perspective

Software Science and Engineering

Series Editor: **Richard A. DeMillo**
Purdue University, West Lafayette, Indiana

High-Integrity Software
Edited by C. T. Sennett

Software Engineering and Environment: An Object-Oriented Perspective
Phillip C.-Y. Sheu

Software Reuse: Guidelines and Methods
James W. Hooper and Rowena O. Chester

Studies in Computer Science: In Honor of Samuel D. Conte
Edited by John Rice and Richard A. DeMillo

A Continuation Order Plan is available for this series. A continuation order will bring delivery of each new volume immediately upon publication. Volumes are billed only upon actual shipment. For further information please contact the publisher.

Software Engineering and Environment

An Object-Oriented Perspective

Phillip C.-Y. Sheu

University of California, Irvine
Irvine, California

Springer Science+Business Media, LLC

Library of Congress Cataloging-in-Publication Data

Sheu, Phillip C.-Y.
    Software engineering and environment : an object-oriented
  perspective / Phillip C.-Y. Sheu.
       p.   cm.
    Includes bibliographical references and index.
    ISBN 978-1-4613-7710-8   ISBN 978-1-4615-5907-8 (eBook)
    DOI 10.1007/978-1-4615-5907-8
    1. Software engineering. 2. Object-oriented programming (Computer
  science)   I. Title.
  QA76.758.S475   1997
  005.1--dc21   96-47606
                                                              CIP

ISBN 978-1-4613-7710-8

© 1997 Springer Science+Business Media New York
Originally published by Plenum Press, New York in 1997
Softcover reprint of the hardcover 1st edition 1997

10 9 8 7 6 5 4 3 2 1

Preface

The term *software engineering* has been used extensively in different contexts. In a broader sense, software engineering encompasses every aspect of software systems; these include models, algorithms, programming, and management. Depending on one's interest, different perspectives of software engineering have been produced: project managers have emphasized managerial aspects of software products, programmers efficient programming, and computer scientists modeling and automating the programming process.

This book first introduces a number of software life cycle models and the basic concepts of object-oriented systems. Subsequently it discusses in more detail different phases of a software life cycle, with an emphasis on the object-oriented paradigm: "Formal Specification and Verification" (Chapter 3), "Design Methodologies and Specifications" (Chapter 4), "Programming and Coding" (Chapter 5), "Program Verification and Testing" (Chapter 9), and "Software Maintenance" (Chapter 10). Two of the six phases, namely, the requirement stage and the integration stage, are not covered extensively in separate chapters; rather in Chapter 1, several approaches to software integration are briefly discussed. It is my understanding that these two stages have been less understood in the past and more systematic approaches are yet to be developed. Several managerial issues related to software project management are covered in Chapter 12. Approaches to distributed software development are discussed in each stage whenever possible.

I cover the following subjects in more detail: "Programming Tools" (Chapter 6), "Declarative Programming" (Chapter 7), and "Automatic Program Synthesis and Reuse" (Chapter 8). The roles played by the preceding are shown graphically in the diagram below. With the aid of software libraries, programming tools allow a program to be composed with off-the-shelf modules, fully tested by experts, to increase the productivity of programmers and the quality of the software produced. Automatic program synthesis, although not a reality yet, can provide a shortcut from requirements specifications to maintenance. Declarative programming on the other hand is somewhat less ambitious but may relieve programmers of many implementation details. These chapters summarize the current status of such issues. Chapter 11 covers advanced software engineering environments that span several stages of the software development process; these

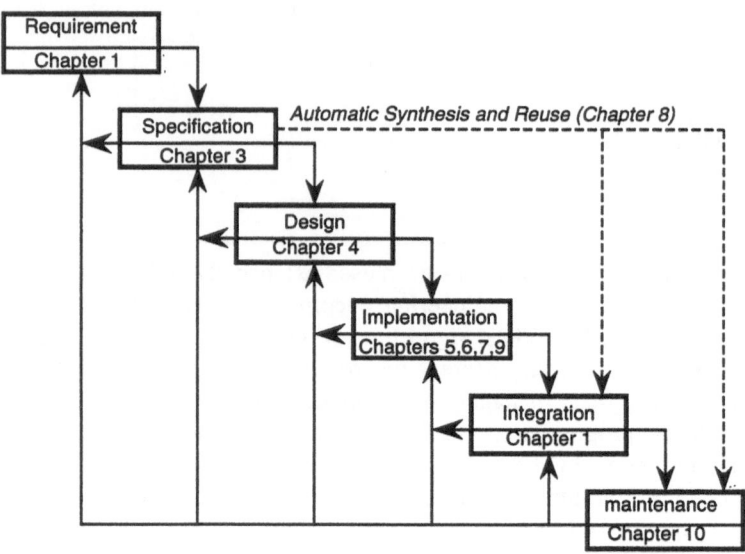

Scope of the book.

include knowledge-based programming environments, visual programming environments, distributed object-oriented programming environments, component software services, and concurrent engineering environments. Chapter 12 discusses issues of interest to software engineers; these include project management, fault-tolerant systems, discrete event simulation, and Internet programming.

I wish to thank Drs. C. V. Ramamoorthy, D. Cooke, R. Reynolds, L. J. Peterson, H. Freeman, T. Kidd, R. L. Kashyap, K. H. Kim, K. C. Tai, F. Calliss, R. DeMillo, P. Dewan, J. Riedl, R. Gordon, D. Yu, D. Lai, and W. T. Tsai for carefully reviewing this book and providing me with many insightful comments.

Although I tried my best to make this book an ideal one, I am sure it is not free of errors, typos, or omissions. I will appreciate it if the reader kindly lets me know of them. Suggestions for improvements will be deeply appreciated as well.

P. C.-Y. Sheu

Irvine, California

Contents

Software Life Cycle Models

The production process of a software system is usually called the *life cycle* of the system. To describe software life cycles, a number of models have been proposed. The earliest may be the *waterfall* model.[1] It describes the software life cycle of a software system in terms of the following steps:

1. *Requirements.* The requirements of the system are informally summarized and analyzed; feasibility of the requirements is assessed, required resources are projected, etc. Requirements must be verified by the client.

2. *Specifications.* In this step requirements for the system are formalized in terms of *inputs, outputs,* and *functionalities,* which define desired relationships between inputs and outputs. In a concurrent system, it is sometimes necessary to specify coordination aspects among different components. In both cases requirements specifications are verified (to eliminate inconsistency, prove that a solution does exist, etc.).

3. *Design.* The architecture of the system is determined, usually through a block diagram. The system, if it is reasonably complicated, in most cases consists of a number of components, called *modules.* Relationships among modules are defined. Functionalities of the modules are further specified. This step is repeated until no further decomposition can be done. The process is a typical instance of *stepwise refinement.*[2] As for requirements, a design specification must be verified (to be consistent, efficient, etc.).

4. *Implementation.* Each module is coded and tested. Implementation can be either top-down, bottom-up, or a mix of both. In the top-down approach, top-level modules are implemented before lower level modules. In the bottom-up approach, lower level modules are implemented first. A program can be formally verified against its requirements, or it can be tested by test cases. To test a module in the top-down approach, lower level modules are assumed to exist and be present as *stubs;* in the bottom-up approach, upper level modules are assumed to exist and be present as *drivers.*

5. *Integration.* Independently implemented modules are integrated in this step. Again, this step can be either top-down, bottom-up, or a mix of

both. In the top-down approach, top-level modules are integrated and tested before lower level modules. In the bottom-up approach, lower level modules are integrated and tested first. Note that in the integration step, drivers or stubs are gradually replaced by real modules. The result of this step should be a functional system.

6. *Maintenance.* As the system is being used, changes may have to be made, and the system may have to be maintained. Common maintenance types include *corrective maintenance* (maintenance due to residual bugs), *perfective maintenance* (maintenance due to upgraded requirements), and *adaptive maintenance* (maintenance due to environmental changes).

The waterfall model is not a linear model; that is feedback is included between two successive steps (see Figure 1.1). Feedback paths are included in the model so that whenever difficulties are found in one step, it may be necessary to go back to the previous step to make corrections. It should be noted however that feedback from the maintenance stage to any previous step may be needed when changes are made to requirements, specification, design, or implementation.

A weakness of the waterfall model is that very often the final product does not address the client's expectations. This is due to the fact that specifications can be very involved and difficult to follow for an untrained person. Many times the

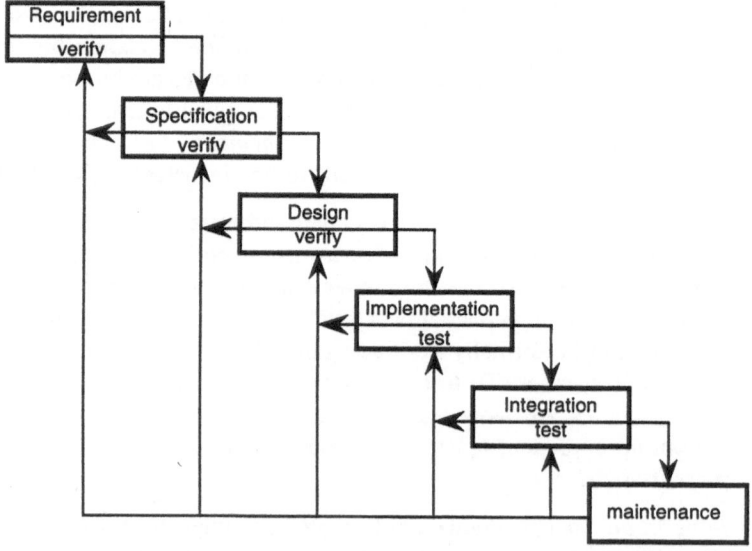

Figure 1.1. The waterfall model.

client approves the specification even though he/she does not have a clear picture of the final product. Once a discrepancy is found in a later stage of the life cycle, the cost involved in making changes to the specification and redoing the design and implementation can be very high. These limitations of the waterfall model are addressed in the *rapid-prototyping* model.[3] The initial requirements stage of this model differs from the waterfall model. Here clients are provided with a prototype to have an idea of how the finished product looks. This prototype then goes into a rapid modification stage where it is worked on until it meets the client's needs and expectations. This aspect of the process gives it its descriptive name.

Prototypes are constructed rapidly, and they only roughly resemble the finished product. The only purpose of these prototypes is to communicate the needs of the client to the developer. This eliminates some of the problems associated with the waterfall model, since the client no longer has to understand the specifications in order to visualize the final product. It should be noted that a prototype is completely discarded after serving its initial purpose. When the actual product is developed, its design and implementation are accomplished in a well thought out manner, with a great deal of attention to detail, unlike the prototype. The original prototype merely aids the design and development process.

Even though rapid prototyping seems like a better way of doing things, it has its own difficulties. One of the things that this process eliminates is a rigorous specification stage. This gives rise to situations where a client can claim that the product delivered is not the one that was promised. This could not be the case in the waterfall model, where detailed specification documents would prove otherwise.

Another shortcoming is that the client sees the prototype being developed and assumes that the final product will be developed just as quickly. This raises some false expectations about the amount of time required to develop the final product that the developer cannot possibly meet. It is therefore a good idea for the developer to inform the client of the degree of functionality of the prototype as well as the time and effort required to develop a fully functional product.

Another important application of the rapid-prototyping model is its use as a risk minimization tool. One type of risk reduced by rapid prototyping involves using new ideas. If a new algorithm is tested on a real system, the cost of failure can be quite high. Associated with this cost is the cost of development, which in terms of time and effort renders using new ideas feasible near the final stages of development. A good solution is to construct a prototype first, then test its feasibility in a simulated environment. This is no guarantee that the idea will work in the real environment, but chances of success are greatly improved, and the risks of development are minimized.

The idea of minimizing risk is also one of the main components of the *spiral*

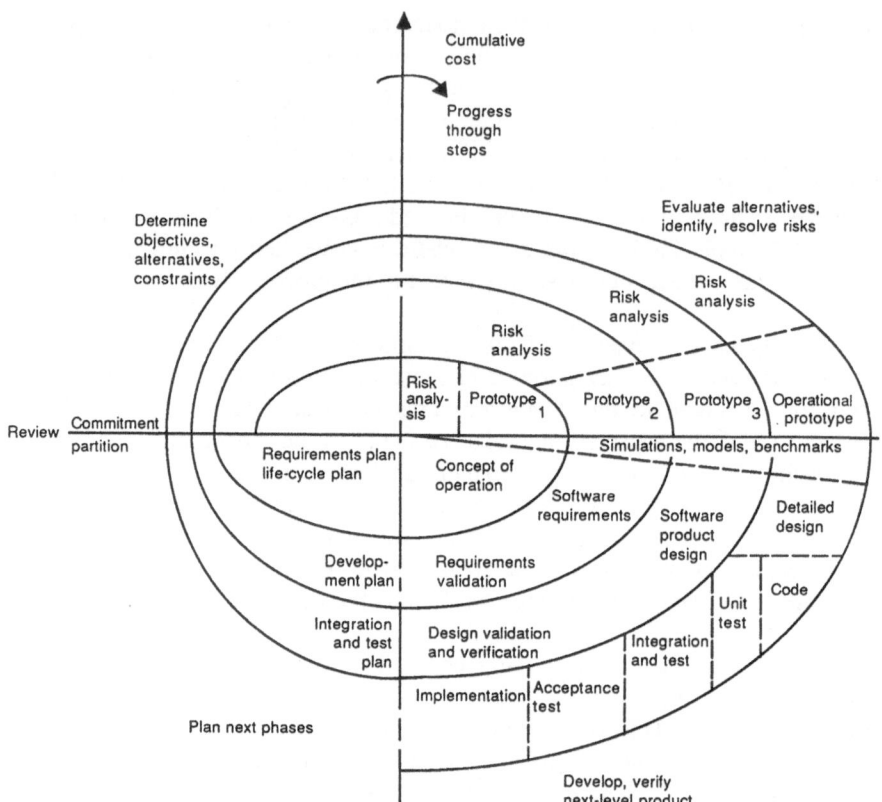

Figure 1.2. The spiral model. Reprinted from Ref. 4 with permission. © 1988, IEEE.

model of software development[4] (see Figure 1.2). The spiral model describes the software process as an iteration over four phases of activities. Each iteration involves a progression through the same sequence of steps, which take each portion of the product through a series of elaboration from conception to code. The phases of each cycle are

1. Identification of objectives to be achieved by the portion of the product under consideration

2. Alternative ways of implementing that part of the system

3. Constraints that affect choices among alternatives

4. Evaluation of alternatives with respect to objectives and constraints

5. Development and verification of the next level of the product

6. Review of the current cycle and development of a plan for the next cycle

Developing a plan for the next cycle can include partitioning the process into separate activities for subsequent development, where partitions may correspond to work on different aspects of the project components to be developed by different groups, individuals or both.[5] The spiral model adds the concepts of risk analysis, prototyping, and iteration to the basic framework provided by the waterfall model. Alternatively this model can be viewed as a waterfall model with each phrase proceeded by risk analysis. The risks are ascertained by the rapid-prototyping method discussed earlier. This type of risk analysis is useful in minimizing risks that involve things like timing constraints (e.g., real-time systems) and testing new ideas and algorithms (as explained earlier). The spiral model is considered by some to be a better model than the previously described models because of its ability to include multiple paradigms in the process model.[5] This makes these models suitable for describing a wide range of software processes. The spiral model on the other hand has development as an iteration of four phases of activities corresponding to the four quadrants in Figure 1.2. These phases combine different approaches, including specification-driven (i.e., waterfall) and prototype-driven (i.e., rapid prototyping) development. While the spiral model represents a significant advancement over the other models, it still has its limitations. This approach works well if the project is confined to one organization; however it is less useful in describing software development under external contract.[4]

The *contractual* model of software development, a more general approach, is capable of describing software development across a wide variety of organizational environments, methods, and application domains.[5] The contractual approach views every task in a software project as a contract, that is, a well-defined package of work that can be performed independently by a contractor for a client.[6] Contract specifications can include an acceptance test for contract deliverables, schedules, requirements for standards that must be met, obligations to make periodic reports, etc. The key point is that the contractor is free to decide how to fulfill the contract specification. This freedom includes the ability to let subcontractors perform all or part of the work and so on recursively. One such contractual approach to software development is ISTAR.[7] The ISTAR provides independent contract databases for the execution of each contract. It also provides additional services, such as contractual operations for assigning contracts, amending or canceling them as necessary, accepting their deliverables, and communicating formal reports to them. The contractual method creates a dynamic hierarchy of contracts reflecting the organization of the contract, and at any level of the hierarchy, the development process can be implemented using any available methods.

At any stage of the hierarchy, project implementation as a whole may involve the waterfall model with Contractor *A* and the rapid-prototyping model with Contractor *B*, while their subcontractors may use still other methods. This gives maximum flexibility in implementing the project and models. Another advantage is that the software is developed at every stage in a manner that best suits that particular stage. This increases the efficiency of development as a whole, unlike the previous models where the development process is inflexible.

One way of evaluating any software development process is to examine what happens when things do not work as planned, which happens very often in real-life situations. In the ISTAR model this situation arises when one of the subcontractors is unable to meet contract constraints. In this case the contractor can do one of two things. The first is to solve the problem within the constraints of the contract that has to be met. This may involve finding additional resources to staff a new subcontract or canceling all existing contracts. The second option is to escalate the problem. The client now has the same options. The essential point is that problems are handled at the organizational level with the competence and responsibility to correct them. Thus the question of where in the hierarchy to resolve a problem has a very natural solution with this approach.

Other process models do exist; a partial list of references include Refs. 8–11. A way of comparing such models is found in Ref. 12.

PROBLEMS

1. One view of a software development process is that it is built incrementally. Each piece is integrated into a partially completed system one by one until done. Develop a life cycle model of this view.

2. Another approach to software development is to build the system first, then revise it until the client's requirements are satisfied. Develop a life cycle model for this process.

3. Discuss how the waterfall model and the rapid-prototyping model can be combined.

4. Give an example software system that can best be guided by the rapid-prototyping model. Do the same for the spiral model.

REFERENCES

1. Royce, W. W. "Managing the development of large software systems: concepts and techniques." *Proc. WESCON* (Aug. 1970).

2. Wirth, N. "Program development by stepwise refinement." *Communication. ACM* **14**:4, 221 (1971).
3. Tanik, M. M. and Yeh, R. T., eds. *IEEE Computer* (Special Issue) **22**:5 (May 1989).
4. Boehm, B. W. *IEEE Computer* **21:5**, 61 (May 1988).
5. Williams, L. G. "Software process modeling: a behavioral approach." *Proc. of the Tenth International Conference on Software Engineering* (Singapore, 1988).
6. Dowson, M., ed. "Iterations in the software process." *Proc. of the Third International Software Process Workshop* (IEEE Computer Society Press, 1987).
7. Dowson, M. "ISTAR and the contractual approach." *Proc. of the Ninth International Conference on Software Engineering* (Monterey, CA, 1987).
8. Gilb, T., *Principles of Software Engineering Management* (Addison Wesley, Reading, MA, 1988).
9. Currit, P. A., Dyer, M., and Mills, H. D. *IEEE Transactions on Software Engineering* **SE-12.1**:3 (Jan. 1986).
10. Lehman, M. M. and Belady, L. A., eds. *Program Evaluation: Processes of Software Change* (Academic Press, 1985).
11. Henderson-Sellers, B. and Edwards, J. M. *Communications of the ACM* **33:9**, 142 (Sept. 1990).
12. Davis, A. M., Bersoff, E. H., and Comer, E. R., *IEEE Transactions on Software Engineering*, **14:10**, 1453 (Oct. 1988).

Object-Oriented Concepts and Modeling

There are two major conceptual models for software systems: the *procedure-oriented* model and the *object-oriented* model. In the procedure-oriented model, a system consists of a number of processes (programs). A program consists of a number of subprograms (procedures and/or functions), and each subprogram owns and manipulates some local data; together they may share some global data. A program is a sequence of subprogram activations and data exchanges arranged by a control algorithm. If the system has multiple programs, data may be transferred among them asynchronously or synchronously through messages or shared variables.

Object-based computation in general is based on three concepts: object, message, and class.[1,2] An object is essentially an encapsulation of a set of private data, and it can be accessed or modified only by activating its interface methods. In most cases an object corresponds directly to a real-world entity, and it is logically meaningful. It accepts messages that ask it to access or modify data. In an object-based system, each object is an instance of some class, and classes can be arranged in a hierarchy, with the property that operations implemented at higher levels of the hierarchy can be automatically recognized at lower levels. A program is a sequence of messages that access the objects.

The choice between the procedure-oriented model and the object-oriented model may not be obvious sometimes. The procedure-oriented model follows a top-down, or algorithmic, approach toward problem solving. The object-oriented model however attempts to model structures and behaviors of domain objects before a solution is composed in terms of local behaviors. It is therefore bottom-up. Many think that the choice of a model should be made according to the nature of the problem to be solved.

Chapter 2 introduces some fundamental concepts of the object-oriented paradigm (Section 2.1). Section 2.2 summarizes some basic constructs for object modeling; these are conceptual tools that can be employed to describe real-world enterprises in a structured fashion. Section 2.3 introduces some advanced object models.

2.1. BASIC CONCEPTS OF THE OBJECT-ORIENTED PARADIGM

Reference 3 provides a detailed survey of the fundamentals and design issues of the object-oriented paradigm. This section summarizes some key results from that survey.

2.1.1. Object, Class, Inheritance, and Message

Objects are collections of operations that share a state. An object consists of variables, called *instance variables,* that represent the state. An object also contains operations, called methods, that determine its interface and its behavior. Variables inside the objects are accessible only through the object's methods. Communications among objects are achieved via messages. If object *A* must activate method *M* of object *B,* it sends a message to *B* asking it to activate *M;* object *B* subsequently executes *M* and returns the result (if requested) via another message.

Classes serve as templates from which objects are created. The similarity between classes and objects is striking. However there is one major distinction: The instance variables of objects represent actual variables; in classes however, instance variables are instantiated. These class-instance variables are private, which means that only the methods of the class can access and change the variables. Though variables of a class cannot be changed directly, the operations of the class have full access to the variables.

The methods of a class are sometimes called the behavior of the class. The object-oriented paradigm allows programmers to reuse behaviors of classes when new classes are defined, so that new classes inherit operations and instance variables from their parent class, thereby adding new operations and new instance variables.

2.1.2. Object Identity

An object's identity is logically distinct from its value—the name given to the object by the programmer—from the address or location at which the object resides. Support of object identity requires operations that allow an identity to be manipulated. A basic operation is testing for object identity. Testing for object identity can be viewed as a special case of testing for object equivalence. Object equivalence can be defined in many ways, such as having the same type or class, some specific common property (e.g., people of the same age), or observational equivalence (having the same behavior in all possible contexts of observation). Unique identifiers are one kind of object identity (determined at object creation).

2.1.3. Imperative and Active Objects

Imperative objects are passive unless activated by a message. In contrast active objects can be executing when a message arrives. Active objects have the following modes: dormant (there is nothing to do), active (executing), or waiting (for resources or the completion of subtasks). Message passing among active objects may be asynchronous.

2.1.4. Object-Oriented Libraries

Programs in procedure-oriented languages are action sequences. In contrast object-oriented programs are collections of interdependent components, each providing service specified by its interface. The object-oriented program structure directly models interactions among objects of an application domain.

Libraries are repositories of software components that serve as reusable building blocks for software development. Libraries in procedure-oriented languages have actions (procedures) as their software components. Components of object-oriented libraries are classes from which objects may be created. Object-oriented libraries contain hierarchically organized collections of classes whose patterns of sharing are determined by inheritance. The behavior encapsulated in classes can be reused in two ways: by creating instances and by subclasses that modify the behavior of parent classes.

2.1.5 Object-Oriented Paradigm

The object-oriented paradigm can be viewed as a paradigm of program structure in terms of the

- Characteristic program structures supported by the paradigm

- Characteristic structure of its execution-time state

- Balance between state transition, communication, and classification mechanisms

In contrast to the shared-memory model of procedure-oriented programming, object-oriented programming partitions the state into encapsulated chunks, each of which is associated with an autonomous, potentially concurrent, virtual machine. Each chunk is responsible for its own protection against access by unauthorized operations. In a concurrent environment, objects protect themselves against asynchronous accesses, thereby removing the synchronization burden from processes that access the object's data. Object-oriented programming emphasizes object management and application design through such mechanisms as classes and inheritance, while distributing programming emphasizes concurrency, implementation, and efficiency. There is also a strong affinity between object-oriented and distributed architectures.

2.1.6. Examples

As a very simple example of the object model just introduced, let us assume that class *matrix*-2 defines a two-dimensional matrix. The objects *a, b,* and *c* are of type *matrix*-2. To compute the following expression:

$$a := b + c;$$

The user sends a message *add:c* to the object denoted by *b,* where *add* is a method inherited from a more general class *matrix.* When the object receives the message; it, in cooperation with the object denoted by *c,* creates a new object that is the result of adding matrices. Then the new object name is sent back to the caller. This mode of computation is illustrated in Figure 2.1. Note that because communication is among the objects and each object is an active entity, a high level of concurrency can be achieved.

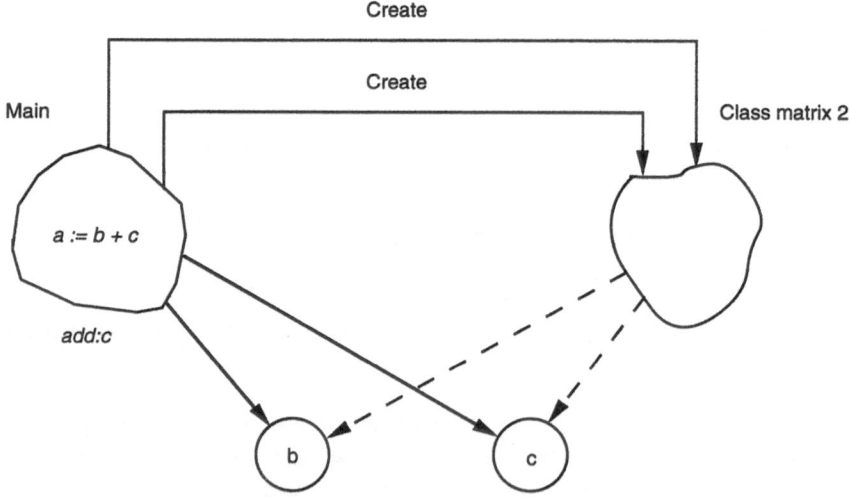

Figure 2.1. An object as a computational entity.

Example 2.1. (Ref. 4) For simplicity we assume that a factory has two departments: *Stock* and *Production*. The responsibility of the Stock department is to maintain a set of SSI parts that are needed for any product the company can make. The responsibility of the Production department is to assemble each product as cheaply as possible at a specified level of quality. The factory accepts product requests on a first-come, first-serve basis; a request is served (i.e., manufactured) if all the resources needed are available. For simplicity the organization of these departments is as follows:

1. The Stock department has only one agent.
2. The Production department consists of two managers: the *assembler planner* and the *process scheduler*. Assembling a product consists of a sequence of jobs performed by different types of work cells; each work cell may have different tools and an industrial robot. Given the identifier of a product, the task of the process planner is to obtain an assembly plant for the product; the task of the process scheduler is to allocate appropriate resources (i.e., work cells) to assemble the product.

The overall organization of the factory is shown in Figure 2.2.

A natural way of mapping this factory into an object-based system is to represent each department as an object. It is also natural to represent the assembly planner, the process scheduler, every customer order, every resource, and every product as separate objects. The object-based system can be programmed to resemble the actual processing of a manufacturing order. Let us assume the following process, depicted in Figure 2.3.

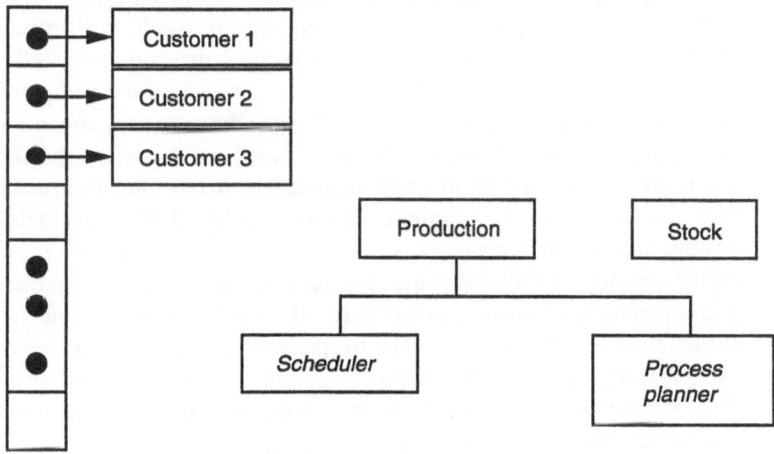

Figure 2.2. The factory's internal organization.

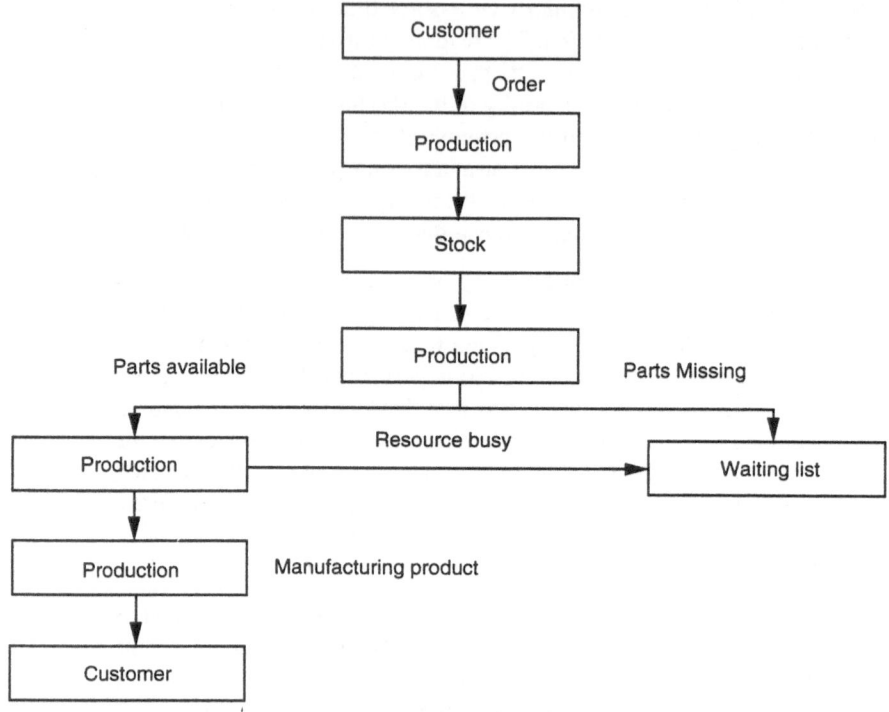

Figure 2.3. Processing a customer's request.

A customer submits an order that specifies the name and the quantity of the SSI part to be assembled. On receiving the message, the Production department creates an order object for the request, determines the SSI parts needed, and consults the Stock department to see if all the SSI paths are available. If some parts are missing, the Stock department issues an order for supply, and the order is placed on a waiting list. Otherwise the SSI parts are reserved, and the Production department determines the resources (e.g., machines, robots) required and their availability through messages communication. If some resources are not available, the request is placed on the waiting list. Otherwise the necessary resources are allocated; a set of job objects are generated and sent to the appropriate resource objects; and the assembly process begins. After the product is assembled, the resources are released. The Production department then examines the waiting queue from the top to see if any request can be served due to the recent release of resources. This process is then repeated.

Now let us examine the internal functions of the *production man-*

ager. Associated to these function is a method called *product_request.* A customer activates this method by sending the production manager a message specifying the method as the selector and the name as well as the quantity of the product as the arguments.

On receiving the message, the production manager creates an order object and the *assembly planner* is asked to define the necessary SSI components and process sequence needed for the product. The assembly planner then requests the Stock manager and the process scheduler to determine if the factory is currently able to manufacture the product. If all required SSI components and resources are available, the process scheduler reserves the appropriate work cells and develops the flow path for the assembly process. In case some resources or SSI components are not currently available, the process scheduler queues the order object.

We can go one step down to see how the assembly planner determines the job sequence of the assembly process. We assume that each product that can be manufactured by the factory is implemented as an object class. Associated with each product class is defined a set of methods. For example the method *retrieve_assembly_plan* develops an assembly plan for the product, and the method *tools_required* reports the tools required to assemble the product.

Consequently when a product is identified, a message with the selector *retrieve_assembly_plan* is sent from the assembly planner to the product object, and the assembly process for that object is returned as the result. Since many classes may be very similar in that they share many methods (e.g., *tools_required*), it is possible to organize product classes into families and let a class object enlist the services of a super-class object whenever it is called on to execute methods it shares with other classes.

Now assume that in our automatic factory there is a third department, *Service.* The function of the Service department is to test and to repair faulty products returned by customers for service. We assume that the Service department has several service experts; naturally we can implement the Service department and each service expert as an object.

To identify a fault associated with a malfunctioning product, a *service* expert object is intended to work in conjunction with a tester that can manipulate and observe a malfunctioning product. The diagnostician accepts from the tester a description of an observed malfunction, prescribes tests, accepts the results, and ultimately identifies faulty components responsible for the malfunction. More likely the service expert uses information about a product's intended structure (a product's part and its interconnection) and its expected behavior (equations, rules, or productions that relate the product's inputs, outputs, and state).

Because a service expert works independently of any particular product, the required information must be stored independently. A natural way of achieving this is to include the design knowledge (intended structure and expected behavior) and diagnostic rules as part of the class definition. A typical product is shown in Figure 2.4. In general terms this product can be described in terms of adders and multipliers. The adders and multipliers can be individually described in terms of their subcomponents, and so on until we reach the level of gates. A full adder is essentially a one-bit adder with carry-in and carry-out, and it is usually used as one of n elements in an n-bit adder. Figure 2.5 shows its design. The adder has three inputs and two outputs, two XOR-gates (X_1 and X_2), two AND-gates (A_1 and A_2), and an OR-gate (O_1).

Of course the structure of any product can be elaborated on and described at gate level. However most of the existing diagnosis expert systems prefer to have *structural abstraction,* which means that much of structural detail is suppressed. The most common example is structural hierarchy as described earlier. The advantage of structural abstraction for diagnosis is that it is often possible to diagnose faults in a hierarchical way. For example it is possible to diagnose the product in Figure 2.4 at a higher level of abstraction to determine the major subcomponents in which the fault lies (e.g., the adder *AA*). This subcomponent can then be diagnosed to identify the fault at the next lower level (e.g., the full adder), and so on until the lowest level failure is determined (e.g., X_1's output stuck at off). By conducting the diagnosis hierarchically, the number of components under consideration at any one time is reduced;

D74

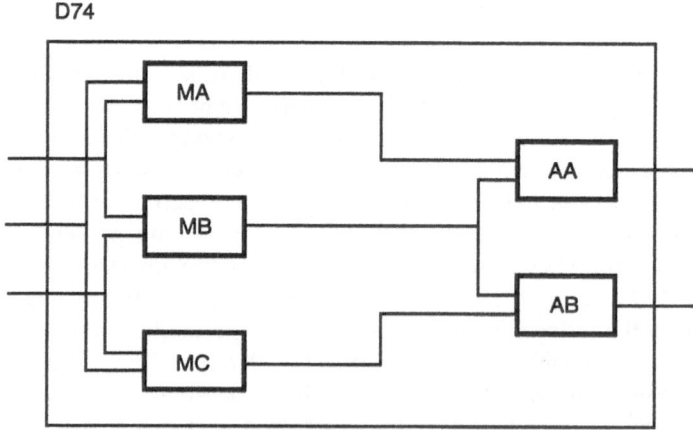

Figure 2.4. A typical product.

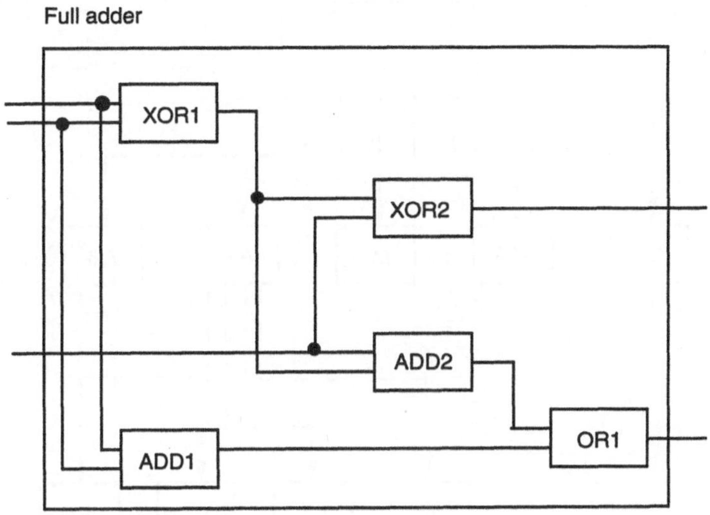

Full adder

XOR1

XOR2

ADD2

OR1

ADD1

Figure 2.5. A typical adder.

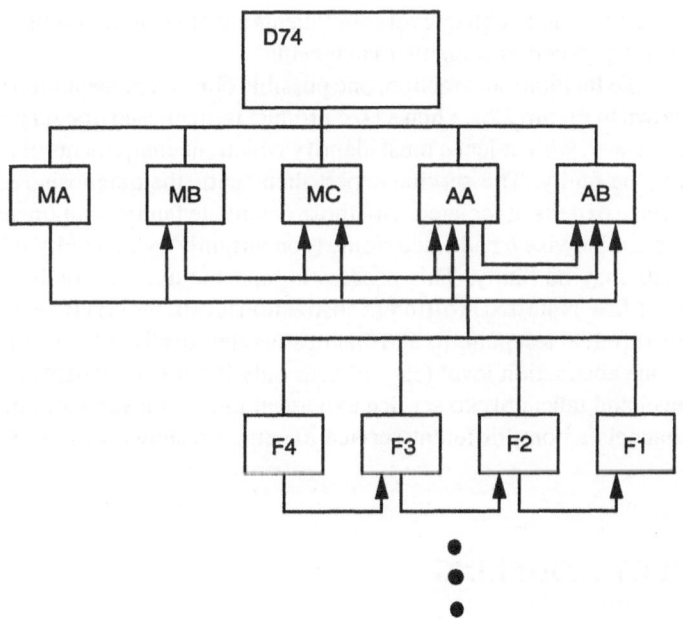

D74

MA   MB   MC   AA   AB

F4   F3   F2   F1

Figure 2.6. An object representation of D74.

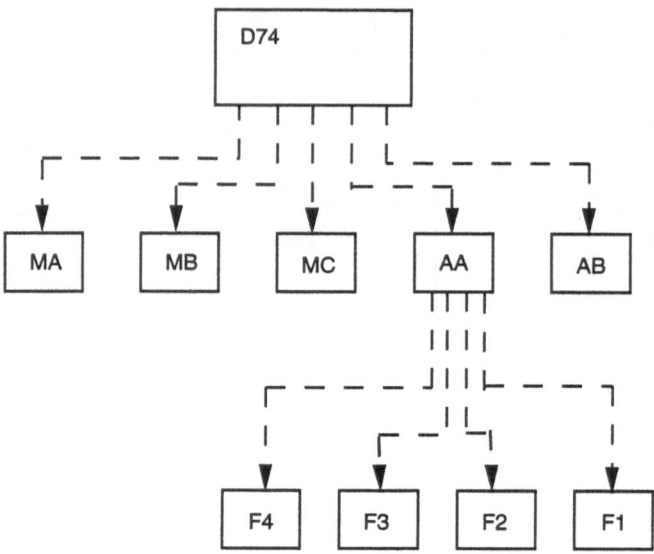

Figure 2.7. Communication channels among different experts.

and even though higher level components are often quite complex, the cost of test generation remains manageable.

To facilitate abstraction, one possible object representation of *D74* is shown in Figure 2.6. When a *D74* product is diagnosed, the *service expert* associated with object *a* must identify which subcomponents of *b, c, d, e, f* may be faulty. The service expert then sends the diagnosis requests to service experts associated with those candidate faulty components, say, *b* and *c*. Likewise *b* and *c* determine (concurrently) which of its subcomponents may be faulty. This process is repeated until the faulty gates are identified. Note that at different abstraction levels, the service experts must use different test patterns and diagnostic rules. In all cases a service expert at one abstraction level (e.g., *a*) sees only its subcomponents at the next level and talks only to service experts at the next level. Communication channels among different service experts are shown in Figure 2.7.

2.2. OBJECT MODELING

Object-modeling techniques are conceptual tools that can be applied to abstract and formulate real-world things. Most object-modeling techniques ex-

tend the *entity-relationship* model (ER model)[5] with object-oriented considerations. In an ER model, real-world enterprises are described in terms of *entities*
and *associations;* entities that share the same structure are grouped into an *entity
set,* and associations of the same kind are group into an *association set.* An ER
diagram is a network of nodes (entity sets) whose connections are labeled by
associations. Most object-oriented modeling techniques extend the preceding
with the concepts of generalization, aggregation, and operations. Typically an
object model consists of a number of classes and their associations (relationships). Graphically an object diagram consists of a set of nodes (classes) whose
connections are labeled by associations. Example 2.2 gives an informal introduction to the object-modeling techniques proposed in Ref. 6.

Example 2.2. Figure 2.8 shows the class diagram of a windowing
system. In the object modeling technique (OMT), an *object diagram* can
be a *class diagram* (which shows classes and their relationships) or an
instance diagram (which shows instances of objects and their relationships). In Figure 2.8 each object class is depicted as a rectangular box
divided into three parts: the name of the class, its attributes, and its
operations. Classes are connected by associations. A superclass and its
subclasses are connected by a special type of association that captures
the *is a* relationship; such an association (called a *generalization* association) is depicted by a triangle in Figure 2.8. For example a *window*
can be a *scrolling window,* a *canvas,* or a *panel;* a *shape* can be a *line* or
a *closed shape,* and so on.

Similar to the ER model, an association can be a one-to-one, one-
to-many, many-to-one, or many-to-many relationship. An association
connecting two classes can have a bubble at either end, where a solid
bubble designates a *many* end and a hollow bubble designates a *one* or
zero end; an end without a bubble designates a *one* end. One end of an
association may have a diamond (in this case the association is an
aggregation association): in this case each object of the class connected
to the diamond end is an assembly of a set of (zero, one, or many,
depending on the other end of the association) objects of the class
connected to the other end. For example each polygon consists of a
number of points, where the points are ordered. The association between
point and *polygon* is called *vertices,* although an association does not
have to be named. As another example, each *choice item* consists of
several *choice entries* as possible choices among which one is chosen as
the current choice. A dotted arrow from the association *current choice*
to the association *choices* designates a constraint labeled as *{subset},*
meaning the current choice has to be a member of the *choice entries.*

Similarly a *panel item,* once selected by the user, generates (is

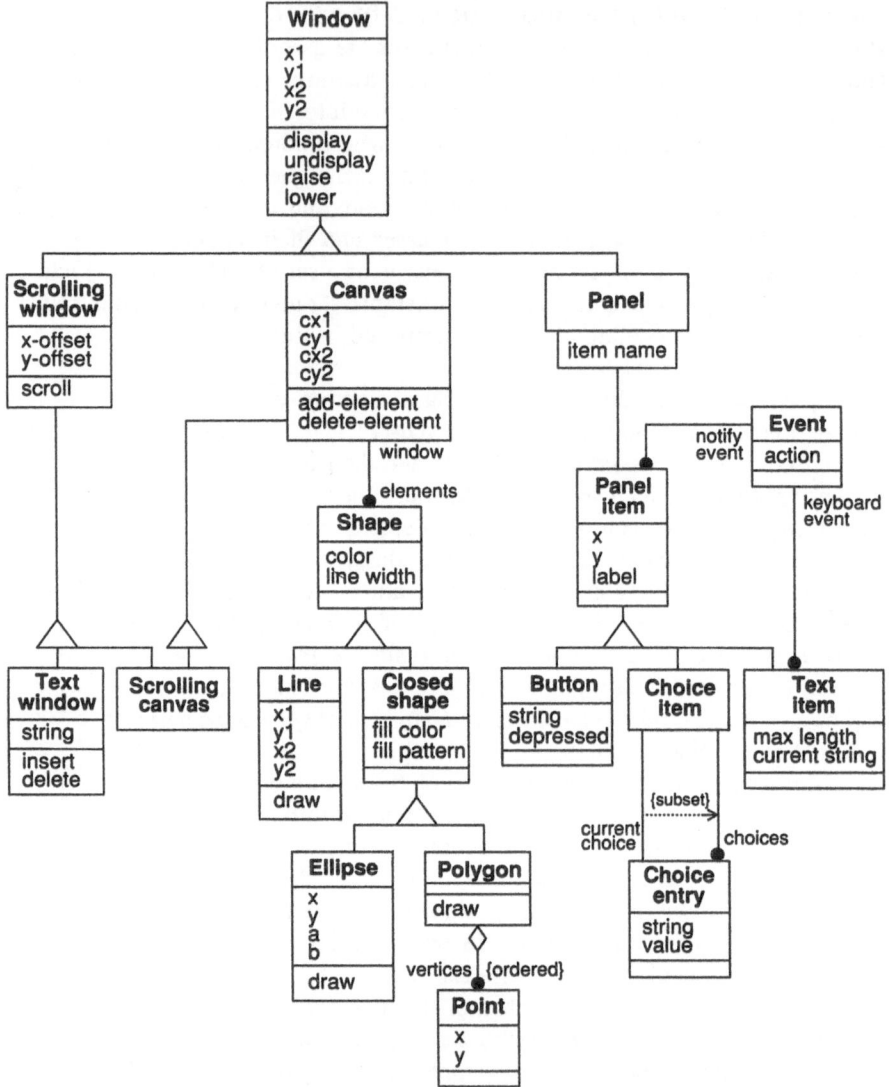

Figure 2.8. The class diagram of a windowing system. Reprinted with permission from Ref. 6 ©
1991, Prentice-Hall.

associated with) a *notify event,* although many *panel items* can be associated with the same *event.* The association between *panel* and *panel item* is a one-to-one association once the name of the panel item is specified. The box associated with the association between *panel* and *panel item* is a qualification, and it can usually be read as *indexed by.* Finally the attributes and operations of a superclass are automatically inherited by its subclasses. Although not shown in Figure 2.8, ternary associations can be expressed as a diamond whose three vertices are connected to the three classes involved.

Example 2.2 illustrates some basic constructs in OMT for object modeling: classes, associations, generalization, and aggregation. Figure 2.9 summarizes the semantics of some of the most commonly used notations in OMT. Most object-modeling techniques provide a rich set of tools for capturing the semantics of real-world enterprises. Some additional constructs include the following:

Multiplicity: The many end of an association can be labeled by a nonnegative integer, an interval, a set of integers, or a set of intervals to identify the possible number of objects that can be associated with the object(s) at the other end of the association.

Join Classes: A class with more than one subclass is called a join class. If some subclasses overlap, the hollow triangle of the related generalization association is replaced by a solid triangle.

Role: Either end of an association is called a role, and it can be labeled by a role name.

Class Descriptors: Attributes and operations of a class that belong to the class only and are not shared by its instances can be listed with a special symbol.

Candidate Keys: A set of attributes from the two classes connected by a binary association can be appointed as a candidate key to identify uniquely a link (which is defined to be an instance of an association) between two object instances.

Constraints: Constraints can be expressed as predicates and imposed on attributes, parameters (of operations), and link attributes. Constraints may also be imposed between attributes, parameters, and link attributes.

Figure 2.10 illustrates some of the preceding and provides brief explanations.

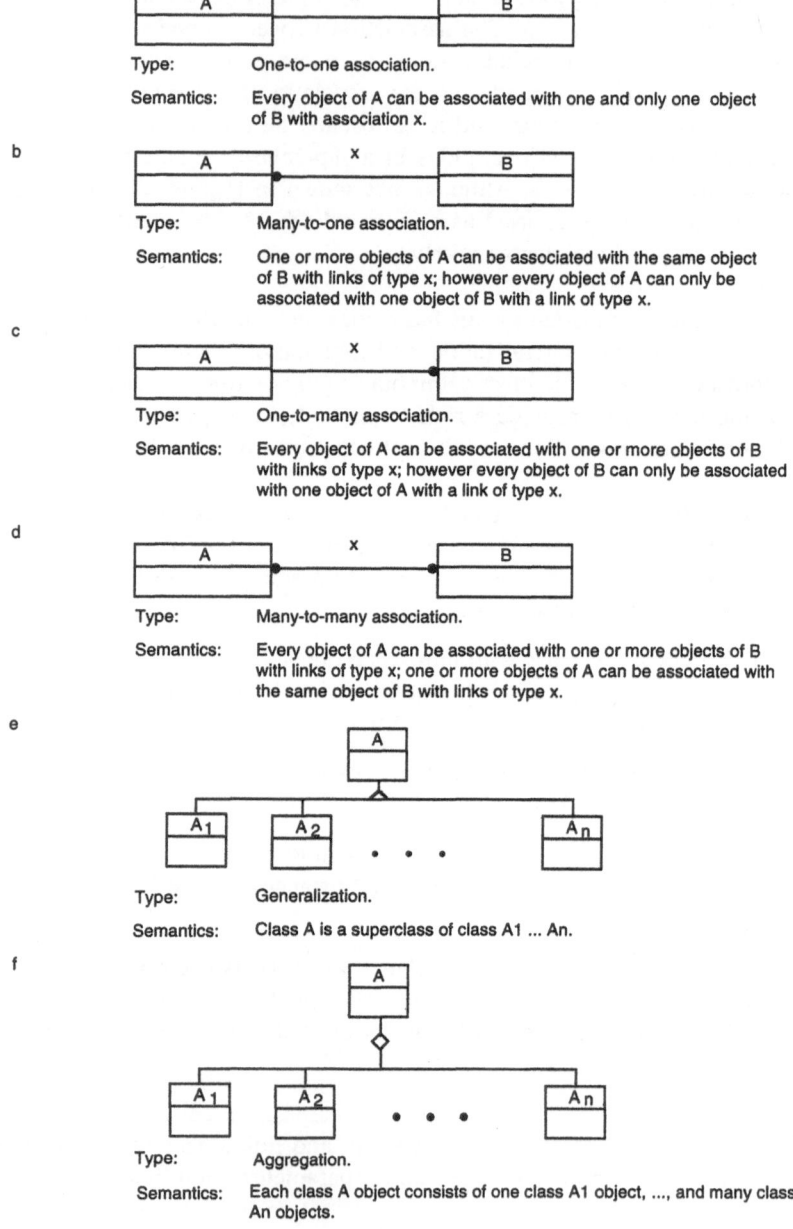

a

Type: One-to-one association.

Semantics: Every object of A can be associated with one and only one object
             of B with association x.

b

Type: Many-to-one association.

Semantics: One or more objects of A can be associated with the same object
             of B with links of type x; however every object of A can only be
             associated with one object of B with a link of type x.

c

Type: One-to-many association.

Semantics: Every object of A can be associated with one or more objects of B
             with links of type x; however every object of B can only be associated
             with one object of A with a link of type x.

d

Type: Many-to-many association.

Semantics: Every object of A can be associated with one or more objects of B
             with links of type x; one or more objects of A can be associated with
             the same object of B with links of type x.

e

Type: Generalization.

Semantics: Class A is a superclass of class A1 ... An.

f

Type: Aggregation.

Semantics: Each class A object consists of one class A1 object, ..., and many class
             An objects.

Figure 2.9. Some commonly used notations in OMT.

a

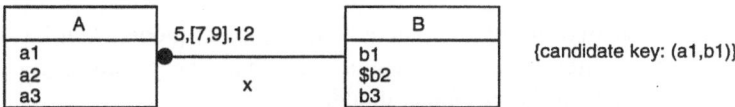

Semantics: Either five, seven, eight, nine, or twelve objects of class
A can be associated with many objects of class B. The
attribute b2 of class B is a class attribute. The tuple (a1,b1)
uniquely identifies a pair of objects (from class A and class
B respectively) associated by an association of type x.

b

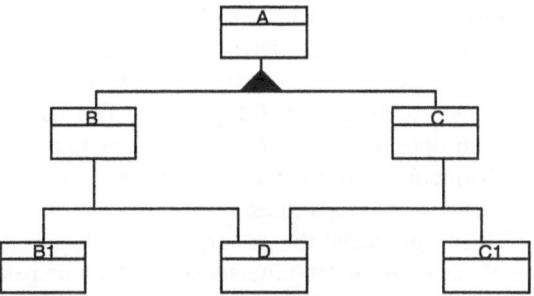

Semantics: Class B and C are subclasses of class A;
Class B1 and D are subclasses of class B;
Class C1 and D are subclasses of class C;
and class D inherits from both classes B and C.

c

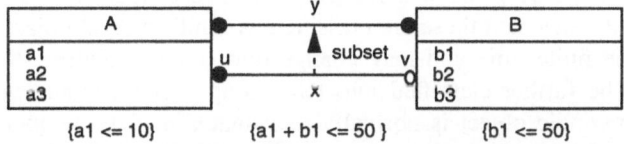

{a1 <= 10}   {a1 + b1 <= 50 }   {b1 <= 50}

Semantics: Many objects of class A can be associated with many objects of
class B with association of type y. Many objects of class A can be
associated with one or zero object of class B with association type x;
the role of a class A object in the association is u and the role of a
class B object (if exists) in the association is v. The value of attribute
a1 of each class A object is less than or equal to 10; the value of
attribute b1 of each class B object is less than 50. The association set
x is a superset of the association set y.

Figure 2.10. Some examples of additional modeling constructs.

2.3. ADVANCED OBJECT MODELS

This section discusses some advanced object models that have been introduced in the literature; these include real-time object models, reflective object models, and agent-based object models.

2.3.1. Real-Time Object Models

Models for real-time systems traditionally focus on system processing and its timing characteristics. For example research on real-time databases emphasizes maximizing the number and/or value of transactions completed by certain deadlines, based on some correctness criteria.[7,8] Proposals that incorporate real-time considerations into an object model have been found recently in the real-time system community. For example the MARS model[9] requires all data values to be included in messages with fixed validity times. The CHAOS project[10] describes the need for multiple, time-constrained value assignments to objects. Time capsules,[11] an abstraction proposed for continuous media systems, also associates validity intervals with data values.

More recently Callison proposed the concept of a time-sensitive object.[12] Specifically the value of such objects are time-sensitive: As time passes the value of the object is expected or even required to change. Examples of such time-sensitive objects for real-world applications include the position of aircraft in an airspace and temperature during a nuclear or chemical reaction. Callison classified time-sensitive objects into three categories: single-interval transient, multilevel, and immutable. Immutable objects have constant values (they do not change). A single-interval transient object is created, remains in the system for a short time, then disappears without changing. Most other objects fall between these two extremes, and these are classified as multi-interval objects: They persist for some finite time and may change during their lifetime. Multi-interval objects can be further classified into two groups: *sporadic* and *periodic*. The value of a periodic object is normally reevaluated at fixed temporal intervals; each new value remains valid for a fixed length period. Sporadic objects are allowed or expected to change but not at precisely regular times.

2.3.2. Reflective Object-Oriented Models

According to Ref. 13, "Reflection is the process of reasoning about and acting on the system itself." A language is considered reflective if it uses uniform structures to represent data as well as control entities.[14] Reference 15 describes a reflective object-oriented system as a collection of objects and a collection of invariants about the object states. Invariants are classified into two groups: derivations that define the value of a computed data element and constraints that assert possible relationships between data elements. The two types of invariants correspond to deductive laws and integrity constraints in a database (see Section 3.2). In a reflective process the database reflects on the contents of its present state, identifies invariants that are not satisfied by the present state, and devises a set of transitions that transfer the database into a consistent state.

Reference 16 describes a reflective object-oriented language that allows an object to extend its behavior by dynamically composing multiple secondary behaviors, with the object's primary behavior defined in the class. This reflective feature is accomplished by using metaclasses that support shadow objects to implement an object's secondary behaviors. Similar features have also been implemented in other object-oriented languages, such as ACTOR[17] and ObjV-Lisp.[18] Reference 19 claims that reflection is especially beneficial in concurrent systems that require customization according to system organization or application program characteristics for achieving efficiency and robustness.

2.3.3. Agent-Based Object Models

Abstractly, agents are executable threads, i.e., an agent is a process executing some program.[20] Typically an agent has input and output ports and a set of methods that actually perform the agent's functions.[21] Most agents are dormant until awakened by messages sent to them. The agent's methods specify what to do when messages are received at the input ports and which messages to send out at the output ports. Preconditions (triggers) can be used to specify when a particular action should be taken (e.g., when messages have been received at all three specified input ports.) In those cases when the agent has to be awakened at certain time intervals, a predicate for waking up the agent may be specified; this predicate need not depend on receiving messages, and it can be as simple as stating the time elapsed before the agent must wake up. When an agent wakes up, all actions whose preconditions are met are executed in the order they are listed. In addition an agent can have state variables. Extensive work has been reported on the specifications of multi-agent systems.[22,23]

PROBLEMS

1. Construct an object model for the file system of your favorite operating system (UNIX, DOS, etc.).

2. Construct an object model for circuits consisting of electronic gates (e.g., AND gates, OR gates, inverters, flip flops) connected by wires.

3. Construct an object model for the structure of a university.

4. The following object model, taken from Ref. 6, describes the structure of automobiles. Translate it into English.

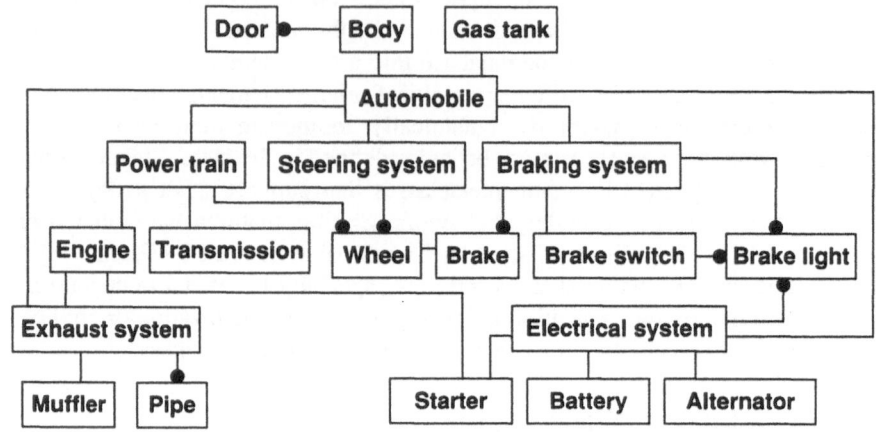

Problem 4. Object model describing the structure of automobiles.

5. Build an object model for the factory discussed in Example 2.1.

6. A *derived class* is a class that can be derived from some existing classes. Extend the object-modeling constructs discussed in this chapter to include derived class.

7. Extend the object-modeling constructs discussed in this chapter with *n*-ary associations (i.e., associations which connect *n* classes). Is it always possible to convert an *n*-ary association into a set of binary associations without losing any information?

8. A *derived association* is an association that can be derived from attributes of some existing classes. For example in a spatial database, the association *to-the-left-of* can be derived from two objects' locations. Extend the object-modeling constructs discussed in this chapter to include derived associations.

9. Is it possible to transform associations in an object model into classes without losing any information? Why or why not?

10. Discuss the impact of any change that could be made to object classes (e.g., adding/deleting attributes/operations, adding/deleting sub-/superclasses, etc.) to an object model. It is possible to develop an incremental maintenance algorithm for an object model? Why or why not?

REFERENCES

1. Blair, Gallagher, Hutchion, and Shepherd, eds. *Object-Oriented Languages, Systems and Applications* (Wiley, New York, 1991).
2. Goldberg, A. *Smalltalk-80: The Language and Its Implementation* (Addison Wesley, Reading, MA, 1983).
3. Wegner, P. *ACM SIGPLAN Notices* **25**:6 (June 1990).
4. Ramamoorthy, C. V., and Sheu, P. C-Y. *IEEE Expert* **3.3**, 9–17 (fall 1988).
5. Chen, P. P. S. *ACM Transactions on Database Systems* **1.1**, 9–36 (Mar. 1976).
6. Rumbaugh, J., Blaha, M., Premerlani, W., Eddy, F., and Lorensen, W. *Object-Oriented Modeling and Design* (Prentice Hall, New York, 1991).
7. Abbott, R., and Garcia-Molina, H. "Scheduling real-time transactions: a performance evaluation." *Proc., 14th International Conference on Very Large Databases* (Morgan Kaufmann, Palo Alto, CA, 1988).
8. Haritsa, J. R., Linvy, M. J., and Carey, M. J. "Earliest deadline scheduling for real-time database systems." *Proc., IEEE 12th Real-Time Systems Symposium* (1991).
9. Kopetz, H., Damm, A., Koza, C., Mulazzi, M., Schwabl, W., Senft, C., Zainlinger, R. *IEEE Micro* **9-1**, 25–40 (Feb. 1989).
10. Bihari, T., Gopinath, P., and Schwan, K. "Object-oriented design of real-time software." *Proc., IEEE Real-Time Systems Symposium* (1989).
11. Herrtwich, R. G. "Time Capsules: an abstraction for access to continuous media data." *Proc. IEEE 11th Real-Time Systems Symposium* (1990).
12. Callison, H. R. "A periodic object model for real-time system." *Proc., IEEE International Conference on Data Engineering* (1994).
13. Yonezawa, A., and Watanable, *ACM SIGPLAN Notice* **24**:4, 50–54 (April, 1989).
14. Ibrahim, M. H., and Cummins, F. A. "KSL: a reflective object-oriented programming language." *Proc., International Conference on Programming Languages* (Oct. 1988).
15. Etzion, O. "An alternative paradigm for active databases." *Proc., IEEE International Conference on Data Engineering* (1994).
16. Kaiser, G. E., Hseush, W., Lee, J. C., Wu, S. F., Woo, E., Hilsdale, E., and Meyer, S. "MeldC: A reflective object-oriented coordination language." *Technical Report CUCS-001-93* (Dept. of Computer Science, Columbia University, New York, 1993).
17. Ferber, J. In *Metalevel Architectures and Reflection* (Maes, ed.) (North-Holland, 1988).
18. Ferber, F. "Computational reflection in class-based object-oriented languages." *Proc., ACM OOPSLA* (New York, 1989) 317–326.
19. Masuhara, H., Matsuoka, S., Watanabe, T., Yonezawa, A. "Object-oriented Concurrent reflective languages can be implemented efficiently." *Proc., ACM OOPSLA* (ACM, New York, 1992).
20. Ciancarini, P. *ACM Transactions on Software Engineering and Methodology* **2**:3, 203–209 (July 1993).
21. Lim, W., and Verzulli, J. *SPIE* **1831**; *Mobile Robots VII* (1992) 285–296.
22. Szczerbicki, E. *International Journal on Systems Science* **24**:11, 2117–2134 (1993).
23. Singh, M., Huhns, M., and Stephens, L. *IEEE Transactions on Data and Knowledge Engineering* **5**:5, 721–739 (Oct. 1993).

3

Formal Specification and Verification

Once requirements are fully understood, it is important to have them documented and verified. This stage is critical, since no one wants to waste hundreds of employee hours developing a software package that does not function as expected. Requirements specification can be done in terms of the logical components involved, their respective inputs, outputs and desired relationships, and constraint to be imposed. *States* and possible *state transitions* can also be incorporated into a requirements specification; in this case the requirements specification may be executable. Indeed some requirements specification languages are executable (e.g., Petri net; see Section 3.6).

Although there are informal requirements specification languages (e.g., RSL),[1] a formal specification attempts to eliminate the ambiguity or uncertainty of an informal requirements specification language. Another advantage is that a formal specification may prove to be internally consistent without conflicts. In some cases a formal requirements specification can be proved to be complete, in the sense that a solution can always be derived from the set of functions provided (e.g., algebraic specification; see Section 3.5). However compared with informal specification languages, formal requirements specification languages can be restrictive in terms of expressive power and difficult to learn.

Chapter 3 begins with a brief introduction to first-order logic and its application to data definition (Sections 3.1 and 3.2). Based on these, Chapter 3 describes some formal requirements specification languages, including two logic-based specification languages, namely, Z (Section 3.3) and the object-oriented logic system (Section 3.4), a number of algebraic specification languages (Section 3.5), and a graphical specification language, namely, Petri net (Section 3.6), which is suitable for specifying the coordination aspects of concurrent processes. Section 3.7 discusses some verification processes that can be applied to formal requirements specifications. Section 3.8 includes some final remarks.

3.1. FIRST-ORDER LOGIC

Logic is just a formal system. Any formal system relies on an object language, a semantics or interpretation of formulas in that language, and a proof theory. For a detailed presentation, see Refs. 2 and 3.

29

3.1.1. First-Order Language

The object language we use is first-order language: lowercase letters represent constants, predicates, and functions; uppercase letters represent variables $(X,Y,Z,\ldots)$. The symbols $\rightarrow$ (implies), $\vee$ (or), $\wedge$ (and), and $\sim$ (not) are used as logical connectors. The *universal quantifier* $\forall$ allows facts about all objects in the universe without enumerating each one; the *existential quantifier* $\exists$ allows an object to be asserted to exist with certain properties without naming the object. A *term* is defined to be a constant, a variable, or a function. A *literal* is defined to be a predicate $p(T_1,\ldots,T_n)$ or its negation $\sim p(T_1,\ldots,T_n)$. Finally a *well-formed formula* (wff, or formula, in short) is defined either by a literal, by connecting or quantifying other wffs. Closed wffs do not contain free variables: they contain quantified variables only.

Two special forms of a wff are sometimes needed: in the *Prenex normal form*, all quantifiers are placed in front of the wff; in the *Skolem normal form*, all existential quantifiers are eliminated by replacing variables they quantify with adequate functions of other universally quantified variables in the Prenex normal form. Formulas built by connecting formulas with $\wedge$s are called *conjunctions;* each component formula is called a *conjunct*. On the other hand, formulas built by connecting formulas with $\vee$s are called *disjunctions;* each component formula is called a *disjunct*. Finally a *clause* is a disjunction of several literals, or a single literal, all of whose variables are implicitly universally quantified. It can be shown that every wff can be put in either the Prenex normal form and the Skolem form and every closed wff can be put in the clausal form, i.e., as a conjunction of clauses.

Example 3.1. The following are wffs:

$(\forall X)(bike(X) \rightarrow two\_wheel(X))$
All bikes have two wheels.
$(\exists X)(student(X) \wedge likes\ (X, software\ engineering)$
There exists a student who likes software engineering.
$(\forall S)\{school(S) \rightarrow (\exists T)\{student\_of\ (T,S) \wedge (\forall R)\{[teacher\_of\ (R,S) \rightarrow taught\_by\ (T,R)]\}\}\}$
Every school has a student who has been taught by every teacher in the school.

3.1.2. Semantics: Model and Interpretation

An *interpretation* of a set of wffs defines a nonempty set or domain E in which variables and constants are given values. Each function symbol is assigned a value, and each *n*-ary predicate is assigned the value true or false. Each wff can be evaluated as true or false by all connectors h and wffs α and β and an evaluation function v:

- $v(\alpha) \wedge \textit{false} = \textit{false}$
- $v(\alpha) \wedge \textit{true} = v(\alpha)$
- $v(\alpha) \vee \textit{true} = \textit{true}$
- $v(\alpha) \vee \textit{false} = v(\alpha)$
  - $\sim \textit{true} = \textit{false}$
  - $\sim \textit{false} = \textit{true}$

A *model* of a set of wffs is an interpretation in which all of the wffs are true; a set of wffs w' has wff w as a logical consequence if w is true in all models of w', noted $w' \rightarrow w$.

3.1.3. First-Order Theory

A *logical axiom* is a wff that is true under all interpretations. The first-order theory uses two inference rules to derive new logical axioms (theorems) from existing ones. The *Modus Ponens* inference rules says $(f_1 \wedge (f_1 \rightarrow f_2))$ infers f_2, where f_1 and f_2 are wffs. The *Generalization* inference rule says that $\sim(\forall X)f(X)$ infers $f(a)$, where a is any constant.

3.1.4. Theorem Proving

Given a set of axioms T, a new *theorem* (expressed as a wff) F can be proved by proving that $T \wedge \sim F \rightarrow \textit{false}$. This process is referred to as *refutational theorem proving*. Assuming F and all axioms in T are expressed in clausal forms, *resolution refutation theorem proving* can be carried out by combining different clauses of $\sim F$ and T based on the resolution principal until a contradiction (i.e., nil clause) is derived. This occurs whenever two clauses to be combined are unified to the form P and $\sim P$, respectively.

3.1.5. Resolution Principle

The resolution principle says two wffs $P \vee Q_1$ and $R \vee \sim Q_2$ can be combined (resolved) to be $P' \vee R'$:

$$
\begin{array}{l}
P \vee Q_1 \\
R \vee \sim Q_2 \\
\hline
P' \vee R'
\end{array}
$$

where P, R, R' are clauses, Q_1 and Q_2 are predicates that are not negated, and

- Q_1 and Q_2 have the same predicate symbol.

- The arguments of Q and the arguments of Q_2 are *unifiable;* i.e., there exists a substitution of variable terms for Q_1 and Q_2, where a variable term can be substituted by another variable term, a constant term, or a function term, so that the arguments of Q_1 and Q_2 become identical.

- Let the notation $\cdot$ be used so that given a wff A and a substitution δ, $A \cdot \delta$ stands for the new wff obtained from A by performing the substitution δ of terms in A. Assume that the substitution for Q_1 is δ_1 and the substitution for Q_2 is δ_2 in 2 such that $Q_1 \cdot \delta_1 = Q_2 \cdot \delta_2$, $P' = P \cdot \delta_1$, and $R' = R \cdot \delta_2$.

Example 3.2. (Ref. 4) Consider the following axioms:

- $(\forall X)(read(X) \rightarrow literate\ (X))$
  Whoever can read is literate.

- $(\forall X)(dolphin\ (X) \rightarrow \sim literate\ (X))$
  Dolphins are not literate.

- $(\exists X)(dolphin\ (X) \wedge intelligent\ (X))$
  Some dolphins are intelligent.

Assume that theorem F to be proved is

- $(\exists X)(intelligent\ (X) \wedge \sim read\ (X))$
  Some who are intelligent cannot read.

$T \wedge \sim F$ can be organized into the following clausal form:

1. $\sim$read (X) $\vee$ literate (X)

2. $\sim$dolphin (Y)$\sim$literate (Y)

3a. dolphin (a)

3b. intelligent (a)

4. $\sim$intelligent (Z) $\vee$ read (Z)

The resolution refutation theorem proving process can be summarized into a *resolution refutation tree,* as shown in Figure 3.1 below, where each node contains a clause. Two arcs from two nodes n_1 and n_2 come into the same node n if n_1 and n_2 can be combined (resolved) into n, with the necessary substitution(s) marking the arc(s). An arc without a mark represents no substitution; i.e., all variables are not substituted.

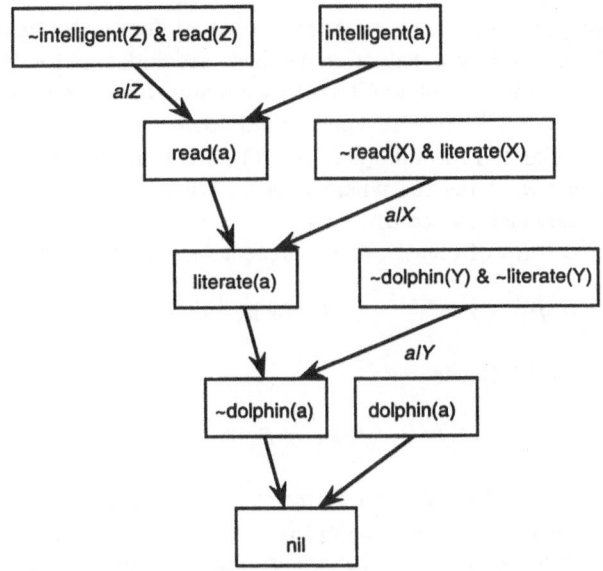

Figure 3.1. A resolution refutation tree. Reprinted with permission from Ref. 4. © 1981, Morgan Kaufmann.

3.2. LOGIC AND DATABASE

Data definition languages were mainly developed for database systems to describe the structures and semantics of information stored in a database system. Among existing data models, the relational model may be the most widely accepted.[5] In the relational theory, a domain is a (usually finite) set of values. The Cartesian product of domains $D_1 , \ldots , D_n$, denoted by $D_1 \times D_2 \ldots \times D_n$, is the set of all n-tuples $(v_1 , \ldots , v_n)$ such that $v_i \in D_i$, $1 \le i \le n$. A *relation R* is a finite subset of a Cartesian product, which is represented by a table. Each row is called a *tuple* and each column, an *attribute*.

A relational database can be visualized as a collection of relations whose contents and semantics can be described as a logic system. This is similar to a PROLOG system (see Chapter 7) without list notations and with a very limited set of procedural predicates, such as $<$, $>$, $<=$, $>=$, $=$, and $\ne$.[6] However, a relational database is a logic system with *integrity constraints,* which are axioms (rules) that state the necessary constraints about the facts and are constantly enforced whenever facts are added and/or deleted.

A *deductive database* is a database in which new facts can be derived from explicitly introduced facts.[6] In general a deductive database consists of a finite set of constants, say, $\{c_1, \ldots, c_n\}$, and a set of first-order clauses without function symbols. Initially a deductive database precludes null values that arise when there are statements such as $(\exists X)p(a,X)$; that is, linked to a in the predicate p, there is a value, but its precise value is unknown.

If we skolemize the formula $(\exists X)p(a,X)$, then transform it into the clausal form, the clause $p(a,w)$ results, where w is a Skolem constant (i.e., a constant whose value is otherwise unconstrained).

The general form of clauses that represent facts and deductive laws is

$$P_1 \wedge P_2 \wedge \ldots \wedge P_k \rightarrow R_1 \vee \ldots \vee R_q$$

It is equivalent to the clause

$$\sim P_1 \vee \ldots \vee \sim P_k \vee R_1 \vee \ldots \vee R_q$$

The conjunction of the P_is is referred to as the left-hand side of the clause and the disjunction of the R_js, as the right-hand side. It is assumed that the clauses are function-free; therefore terms that are arguments of the P_is and R_js are either constants or variables. Whenever any variable on the right-hand side of a clause also occurs on the left-hand side, the clause is said to be range-restricted. The following summarizes the possible types of clauses of a deductive database, depending on the values of k and q, as discussed in Ref. 6:

1. *Type 1 ($k = 0$, $q = 1$)* clauses take the form $\rightarrow p(T_1, \ldots, T_m)$:

    (a) If all T_is are constants, $c_{i1}, \ldots, c_{im}$, then $\rightarrow p(c_{i1}, \ldots, c_{im})$, which represents an assertion of a fact in the database. The set of all such assertions for the predicate p corresponds to a table in a relational database. The arrow preceding an assertion is generally omitted.

    (b) When some, or all, of the T_is are variables, the clause corresponds to a general statement in the database. For example the clause $\rightarrow$ *ancestor(adam,X)* states that *adam* is an ancestor of all individuals in the database (the database consists only of human beings). Clearly such data, which are not range-restricted clauses and therefore assume that all the individuals in the database are of the same type, appear very seldom.

2. *Type 2 ($k = 1$, $q = 0$)* clauses take the form $p(T_1, \ldots, T_m) \rightarrow$

    (a) When all T_is are constants, then $p(c_{i1}, \ldots, c_{im}) \rightarrow$, which represents a negative fact. Negative statements may seem peculiar, since relational databases do not contain negative data.

    (b) Some of the T_is are variables. This may be thought of as either an integrity constraint (as a particular Type 3 clause) or as meaning the value does not exist (null value).

3. *Type 3 (k > 1, q = 0)* clauses take the form $P_1 \wedge \ldots \wedge P_k \rightarrow$. Such axioms may be thought of as integrity constraints. That is data to be added to a database must satisfy the laws specified by the integrity condition to be allowed in the database. For example we can specify an integrity law that states no individual can be both a father and a mother of another individual. This may be specified as *father(X,Y)* $\wedge$ *mother(X,Y)* $\rightarrow$. If *father(jack,sally)* is already in the database, an attempt to enter *mother(jack,sally)* into the database leads to an integrity violation. This does not rule out other kinds of integrity constraints.

4. *Type 4 (k ≥ 1, q = 1)* clauses take the form $P_1 \wedge P_2 \wedge \ldots \wedge P_k \rightarrow R_1$. The clause may be considered either an integrity constraint or a definition of the predicate R_1 in terms of the predicates $P_1, \ldots, P_k$ (such a definition is a *deductive law*).

5. *Type 5 (k = 0, q > 1)* clauses take the form $\rightarrow R_1 \vee R_2 \vee \ldots \vee R_q$. If all arguments for R_i, $i = 1, \ldots, n$ are constants, then we have an indefinite assertion; that is, any combination of one or more R_i is true, but we do not know which ones are true.

6. *Type 6 (k ≥ 1, q > 1)* clauses take the form $P_1 \wedge P_2 \wedge \ldots \wedge P_k \rightarrow R_1 \vee R_2 \vee \ldots \vee R_q$. The clause can be interpreted as either an integrity constraint or the definition of indefinite data. An integrity constraint that states that each individual has at most two parents can be written as *parent(X_1,Y_1)* $\wedge$ *parent(X_1,Y_2)* $\wedge$ *parent(X_1,Y_3)* $\rightarrow (Y_1 = Y_2) \vee (Y_1 = Y_3) \vee (Y_2 = Y_3)$. As a general rule of deduction, we can have *parent(X,Y)* $\rightarrow$ *mother(X,Y)* $\vee$ *father(X,Y)*. This general law can also be interpreted as an integrity constraint.

Finally, a clause where $k = 0$, $q = 0$ (the empty clause) denotes falsity and should not be a part of a database. Furthermore we call a clause definite if its right-hand side consists of exactly one atom (i.e., Type 1b or Type 4).

All the clause types just defined, except ground facts (Type 1a), are treated as integrity constraints in conventional databases. In a deductive database, some of types may be treated as deductive laws. We distinguish two classes of databases: *definite databases* in which no clauses of either Type 5 or Type 6 appear and *indefinite databases* in which such clauses do appear.

3.3. FORMAL SPECIFICATION IN Z

The Z is a formal specification language based on predicate logic and set theory.[7,8] In Z a system is formally described in terms of a number of schemas; a *schema* consists of two parts: the *signature* and the *predicate*, presented in the following form:

```
---Schema Name ---
  Signature Part
------------------------
  Predicate Part
------------------------
```

Typically a schema describes a state space of the system (the complete state space can be decomposed into a number of subspaces), the initial value of a state space, or an operation that can be executed on objects in the system and the effects of the operation (to the current state). To describe a state space or the initial value of a state space, the signature of a schema specifies a number of objects that constitute the state space and some related objects. The predicate specifies a number of relationships (i.e., *invariants*) that have to hold among the objects declared in the signature. To support modularity the signature may contain some other schemas. In this case all objects specified in each of these schemas are included in the current schema.

To describe an operation, the predicate specifies a set of state spaces (in terms of schemas) involved in the operation and possibly some other objects (e.g., arguments to the operation, input objects, and output objects), and the predicate specifies a number of preconditions (if these exist) and postconditions (if these exist) among the objects involved for the operation.

For schemas of this type, the notion s' (called *after state*) denotes the value of the schema s (called *before state*) after the operation is applied. The notion v' denotes the value of any object v in a state space after the operation is applied. With such postconditions can be established. Note that preconditions do not involve after states. In addition the notion $v?$ denotes an input object, and the notion $v!$ denotes an output object. Given a schema S, the schema ΔS (called *delta S*) is defined to be

```
---ΔS---
   S
   S'
----------
```

The schemas ΣS (called *xi S*) is defined to be the same as the schema ΔS with the constraint that the after state of S is the same as the before state. Schema modularity is also supported in Z by a set of operators that can be used to combine several schemas into a more complicated schema.

Finally for purpose of illustration, the following notations are employed in Z in addition to commonly adopted conventions (such as $\in$, $\cup$):

• $\#A$, which denotes the cardinality of set A

- $\{x{:}T\,|\,P\}$, which denotes the set of all *x*s of type *T* such that *P* is true

- *A/B*, which denotes the difference between set *A* and set *B*

- *S: P X*, which denotes that *S* is a set of *X*s

- *S: F X*, which denotes that *S* is a finite set of *X*s

Example 3.3 shows a Z specification for a simple computerized library system.

Example 3.3. (Ref. 8) Consider a computerized library system that consists of a set of books; a book may be either on loan, reserved (in this case it is either on loan or kept at the counter), or on the shelves. Assuming the library does not keep multiple copies of a book and a book can be reserved by only one person, the following library operations can be performed:

- *NewBook,* which adds a new book to the library
- *TakeOutBook,* which checks out a book
- *Returns,* which returns a book
- *ReserveBook,* which reserves a book
- *BookQuery,* which checks the status of a book

The following Z schemas formally describe the computerized library; comments are preceded by two slashes:

```
// The Library state space
---------------------------------Library----------------------------------
books : P BARCODE // assuming BARCODE is a basic type
shelved, reserved, loaned: P BARCODE
-----------------------------------------------------------------------------
books = loaned ∪ reserved ∪ shelved ∧
// A book on reserved or on loan is never shelved
shelved ∩ reserved = Ø ∧
shelved ∩ loaned = Ø
-----------------------------------------------------------------------------

// The initial state space of Library
---------------------------------InitLibrary----------------------------------
Library
-----------------------------------------------------------------------------
shelved = Ø ∧
loaned = Ø ∧
reserved = Ø
-----------------------------------------------------------------------------
```

// *The NewBook operation*

-------------------------------*NewBook*-------------------------------

$\Delta Library$

$bcode?$: $BARCODE$ // *it's an input object*

// *precondition*

$bcode? \notin books \land$

// *postconditions*

$shelved' = shelved \cup \{bcode?\} \land$

$loaned' = loaned \land$

$reserved' = reserved$

// *The TakeOutBook operation*

-----------------------------*TakeOutBook*-----------------------------

$\Delta Library$

$bcode?$: $BARCODE$

// *Only a book on shelve or on loan can be checked out;*

// *it's a precondition*

$bcode? \in (shelved \cup (reserved / loaned)) \land$

// *postconditions*

$shelved' = shelved / \{bcode?\} \land$

$reserved' = reserved / \{bcode?\} \land$

$loaned' = loaned \cup \{bcode?\}$

// *The Return operation*

-------------------------------*Return*-------------------------------

$\Delta Library$

// *a number of books can be returned at once*

$bcodes?$: $BARCODE$

// *Only a book on loan can be returned;*

// *it's a precondition*

$bcodes? \subset loaned \land$

// *postconditions*

$shelved' = shelved \cup \{x{:}BARCODE | x \in bcodes? \land x \notin reserved\}$

$\land$

$reserved' = reserved / \{bcode?\} \land$

$loaned' = loaned / bcodes? \land$

$reserved' = reserved$

// *The ReserveBook operation*

```
-----------------------------ReserveBook-----------------------------
ΔLibrary
bcode? : BARCODE
report! : {"ok","on_shelves","cur_reserved"} // an output mes-
```
sage
```
-------------------------------------------------------------------
// Only a book in the library can be reserved;
// it's a precondition
bcode? ∈ books ∧
// postconditions
// The following are a number of rules
// If the book is on shelves then the librarian is informed
// If the book is on loan but not reserved, it's added to the reserved
```
list
```
(bcode? ∈ reserved → report! = "cur_reserved" ∧ reserved' =
reserved) ∧
(bcode? ∈ shelved → report! = "on_shelves" ∧ reserved' =
reserved) ∧
(bcode? ∈ loaned/reserved → report! = "ok" ∧ reserved' =
reserved ∪ {bcode?}) ∧
loaned' = loaned ∧
shelved' = shelved
-------------------------------------------------------------------
// The BookQuery operation
-----------------------------BookQuery-----------------------------
// The Library state space remains intact after the operation
ΣLibrary
bcode? : BARCODE
report! : {"unknown", "shelved", "reserved", "loaned"}
-------------------------------------------------------------------
// postconditions
(bcode? ∉ books → report! = "unknown") ∧
(bcode? ∈ shelved → report! = "shelved") ∧
(bcode? ∈ loaned/reserved → report! = "loaned") ∧
(bcode? ∈ reserved → report! = "reserved")
-------------------------------------------------------------------
```

To cover illegal inputs and errors, the following schemas can be defined and later combined with preceding schemas to complete the specification:

Define the new type LIBMESS:
LIBMESS : {

"operation was successful",
"no multiple copies of books allowed",
"barcode does not match any library book",
"some barcodes don't match any library books",
"some barcodes are of books not on loan",
"barcode corresponds to book already on loan"}

---------------------------------*Success*----------------------------------
mess! : *LIBMESS*
----
mess! = *"operation was successful"*

---------------------------------*NoMultiples*-------------------------------
Σ*Library*
bcode? : *BARCODE*
mess! : *LIBMESS*
----
bcode? $\in$ *books* $\wedge$
mess! = *"no multiple copies of books allowed"*

---------------------------------*TakeOutErrors*-----------------------------
Σ*Library*
bcode? : *BARCODE*
mess! : *LIBMESS*

(bcode? $\notin$ *books* $\rightarrow$
mess! = *"barcode does not match any library book")* $\wedge$
(bcode? $\in$ *loaned* $\rightarrow$
mess! = *"barcode corresponds to book already on loan")*

---------------------------------*ReturnErrors*------------------------------
Σ*Library*
bcodes? : *BARCODE*
mess! : *LIBMESS*

(bcodes? $\subseteq$ *books* $\rightarrow$
mess! = *"some barcodes don't match any library book")* $\wedge$
(bcodes? $\subseteq$ *loaned* $\wedge$ *bcodes?* $\subset$ *books* $\rightarrow$
mess! = *"some barcodes are of book not on loan")*

---------------------------------*NotLibraryBook*----------------------------
Σ*Library*
bcode? : *BARCODE*
mess! : *LIBMESS*

(bcode? ∉ *books* →
mess! = *"barcode does not match any library book")*

Now the specification can be completed with the following composite schemas:

NewBook2 := *(NewBook* ∧ *Success)* ∨ *NoMultiples*
TakeOutBook2 := *(TakeOutBook* ∧ *Success)* ∨ *TakeOutErrors*
Return 2 := *(Returns* ∧ *Success)* ∨ *ReturnErrors*
ReserveBook2 := *(ReserveBook* ∧ *Success)* ∨ *NotLibraryBook*
BookQuery2 := *BookQuery* ∧ *Success*

Note that when two schemas are combined with a logical operator α (where α could be ∧ or ∨), the signature of the resulting schema contains all declarations from the two schemas and the predicate of the resulting schema contains the predicate of the first schema in parentheses followed by the predicate part of the second schema. For instance the composite schema *NewBook2* is actually:

-----------------------------*NewBook2* -------------------------------
Δ*Library*
bcode? : *BARCODE*
mess! : *LIBMESS*

((bcode? ∉ *books* ∧
shelved' = *shelved* ∪ *{bcode?}* ∧
loaned' = *loaned* ∧
reserved' = *reserved)* ∧
mess! = *"operation was successful")* ∨
(bcode? ∈ *books* ∧
mess! = *"no multiple copies of books allowed")*

Note that in the predicate part of *NewBook2*, either of the two formulas connected by the ∨ is true, depending on which pre-condition is true.

3.4. OBJECT-ORIENTED LOGIC SYSTEM

An object-oriented logic system[9] is a logic system that describes the structure and semantics of an object-oriented system. In Section 8.4, it is used as the basis for an automatic software reuse system.

Formally we define an object-oriented logic system to be a two-level system. The first level, or the *object level*, is a tuple $L_O = (O, G_O, D_O, P_O)$, where O is a first-order object language, G_O is an object representation of O, D_O is a set of axioms, and P_O is a set of productions. Similarly the second level, or the *schema level*, is a tuple $L_S = (S, G_S, D_S)$, where S is a first-order object language, G_S is an object representation of S, and D_S is a set of deductive laws.

Consider an object base G_O, namely, a set of classes and their associated methods. We define the first-order schema language consisting of a set of constants (beginning with a lowercase letter), a set of variables (beginning with an uppercase letter), and the following predicates (beginning with a lowercase letter) to describe object classes and relations:

- *class* $(a, a_1, \ldots, a_n)$ is true if a is the name of a class of objects and the attributes of each object of class a is $a_1, \ldots, a_n$. The symbol *set_of_a* designates the class of all possible ordered sets that can be derived from the objects in class a.

- *a :method* $(m, d_1, \ldots, d_n)$ is true if a is a class, m is a method, and the domain of the *ith* parameter of the method is d_i.

- *attribute(a,b,c)* is true if the attribute b of class a has the domain c, where c is a set.

- The predicate *instance_of(a,b)* is true if object a is an instance of class b. The predicate *member_of(a,b)* is true if object a is an instance of set b.

Negated predicates in L_S are interpreted by the closed world assumption; i.e., a literal $\sim f$ is evaluated as true if f is not asserted. The first-order object language is defined to consist of a set of constants (beginning with a lowercase letter), a set of variables (beginning with an uppercase letter), an n-place predicate symbol m for each n-ary method m (for simplicity we assume that all method names are distinct), and the following predicates (beginning with a lowercase letter) to describe objects and relationships among a set of objects:

- The predicate $a.m(x_1, \ldots, x_r)$ is true if the method of m of some class is applied to the object a of the same class with the arguments $x_1, \ldots, x_r$ of legal values; it is false otherwise. The predicate is called a *method predicate*.

- The predicate $a(t)$ is true if t is an instance of class a; it is false otherwise. The predicate *set_of_a(t)* is true if t is an instance of the class *set_of_a* (i.e., t is a set whose elements are of class a); it is false otherwise.

- The predicate *member_of(a,b)* is true if the object a is an element of the set b; it is false otherwise. The notation $[H|T]$, where H and T are variables or constants, designates a set whose first element is H and the rest of the set is T.

Both a schema-level axiom and an object-level axiom associated with a method predicate f are expressed in the following form, where e is assumed to be a well-defined formula assumed to be free of implications for convenience:

$$e \to f$$

If and only if the following are defined:

$$e_1 \to f$$
$$\cdots$$
$$e_m \to f$$

The following is true:

$$f <-> e_1 \lor e_2 \lor \ldots e_m.$$

If $m = 1$, this results in $f <-> e_1$.

The L_O and L_S communicate by the predicate *instance_of*. It is assumed that whenever an assertion *instance_of(a,b)* is made in L_S, the assertion $b(a)$ is made in L_O, and vice versa. Despite their appearances L_O and L_S are not PROLOG (see Chapter 7), since no procedural predicate, such as assignment is defined in the language.

For simplicity, from now on, we use the notation:

$$class(a,a_1:d_1 , \ldots , a_n :d_n)$$

in place of the set of predicates:

$$class(a,a_1 , \ldots , a_n)$$
$$attribute(a,a_1,d_1)$$
$$\cdots$$
$$attribute(a,a_n,d_n)$$

Furthermore we use the symbol , instead of $\land$ for convenience.

Example 3.4. Suppose we have an object class called *city* with only one attribute, *state* , whose domain is *string* , and an object class called *flight* with the following attributes:

- *source*, whose domain is *city*

- *destination*, whose domain is *city*
- *fare*, whose domain is *float*

Also assume that we have a class called *airline* with the following attributes:

- *cs*, whose domain is *set_of_city*
- *fs*, whose domain is *set_of_flight*

Associated with the class *airline*, assume there is a method called *connection* that takes two cities as the input and returns a set of flights that connect the two cities. The structure of this system can be described as follows, where expressions at schema level and expressions at object level are separated by a line. The same convention is followed in the rest of Chapter 3:

class(city,state:string)
class(flight,source:city,destination:city,fare:float)
class(airline,cs:set_of_city,fs:set_of_flight)
airline:method(connection,set_of_flight,city,city,float)
airline:method(cheapest_fare,city,city,float)

---

airline(A) → *instance_of(A.cs,set_of_city), instance_of(A.fs,set_of_flight)*.
A.connection(C,S,T,Fare) <-
member_of(S,A.cs), member_of(T,A.cs),
member_of(F,A.fs), (F.source = S), (F.destination = T),
(C = [F]), (Fare = F.fare).
A.connection(C,S,T,Fare) <-
member_of(S,A.cs), member_of(T,A.cs),
member_of(F,A.fs), (F.source = S), (∃ C1) (set_of_flight(C1),
A.connection(C1,F.destination,T,Fare1),
C = [F|C1], (Fare = F.fare + Fare1)).
A.cheapest_connection(D,S,T,Fare) <-
A.connection(D,S,T,Fare),
~((∃ C) (∃ Fare1) (set_of_flight(C), float(Fare1), A.connection(C,S,T,Fare1),
(Fare1 < Fare)))

The presence of variables and constants at object level that are structured objects makes unification at that level a rather complicated task. At first glance given a predicate $c(A)$ and assuming the structure of c is declared as the predicate *class*($c,a_1:d_1 , \ldots , a_n :d_n$), the predicate can be translated into the following set of predicates:

$$c(A)$$
$$attribute\_value(A,a_1,A_1)$$
$$\cdots$$
$$attribute\_value(A,a_n,A_n)$$

where a predicate *attribute_value(a,b,c)* is true if object a has c as the value of its attribute b. Now any object expressed as $A.a_j$, $1 \le j \le n$, can be translated into A_j. The same rule can be applied recursively if any A_j is a structured object. This mechanism seems to work well if the type of A is known exactly. However if c is *object* (which means a can essentially be any type of object) or some unknown attribute of A is referenced (in the form $A.B$, for example, where B is a variable), the preceding mechanism does not work.

In the following, we extend the conventional unification algorithm to handle structured objects in general. Before proceeding let us recall that the *disagreement set* of a nonempty set W of expressions is obtained by "locating the first symbol (counting from left) at which not all the expressions in W have exactly the same symbol, and then extracting from each expression in W the subexpression that begins with the symbol occupying at that position."[10]

The object-oriented unification algorithm is extended to include structured objects as follows:

Step 0: Retrieve the types of each expression if known.

Step 1: $k = 0$, $W_k = W$, $\alpha_k = \phi$, $\beta = \phi$

Step 2: If W_k is a singleton, stop with success and return α_k; otherwise find the disagreement set D_k of W_k.

Step 3: If there exist elements u and v in D_k, consider the following:

1. If both u and v are predicate symbols, u and v cannot be unified (as they are different) and stop with failure.
2. If $u = A_1.A_2 \ldots A_n$ and $v = B_1.B_2 \ldots B_m$, where each A_i, $1 \le i \le n$, or B_j, $1 \le j \le m$, is a constant or a variable:

(a) If u and v cannot be the same type, with a unifier or a unifier that was not applied before and backtracking is possible, backtrack to the previous decision point; otherwise stop with failure.

(b) If u and v can be the same type, with a unifier δ' that was not applied before, add this step as a decision point. Let $\delta = \{(u \cdot \delta')/u, (v \cdot \delta')/v\}$. Also let $\beta = \beta \cup \{(\delta' \cdot u)/u, (\delta' \cdot v)/v\}$. If at this point there exists a set of unifiers of the form $\{w_1/y_1, \ldots, w_r/y_r\}$, where each w_i has the form $D_1.D_2 \ldots D_q.T_i$, where T_i is a constant or a variable and each y_i has the form $C_1.C_2 \ldots C_p.S_i$, where S_i is a constant or a variable, consider the following. If $\{T_1, \ldots, T_r\}$ covers all attributes of $D_1 \ldots D_q$ and $\{S_1, \ldots, S_r\}$ covers all attributes of $C_1 \ldots C_p$, then add $D_1 \ldots D_q/C_1 \ldots C_p$ to δ. If $\{S_1, \ldots, S_r\}$ covers all attributes of $C_1 \ldots C_p$, but $\{T_1, \ldots, T_r\}$ does not cover all attributes of $D_1 \ldots D_q$, then add $D_{t1}, \ldots, T_r/C_1 \ldots C_p$ to δ. Otherwise go to Step 4.

Step 4: Let $\alpha_{k+1} = \alpha_k \cdot \delta$, $W_{k+1} = W_k \cdot \delta$

Step 5: $k = k + 1$ and go to Step 2.

Example 3.5. Consider the following two expressions, assuming *airline* (G) and *airline* (A), where the class *airline* is defined as in Example 3.4:

$$W = \{p(G \cdot ES, G \cdot NS, G), p(A \cdot fs, A \cdot cs, A)\}$$

According to the extended unification algorithm, initially β is ϕ. The unifier $\delta' = \{A/G, fs/ES\}$ unifies $G \cdot ES$ and $A \cdot fs$. Let

$$\delta = \{(G \cdot ES \cdot \delta')/G \cdot ES, (A \cdot fs \cdot \delta')/A \cdot fs\}$$
$$= \{A \cdot fs/G \cdot ES, A \cdot fs/A \cdot fs\}$$

Also set

$$\beta = \beta \cup \{A \cdot fs/G \cdot ES, A \cdot fs/A \cdot fs\}$$

At the end of the first iteration,

$$W_1 = \{p(A \cdot fs, G \cdot NS, G), p(A \cdot fs, A \cdot cs, A)\}.$$

Similarly a unifier for the second argument can be obtained as $\{A \cdot cs/G \cdot NS, A \cdot cs/A \cdot cs\}$ and β becomes

$$\{A \cdot fs/G \cdot ES, A \cdot fs/A \cdot fs, A \cdot cs/G \cdot NS, A \cdot cs/A \cdot cs\}$$

At this point $A \cdot fs$ and $A \cdot cs$ cover all attributes of A, and $\{G \cdot ES, G \cdot NS\}$ covers all the attributes of G (based on their types), so that the unifier $\{A/G\}$ is added, and the resulting set of unifiers is returned successfully.

3.5. ALGEBRAIC SPECIFICATIONS

An algebraic specification is a mathematical representation that is particularly powerful in specifying abstract data types (ADTs). The underlying mathematical model of the algebraic specification is many-sorted algebra, which is an abstract structure consisting of a family of sets of objects and a number of functions whose arguments and results belong to their sets.[12] Formal specifications, such as algebraic specifications, aid the software designer in applying rigorous mathematical reasoning about specifications.[13,14]

Example 3.6. (Ref. 11) The following example describes the abstract data type *Stack* in terms of an algebraic specification:

> *sort Stack;*
> *operations*
> *newstack: → Stack;*
> *push: Stack * Nat → Stack;*
> *isnewstack: Stack → Bool;*
> *pop: Stack → Stack;*
> *top: Stack → Nat;*
> *declare s: Stack; n; Nat;*
> *axioms*
> *isnewstack(newstack) == true;*
> *isnewstack(push(s,n)) == false;*
> *pop(newstack) == newstack;*
> *pop(push(s,n)) == s;*
> *top(newstack) == zero;*
> *top(push(s,n)) == n;*

In the preceding example, *sort* lists the name of the ADT being represented. The *operation* lists the services or functions available on instances of the type *Stack* and syntactically describes how they have to be called; this is called the *signature*. For example,

> *push: Stack * Nat → Stack;*

means that *push* is a two-argument operation; the arguments are of types *Stack* and *Nat*, and the result is of the type *Stack*. Functions in an algebraic specification have no side effects. In Example 3.6 *push* takes two arguments: a stack *s* and a natural number *n* to create a new stack that is identical to the input stack but has one extra element on its top. By systematically avoiding any kind of side effects, properties of the abstract data type can be expressed simply.

Example 3.7. This example describes the abstract data type TABLE in the Larch Shared Language.[15]

> *TableSpec: trait*
> *introduces*
> *new: → Table*
> *add: Table, Index, Val → Table*

 # ∈ #: Index, Table → Bool
eval: Table, Index → Val
isEmpty: Table → Bool
size: Table → Card
constrains new, add, ∈, eval, isEmpty, size so that
for all [ind, ind1: Index, val: Val, t: Table]
eval(add(t,ind,val),ind1) =
if ind = ind1
then val
else eval(t,ind1)
ind ∈ new = false
ind ∈ add(t,ind1,val) = (ind = ind1) | (ind ∈ t)
size(new) = 0
size(add(t,ind,val)) = if ind ∈ t
then size(t) else size(t) + 1
isEmpty(t) = (size(t) = 0)

In this example a *trait* is the building block for a Larch algebraic specification. The keyword *introduces* starts the signature (i.e., sort), and the keyword *constrains* starts the axioms. The meaning of the specification should be reasonably clear to the reader.

As expected given an algebraic specification, new operations can be derived from existing ones. Axioms can be employed to prove some desirable properties about an ADT; they may also be used to discover inconsistencies among specifications. In Example 3.6 for instance, such operations as *newstack* and *push* are called *constructors,* since they either create a stack or add something into a stack. Operations like *pop* are called *modifiers,* since they remove or replace something from a stack. Finally such operations as *isnewstack* and *top* are called *behaviors,* since they return some properties about a stack. A sufficiently complete set of axioms associated with an ADT includes axioms of the forms

modifier(constructor(. . .)) = . . .
and
behavior(constructor(. . .)) = . . .

This can be used as a guideline to establish a complete specification of an ADT.

3.6. PETRI NETS

In this section, we discuss a specification language particularly useful for specifying concurrent systems. In general a concurrent system consists of a number of tasks (processes) working asynchronously, where each task is sequential. While each task can be specified as described in previous sections, communication and coordination aspects of a set of concurrent processes must be specified separately; Petri net is a powerful specification language for this purpose.

A Petri net is a mathematical representation of a system.[16] Petri nets are very useful for modeling control aspects of systems. Analyzing a Petri net reveals both the structure and the dynamic behavior of a system. The four components of a Petri net are a set of *places P*, a set of *transitions T*, an input function *I*, and an output function *O*. A Petri net is often denoted as *PN* = (*P, T, I, O*). In this description input and output functions relate places and transitions. *Tokens* are associated with Petri nets. A token is a primitive concept of Petri nets. Tokens are assigned to, and can be thought to reside in, a Petri net, and these are used to define the execution of a Petri net.

The execution of a Petri net is controlled by the number and distribution of tokens in the Petri net. A Petri net executes a loop that consists of three steps:

1. Identify the set of enabled transitions, where a transition is enabled if each of its input places has at least as many tokens in it as the number of the arcs from the place to the transition.

2. Arbitrarily select a transition to fire from the set of enabled transitions.

3. The selected transition fires by removing tokens from its input places and creating new tokens that are distributed to its output places.

Example 3.8. (Ref. 17) The Petri net in Figure 3.2 shows the different states (places) and transitions in a single-processor system. Clearly when a job enters the system and the processor is idle (i.e., when a token is present at the associated places), processing the job can begin, so the system enters a new state: job being processed. Whenever the job is done, it is placed on the output list, and the processor becomes idle again.

Example 3.9. (Ref. 18) The Petri net model in Figure 3.3 shows the different states and transitions associated with two communicating processes. When one process is ready to send information, the information is sent, then the process waits for an ACK (acknowledgment) message. In the mean time, the buffer becomes full. When the buffer is full and the second process is ready to receive information, it receives the message, then sends an ACK message; in the meantime it processes the data. The first process resumes its operation when an ACK is received.

By nature the firings of transitions in a Petri net are nondeterministic. This means if two transitions are enabled at the same time, either one can fire first. It is

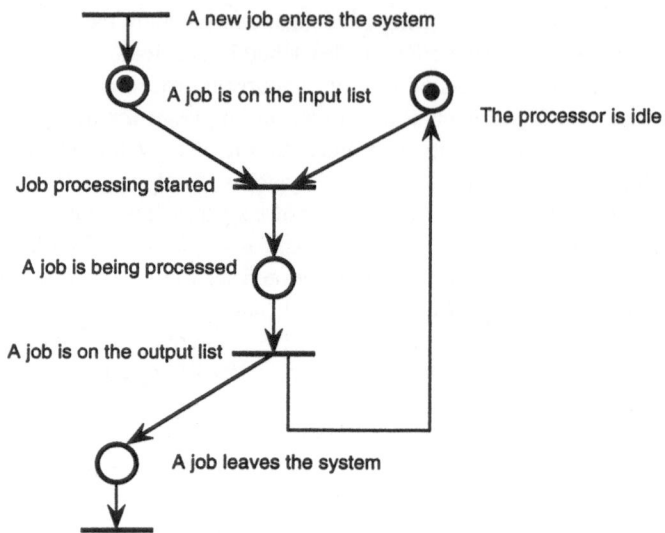

Figure 3.2. A Petri net model for a single-processor system. Reprinted with permission from Ref. 17. © 1977, ACM.

also possible that two transitions are conflicting; this means that the firing of one disables the other (see Figure 3.4).

To model complex systems, Petri nets can be used in a hierarchical fashion. This means a net at a lower level of abstraction can be replaced by a single place or transition at a higher level of abstraction. The modeling power of Petri nets is just below the Turing machine, so that any significant extension results in a Turing-machine equivalence.[17] One significant extension is the introduction of

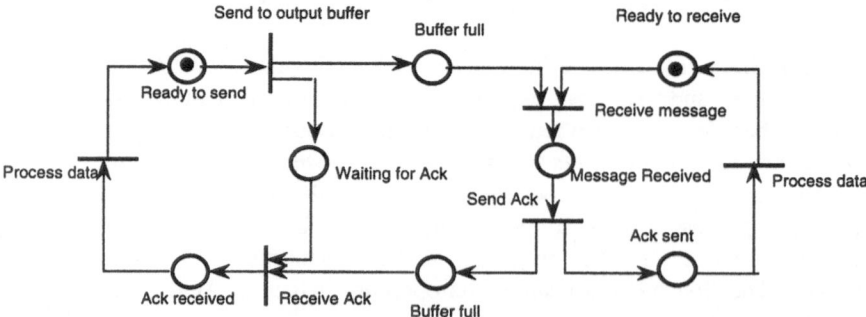

Figure 3.3. A Petri net model for two communicating processes. Reprinted with permission from Ref. 18. © 1980, IEEE.

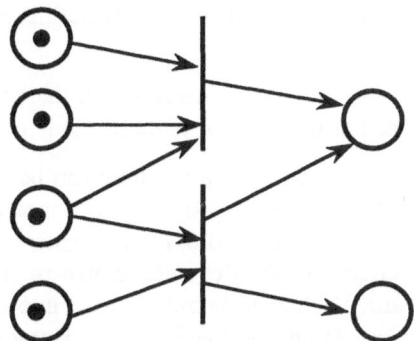

Figure 3.4. Undeterminism in Petri nets.

the *inhibitor arc*—an arc that is active only if its associated source place does not hold a token. For example as shown in Figure 3.5, transition c_2 is enabled only if p_4 and b_2 have a token and b_1 does not.

Other extensions to Petri nets have also been proposed

1. *Generalized Petri nets:* Allow multiple arcs between a place and a transition. A transition is enabled in a generalized Petri net only if each of its input places has as many tokens as the number of arcs connecting the place and the transition. These nets can be shown to be equivalent to ordinary Petri nets.

2. *Extended Time Petri nets:* An execution time r is associated with each

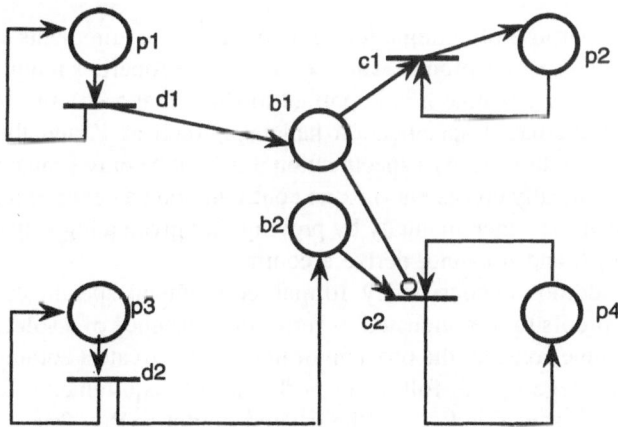

Figure 3.5. A Petri net with an inhibitor arc. Reprinted with permission from Ref. 17. © 1977, ACM.

transition. Such nets are useful in predicting the performance of a concurrent system.

Subclasses of Petri nets have been studied with the hope that their decision power can be strengthened at the price of reduced modeling power:

1. *Finite-State Machines:* Such a machine can be converted into a Petri net whose transitions have exactly one input and one output. For example as shown in Figure 3.6, the finite-state machine shown in (a) can be converted into the Petri net shown in (b). The conversion is straightforward: Each state is transformed into a place; each input is transformed into a transition; and each arc is transformed into two arcs in the net. The net shown in (b) is equivalent to the state machine shown in (a), since a string that can be accepted by (a) corresponds to a sequence of transitions that can be fired if a token is placed in place p_A, and vice versa.

2. *Marked Graphs:* A marked graph is a Petri net whose places have exactly one input transition and one output transition.

3. *Free Choice Petri nets:* A Petri net is a free choice net if each arc from a place is either the unique output from the place or the unique input to a transition.

See Ref. 19 for a discussion of the relationships between Petri net theory and algebraic specifications.

3.7. VERIFYING SPECIFICATIONS

The purpose of taking a formal approach to requirements specification is to prove that a specification satisfies certain basic properties required for all correct programs. For example it is important to show that a specification is consistent. With a logic-based specification language, such as Z and the object-oriented logic system, this means a specification must not be only syntactically correct but also semantically consistent (i.e., no contradiction can exist among axioms). This can be achieved incrementally by proving that given a logic system L and a new axiom A, L and A cannot derive a contraction.

In addition to consistency, formal requirements specification allows mathematical proofs to be conducted to verify the existence of a solution to a problem. For example consider the problem of finding the greatest common divisor of two positive integers. The following is the set of requirements for the two input parameters, say, x and y, and the desired output z (Ref. 20):

1. z divides x.

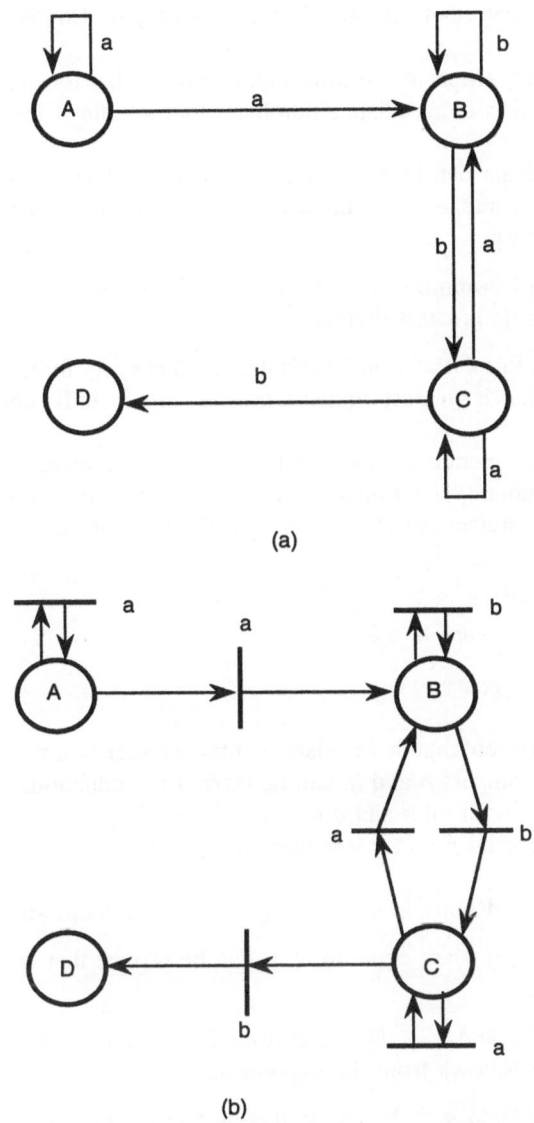

(a)

(b)

Figure 3.6. Transformation from a finite-state machine (a) to a Petri net (b). Reprinted with permission from Ref. 17. © 1977, ACM.

2. z divides y.

3. z is the greatest of the set of integers satisfying Conditions 1 and 2.

The following proof, stated informally, verifies that for every pair of positive integers x and y, there exists a number z that satisfies Condition 3:

1. Every integer can be divided by 1. Therefore 1 is a common divisor of any pair of integers; i.e., the set of common divisors of any two integers is not empty.

2. The set of common divisors of any two integers is finite, since each integer is its greatest divisor.

3. Based on Properties 1 and 2 and the fact that every finite nonempty set of integers has a greatest element, the statement can be concluded.

The same statement can be verified by an algebraic specification. Considering the same problem, the following is a set of axioms for determining the greatest common divisor (gcd) between two positive integers:

1. $x = gcd(x,x)$

2. $gcd(x,y) = gcd(x + y,y)$

3. $gcd(x,y) = gcd(y,x)$

Now the statement that there exists an integer r such that $r = gcd(p,q)$, given any two positive integers p and q, can be proved by induction. We assume that the statement is true for all p and q less than N (the hypothesis), then prove that the same is true for all p and q less than or equal to N:

1. If both p and q are less than N, it is true by hypothesis.

2. If both p and q are equal to N, it can be proved that $N = gcd(N,N)$ by Axiom 1.

3. Let $p = N$ and $q < N$. By Axiom 2, $gcd(p,q) = gcd(p - q,q)$. The statement follows from the hypothesis.

4. Let $p < N$ and $q = N$. The statement can be proved as in Axiom 3.

Reference 20 suggests that formal specifications orthogonal to each other, such as algebraic specification and logic-based specification are complementary. Reference 20 also suggests writing and verifying separately different specifications to provide a secure basis for software engineering.

Many properties of concurrent systems can be proved formally based on theorem proving; these can be divided into two categories[21]:

1. *Safety properties:* Concerning a program not entering an unacceptable state.

2. *Liveness properties:* Concerning a program eventually entering a desirable state.

Examples of safety properties include the following:

1. *Partial correctness:* If the precondition of a program is true when the program starts, then the postcondition has to be true after the program terminates.

2. *Deadlock freeness:* A program can never enter a state in which no further progress can be made.

3. *Mutual exclusion:* Two different processes can never be in their critical sections at the same time.

Some examples of liveness properties include the following:

1. *Proper termination:* A program eventually terminates.

2. Each request for service is eventually answered.

3. A process eventually enters its critical section.

A substantial amount of work with *temporal logic*[21] has been done to prove that a program satisfies certain properties. Temporal logic is another formal specification language that extends ordinary logic with two temporal operators:

1. $\Box$: meaning *now and forever*

2. $\Diamond$: meaning *now or sometime in the future*

For example the assertion $x > 0$ is interpreted as x is positive now. The assertion $\Box(x > 0)$ is interpreted as x is positive now and forever; and the assertion $\Diamond(x > 0)$ is interpreted as x is positive now or will be positive sometime in the future. Temporal operators are useful in dealing with dynamics (i.e., sequences of state charges) that could be created by a program.

Three kinds of assertions are used to refer to any control component A (i.e., statement) of a program: *at A, in A,* and *after A,* meaning the control is at the beginning of A, during the execution of A, and after A is executed, respectively. Therefore partial correctness for example can be expressed as:

$$(at\ S \wedge P) -> \Box(after\ S -> Q)$$

This means if before program S starts, precondition P is true, then it is always true (i.e., for all possible sequences of states that may be obtained due to S's execution) that S terminates with the postcondition Q true. Similarly mutual exclusion can be expressed as:

$$at\ S -> \Box\ \sim(in\ CS_1\ and\ in\ CS_2)$$

To prove such properties, temporal logic employs all the axioms and rules of inference available in ordinary logic and some additional theorems, such as the following[21]:

1. $\Box(P -> Q) -> (P ->-> Q)$, where the notion $->->$ is interpreted as *eventually leads to.*

2(a) $\Box(P \wedge Q)$ is equivalent to $(\Box P \wedge \Box Q)$.

2(b) $\Diamond(P \Diamond Q)$ is equivalent to $(\Diamond P \vee \Diamond Q)$.

3. $(\Box P \wedge \Box(P -> Q)) -> \Box Q$

4. $\Diamond P \vee \Box \sim P$

5. $((P ->-> Q) \wedge (Q ->-> R)) -> P ->-> R$

6. $((P ->-> R) \wedge (Q ->-> R)) -> ((P \vee Q) ->-> R)$

7. $\Box(P \vee Q) -> (\Box P \vee \Diamond Q)$

8. $[(P \wedge \Box Q) ->-> R] -> [(P \wedge \Box Q) ->-> (R \wedge \Box Q)]$

Reference 21 contains detailed proofs for some interesting examples. Reference 22 presents some additional theorems that deal with the synchronous communication constructs available in CSP.[20] Real-time constructs, such as *wait*, is considered in Ref. 23.

Instead of theorem proving, a graph-based approach can be employed to verify a specification presented as a Petri net. For the purpose of analysis, a *marked* Petri net (P,T,I,O,α) can be defined as a Petri net (P,T,I,O) augmented with a marking function α, which assigns tokens to places in the net. The number and positions of tokens in a net may change when a net is being executed. Therefore the state of a Petri net with n places $p_1 \ldots p_n$ can be defined as a vector $(\alpha_1 \ldots \alpha_n)$, where α_i, $1 \leq i \leq n$, is the number of tokens in place p_i at any particular instance of time. The change of states in a net can be described in terms of the *next-state function* δ, where $\delta(\alpha,t_j)$ gives the marking resulting from the marking α with transition t_j. Based on this two sequences can be produced from the execution of a Petri net: a sequence of markings $(\alpha_0, \alpha_1, \dots)$ and a sequence of transitions $(t_{j(0)}, t_{j(1)}, \dots)$ such that $\delta(\alpha_k, t_{j(k)}) = \alpha_{(k+1)}$, where $k = 0, 1, 2$, etc. The *reachability set* $R(M)$ for a marked Petri net $M = (P, T, I, O, \alpha)$ is defined to be the set of all possible markings that can be reached from α. In other words it defines all possible states that can be reached in M, assuming the initial state is α.

The most fundamental problem associated with a Petri net is the *reachability problem:* Given a marked Petri net with a marking α and another marking, α, is α reachable from α? The following are some other properties defined in Petri net theory:

1. *Boundness*[24]: The number of tokens in each place at any instance of time should be bounded. A Petri net is *k-bounded* if at any time the number of tokens in any place is bounded by k. A *1-bounded* Petri net is called a *safe* net. Such properties are important for verifying mutual exclusions (i.e., only one token in one place) and finite capacities of places (e.g., buffer spaces).

2. *Liveness*[25]: A Petri net is live if there always exists a transition to fire from a reachable marking in the net. This property implies the system is *deadlock free.*

3. *Conservativeness:* A Petri net is conservative if the number of tokens in the net is a constant.

4. *Proper Termination*[26]: A Petri net is properly terminating if it always terminates in a well-defined manner such that no tokens are left in the net. With this property the system is guaranteed not to produce side effects on the next initiation.

Some of the preceding properties can be established by constructing a *reachability tree* from the net. This gives a finite representation for the reachability set. A reachability tree avoids enumerating a potentially infinite number of markings (states) of the net by introducing a special symbol w, which stands for *arbitrarily large*. Specifically, a reachability tree is constructed as follows:

1. The root of the tree is labeled with the initial state (marking).

2. From any leaf node on the tree that is not terminal and marked with α, a node is added to the tree and marked with β if there exists an enabled transition t for which $\delta(\alpha, t) = \beta$. If β repeats a marking associated with a node that belongs to the path from the root, the added node becomes a terminal node, and it is not expanded further. In addition if all components

of β are greater than or equal to the corresponding components of a marking associated with a node that belongs to the path from the root, those components strictly greater than the corresponding components (of the marking of the node on the path) are replaced by the special symbol w. This is necessary because otherwise those components (i.e., those replaced by w) can ultimately become very large by repeating transitions in between the two nodes. Such repetitions do not discover new markings that are reachable from the first node by simply repetitively visit the same set of nodes between the two nodes.

The reachability tree produced is finite, since loops are avoided. As a simple example, consider the marked Petri net shown in Figure 3.7(a). The corresponding reachability tree is established in Figure 3.7(b). From the node labeled $(1,0,0,1)$, transition t_2 is enabled, and the new marking should be $(1,1,1,0)$. Now since every component of $(1,1,1,0)$ is greater than or equal to the corresponding components of the marking associated with the root, which is of course on the path from the root to the new node, the new node should be labeled $(1,w,1,0)$.

The properties discussed earlier can now be visually obtained from the reachability tree:

- If a Petri net is *k-bounded,* then the reachable state space must be finite. This is because there are only $k + 1$ possible values that can be assigned to each place in a marking. Consequently no w can exist in the reachability tree.

- If a Petri net is conservative, then the reachable state space must be finite. This is because there are only a finite number of ways of partitioning tokens among places. Consequently no w can exist in the reachability tree.

Some problems associated with Petri nets are solvable but difficult to solve; these include the reachability problem and the liveness problem, which can be proved to be equivalent to the reachability problem. Some other problems associated with Petri nets, are not, however, decidable; these include the following:

- Given two marked Petri nets, is the reachability set of one a subset of that of the other?

- Given two marked Petri nets, is the reachability set of one equal to that of the other?

As mentioned earlier, subclasses of Petri nets have higher decision power (but a weaker modeling power): A state machine is conservative and finite and a marked graph is live and safe. The reachability problem is solvable.

References 27–29 present other work on applying Petri net analysis. We see from the structure of a Petri net that it can be converted into a production system.[30] A production system consists of a set of rules, or productions, which take the form (condition) -> (action); a database or context, which maintains state/data of the system; and a rule interpreter. The condition portion of each rule (LHS) is composed of some logical combination of results obtained from comparing some state variable(s) to a fixed value or to some other state variable(s). These results are tested continuously. If the condition is true, the consequent action (RHS) of the rule is executed. In a pure production system, rules are in a sequential list, and these are evaluated one at a time according to their order on the list. When a rule is found to be true in the current context, the RHS is

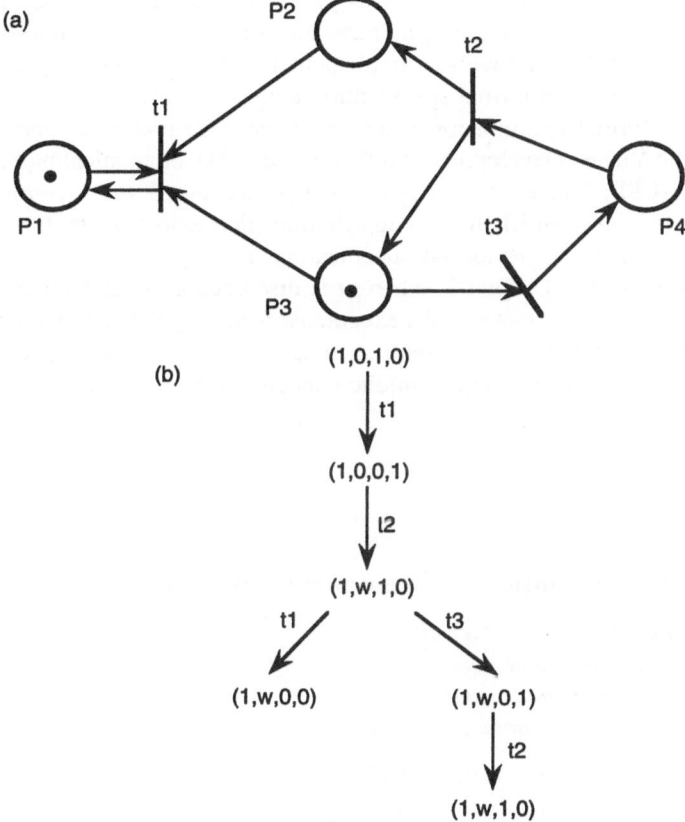

Figure 3.7. A Petri net and its reachability tree. Reprinted with permission from Ref. 17. © 1977, ACM.

executed, then rule testing begins again at the top of the list of rules. If no rules have true LHSs or a halt RHS is executed, the system terminates processing.

3.8. FINAL REMARKS

In the past many argued that formal specification methods, such as those discussed in this chapter, are too complex to be useful in real applications. In addition these methods require complex mathematics, which is difficult to learn; they tend to increase the cost of development; and they are incomprehensible to clients. However Ref. 31 points out that such arguments are not true; in particular formal specifications have the ability to expose more errors than informal methods.

In addition to requirements specification and verification, Ref. 32 shows that many formal specification languages (e.g., Z) are especially suitable for system design via decomposition and refinement and for system validation—a formal specification can be used with an implementation to reveal missing paths.

In addition to the formal specification languages described in this chapter, many other formal specification languages have been proposed. Some notable ones are the Vienna Development Method (VDM),[33] Communicating Sequential Processes (CSP)[35] (see Chapter 5 where it is discussed with a programming language derived from it), and Lamport's transition axiom method.[34]

Like Petri net some formal specification languages are executable; these include PROLOG (see Chapter 7, where it is discussed as a declarative programming language) and PAISLEY.[36] An executable formal specification language can provide many additional advantages, such as immediate feedback about specification, rapid prototyping, and symbolic execution (see Chapter 9).[32]

PROBLEMS

1. Consider a first-order system with the following predicate definitions:

lives(person_name,street city)
works(person_name,company_name, salary)
located_in(company_name,city)
manages(person_name,manager_name)

Convert each of the following queries into first-order logic:

- Does anybody work for Bank of America?
- Does anybody work for Bank of America and earn more than 10,000?

- Does anybody live in the same city as the company he/she works for?
- Does anybody live in the same city and on the same street as his/her manager?
- Is there anybody who does not work for Bank of America?

2. Suppose that each edge from node x to node y in a directed graph is asserted as a fact of the form $edge(x,y)$. Write a functional specification in first-order logic for the Boolean function $hamiltonian(Node\_list)$, where $Node\_List$ is a list representation of the set of *all* graph nodes and the graph contains a *hamiltonian circuit*, i.e., a path that begins and ends at the same node and passes through each node in $Node\_List$ exactly once.

3. Suppose each edge from node x to node y in a directed graph g is asserted as a fact of the form $edge(g,x,y)$. Also assume that each node x of g is asserted as a fact of the form $node(g,x)$. Write a functional specification in first-order logic for the procedural predicate $min\_span\_tree(g,L)$, where L is a list representation of the set of edges that forms a minimal spanning tree for the graph g.

4. Write the following integrity constraints for the database described in Problem 1:

(a) No employee of Bank of America can make more than his/her manager.
(b) Every employee has to live in the city in which his/her company is located.

5. Write a Z specification for the abstract data type *Queue*.

6. Write a Z specification for the abstract data type *Binary Search Tree*.

7. Describe the finite-state machine in Figure 3.6(a) in terms of a production system. You may assume a set of actions.

8. Describe the Petri net in Figure 3.3 in terms of a production system.

9. Develop an general algorithm to convert a Petri net into a production system.

10. Find the set of reachable states for the Petri net in Examples 3.8 and 3.9.

REFERENCES

1. Alford, M. *IEEE Computer* **18**:4, 36–46 (Apr. 1985).
2. Shoenfield, J. R. *Mathematical logic* (Addison-Wesley, Reading, MA, 1967).
3. Genesereth, M. R., and Nilsson, N. J. *Logical foundations of artificial intelligence* (Morgan-Kaufmann, Palo Alto, CA, 1988).
4. Nilsson, N. J. *Principles of artificial intelligence* (Morgan Kaufmann, Palo Alto, CA, 1980).
5. Ullman, J. D. *Principles of database systems,* 2d ed. (Computer Science Press, Potomac, MD, 1982).
6. Gallaire, H., Minker, J., and Nicolas, J. M. *ACM Computing Surveys* **16**, 153–185 (June 1984).
7. Spivey, J. M. *Z notation: a reference manual* (Prentice-Hall, New York, 1988).
8. Imperato, M. *An introduction to Z* (Chartwell-Bratt, Bromley, Kent, U.K., 1991).
9. Sheu, P. C-Y., and Yoo, S. B. "A deductive approach to software reuse." *Proc. of 1994 International Conference on Software Engineering and Knowledge Engineering* (Latvia, June, 1994).
10. Chang, C. L., and Lee, R. C. T. *Symbolic logic and mechanical theorem proving* (Academic Press, New York, 1973).
11. Horebeek, I. V., and Lewi, J. *Algebraic specifications in software engineering, an introduction* (Springer-Verlag, New York, 1989).
12. Reichel, H. *Initial computability algebraic specifications and partial algebras* (Oxford Science Publications, New York, 1987).
13. *IEEE Transactions on Software Engineering,* Special Issue on Algebraic Specifications **SE-11**:3, 242–251 (Mar. 1985).
14. Ehrig, H., and Mahr, B. *Fundamentals of algebraic specification 1: equations and initial semantics* (Springer-Verlag, New York, 1985)
15. Guttag, J. V., Horning, J. J., and Wing, J. M. *IEEE Software* **2**:5, 24–36 (Sept. 1985).
16. Peterson, J. L. *Net theory and the modeling of systems* (Prentice-Hall, New York, 1981).
17. Peterson, J. L. *ACM Computing Surveys* **9**:3, 223–252 (Sept. 1977).
18. Ramamoorthy, C. V., and Ho, G. *IEEE Transactions on Software Engineering* **SE-6**:5, 440–449 (Sept. 1980).
19. Reisig, W. *Theoretical Computer Science* 80, 1–34 (1991).
20. Hoare, C. A. R. *IEEE Computer* **20**:9, 85–91 (Sept. 1987).
21. Owicki, S., and Lamport, L. *ACM Transactions on Programming Languages and Systems* **4**:3, 455–495 (July 1982).
22. Lamport, L., and Schneider, F. B. *ACM Transactions on Programming Languages and Systems* **6**:2, 281–296 (Apr. 1984).
23. Liu, L. Y., and Shyamasundar, R. K. *IEEE Transactions on Software Engineering* **SE-16**:3, 373–388 (Apr. 1990).
24. Karp, R. M., and Miller, R. E. *SIAM Journal of Applied Math.* **14** (Nov. 1966).
25. Hack, M. *Decidability questions for Petri nets* (Ph.D. diss., MIT, 1975).
26. Gostelow, K. P., *Flow of control, resource allocation, and the proper termination of programs* (Ph.D. diss., University of California, Los Angeles, 1971).
27. Leveson, N. G. *IEEE Transactions on Software Engineering* **SE-13**:3, 386–397 (Mar. 1987).
28. Leveson, N. G. *Communication ACM* **34**:2, 36–46 (Feb. 1991).
29. Coolahan, J. E., and Roussopoulos, N. *IEEE Transactions on Software Engineering* **SE-9.9**, 603 (Sept. 1983).
30. Davis, R., and King, J. In *Machine intelligence,* vol. 8 (Elcock and Michie, eds.) (Wiley, New York, 1976), pp. 279–90.
31. Hall, A. *IEEE Software* **7**:9, 11–20 (Sept. 1990).
32. Wing, J. M. *IEEE Computer* **23**:9, 8–24 (Sept. 1990).

33. Jones, C. B. *Systematic software development using VDM* (Prentice-Hall, New York, 1986).
34. Lamport, L. *ACM Transactions on Programming Languages and Systems* **5**:2, 190–222 (Apr. 1983).
35. Hoare, C. A. R. *Communication ACM* **21**:8, 666 (Aug. 1978).
36. Zave, P., and Schell, W. *IEEE Transactions on Software Engineering* **SE-12**:2, 312–325 (Feb. 1986).

Design Methodologies and Specifications

In the design phase of the software life cycle, the architecture of the system is determined. If it is reasonably complicated, the system in most cases consists of a number of components, called *modules*. During the design phase, those modules, relationships among modules, and possibly some control sequences are identified. Requirements for the modules are further specified, and this step is repeated until no further decomposition can be made and each module can be realized directly.

The preceding description reflects two important concepts commonly employed in the design process: *decomposition* and *refinement*. Clearly these concepts were employed in some of the formal specification languages discussed in Chapter 3 (e.g., Z). However we emphasize here that a design specification must often identify the control aspects of a system in addition to its structure.

Chapter 4 begins with a discussion of some of the concepts behind most of the existing design methodologies (Section 4.1). Section 4.2 summarizes some design specification languages, which are usually semiformal or informal, proposed for procedure-oriented software systems. One particular design specification language, namely, *structured design analysis,* and its associated design methodology are discussed in detail. Section 4.3 introduces some design issues related to object-oriented programming. Section 4.4 describes how to apply structured design analysis to express the dynamic and functional semantics of an object-oriented system. Section 4.5 summarizes some object-oriented design methodologies. Finally Section 4.6 introduces some CASE tools that can be used to automate many tasks involved in the design process.

4.1. DESIGN CONCEPTS

A number of design concepts have been proposed for software systems. A fundamental one may be stepwise refinement, which begins with the highest level of abstraction—program specification. The program is then decomposed into a number of major components, and the major components are designed. The major components are subsequently decomposed. This process is repeated until sufficient details about the program can be developed to implement it with a programming language. According to Ref. 1, stepwise refinement requires post-poning decisions about representation details as long as possible and carefully demonstrating that each successive step is a faithful expansion of previous steps. This concept is important for both structured and object-oriented programs.

Other important design concepts include the following:

- *Abstraction*[2]: Functions of a system should be hierarchically structured so that lower modules provide services to higher level modules. A module at each level of abstraction should have the capability of summarizing ser-vices provided to it from lower level modules.

- *Information Hiding*[3]: Each module hides its internal details, and modules communicate only through well-defined interfaces.

- *Modularity:* A system should be decomposed into a set of well-defined and manageable units whose interfaces are well-defined. A number of criteria are proposed to decompose a system into modules. An important one is based on *coupling* and *cohesion*,[4] so that modules are chosen to minimize intermodule coupling and maximize intramodule cohesion. The degrees of coupling between two modules can be ranked (from the highest to the lowest) as follows:

  —*Content Coupling:* Occurs if one module modifies some data or control components within another module.
  —*Common Coupling:* Occurs if two modules share some global data.
  —*Control Coupling:* Occurs if one module passes some control flags to another module to impact its control flow.
  —*Stamp Coupling:* Occurs if only data structures (e.g., arrays) are passed as parameters between two modules but not all of the passed data are used by the called module.
  —*Data Coupling:* Occurs if only data are passed as parameters between two modules and all of the passed data are used by the called module.

  The degrees of cohesion within a module can be ranked (from the lowest to the highest) as follows:

  —*Coincidental Cohesion:* Occurs if elements of the module have no obvious relationships to one another.
  —*Logical Cohesion:* Occurs if elements of the module have some logical associations. A typical example of this type of cohesion is a module containing elements that perform the same type of functions (e.g., I/O). Another example is a module whose elements are executed in sequence to accomplish one function (e.g., initialization). In essence, elements of this type of module are grouped by some logical associa-tions.

—*Temporal Cohesion:* Logical cohesion, but elements are executed in sequence.

—*Sequential Cohesion:* Temporal cohesion with the additional property that the input of one element is the output of another.

—*Communication Cohesion:* Occurs if elements of the module refer to the same data set.

—*Informational Cohesion:* Occurs if elements of the module are related to manipulate the same data structure.

—Functional Cohesion: Occurs if elements of the module are related to perform a single data structure function.

4.2. PROCESS DESCRIPTION LANGUAGES AND DESIGN METHODOLOGIES

As stated in Ref. 5, "While a process is a vehicle for doing a job, a process description is a specification of how the job is to be done. Thus cookbook recipes are process descriptions, while carrying out the recipes are processes." The essence of some of well-known process description languages and their associated design methodologies (if these exist) are summarized in the following.

4.2.1. Data Flow Diagrams and Design Methodology

Data flow diagram was first used by Ref. 6 as a model for graphically capturing a description of the information flow within a system. The captured information was then used to perform a structured analysis, which involves studying systems of all sizes. This study can lead to their specifications.

A data flow diagram is made up of five types of elements: data flows, activities, files, sources, and sinks. Each flow is represented by an arc with an arrow to show the direction of flow. A labeled arc denotes a data flow of the named information or object that is passed between other entities in the process. An activity is denoted by a circle, and it represents a conversion of incoming data flow into outgoing data flow. The uniqueness of an activity in the data flow diagram is determined by its name, so each activity must have its own unique name within a process. A file is denoted by an open ended box in a data flow diagram, and it represents a storage of information. Sources, sinks, and external elements are denoted by boxes. A source provides data to an activity, while a sink receives data and information from the activity.

The language introduced in the preceding discussion is substantiated by the so-called *data flow design methodology,* which maps information flows and processes into a program structure. One of two types of analysis are used to derive the program structure: *transform* or *transaction* analysis. Transform analysis is used if the information flow can be separated into input and output. However if one data item determines the flow of data through various paths, transaction analysis should be used. A system can have both transform and transaction flows; however the prevalent of the two must be identified. The following list shows the primary steps of data-flow-oriented design:

1. Refine data flow diagram.

2. Determine type of flow:
   - If transaction:
     —Identify transaction center and data acquisition path.
     —Map into transaction structure.
   - If transform:
     —Identify incoming/outgoing branches.
     —Map into transform structure.

3. Factor the structure.

4. Refine the structure using design heuristics.

5. Develop interface description and global data structure.

6. Review, then return to Step 2 if necessary.

7. Prepare design details.

For transform analysis, the first step is to review the Level 0 data flow diagram (DFD), the system specification, and the software requirements specification. The second step is to refine the DFD to include more details. Refinement continues until all required details are present. Then the DFD is inspected to identify transform and transaction flows. If an information flow is transform, transform analysis is used to map the DFD into a program structure. If a transaction flow is present, transaction analysis is used. The last step involves factoring the DFD diagram. This is the process of mapping the DFD into a program structure that can be represented by a structure chart.

By the mid-1980s structured analysis techniques were found to lack provisions for real-time control-oriented systems. Real-time extensions were made by Refs. 7 and 8. The Ref. 7 extensions basically provide time-continuous information flow, control information and processing, multiple instances of the same process for multitasking systems, and state-transition mechanisms.

Reference 8 added three extensions/modifications. First data flow and control flow were separated into two diagrams. Second control specifications

(CSPECS) and process specifications (PSPECS) were associated with the diagrams. A CSPECS does two things: It determines how the process behaves when a control signal is sensed, and it determines which processes are invoked by the signal. A PSPEC describes the inner workings of a process in the flow diagram. Third, the state-transition diagram was added. By following state-transition diagrams, we can easily see what states cannot be reached nor exited, then correct these errors. The requirements dictionary is a relational database containing all data, composite or singular, used in a system. This is another extension to DFD. It allows us to know exactly what is flowing in the DFD. Example 4.1[9] shows the DFD, CFD, CSPEC, PSPEC, and data dictionaries of a simple system: a vending machine.

Example 4.1. (Ref. 9)   The operations of a typical vending machine can be explained as follows. Initially the machine waits for a customer selection. Once a valid selection is made, the machine waits for payment. If the selected product is available and the payment is sufficient, the machine dispenses the product, then returns the correct change. If payment is insufficient, the machine returns the payment. In both cases change is returned after the customer presses the return coins button.

As shown in Figure 4.1, the DFD diagram consists of a number of

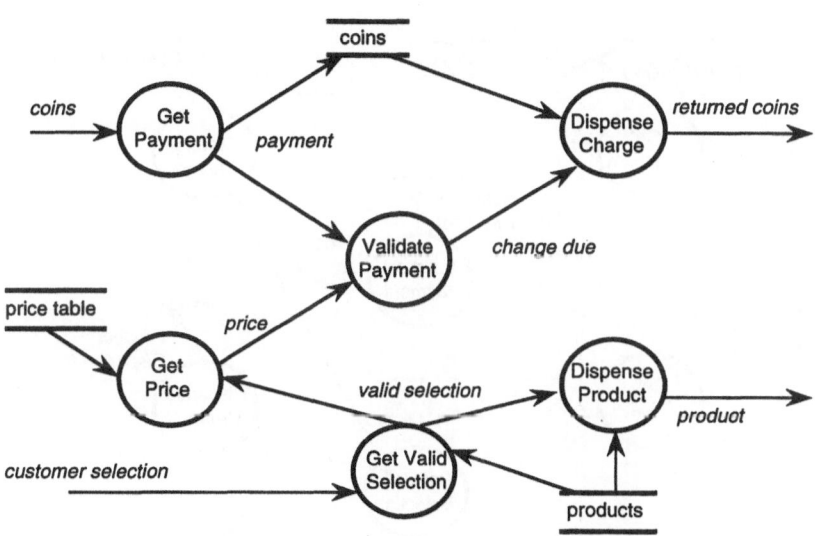

Figure 4.1. The DFD for the vending machine example.

Valid Payment

```
input: price, payment
output: change due,
        Sufficient_Payment (Boolean)
if payment >= price
   Sufficient_Payment = True
   change due = payment - price
else
   Sufficient_Payment = False
```

Figure 4.2. The PSPEC for valid payment.

modules associated with the system: *Get Payment, Validate Payment, Dispense Payment, Get Product Price, Get Valid Selection,* and *Dispense Product.* Among these are the information flows. For example the *Validate Payment* module obtains the correct price and the amount of payment from *Get Product Price* and *Get Payment,* respectively. The module then produces the output *Change Due,* which serves as the input to the module *Dispense Change.* Thus a DFD shows the modules of a

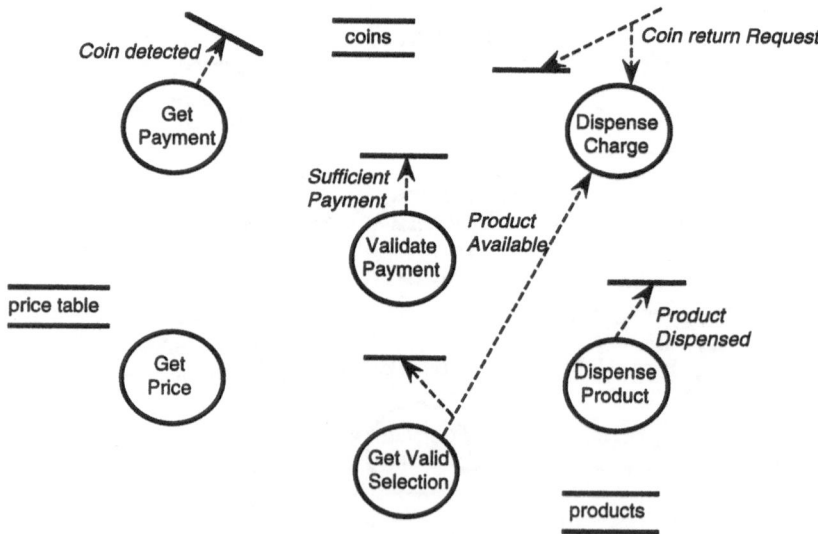

Figure 4.3. The CFD for the vending machine example.

system and data flows among the modules, i.e., inputs to, and outputs from, those modules. The functionality (i.e., relationships between in puts and outputs) of each module is described in the associated PSPEC of the module, as in Figure 4.2. The events produced by the modules are shown in the CFD, as shown in Figure 4.3, where a short vertical bar designates the CFD/CSPEC interface, and control flows are designated as dotted arcs. In Figure 4.3, for example, the control flow from the module *Get Payment* to the CFD/CSPEC interface means the event *Coin detected* is set by the module *Get Payment* and used in the associated CSPEC. Two control flows enter the module *Dispense Change—Coin Return Request* and *Product Available;* therefore values of both events (flags) are used in the module *Dispense Change* to take the correct action (e.g., if the product is not available, then return the payment; if the product is available and the return coin button is pressed, then return the correct change, etc.). Finally as shown in Figures 4.4 and 4.5, the CSPEC consists of two parts: a state-transition diagram (STD) and a process activation table (PAT). In the STD each rectangle designates a state, and arcs correspond to state transitions labeled by the pair event/control signal. The PAT records the actions (module activations) triggered by each control signal.

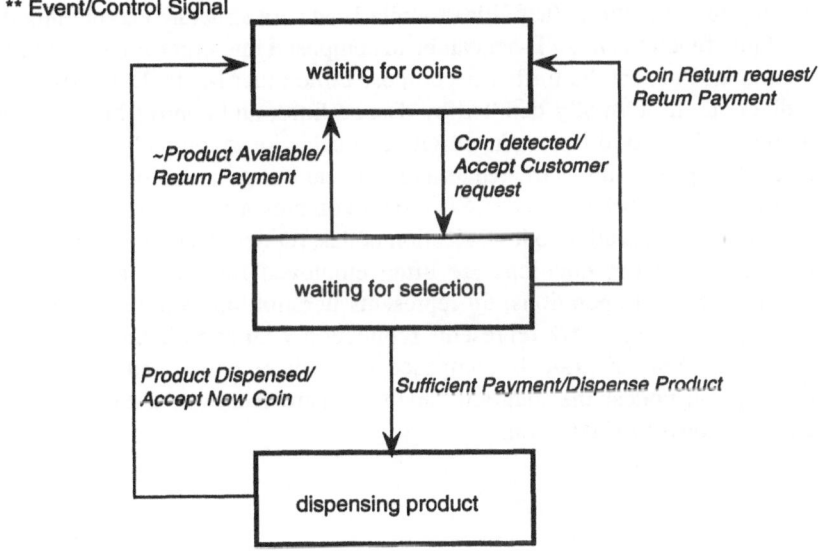

Figure 4.4. The STD for the vending machine example.

	Dispense Charge	Dispense Product	Get Valid Selection	Get Payment
Accept Customer Request	0	0	1	0
Return Payment	1	0	0	0
Accept New Coin	0	0	0	1
Dispense Product	1	1	0	0

Figure 4.5. The PAT for the vending machine example.

4.2.2. SSL

System Specification Language (SSL) is a portion of Distributed Computing Design system (DCDS).[10,11] Using SSL to specify products was first proposed by Mack Alford; SSL can also be used to capture processes behavior.

The SSL structures are made of F-nets and I-nets. The F-nets are structures containing time functions (activities), while I-nets are structures containing data items. Time functions in an F-net can be decomposed into other F-nets. Similarly an item in an I-net can be further decomposed into other I-nets. Data flows in an SSL diagram are normally denoted by dashed lines, and control flows are normally denoted by solid lines. An activity is a behavior graphically denoted by a box. A data type or a file is treated as an item, and it is graphically denoted by an oval. To represent behavior the SSL model contains a variety of nodes: begin nodes, end nodes, parallel nodes, selection nodes, replication nodes, and iteration nodes. The following notations are often employed for these node types: + represents selection operations, @ represents iteration operations, & represents parallel operations, and *& represents replication with coordination operations. In general an SSL diagram is composed of a set of nodes and a set of arcs connecting the nodes; the diagram can be constructed from a set of building blocks, as shown in Figure 4.6.

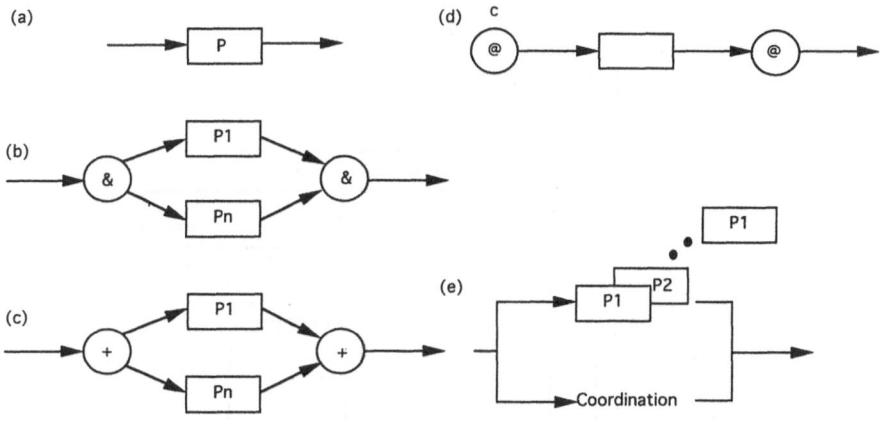

Figure 4.6. The Building blocks for SSL.

4.2.3. HIPO

Since it is estimated that one-third of reworking costs can be traced to errors in the analysis and design phases of a project, it is extremely important to place more emphasis on the quality of analysis and design. Hierarchy Input-Process-Output (HIPO)[12] allows the software designer to use an integrated method that can specify all levels of a system, from the highest functional level to the lowest code level. An HIPO specification has two basic components: a hierarchy chart and input-process-output charts. The hierarchy chart provides a functional break-down of the system, its functions and subfunctions. An input-process-output chart explains each function or subfunction of the hierarchy chart in terms of its input and output characteristics. Figure 4.7 shows a hierarchy chart and input-process-output chart.[12] This method provides a top-down, comprehensive functional breakdown of the whole system. It also allows different people to work on different functions as long as the functional interface specified in the HIPO charts is followed.

4.2.4. INTERCOL

The INTERCOL[13] is a language describing how modules are interconnected. It provides two facilities at the module level: interface control and version control. It defines *resources* as all things that can be named in a programming

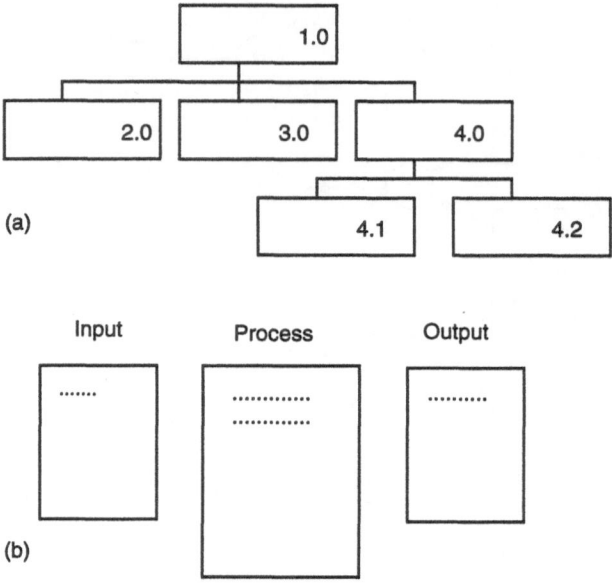

Figure 4.7. Hierarchy chart (A) and input-process-output chart (b). Reprinted with permission from Ref. 12. © 1976, IEEE.

language, e.g., variables, procedures, type definitions, etc. A subresource is a resource that is part of another resource, e.g., a field of a record. The INTERCOL uses a combination of incremental type checking with incremental compilation. Incremental type checking checks interface requirements and provides directives in a INTERCOL program to assure that the interface between modules is consistent. The INTERCOL also insists that no module be given more access rights than it actually needs. This can be done in the following ways:

- *Heterogenous Interfaces:* Different modules can use only resources specified in their require clause.

- *Name Control:* A module may be given access to only one subresource X of a resource N even if N has more than one subresource.

- *Write protection:* It allows explicit control of write protection of a resource.

The following is an example of an INTERCOL program[13]:

```
system PARSER
  module IO
    provide
    function SrcChar : char;
    const Line = record { lineNum : int;
                lineBuf : array[1 . . lineLn] of
                char;};
    procedure ListLine(outline : |Line);
  endIO
  module LEXAN
    provide
    type Lexeme = (Keyword, Operator, Identifier);
    function NextLex : Lexeme;
    require SrcChar,LineLn, Line.{lineNum,linebuf},
ListLine
  end LEXAN
end PARSER
```

In the preceding program, the system PARSER consists of two modules, IO and LEXAN. Module IO provides a function, a procedure, a constant, and a user-defined resource, called Line. Module LEXAN provides a user-defined type Lexeme and a function, and it requires all resources provided by IO.

To facilitate version control, "Each module or system in an INTERCOL description is viewed as a family, whose members are the various versions."[13] A module family contains three different types of members:

- *Implementations:* Actual source programs that share the same interface but are implemented in different ways

- *Revisions:* Revisions of implementations due to changes in one implementation, to fix bugs or other small problems

- *Derived versions:* Versions generated automatically

A system family is composed from module families, and a module family is composed from specific module versions. A complete example of an INTERCOL description, including interface control and version control, can now be presented in the following:[13]

```
system PARSER
  module IO
    provide
    function SrcChar : char;
    const Line = record { lineNum: int ;
                  lineBuf  :  array[1 . . lineLn] of
                  char;};
    procedure ListLine(outline : |Line);
    implementation HYDRA.bliss
    implementation TOP.bliss
  end IO
  module LEXAN
    provide
    type Lexeme = (Keyword, Operator, Identifier);
    function NextLex : Lexeme;
    require SrcChar, LineLn, Line.{lineNum,linebuf},
ListLine
  end LEXAN
  composition CMMP = { LEXAN, IO.HYDRA }:Target-
.PDP11
  composition PDP10 = { LEXAN, IO.HYDRA }:Target-
.PDP10
end PARSER
```

In the preceding program, there are two implementations for IO: one for the HYDRA operating system and the other for the TOPS10 operating system. Both implementations are written in the language BLISS, and the whole system is compiled for two different target machines, PDP10 and PDP11.

4.2.5. Others

Process description languages has been a very active research area; languages other than those just discussed include flowcharts, pseudocodes, structure charts (which show hierarchical structures of modules), decision tables, Problem Statement language (PSL),[14] Requirements Statement language (RSL),[10] SADT,[15] Structured System analysis (SSA).[6] Many of these were also accompanied by an automated analysis system, e.g., Problem Statement analyzer (PSA)[14] for PSL and Requirements Engineering Validation system (REVS)[10] for RSL.

4.3. DYNAMIC AND FUNCTIONAL MODELING

An object model describes the data aspects of the system; these include the static structures of objects involved in the system. In OMT the behavior of an object-oriented system is described in terms of two models: the *dynamic model* and the *functional model*. The dynamic model describes the control, or dynamic, aspects of the system; the functional model describes the transformational, or functional, aspects of the system. The dynamic model consists of a set of state diagrams, one for each class and one for each process that accesses objects in the system. The states of a state diagram can be defined in terms of existing attributes or by creating separate state variable(s). Operations can be assigned to a state so that they are executed whenever the state is entered. State transitions are triggered by *events*, which are special objects used solely for control purpose. In OMT the term event is somewhat vaguely defined. A more precise definition of events can be found in recent research on active databases. For example in SAMOS,[16] five types of primitive events are defined

- *Message Events:* Point in time when a message is arriving at an object and the point in time when the object has finished executing the appropriate method requested by the message

- *Value Events:* Point in time when the value of an object is being modified

- *Time Events:* Absolute points in time (e.g., 22:00:00, Feb. 28, 1995), periodically reappearing events (e.g., every hour), or relative to occurring events (e.g., one minute after event $E1$)

- *Transaction Events:* Defined by the beginning or termination of (user-defined) transactions

- *Abstract Events:* Events defined by users and applications according to their specific semantics

The following composite events can be specified given two (composite or primitive) events $E1$ and $E2$:

- *(E1|E2):* Occurs when either *E1* or *E2* occurs.

- *(E1,E2):* Occurs when $E1$ and $E2$ occur, regardless of the order.

- (E1;E2): Occurs when $E1$ and afterward $E2$ occurs.

- *(~E1):* Occurs when $E1$ does not occur in a specified (named) transaction or in a predefined time interval.

In HiPAC[17] three kinds of primitive events are defined: data manipulation operations, clock time and external notifications, which roughly correspond to value events, time events and abstract events in SAMOS, respectively. In addition to the composite events just listed, HiPAC includes the *closure* constructor. Specifically given an event E, the event $E*$ is signaled after E has been signaled an arbitrary number of times in a transaction.

The OMT employs data flow diagrams to construct the functional model. Like the dynamic model, the functional model consists of a set of data flow diagrams, one for each class and one for each process of the system. Each node in a data flow diagram typically corresponds to an operation. A data store corresponds to a class or an object. Finally flows in a data flow diagram correspond to information (including events) transferred between operations.

Example 4.2. (Ref. 18) Consider the object (class) diagram shown below that describes a bank application.

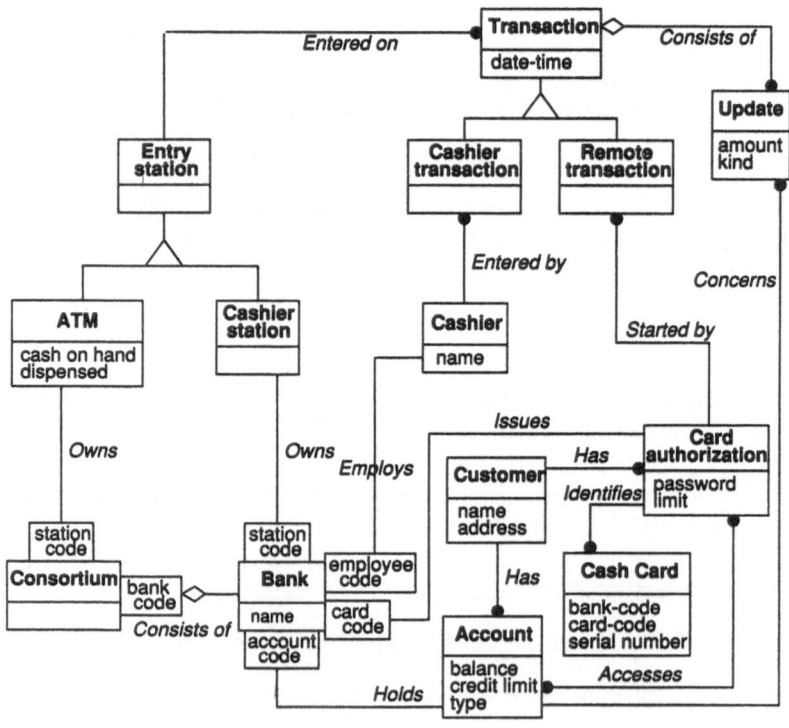

Object diagram for a bank application. Reprinted with permission from Ref. 18. © 1991, Prentice-Hall.

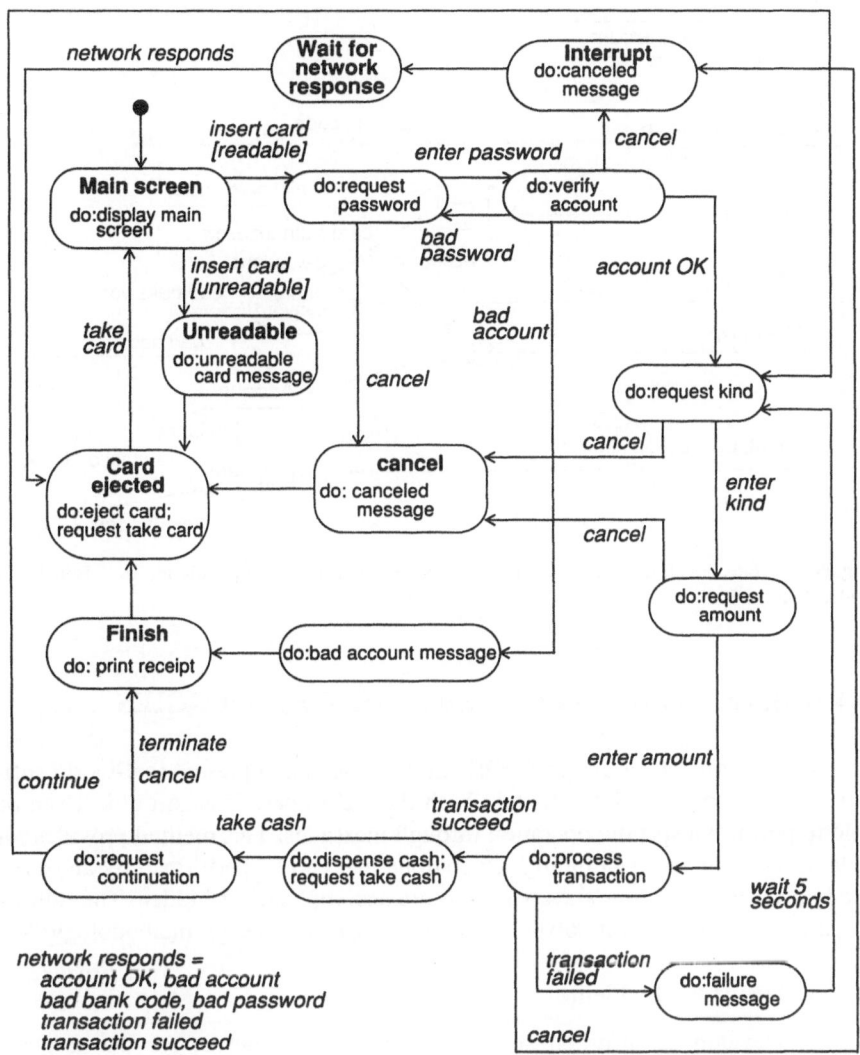

Figure 4.8. Dynamic model for the bank application. Reprinted with permission from Ref. 18. © 1991, Prentice-Hall.

Figures 4.8 and 4.9 show the dynamic model of the ATM class and the functional model of a transaction process that accesses an ATM, respectively. The semantics of the two diagrams should be clear to the reader. Note that events in the dynamic model can be characterized as user-defined according to our earlier discussion.

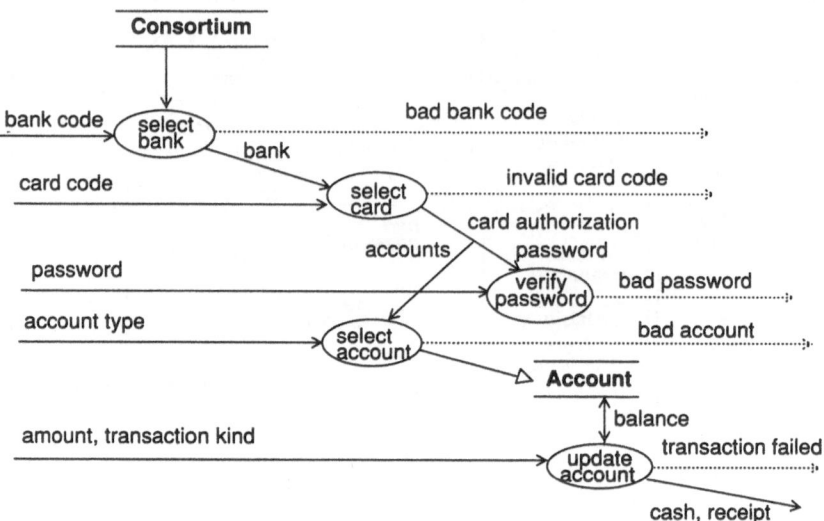

Figure 4.9. Functional model for the bank application. Reprinted with permission from Ref. 18. ©
1991, Prentice-Hall.

4.4. OBJECT-ORIENTED DESIGN METHODOLOGIES

In *object-oriented design* (OOD) method objects represent real-world software requirements. Objects contain both data and operations. An object can be
told to perform a specific operation through messages. This method provides for
data abstraction and data hiding. Operations that can be performed by an object
are known; however how the operations are accomplished is hidden. The following are the major steps involved in an object-oriented design methodology[19,20]:

1. Define the problem.

2. Develop an informal strategy (processing narrative) for the software
   realization of the real-world problem domain.

3. Formalize the strategy using the following steps:
   - Identify objects and their attributes.
   - Identify operations that may be applied to objects.
   - Establish interfaces by showing the relationship between objects and
     operations.
   - Decide on detailed design issues to provide an implementation descrip-
     tion for objects.

4. Repeat Steps 2–4 recursively. Previous steps are part of software requirement analysis; Steps 5–7 are design steps.

5. Refine the work done, looking for subclasses, message characteristics, and other details.

6. Represent the data structure(s) associated with object attributes.

7. Represent the procedural detail associated with each operation.

Another methodology, called the object-modeling technique (OMT), was introduced in Ref. 18. The methodology includes the following stages:

1. *Analysis:* A model of the real-world situation is built. The model consists of three views: the object model, the dynamic model, and the functional model, as described earlier.

2. *System Design:* A system is decomposed and structured into subsystems; a subsystem is a package of object classes, associations, operations, events, and constraints that are modular with respect to each other. Although ideally all objects can be active at the same time, typically a subsystem is the basic unit for concurrent processing; i.e., a subsystem corresponds to a task in a concurrent program. Consequently at this stage potential concurrency in the system has to be identified as a guideline to forming subsystems. In addition databases and other global resources have to be identified and how these are accessed has to be determined.

3. *Object Design:* This stage includes the following steps:
   (a) Obtain operations for the objects based on system design.
   (b) Design algorithms and data structures for the operations.
   (c) Minimize the cost of data accesses, such as using indices or hashing, for large set of data.
   (d) Maximize inheritance.
   (e) Determine how each association is implemented (e.g., as a class or an operation).
   (f) Determine the exact representation of object attributes.
   (g) Package classes and associations into modules.

The following example, although not complete, attempts to illustrate the different stages discussed in the OMT. It takes a bottom-up approach; i.e., it starts an object-oriented solution with the finest granularity. Obviously a top-down approach (i.e., starting a solution with a large granularity) or a mixture of both can be applied as well. Regardless if it is top-down, bottom-up, or a mix, a solution must be object-oriented in nature (i.e., in terms of objects and messages).

As shown in Example 4.3, it may be appropriate to call such informal solutions *object-oriented algorithms.*

> **Example. 4.3.** Consider the problem of displaying a set of three-dimensional objects on a two-dimensional screen of 256×256 pixels. A solution is to first project the three-dimensional objects (with depth) to the screen, then compute the density of each pixel based on the density of the object not hidden by any other object with respect to the pixel (i.e., whose depth is the smallest). Let us assume the finest granularity; identify objects in this problem as three-dimensional objects and pixels. An object-oriented approach assumes that each three-dimensional object is active. In addition each pixel (called a *pixel object*) is active. A scene is composed from pieces of contributions made by the objects, subject to available light sources and the position of the camera(s). For simplicity assume that three-dimensional objects are convex. Each of these can execute the following to compute its contribution to the scene:
>
> ```
> let projection be the result of projecting and
> clipping the object;
>     send acknowledgment to each pixel object in pro-
> jection;
> ```
>
> Each of the pixel objects can execute the following to determine which object occupies the pixel:
>
> ```
> set depth = infinity;
> for each acknowledgment received from object p do
> {
>   if (p.depth < depth)
>   {
>     depth = p.depth;
>     occupied_by = p;
>   }
>   send a reply to p;
> }
> ```

To make sure the program can terminate properly, let us assume that there exists a *controller* object and each three-dimensional object uses a counter to keep track of the number of the messages sent. Also assume that all messages in the system are time-stamped and delivered and processed according to the time stamp. The controller can execute the following:

```
set count = 0;
send an init message to each 3D object;
while a done message is received from a 3D object
{
  count++;
  if(count == #object)
  {
    send a display message to each pixel object;
    stop;
  }
}
```

On receiving an *init* message from the controller, each three-dimensional object can do the following:

```
let projection be the result of projecting and
clipping the object;
set count = 0;
set received = 0;
for each pixel object r in projection do
{
  send acknowledgment to r;
  count++;
}
while a reply is received from a pixel object do
{
  received++;
  if(received == count)
  {
    send a done message to controller;
    break;
  }
}
```

The algorithm for each pixel object is modified accordingly:

```
set depth = infinity;
while receiving a message do
{
  if the message is an acknowledgment message from
an object p;
  {
    if(p.depth < depth)
```

```
        {
           depth = p.depth;
           occupied_by = p;
        }
        send a reply message to p;
     }
     else if the message is a display message from
the controller
        {
           display the pixel according to occupied_by;
           break;
        }
  }
```

The preceding program constitutes an informal specification of an object-oriented solution to the problem. In the specification objects, their associated events and operations, and the dynamics of the solution are identified. It should be straightforward to convert the specification into an object model, a dynamic model, and a functional model, as required by the OMT to complete the analysis stage.

The next step is the system design stage according to the OMT. At this stage system performance is taken into consideration, and packages (logical processes) are formed. This is quite an obvious requirement in Example 4.3, since an excessive amount of communication is needed among the large number of objects (i.e., three-dimensional objects and 256 × 256 pixel objects). One possible approach is to group the pixel objects into a process called *screen* so that computations within *screen* are sequential. By doing this all pixels are implemented as records (i.e., passive objects). The object-oriented solution can then be modified as follows:

```
Controller
set count = 0;
send an init message to each 3D object;
while a done message is received from a 3D object
{
   count++;
   if(count == #object)
   {
      send a display message to screen;
      stop;
   }
}
```

On receiving an *init* message from the controller, each three-dimensional object can do the following:

```
let projection be the result of projecting and
clipping the object;
send projection to screen;
if a reply is received from screen do
  send a done message to controller;
```

The screen object executes the following:

```
for each pixel (x,y) do
  set depth = infinity;
while receiving a message do
{
  if the message is an acknowledgment message
from an object p
  {
    for each pixel (x,y) do
      if (x,y) belongs to the projection of p
      {
        if(p.depth < (x,y).depth)
        {
          (x,y).depth = p.depth;
          (x,y).occupied_by = p;
        }
      }
    send a reply message to p;
  }
  else if the message is a display message from
the controller
  {
    display the screen;
    break;
  }
}
```

An alternative way of grouping is to cluster three-dimensional objects into a single process while leaving pixel objects active. Yet another approach is to cluster pixel objects into several groups so that each group corresponds to an area on the screen.[21] The programmer must decide which approach to take based on available resources. Simulations or some performance analysis may have to be performed. It should be obvious to the reader that the decision made at this stage affects object structures in the implementation. For example in the pure object-oriented solution (i.e., all pixels and three-dimensional objects are active), each pixel has the capability of looping on itself and interpreting messages, while in the second solution (i.e., all pixels are grouped into a screen object), each pixel is passive, and a new object (and its associated methods) has to be provided.

The last stage according to the OMT is object design. At this stage object structures are finalized, implementation detail for each object class are determined, class inheritance is determined, and optimization is completed. For example, if the second solution is taken, pixels associated with the *screen* object can be implemented as an array, a hash table, or a linked list (although it is obvious in this case). Parameters needed for each type of messages (i.e., acknowledgment, reply, display, etc.) are determined, and so on.

In addition to Refs. 18 and 20, object-oriented methodologies are discussed in Refs. 22 and 23. As suggested in Ref. 18, "All of the object-oriented methodologies, including ours, have much in common, and should be contrasted more with non-object-oriented methodologies than with each other" (p. 274). The reader is encouraged to map the steps identified in Example 4.3 to the Booch methodology (see Problem 4.6).

4.5. DESIGN VERIFICATION AND CASE TOOLS

Once a design is finished, it is important to verify that the design incorporates every aspect stated in the requirements specification; it is also important to verify that the design itself is consistent (i.e., no contradictions). A number of CASE tools are available in the commercial market to support structured design methodology. Such CASE tools are referred to as Upper CASE tools.

A popular graphical design tool in the UNIX environment is Software through Pictures (StP) by Interactive Development Environments (IDE),[24] which runs on workstations and makes efficient use of their windowed interfaces and graphic capabilities. The StP consists of a collection of editors that draw such objects as structure charts, data structures and data flow diagrams. These editors are usually used jointly to represent a system. For example the data flow editor (DFE) can be used to represent data flow diagrams for the system, and the data flows can be linked to data structures drawn using the data structure editor (DSE). A brief description of each of the editors follows.

- *Structure chart editor (SCE):* Supports software architecture design, including input and output parameters for every module in the system, by creating and using structure charts; also checks for consistency between input and output parameters.

- *Data structure editor:* Supports definition of such data items as object name and type; also generates types and data declarations in C.

- *Data flow editor:* Supports creating, changing, and updating data flow diagrams; also checks for incompleteness, invalid diagrams of designs, and the level and ancestry of nodes.

- *Control flow editor (CFE):* Supports creating, changing and analyzing control flow diagrams.

- *Transition diagram editor (TDE):* Takes care of interactive changes and creations. For example TDE allows the description of screen layouts, inputs causing transitions, and output prompts. One of its more important facilities is that it automatically generates an executable version of the dialog, represented by a transition diagram. This executable file can be used as a prototype.

- *Entity relationship editor (ERE):* Automatically creates a relational database schema given an entity relationship diagram.

- *Picture editor:* Used for drawing; provides many commonly used symbols.

- *Graphical output:* Outputs from any of the StP editors can be generated in several formats, such as pic and postscript.

TurboCASE,[25,26] a CASE tool made for Apple Macintosh, includes comprehensive coverage of functions needed for requirements specification and analysis. Some of these include data modeling, techniques for structured design, and object-oriented analysis. To support these TurboCASE allows many diagrams to be produced by the user, such as data flow, control flow, state-transition, entity relationship, structure charts (SC), decision tables, control specifications, and minispecifications. TurboCASE also allows the user to draw flowcharts, block diagrams, and ordinary organization charts. All objects created by the user are integrated using a central data dictionary that ties them together. Needless to say Macintosh software, which uses object-oriented pop-up menus for frequently used modeling commands provides extraordinary ease of use.

Another feature of this software is its structured design methodology, whose basic modeling mechanism is *structure chart*. This shows how software works by depicting program modules, their hierarchical structure, and how they interface. Structure charts provide the ability to link to specification tables, which in turn allow the user to define details of each module and interface. TurboCASE eliminates using traditional *couples* to specify parameters passed between modules.

Instead pop-up tables show how parameters are passed between modules and which parameters a particular module accepts.

Design Generator is a fully integrated CASE tool[27] that assists in specifying what the system has to do and in verifying this specification for accuracy and completeness. This tool automates the requirements specification/analysis phase and integrates it with other phases of the software life cycle. There is a rule base in the tool that allows specification inputs presented in a strict format. This reduces specification ambiguity, since a system analyst must comply with the format when inputting specifications. Design Generator automates requirements specification and design phases of the software development cycle by providing an appropriate design based on specification analysis. A central repository information from all phases together and cross-references to identify stores discrepancies and conflicts.

Like procedure-oriented software, a number of CASE tools are available on the market to support one or several of the object-oriented design methodologies discussed earlier. For example Software through Pictures/OMT (StP/OMT)[27] is an object-oriented extension of StP that supports OMT. The StP/OMT has an object model editor, a dynamic model editor, and a functional model editor that allow the object, model, and functional models to be visually constructed. Class interface and definition files can be generated automatically from object models. The StP/OMT stores the semantics of all diagrams in a multiuser, shared repository built on top of a commercial DBMS. The environment offers the following features for design checking:

- Verifies that all classes and associations are appropriately modeled and meaningfully named

- Flags cycles in generalization hierarchies, illegal join classes, and inconsistent inheritance relationships

- In the dynamic model, checks the logic of how objects of a class change state by ensuring that a superstate has only one initial state and only one exiting transition; flags (a) states with nondeterministic transitions, (b) split flows not destined for concurrent activities, or (c) merged flows not originating from concurrent activities

- Ensures completeness within the object model by scanning each class to be sure that it (a) appears in at least one object model diagram and (b) has a class table definition and at least one attribute or operation

- Assures completeness and consistency between the object and dynamic models; endures that (a) all classes have a dynamic model, (b) operations modeled in a class map to activities in a dynamic model, (c) send events in a dynamic model have a corresponding operation in a receiving class, and (d) dynamic models are not orphaned

- Assures completeness and consistency between the object and the functional models; ensures that (a) all operations have functional models, (b) class or operation attributes correspond to data flows or data stores in the functional model, and (c) all operations in a functional model belong to a class.

Other CASE tools, such as Paradigm Plus,[27] offer features more or less compatible with those of StP/OMT.

PROBLEMS

1. Consider an inserting machine and a robot in a factory that cooperate to insert parts into a printed circuit board (the robot places a board on the inserting machine, then removes it once the insertion is done). Clearly the inserting machine and the robot controller have to work in an interlock manner. Design a controller for the robot and the inserting machine using the structured design methodology. Assume that the following simplified communication primitives are used—*send(q,c)* means that object *c* is sent to process *q*, and *received(c)* means that object *c* is received.

2. Transform the design obtained in Problem 1 into a flowchart. Label the flowchart with the distinctive states for the inserting machine and the robot.

3. Describe the behavior of the controllers in terms of a Petri Net.

4. Given a flowchart of a program, can a procedure be provided so that it automatically converts the program into a Petri Net?

5. Design a voice mail system using the structured design methodology.

6. Map the approach described in Example 4.3 into the Booch methodology. Subsequently compare the OMT and Booch methodologies.

7. Develop the finite-state model for each three-dimensional object and each pixel object. Also develop a data flow diagram for the graphics systems discussed in Example 4.3.

8. Write an object-oriented algorithm with the finest granularity to realize the ray-tracing algorithm. Ray tracing is another technique that can be applied to

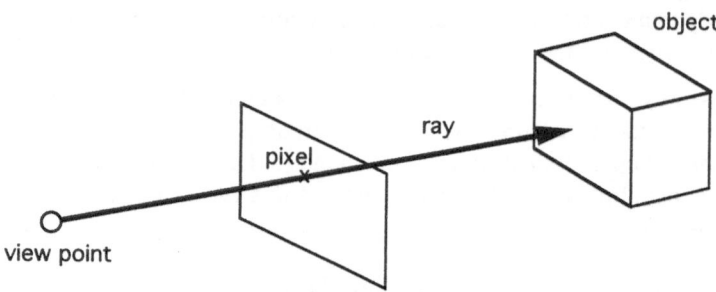

Figure 4.10. The Ray-tracing algorithm.

three-dimensional graphics. In the original ray-tracing algorithm, rays are traced from the view point through each pixel of the virtual screen and into the environment (see Figure 4.10), i.e., in the reverse direction from that in which rays of light propagate in a physical environment. Of all the objects that intersect with the ray, the closest of which corresponds to the visible surface.

9. Complete an object-oriented version of the ray-tracing algorithm with system design and object design.

10. Use a top-down approach in Problems 8 and 9.

REFERENCES

1. Wirth, N. *Communication ACM* **14:**4, 221–227 (1971).
2. Dijkstra, E. W. *Communications of the ACM* **11:**5, 341–346 (May 1968).
3. Parnas, D. L. "Information distribution aspects of design methodology." *Proc., IFIP Congress* (Ljubljana, Yugoslavia, 1971), pp. 339–44.
4. Stevens, W. P., Myers, G. J., and Constantine, L. L. *IBM Systems Journal* **13:**2, 115–139 (1974).
5. Osterweil, L. "Software processes are software too." *Proc. of the Ninth International Conference on Software Engineering* (Monterey, CA, Apr. 1987).
6. DeMarcio, T. *Structured analysis and system specification* (Yourdon, Englewood Cliffs, NJ, 1978).
7. Ward, P. T., and Mellor, S. J. *Structural development for real-time systems,* vols. 1–3 (Yourdon Press, Englewood Cliffs, NJ, 1985).
8. Hatley, D. J., and Pirbhai, I. A. *Strategies for real-time system specification* (Dorset House, New York, 1987).
9. Hatleg, R., *Software Processes* (Prentice-Hall, Englewood Cliffs, NJ, 1981).
10. Alford, M. *IEEE Computer* **18:**4, 36–46 (Apr. 1985).
11. Loshbough, R. P. *DCDS methodology capability demonstration,* vol. 2. TRW System Development Division, Defense Systems Group, Huntsville Operations, (Huntsville, AL, Jan. 1987).
12. Stay, J. F. *IBM Systems Journal* **15:**2, 143–154 (1976).

13. Tichy, W. F. *IEEE Transactions on Software Engineering* **SE-5.1**, 29–41 (Jan. 1979).
14. Teichroew, D., and Hershey, E. *IEEE Transactions on Software Engineering* **SE-3.1**, 41–48 (Jan. 1977).
15. Ross, D. T. *IEEE Transactions on Software Engineering* **SE-3**:1, 2–5 (Jan. 1977).
16. Gatziu, S., Geppert, A., and Dittrich, K. R., "Integrating active concepts into an object-oriented database system." *Proc., the Third International Workshop on Database Programming Languages* (Nafplion, Aug. 1991).
17. Dayal, U., Buchmann, A. P., and McCarthy, D. R. *Proc., second international workshop on object-oriented database systems* (Dittrich, K. R., ed.) Lecture Notes in Computer Science 334 (Springer, New York, 1988).
18. Rumbaugh, J., Blaha, M., Premerlani, W., Eddy, F., and Lorensen, W. *Object-oriented modeling and design* (Prentice-Hall, New York, 1991).
19. Booch, G. *IEEE Transactions on Software Engineering* **SE-12**:2, 211–221 (Feb. 1986).
20. Booch, G. *Object oriented design with applications* (Benjamin/Cummings, Redwood City, CA, 1991).
21. Green, S. *Parallel Processing for Computer Graphics* (MIT Press, Cambridge, MA, 1991).
22. Shlaer, S., and Mellor, S. *Object-oriented systems analysis* (Yourdon, Englewood Cliffs, NJ, 1988).
23. Coad, P., and Yourdon, E. *Object-oriented analysis* (Yourdon, Englewood Cliffs, NJ, 1991).
24. Frakes, W. B., Fox, C. J., and Nejmeh, B. A. *Software engineering in the UNIX/C environment* (Prentice-Hall, New York, 1991).
25. Oman, P. W. *IEEE Software* **7**:5, 37–43 (May 1990).
26. Oman, P. W. *IEEE Software* **7**:1, 133–135 (Jan. 1990).
27. Computer Science Corporation. *Software World* **19**:4, 15–20 (Apr. 1988).
28. Blake, J. *Advanced Systems* 84 (June 1994).

Programming and Coding

Chapter 5 discusses some fundamentals of object-oriented programming languages (Section 5.1) and distributed programming languages (Section 5.4). It also specifically summarizes the major features of two object-oriented programming languages: c++ (Section 5.2) and SMALLTALK (Section 5.3), and one distributed programming language, namely, OCCAM and its predecessor CSP (Section 5.5). Although there are other object-oriented languages (e.g., ACTOR[1] and EFFEL[2] and distributed programming languages (see Section 5.4), these three languages are chosen to illustrate some basic ideas behind object-oriented programming and distributed programming. It is assumed that the reader is familiar with c.

5.1. OBJECT-ORIENTED PROGRAMMING LANGUAGES

Reference 3 discusses design issues for object-oriented programming languages. This section summarizes the following dimensions of the object-based design space: objects, classes and types, inheritance and delegation, data abstraction, strong typing, concurrency, and persistence.

5.1.1. Objects

Functional, imperative, and active objects are, respectively, like values, variables, and processes.

5.1.1.1. Functional Objects

Functional objects have an objectlike interface, but no identity that persists between changes of state. Their operations are invoked by function calls in expressions whose evaluation is side-effect-free, as in functional languages.

5.1.1.2. Imperative Objects

Imperative objects are traditional objects as defined in SIMULA, SMALLTALK, or c++. They have a name (identity), a collection of methods activated by receipt of messages from other objects, and instance variables shared by object methods but inaccessible to other objects. Mainstream object-oriented languages, such as SMALLTALK, have imperative objects, so these languages may be referred to as imperative object-oriented languages. When used without qualification, the term object or object-oriented language generally implies that objects are imperative.

5.1.1.3. Active Objects

Imperative objects are passive unless activated by a message. In contrast active objects may be executing when a message arrives. Active objects have the following modes: dormant (there is nothing to do), active (executing), or waiting (for resources or the completion of subtasks). Message passing among active objects may be asynchronous.

5.1.1.4. Actors

An actor has a mail address, an associated mailbox that holds a queue of incoming messages, and a behavior that at each computation step may read the next mailbox message and perform one of the following actions: create new actors, send communications (messages) to other actors (its acquaintances), or become a replacement behavior for executing the next message in the mailbox. Newly created actors initially have an empty mailbox and a behavior specified by a script.

5.1.2. Types

Types are useful in classifying, organizing, abstracting, conceptualizing, and transforming collections of values. Types are specified by predicates over expressions used for type checking, and types determine a type checking interface for compilers. However classes are specified by templates that determine a system evolution interface and are types. Many object-oriented languages have abandoned types in favor of classes. Classes represent behavior. Inheritance facilitates composing incomplete behavior. Object-oriented database languages keep track of the set of all instances of a class and allow operations made to such instances.

5.1.3. Inheritance

Inheritance is a mechanism for sharing code and behavior. *Multiple inheritance* facilitates sharing by a descendant of the behavior of several ancestors. There are four design dimensions for inheritance: modifiability, granularity, multiplicity, and quality.

5.1.3.1. Inheritance As an Incremental Modification Mechanism

Incremental modification is a fundamental process not only in software systems but also in physical and mathematical systems. Incremental modification of software systems by inheritance spans two distinct notations: refinement and similarity (likeness). There are four progressively powerful mechanisms for modifying attributes of a parent class: behavior compatibility, signature compatibility, name compatibility, and cancellation.

5.1.3.2. Granularity of Inheritance

Uniform inheritance of several kinds of behavior by all instances of a class can be accomplished by multiple inheritance; differential inheritance of behavior requires a finer granularity of sharing at the level of individual objects. Behavior sharing at the level of objects is referred to as *delegation*. Objects may delegate responsibility for performing nonlocal operations to parent instances, called prototypes, that serve both as instances and as templates for behavior sharing and cloning other instances. Prototyping languages do not distinguish between behavior and values at the language level, and they may use inheritance to share both behavior and values. Languages based on prototypes eliminate the need for classes, thereby reducing the number of primitive language concepts, which could be dangerous. Classes separate concerns of structure and behavior from those of execution time computation. Classes are required when the number of instances increases.

5.1.3.3. Single versus Multiple Inheritance

The real world abounds in situations of multiple inheritance. In software multiple inheritance is conceptually difficult, since there are so many ways of combining inherited entities when designing a new entity. There are problems in linearizing multiple inheritance hierarchies because a class may become separated from its immediate parents by intervening classes that disrupt communication.

5.1.3.4. What Should Be Inherited? Behavior or Code?

Behavior and code hierarchies are rarely compatible, and they are often negatively correlated because shared behavior and shared code have different requirements.

5.1.4. Strongly Typed Object-Oriented Languages

Programming languages in which the type of every expression can be determined at compile time are statistically typed languages. Languages in which all expressions are type-consistent are called strongly typed languages. Whether a language should be strongly typed or not depends on the importance of the structure versus flexibility. SMALLTALK compromises on this issue, supporting class abstraction but not strong typing. Languages like c++ are strongly typed.

5.1.5. Models of Concurrency

Object-based concurrent programming combines object-based and concurrent paradigms. It combines the object-based notions of encapsulation, classes, and inheritance with concepts of threads, synchronization, and communication. Objects mesh nicely with concurrency, since their logical autonomy makes them a natural unit for concurrent execution. However concurrent sharing is more complex than sequential sharing. The goal of both sequential and concurrent object-based programming is to model the real world directly and naturally.

5.1.5.1. Process Structure

Processes are active objects that must synchronize with messages arriving from other active objects. Design issues for processes include protection and encapsulation, tasks versus monitors, logical versus physical distribution, and weak versus strong distribution.

5.1.5.2. Unprotected versus Encapsulated Data

In an object-based model, input and output buffers are server processes responsible for their own protection. Input and execute (client) processes no longer need to use low-level primitives to protect data in the input buffer. ADA tasks and monitors illustrate two distinct forms of interaction between calling clients and called server processes.

5.1.5.3. Logical versus Physical Distribution

A system of modules is logically distributed if each module has its own separate name space. Local data are not directly accessible to other modules. Conversely modules cannot directly access nonlocal data but must communicate with other modules by messages. Physical distribution usually implies logical distribution, since physical separation is most naturally modeled by logical separation. Object-based systems are logically distributed, but these are usually implemented on nondistributed computers. Logical distribution supports autonomy of software components and thereby facilitates concurrent execution.

5.1.5.4. Weakly and Strongly Distributed Systems

A system is *weakly distributed* if its modules know the names of other modules. It is *strongly distributed* if its modules cannot directly name other modules. Traditional object-oriented languages are weakly distributed.

5.1.5.5. Internal Process Concurrency

Processes of object-based concurrent systems may be internally sequential, quasi-concurrent, or fully concurrent.

5.1.5.6. Synchronization

For unprotected data synchronization must be performed by each process that accesses the data. Synchronization may require cooperative protocols: For example using semaphores to specify mutually exclusive accesses to critical regions. Protected data assume responsibility for their own protection, removing the burden from processes that access data. Object-based systems focus on synchronization for protected data. There are three kinds of synchronization mechanisms: rendezvous, conditional variables, and locking.

5.1.5.7. Asynchronous Messages, Futures and Promises

Design alternatives for message passing include synchronous, asynchronous, and stream-based message passing. Synchronous message passing, which requires the sender to suspend until a reply is received, is essentially remote procedure call. Asynchronous message passing allows the sender to continue, but requires synchronization if subsequent execution depends on the reply. Steam-based message passing supports streams of messages that likewise require synchronization at message-use time to check that replies have been received. Asynchronously computed results may be handled by data structures created at the time of message-send.

5.1.5.8. Interprocessing Communication

Design alternatives for interprocess communication include two-way interconnected distributed processes, one-way interconnected client/server processes, and dynamically interconnected strongly distributed processes. In strongly distributed processes, the names of nonlocal ports are stored as data in local port variables, so connection to other processes is dynamic.

5.2. c + +

One of the disadvantages of regular c is that data structures are not extensible; i.e., new data types can be built only from fundamental data types. Furthermore there is no provision for operator overloading. The c++ overcomes both of these shortcomings. It is a superset of c. It was primarily designed to be a better c and support data abstraction and object-oriented programming.

The c++ code is centered around the notion of class and object. Each class has an associated set of data and functions. The c++ also allows several levels of protection for data and members. One major disadvantage of c++ is that it does not have a good mechanism for passing messages between objects. The following summarizes some major features of c++; details of c++ can be studied in Ref. 4.

5.2.1. Program

A c++ program usually consists of a number of classes, and each class consists of a number of attributes (members) and member functions. A program may also contain a number of globals and global functions. Among the global functions, one is called *main;* this is the main function of the program. It starts and terminates the control flow of the program.

5.2.2. Classes

A c++ class is an extension of a c structure that realizes the concept of data types. This class consists of a number of fields, called *members*, and a number of functions, called *member functions*. Depending on how they are accessed, members and member functions are divided into three categories: private, public, and protected. Public members can be accessed (called) by any other function; private and protected members can be accessed (called) only by member or friend functions. A friend function of a class can be any (global or member of another class) function declared to be a friend of the class. A simple form of class declaration follows:

```
class <new_class_name> {
  private members and functions
protected:
  protected members and functions
public:
  public members and functions
}
```

Members and member prototypes are declared in the same way as in c:

```
<class_name>  <member_name> ,  . . .  ,  <member
_name>;
<class_name>   <member_function_name>   (argu-
ments);
```

The *body* of a member function is usually declared separately in the following form:

```
<class_name>    <class_name>::<member_function
_name> (arguments)
{
  // body
}
```

The first class name specifies the type of the returned object, and the second class name specifies the type to which the function belongs.

Once a class is defined, it can be instantiated by declaring objects of the class as in C. Pointers to the class can also be declared as in C. A member *m* of an object *a* is accessed by another object with the notation *a.m;* this member is accessed as *m* directly within the same object. A member function *f* of *a* is called by another object as *a.f* (arguments); it is accessed as *f* directly within the same object. A member *m* of an object pointed to by a pointer *p* is accessed by the notation *p → m;* a member function *f* of the object is called as *p → f* (arguments).

The member function named after the class name is called the *constructor* function. The constructor function realizes any customized initialization process when an object is declared to be an instance of the class. The member function named after the class name but proceeded by the symbol ~ is called the *destructor* of the class. The destructor of a class is automatically called when an object is freed. Both the constructor and the destructor of a class return no object (void), but they may take some arguments; their definitions are optional. If a constructor is defined to take some arguments, the arguments are supplied when an object is declared.

Example 5.1. The following is a simple C++ program:

```
#include <stdio.h>
class first {
  int first_i;
  float first_f, first_ff;
  first *first_next;
protected:
  float first_pf;
  public:
  int first_op;
  void first(int n);
  void ~first(void);
  float get_f(void);
  void assign_f(float f);
}
void first::first(int n)
{
```

```
      first_i = n;
      printf("initializing first with %d",n);
    }
    void first::~first(void)
    {
      printf("freeing first");
    }
    float first::get_f(void)
    {
      return first_f;
    }
    void first::assign_f(float f)
    {
      first_f = f;
    }
    int good_friend(first f)
    {
      printf("i is %d",f.i);
    }
    int main(void)
    {
      /* note that any single-line comment in C++ can
be started by two slashes */
      first a(6), *b; // a has 6 as the val of first_i
      b = new first(4); /* This is dynamic initializ-
ation */
          // *b has 4 as the val of first_i
      a.assign_f(3.67);
      b->assign_f(4.55);
      print("the first_f of a is %f",a.get_f());
      printf("the first_f of b is %f",b->get_f());
      good_friend(a);
      good_friend(*b);
    }
```

5.2.3. Inheritance

A c++ class can be derived from a number of other c++ classes as follows:

```
class <class_name> : <access> <inherited_class>
. . . <access> <inherited_class>
```

```
{
// members and member functions
}
```

Each of the inherited classes is called a *base* class with respect to the class defined. For each base class, if *<access>* is *public,* the child class inherits all public/protected members and member functions from the inherited class as public/protected members and member functions. If *<access>* is *private,* the child class inherits all public/protected members and member functions from the inherited class as private members and member functions. In both cases the private part of the inherited class is not inherited.

When an object is declared to be an instance of the derived class, the constructor of the derived class (if it exists) is called first, then the constructor of the first base class is called, and so on. As long as no base class takes an argument, the derived class does not have to provide a constructor function. However, if a base class requires an argument, the derived class must provide a constructor function, which again takes arguments, so that arguments can be passed to those constructors of base classes that require them. Destructors are called in the reversed order. The c++ allows a pointer that is declared to be a pointer to a base class to be used as a pointer to the derived class.

A function of a base class can be declared to be a *virtual* function so that any derived class of it can refine the virtual function. A virtual function is declared in the following format:

```
virtual  <class_name>  <function_name>  (argu-
ments);
```

When refined in a derived class, the keyword *virtual* is dropped. This feature is called *function overriding.* By using this feature, a generic function can be defined to a generic class, and its specifics do not have to be given until the generic class is fully specialized.

Example 5.2. In the following, class *C* is derived from classes *A* and *B.* Based on the inheritance rules, *C* has the following public members: *pa* (inherited from *A*), *pb* (inherited from *B*), and *caa* (added by itself); class *C* has the following public member functions: *evaluate* (inherited from *A* and refined in *C*), *A::A* (inherited from *A*), *B::B* (inherited from *B*), and *C* and *get_ca* (added by itself). Note how *C::C* is specified: It takes one argument that is passed to *A::A.*

```
#include <stdio.h>
    class A {
```

```
int in1, in2, out;
  protected:
    int pa;
  public:
    virtual int evaluate(void);
    void A (int n);
  }
  class B {
    float ba;
  protected:
    int pb;
  public:
    void B (void);
  }
  class C : public A, public B {
    int ca, cb;
  public:
    int caa;
    void C (int r);
    int evaluate (void);
    int get_ca(void);
  }
  void C::C (int r) : A(r), B() {
    // some code
  }
  int C::evaluate(void)
  {
    return ca * cb / pb * pa;
  }
  void main(void)
  {
    A *ptc; /* note that a pointer to A can be used as a
C pointer below */
    ptc = new C(2);
    ptc->ca = 12;
    ptc->cb = 3;
    ptc->pa = 4;
    ptc->pb = 9;
    printf("The val is %d",ptc->evaluate());
  }
```

5.2.4. Operator Overloading

The c++ allows such operators as +, −, = (assignment), and == to be overloaded (i.e., defined separately but using the same name) for different classes of objects. An operator can be redefined for a class as follows:

```
<class_name> <class_name>::operator <operator_
name> (arguments)
```

where the first class name designates the type of the returned object, and the second class name designates the class to which the operator is defined. The precedence, the number of arguments, and the associativity of an operator cannot be changed by overloading.

Example 5.3. Consider the following:

```
#include <stdio.h>
    class twoD {
      int x,y;
    public:
      twoD operator + (twoD t);
      twoD operator = (twoD t);
      void twoD(int a, int b);
    }
    twoD::twoD(int a, int b)
    {
      x = a;
      y = b;
    }
    twoD twoD::operator + (twoD t)
    {
      twoD a;
      a.x = x + t.x;
      a.y = y + t.y;
      return a;
    }
    twoD twoD::operator = (twoD t)
    {
      x = t.x;
      y = t.y;
      return (this); /* note that this is a special
pointer that points to itself */
    }
    void main(void)
```

```
{
        twoD ta(1,2),tb(2,3),tc(0,0);
        tc = ta + tb; // tc.x is 3 and tc.y is 5 now
        ta = tb; // ta.x is 2 and ta.y is 3 now
}
```

5.3. SMALLTALK

In the early 1970s, the Xerox Palo Alto Research Center (PARC) Learning Research Group (later the Software Concepts Group [SCG]) began research that eventually paved the way for many modern programming tools used today. The group began to

> concentrate on two principal areas of research: a language of descrip-
> tion (a programming language) which serves as an interface between
> the models in the human mind and those in computing hardware, and
> a language of interaction (a user interface) which matches the human
> communication system to that of the computer. (Ref. 5)

This research was realized as a system called SMALLTALK.[6] In 1972 the first SMALLTALK system, loosely based on the SIMULA language, was implemented. This system was then continually tested, refined, and redesigned until its eventual release to the outside world as SMALLTALK-80.

The SMALLTALK-80 is such a rich system that it is difficult to present all of its components completely. It is a programming language and a programming environment. The SMALLTALK also contains much of the functionalities normally found in operating systems, including storage management, a file system, display handling, text and picture editing, keyboard and pointing device input, a debugger, a performance spy, processor scheduling, compilation, and decompilation.[5]

The traditional approach to program development can be described as *modular*—programming is achieved by advancing through a sequence of modules. Normally these modules consist of an editor, compiler, linker, and run-time debugger. Each module is a separate entity. A normal sequence consists of loading the editor, entering code, leaving the editor, executing the compiler, executing the linker, and running a debugger. The drawback is that a mode change requires exiting to the operating system to load the next module. Although some modern systems allow mode switching without exiting to the operating system, each module is still a separate entity. For example, most programming systems are composed of a number of separate command line tools: editor, compiler, etc. All of these tools can be integrated into some type of shell; nevertheless they are separate programs.

The SMALLTALK system achieves a total integration of tools: Every tool is an integral part of the environment, and it is available at all times. Not too long ago this concept would have been dismissed as impossible. SMALLTALK achieves such integration through the use of a windows, icons, menu, and pointer (WIMP) based user interface.

SMALLTALK is an object-oriented language. Programming in this type of language promotes three ideas:

An interactive, incremental approach to software development can produce qualitative and quantitative improvements in productivity.

Software should be designed in units that are as autonomous as possible.

Developing software should be thought of in terms of building a system rather than as black box applications.

The SMALLTALK language was based on the concepts of object, message, class, instance, and method, as described in Section 2.1. The classical example demonstrating these ideas is as follows. Take the expression 1 + 5. We normally view this as an addition operation with two operands, 1 and 5. Note that the addition operator is dominant. SMALLTALK consists entirely of objects and messages. Looking at the expression as an object–message relationship then, we see an integer object 1 receiving the message + 5. The receiver of the message, in this case the object 1, determines how the expression is evaluated. In SMALLTALK, object 1 is dominant. In the classical example, 1 and 5 are examples of literal objects. Literal objects can be used to describe numbers, symbols (characters), strings, and arrays.

All variables in SMALLTALK are pointers to objects. Variables are not typed; A variable can point to any type of object. Assignment statements (or messages) merely change the object that a variable points to. For example the statement x <- 1 means that integer object 1 is bound to (pointed to by) *x;* the statement *x <- y* means *x* is bound to the same object that *y* is bound to; and *x <- x + 1* means that the message +1 is sent to the object bound to *x:* The object returned is then bound to *x.* In addition to messages that consist of such operators as + and <-, SMALLTALK also allows keyword messages. For example *x equals: y, 2 factorial,* or *12.48 rounded.* Consider the following program, which computes the sum of the first 100 integers[7]:

```
sum <- 0.
number <- 1.
[number <= 100] whileTrue:[
```

```
      sum <- sum + number.
      number <- number +1].
   sum
```

The SMALLTALK version of the while . . do statement is interpreted as follows:

- The message whileTrue: [. . .] is sent to the block [number <=100].

- In response to the whileTrue: message, the receiver, the block [number <=100] evaluates itself.

- If evaluating the block returns the object true, the whileTrue: argument block is evaluated and the whileTrue: message is again sent to the block [number <=100], and steps 1, 2, and 3 are repeated.

The true power of SMALLTALK lies within its huge system class library. There are classes of almost every imaginable type. An incomplete list follows[8]:

- *Magnitude:* Includes characters, dates, numbers, time, and mathematical functions.

- *Stream:* Includes input and output streams.

- *File/Directory*

- *Collection:* Includes such data structures as arrays, linked lists, trees, strings, ordered collections, and sets.

- *Windows*

- *Graphics:* Includes geometric shapes, mathematical functions, bitmaps, and animation.

> **Example 5.4.** This example is a slight modification from an article in *Byte* magazine (Aug. 1986). The article itself was adapted from the book *A Taste of Smalltalk.*[9] The towers of Hanoi is a classic computer problem used to demonstrate recursion in many computer texts. The towers of Hanoi problem involves moving a number of disks, each having a different diameter, from one peg to another. There are a total of three pegs. Initially all disks are stacked on one pin in order of increasing diameter. The goal is to move all disks from the first pin to the third pin. The catch is that no disk may ever be placed on top of a smaller one. This is why there is another pin.
>
> The c++ program that follows gives the basic solution to the problem:

```
void move_disk(int from_pin, int to_pin)
{
  cout <<from_pin << "->" <<to_pin <<endl;
}
void move_tower(int from_pin, int height, int
to_pin, int using_pin)
{
  if(height > 0)
    {
    move_tower(height-1,from_pin,to
_pin,using_pin);
    move_disk(from_pin, to_pin);
    move_tower(height-1, using_pin, to_pin,
from_pin);
    }
}
void main()
{
  int total;
  cin >> total;
  move_tower(total, 1, 3. 2);
}
```

The SMALLTALK solution to the towers of Hanoi program follows:

```
moveTower: height from: fromPin to: toPin using:
usingPin
  "Recursive procedure to move the disk at a height
from one pin to another using a third pin"
  (height > 0) ifTrue: [
  self moveTower: (height -1) from:
    fromPin to: usingPin using: toPin.
  self moveDisk: fromPin to: toPin.
  self moveTower: (height -1) from:
    usingPin to: toPin using: fromPin]
"moveDisk:to: method"
moveDisk: fromPin to: toPin
"Move disk from a pin to another pin.
Print results in the transcript window"
  Transcript cr.
  Transacript show: (fromPin printString,
                    '->', toPin printString).
```

A SMALLTALK procedure is called a method. As shown each part of a method name ends with a colon, then the argument it describes follows. The four words ending in colons in the first line of the SMALLTALK program are the four parts of the name of the method being defined. The actual name of this method is *move-Tower:from:to:using:*. This method uses calls to three other methods (itself twice and *moveDisk:to:* once). It may be easier to think of the SMALLTALK method as a function name followed by its parameters, for example, *moveTower:from:to:using: (height,fromPin,toPin,usingPin)*. All of these arguments are local names.

Text between double quotes is a comment. Next is an expression *(height > 0)* that is evaluated as true or false. The SMALLTALK if statement is like its c counterpart except that the Boolean expression precedes instead of follows the if. Next is a block of three statements. The SMALLTALK surrounds a block with square brackets instead of using c's curly braces. Periods separate statements instead of semicolons.

To see how the program is executed, recall that SMALLTALK has exactly one way of working: It sends messages to objects. A message is a message selector with its operands. The object that receives a message, the receiver, appears just to the left of the message. In the sample program, everything that is not an object (comments, brackets, periods) is a message selector. The SMALLTALK returns a value as the result of each method. These results are also objects. For example *height −1* returns an integer object, and *height >0* returns a Boolean object. When an object receives a message, it first looks up the message name to see if it understands the message. If the message is found, it starts executing the method that tells how to respond to the message. Just as a c function may call other functions, a SMALLTALK method can call other methods; this is accomplished by sending messages. To send a message to the same object that just received the current message, the keyword *self* is used. This is similar to the *this* keyword in c++. When a piece of code happens to send a message to the same selector as the current method, the program is using recursion.

The method *moveDisk:to:* includes a few new things. The method accomplishes the same thing as c's *cout* or *printf( )*. It does so using the System Transcript window. This behaves like the traditional character-oriented terminal. The object that represents the transcript is held in the global variable *Transcript*. The message *cr* is equivalent to c's *newline*. The message *show:* takes a string as an argument, then appends it to the transcript. It also redisplays the text in the transcript window. Finally the *printString* operator converts the variable name in front of it to a string.

The strings are concatenated to an array, and the array is output to the string.

The SMALLTALK programming environment provides tools for finding, viewing, writing, and running SMALLTALK methods. The system can tell that a particular piece of text is a method by the window in which it is typed. With traditional programming systems, a program is loosely linked to other programs via the operating system. In SMALLTALK however every program is just a piece of the whole system, and the pieces are linked together.

5.4. DISTRIBUTED PROGRAMMING LANGUAGES

Due to the many different ways of configuring distributed systems, it may be desirable to separate programming into several phases: it could have a component programming phase and a system configuration phase. In this way, a programmer can develop software for the system without worrying about the physical configuration of the system on which it will run. System configuration is handled by the underlying supporting environment rather than the application program itself. General sequential programming languages have these two phases mixed together in the language, so these are not suitable for a distributed system environment.[10]

In the component programming phase, each component and how it interacts with other components are defined. Depending on the language, a component may be a process, an object, a statement, an expression, or a clause. Each component may communicate with another through message passing or data sharing. Then in the system configuration phase, the underlying environment (the operating system) assigns a configuration specification that maps the program to specific software nodes, then determines how these software nodes are distributed (mapped) among the physical nodes of the network. The programmer does not have to be concerned with how the system is configured. The programmer can use the same language primitives for both local and remote communication, and he/she can be unaware of how the communication message is actually sent to another node. This is the basis of *communication transparency*.

A language for distributed systems that uses this idea is Network Implementation language (NIL).[11] Its model of a distributed system consists of a logical view and a physical view; the programmer sees only the logical view. The programmer creates a NIL virtual machine, which consists of interconnected processes. This virtual machine is actually implemented on the physical view as one or more physical processors. Messages are used to communicate between the processors. The NIL compiler maps the programmer's logical view to the network's actual physical view. Therefore the programmer can concentrate on designing a correct working algorithm while the compiler adjusts the algorithm's performance to the actual physical implementation of the network. This is one of the main ideas behind many (but not all) distributed system language designs. Many argue that the actual placement of a program on the network should be hidden from the user. However there are applications where explicit placement of components on processors may be better, since a compiler does not know the intentions of the programmer's and what the program actually does.

The following sections discuss issues that should be considered for distributed system language design.

5.4.1. Parallelism

Parallel execution of different components of a program to achieve faster execution time and hence better performance of the program is one of the main reasons for using a distributed system. With good designs a program can have components that successfully run in parallel. If the program is developed in strict sequential manner so that many parts rely on values from other parts, it may not gain much in performance even if run on a distributed system. Therefore a language for a distributed system should be designed to take advantage of parallel execution.

5.4.2. Communication

Depending on the amount of computation a program performs, different types of systems may be desired. A program that performs much computation but communicates infrequently is well suited to such a distributed system as a LAN or a WAN. Since such a program does not communicate often between its parallel components, the cost of communication through the network is small. However a program that must often communicate between its parallel components may be affected by the amount of time it takes to send messages through the network. Communication overhead can become very expensive then. These programs should be run on a very closely coupled distributed system, such as a multiprocessor. It may be even better not to use a distributed system at all but to use a system of multiple processors that access shared memory. As faster communication rates become available through advances in technology however, boundaries between these different distributed systems may blur.

There are many ways of sending messages between processes to control communication costs. Messages can be sent through point-to-point message passing; directly from one processor to another, using remote procedure calls to call procedures running on some other processor; or through one-to-many messages that are broadcast through the network to several or all processors. In addition to message passing, communication between processors can be done by data sharing, using either distributed data structures or shared logic variables. Which forms of communication primitives are used depends on the particular distributed system and what applications are designed to run on it.

5.4.3. Synchronization

Synchronization between processors goes hand in hand with communication primitives. In some programs a procedure may need information from another procedure. If that procedure is located on another processor, then a message must be sent requesting the information. Depending on the design of the system and programming language, the calling procedure may have to wait until the other procedure sends back the desired results. On other systems the procedure may be able to continue running while it waits for its request to be answered. When a program component must wait until another component returns the results of a request, the system has *synchronous* communication. If a component can continue working while it waits for its reply, the system has *asynchronous* communication. Distributed programming languages may implement communication either synchronously, asynchronously, or both, depending on its design goals.

Since a component may have to wait for results from several other components on different processors, there is an amount of nondeterminism present. The order in which results are sent back is unknown to the calling procedure. There must be some way of handling this situation. Primitives designed for this purpose include select statements and guarded horn clauses.

5.4.4. Partial Failure/Fault Tolerance

The final issue in distributed system design is increased reliability through partial failure and fault-tolerant systems. Partial failure is based on the fact that since each processor operates on its own, failure in one processor should not affect the others. If a program has several components running in parallel that are replicated on several different processors, then when some processors fail, backups can continue, so that the user does not know a fault has occurred. In this way a program can execute more reliably.

Depending on the applications being run on a distributed system, different combinations of the preceding ideas are required. An application may be inherently distributed in that each processor primarily runs its own components and communicates only through messages for specialized functions. An example of this is electronic mail (E-mail) communication between workstations. In this case a distributed system is used so that people can communicate with each other. Another area for distributed systems is specialized services: Each service is given several dedicated processors, which increases their reliability and performance. The distributed system then allows these services to share printers, tapes, and disk drives. Other applications are spread out across the system, using many different nodes, and each component must communicate with others often to run efficiently.

Some systems may need faster communication schemes, whereas others may be able to tolerate a slower communication scheme. Some applications are very important and may therefore need heavy protection against faults in the system. Others are less important and may not need the added expense of a serious fault detection and recovery scheme. In such cases if the system crashes, the application is rerun once the system is fixed. In designing a programming language for a distributed system, the applications to be run on this particular system must be considered in the design process.

All of the preceding features could be provided by the operating system for the distributed system or by a language designed specifically for distributed programming. If these features are provided by the operating system, programs being run call special library routines to execute operating system commands to perform desired distributed system actions (i.e., message passing). This approach has the disadvantage that the sequential language used cannot take full advantage of the distributed environment. Since the operating system does not know exactly what the programmer wants to happen, special coding is needed for certain situations.

Using a language designed for distributed systems has several advantages. One advantage is the ability to move programs from one machine to another without side effects; that is programs can be ported to different platforms more easily. Also since the language is designed for a distributed system, the code will be easier to read without numerous strange operating system calls. The programming language is at a much higher level than the operating system, and it may be able to do much more than the operating system's message-passing capabilities and to do it more easily.

For a given distributed system, a language designed for it should be able to run efficiently on it and to implement common applications run on this particular distributed system. Different applications use different models; one very basic model involves a number of sequential processes running in parallel and communicating through message passing. Such languages as CSP[12] (see Section 5.5) belong to this category.

Some languages have parts inherently designed to be run in parallel; some examples are functional languages, logic languages, and object-oriented or object-based languages. Expressions can be evaluated in any order in functional languages. Similarly logic languages have many parts that can be run in parallel. A concurrent version of PROLOG was designed in this fashion.[13] In object-oriented or object-based languages, objects are active parts of a program, and individual objects can be placed on devoted processors to be run in parallel. Another method involves communicating through procedure calls, where some procedure is located on another processor. Shared data can also be used for communication between processors, and this can be done even through distributed systems in our case do not have shared memory.

Before analyzing some actual programming languages for distributed systems, we must discuss what methods are used to implement the preceding ideas; that is what methods are used to implement parallelism, communication, and partial failures.

5.4.5. Primitives for Parallelism

Depending on the language, parallelism can occur among many different types of components: parallel processes, statements, objects, expressions, or clauses. Each one offers advantages and disadvantages depending on the particular system. Many languages support processes as their unit of parallelism. A process acts as both a unit of concurrency and data ownership; how processes are declared varies from language to language. In CONCURRENT C[14] for example, they are declared implicitly. A process data type is defined, then a process is declared by declaring a variable of that data type. A process in CONCURRENT C contains its own stack, program counter, machine registers, and its own flow of control. Other languages however declare processes explicitly using a special statement to create the process. In this way values may be sent to the process on creation that can be used to set it up in special ways. In both cases every process runs in parallel performing its designated functions. Processes may either terminate themselves or be terminated by some other process; termination methods depend on the system.

Another primitive for expressing parallelism is statements, which can be put together in groups to run in parallel. For this a keyword (such as PAR) specifies that the following statements in the program are to be executed in parallel. Likewise a keyword (such as SEQ) can be used to specify sequential execution of statements. Although this is very easy, large programs cannot be handled very well with this method.

In object-oriented and object-based programming languages each individual object could essentially have a processor to itself. Unlike sequential languages, which use objects, an object in a distributed language remains active once it begins and runs as a separate process. Communication between objects occurs through some form of message passing. Although objects lend themselves to parallel execution, many small objects running on separate processors may be costly in terms of communication costs. In a system, such as a WAN, high communication costs may outweigh the advantages of executing each object in parallel.

In functional languages functions compute results based only on their input values. Since these functions cannot affect any other function, they are well-suited to be run in parallel. However as in object parallelism, many small functions may cause too much communication overhead. Similarly logic programming languages can be executed in parallel through AND/OR parallelism. If a goal has several clauses that can be evaluated to determine if the goal is true, they can be executed in parallel.

There are two ways for this parallel execution to occur. Given the following clauses[15]:

```
A:- B,C,D
A:- E,F
```

The two clauses for A can be executed in parallel until one of them succeeds or both fail (OR-parallelism). Alternatively for each of the two clauses, the subgoals can be solved in parallel until they all succeed or any one of them fails (AND-parallelism). However certain conflicts could arise. These situations must be checked, but doing so may restrict the amount of parallelism that can be achieved.

For parallelism to be useful, program performance should be increased. For this to occur there must be efficient program mapping to the physical processors. Certain components of a program should not be run in parallel if communication costs outweigh the added advantage of parallel distribution among these components. Languages may allow component mapping to be performed directly by the programmer or made invisible to the programmer as in NIL. A few languages even allow program components to move between processors during their lifetime.

5.4.6. Primitives for Communication and Synchronization

For parallel running components of a program to work efficiently, there must be some way of exchanging data among parallel components. Therefore good communication primitives are needed. The two basic types of communication are message-passing and data-sharing. Since some program components may need information from another component before it can continue, there must be some synchronization primitives to handle this situation. Both communication and synchronization primitives are needed to run parallel components efficiently. Although the unit of parallelism in a distributed system can be processes, statements, objects, and the like, we refer to parallel-running components as processes in the following discussions.

Message passing can be broken down into four basic groups to include *point-to-point messages, rendezvous, remote procedure call,* and *one-to-many messages.* A point-to-point message is sent from a sender to a receiver. Usually the sender executes some from of *send* command to send a message. The receiver then either issues an *accept* command to receive a message or has automatic code that is executed when a message is waiting at its input port. An advantage of the *accept* command is that the programmer can specify conditions telling the process what message to look for and receive. This can be good for security purposes, for example (from Ref. 15):

```
accept open(f) such that not_locked(f) { . . . }
```

To specify which process to send a message to or receive a message from, there must be a way of naming the process. This can be done directly, as in CSP, where a process name is specified, or indirectly, where the message is sent to an intermediate location. The receiver then accesses this location to receive the message. Another issue in point-to-point messages is whether they execute synchronously or asynchronously. In synchronous message passing, the sender waits for the receiver to acknowledge that it has received the message; in asynchronous message passing, the sender does not wait. Therefore a queuing mechanism is needed for asynchronous message passing. A disadvantage of the synchronous case is that the sender must always wait for the receiver to accept the message even if no data are sent back. Rendezvous message passing (as defined in ADA or CONCURRENT C) is similar to a procedure call: Each entry must be declared in the same way that a procedure is declared, and the entry can be called in the same way that a procedure is called. Then an accept statement is defined that contains the code to execute when its entry is called.

A Remote Procedure Call (RPC) form of message passing is also similar to a regular procedure call. The sending process calls a remote procedure in the same way as a normal procedure. The sender is blocked until output parameters of the remote procedure are returned. The RPC is fully synchronous and can be transparent to the programmer. If transparent, the programmer does not need to worry about where the procedure is located; however making the procedure completely transparent is very difficult. If a fault occurs, there must be some way of telling the sender that something is wrong. One way of doing this is through time-outs.

Sometimes a message needs to be sent to several processes; this is where one-to-many message passing can be used. In this case the message can be broadcast to all processes or multicast to several specific processes. Both are unreliable, since the message cannot be guaranteed to reach all its destinations. However sending a one-to-many message may be faster than sending several point-to-point messages.

In data sharing data can be passed from one process to another if each process can access the same variable. Since any process could access this variable, security precautions are needed. One method of data sharing is distributed data structures. This requires storing the data structures in a specific space that can be accessed by all processors. Then using special commands, data can be sent, read, and deleted from this space. The language LINDA[16] used distributed data structures in a method called Tuple Space. One disadvantage to this approach is that processes do not know which processes will read the message they send; that is a process that reads a message does not necessarily know which process it came from.

Another method of data sharing involves shared logical variables. Once a logical variable is assigned a value, it cannot be changed. Processes generate a binding on certain variables. The processes are blocked when the variables they try to use are still unbound. The process remains blocked until a value is given to the variable.

In addition to communication between processes, synchronization is also needed. Since the order that processes interact cannot always be predetermined, primitives must be set up to handle this nondeterminism. This is done through two primitives: the *select* statement and *guarded horn clauses*. A *select* statement consists of a guard (a Boolean expression), which if evaluated as true causes certain statements to be executed. The CSP language has a form of select statements. If several guard expressions evaluate to true, then one is chosen nondeterministically, and the statements are executed.

Select statements can be used to wait for specific messages from specific processes without considering the order in which the messages arrive. They can also be used to implement time-outs and control process terminations. However since guards are selected nondeterministically from the true Boolean expressions, there is no way of telling which one will be executed.

Guarded horn clauses are another form of nondeterministic control. Since backtracking on sequential systems is too complicated to be implemented easily in a distributed system, some other method must be used.

> Rather than trying the clause for a given predicate one by one and backtracking on failure, parallel logic languages (1) search all these clauses in parallel and (2) do not allow any bindings made during these parallel executions to be visible to the outside until one of the executions is committed to do. (Ref. 15)

Guarded horn clauses are used to implement this. According to the preceding quotation, a guard should not affect its environment unless it is selected. If any guards abort, nothing should happen to the environment.

5.4.7. Primitives for Partial Failure/Fault Tolerance

For higher reliability to be realizable, there must be mechanisms to handle crash situations. If a processor crashes, the rest of the system should be able to continue working on a program. Replicating a program on various processors in case of a crash is one solution. If a system can do this, it is said to be fault-tolerant. Several primitives have been designed to program fault tolerance. One primitive uses failure detection. The operating system detects when a processor fails, then returns an error when a program wants to communicate with the crashed processor. Then either the programmer can write routines to handle the crash or the operating system can repeat requests to redo the work. The process that was on the processor that crashed can be restarted on another processor. Messages can then be resent to the process. If a process does not run to completion, there should be no side effects.

Atomic transactions ensure that a process either commits its actions or aborts. Data from a process cannot be relied on until the process commits the data. If the process fails, then no other process is affected because it did not rely on those data. A transaction on a process should be recoverable so that data changed by a process that failed can be restored to its prefailure state.

Transparent fault tolerance can also be used. Backup processes are created on other processors. If a process fails, its backup begins executing and continues what the main process was working on. The backup processor checks to make sure it does not repeat unnecessary messages. Checks are taken every so often to update the backup processor on the state of the main processor. Checking and logging messages to disk or tape can also be used.

In the preceding paragraphs, we discussed distributed programming languages. Each has advantages and disadvantages depending on the distributed system on which they are used. One language briefly discussed earlier is NIL, which uses processes as its unit of parallelism. A NIL process has only local data visible to it. Local data include input and output ports connected to the input and output ports of other communication processes. The actual physical mapping of a NIL program to processors cannot be seen by the programmer. Security is provided by a NIL program because all data are private to a process and communication occurs only through a communication channel; there is no sharing of variables in any form.

There is also a mechanism for checking type state that prevents malfunctioning modules from affecting other modules. A message variable has three type states: UNINITIALIZED, EMPTY, and FULL. A message is UNINITIALIZED if its fields are unallocated, EMPTY if its fields are allocated but uninitialized, and FULL if they are allocated and initialized. The compiler enforces the type state checking rules. As a result NIL programs can contain many small processes without requiring physical memory protection hardware.

Communication in a NIL program occurs by connecting input and output ports to make a communication channel. The NIL supports synchronous communication through rendezvous calls and asynchronous communication through message sending. Guarded commands are used in the communication process, and several output ports can be connected to a single input port. Synchronous message passing through rendezvous calls uses *call* and *accept* statements. Ownership of a data object is temporarily transferred from sender to receiver, since data sharing is not allowed. Ownership is then either transferred back or permanently given to another process. Asynchronous message passing is done through send and receive statements. Multiple messages to a port are received in the same order in which they were sent. The NIL uses transparent fault tolerance to handle partial failures in the system. This is done through optimistic recovery techniques. The NIL compilers have been implemented for a uniprocessor as well as a distributed system. For more about NIL, see Ref. 11.

Another programming language used in distributed systems is CONCURRENT C, in which C is extended for distributed programming through a process data type and related operations. CONCURRENT C also uses the process as its unit of parallelism. Processes are an instantiation of the process data type; they are declared using the *create* statement. Unlike NIL it is possible to assign a process to a specific processor. Process declaration in CONCURRENT C has process specification and a process body. Process specification is the part that other processes see and communicate with. Information in the process body is hidden and accessible to that process only. Communication in CONCURRENT C occurs through the rendezvous mechanism, so communication takes place via transaction calls. Communication is synchronous, although asynchronous transactions are possible. Nondeterminism is possible through a select statement. CONCURRENT C itself is not fault tolerant, although a fault tolerant version was designed using replication of processes. A CONCURRENT C program can be implemented as one or more UNIX processes, and it has been implemented on several systems. A distributed version of C++ is also being designed.

Another distributed programming language is the Synchronizing Resources language (SR).[17] An SR program is made up of resources which are dynamically created modules that run on a single or multiple processors. Several processes can be included in a single resource. Since distributed programs must change dynamically in size to accommodate different hardware configurations, many different primitives are provided in SR. Concepts used in SR are adapted from sequential programming for the distributed programming environment but use similar interfaces. Resources interact through operations that are called by using a *send* for asynchronous communication or a *call* for synchronous communication, which is similar to NIL's implementation. Since these primitives can be combined in different ways, many forms of communication are possible, including remote procedure call, rendezvous, message passing, and semaphores, which uses a select statement with a guard similar to CSP. Fault tolerance is handled by asking the run-time system to keep track of a certain processor and to execute a programmer's code if it fails. The SR is implemented on UNIX and Sun workstations.

As a final example of a distributed programming language, we take a look at EMERALD,[18] an object-based programming language. All entities in EMERALD are passive or active objects. Unlike the other languages previously described, the object is the unit of parallelism in EMERALD, and an object does not need to stay on the same processor throughout its life: It can migrate from one processor to another. Since objects may be small, many objects can run in parallel. Basically an object in EMERALD has four parts: Its *name* uniquely identifies it; its *representation* contains the object's data; its *operations* are called to communicate to the object; and its *process* can run in parallel with called operators. Although an object can move from processor to processor throughout its life, it is in only one location at any instance of time. An object's location can be controlled by the compiler to create efficient program execution. The method used to invoke an object is independent of the object's location; therefore programmers need not worry where an object is located. EMERALD's implementations should be designed efficiently to find objects and update their locations so that messages can be given to them in a low-cost, efficient manner. EMERALD is implemented on distributed Sun workstations connected through an Ethernet. Other distributed object-oriented programming languages include CONCURRENT SMALLTALK,[19] ABD/1,[20] and COOL.[21] A comparison of such languages is found in Ref. 22.

5.5. COMMUNICATING SEQUENTIAL PROCESSES AND OCCAM

As discussed in Section 5.3, communicating sequential processes (CSP) is a programming language designed for distributed environments. A CSP process with name π has the following general form:

$$\pi : [\pi 1 \parallel \pi 2 \parallel \ . \ . \ . \ \parallel \pi n]$$

where each πi, $1 \leq i \leq n$, is a sequential process executing a sequence of commands, and all πs are executed concurrently. Processes communicate and synchronize among themselves with input and output commands. An input command, presented in the form

```
α?var
```

inputs a value from the process with name α, then assigns the value to the variable *var*. On the other hand, an output command, presented in the form

α!exp

outputs the value of the expression *exp* to the process with the name α. An output command α!*exp* issued by a process β is evaluated only if a *matching* input command β?*var* is issued by α; otherwise it is delayed until such a matching command is issued.

In addition to communication commands, a command can be an assignment command, presented in the form

variable := expression

Or a command can be a guarded command, which in turn can be an alternative or a repetitive command. The syntax of an alternative command is

[G1 -> CL1 □ G2 -> CL2 □ . . . □ Gn -> CLn]

This command arbitrarily evaluates any *CLi* whose guard condition *Gi* is true. If none of the *Gi*s is true, the control moves to the exit point of the command.

A repetitive command takes the form

*[G1 -> CL1 □ G2 -> CL2 □ . . . □ Gn -> CLn]

This is like an alternative command except the command is evaluated repetitively until none of the *Gi*s is true.

A command can also be a command list, presented as a list of declarations and commands separated by semicolons, where the scope of a new variable introduced by a declaration ranges from its declaration to the end of the command list.

A command can be a parallel command, such as

[π1 ∥ π2 ∥ . . . ∥ πn]

where each *pi*, $1 \leq i \leq n$ is a process.

Example 5.5. (Ref. 12) The following CSP program solves the dining philosophers problem:

Five philosophers spend their lives thinking and eating. The philosophers share a common dining room where there is a circular table surrounded by five chairs, each belonging to one philosopher. In the center of the table there is a large bowl of spaghetti, and the table is laid with five forks. On feeling hungry, a philosopher enters the dining room, sits in his own chair, and picks up the fork on the left of his place. Unfortunately, the spaghetti is so tangled that he needs to pick up and use the fork on his right as well. When he has finished, he puts down both forks, and leaves the room. The room should keep a count of the number of philosophers in it. (Ref. 12)

Note that deadlocks can occur in the following program; these may be avoided by, for instance, not allowing more than four philosophers in the room:

```
PHIL = *[ . . . during ith lifetime . . .->
        THINK;
        room!enter();
        fork(i)!pickup();fork((i+1) mod 5)!pick-
up();
        EAT;
        fork(i)!putdown()fork((i+1)mod    5)!put-
down();
        room!exit();
    ]
    FORK  = *[phil(i)!pickup()  -> phil(i)?put-
down();  □
        phil((i-1) mod 5)?pickup() -> phil((i-1) mod
5)?putdown();
    ]
    ROOM = occupancy:integer; occupancy := 0;
    *[(i:0 . . 4)phil(i)?enter() -> occupancy :=
occupancy + 1;
        □ (i:0 . . 4)phil(i)?exit() -> occupancy :=
occupancy - 1;
    ]
    [room::ROOM∥fork(i:0 . . 4)::FORK∥phil(i:0 . .
4)::PHIL]
```

For applications of CSP, see Ref. 23. Although CSP is well-known, little effort has been made to make it a real programming language. Nevertheless the programming language OCCAM and its successors,[24] which have been realized mainly on transputers, was largely based on concepts proposed by CSP. Example 5.6 illustrates the syntax and semantics of OCCAM.

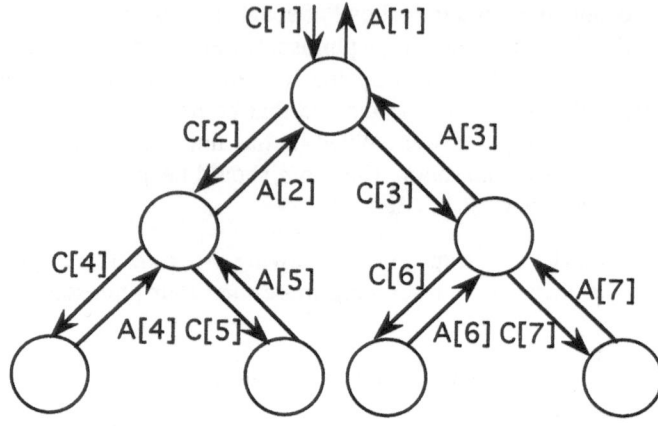

Figure 5.1. A parallel search tree. Reprinted with permission from Ref. 24. © 1988, Addison-Wesley.

Example. 5.6. (Ref. 24) Consider a database consisting of four integers. To search for an item in the database in parallel, we can organize a parallel search tree consisting of seven processes, as shown in Figure 5.1, where each leaf process stores one of the four integers and the other three processes serve as branch processes. To perform a parallel search, the key given is sent to the root branch process; in turn the key is duplicated, then passed to the two children branch processes of the root process in parallel. In turn each key is duplicated, then passed to each leaf process in parallel. Each leaf process compares the integer stored in itself with the key passed, then returns an answer (true or false) to its parent. Each of the two branch processes in the middle, on receiving replies from both children, performs a logical OR of the replies, then returns the result to the root process. The root process performs a logical OR of the two replies sent from its children, then returns the result as the final answer.

The following OCCAM procedure realizes a branch process:

```
PROC branch (CHAN OF INT req, Lreq, Rreq, CHAN of BOOL
ans, Lans, Rans)
      WHILE TRUE
      INT key:
      BOOL al, ar;
      SEQ
        req ? key
```

```
PAR
     Lreq ! key
     Rreq ! key
PAR
     Lans ? al
     Rans ? ar
ans ! al OR ar
:
```

The following OCCAM procedure realizes a leaf process:

```
PROC leaf (CHAN OF INT req, CHAN of BOOL ans)
    INT Data, key:
    SEQ
    - load data
    WHILE TRUE
    SEQ
      req ? key
      ans ! key = Data
    :
```

Based on the preceding, the following is a complete OCCAM program:

```
[8]CHAN OF INT C:
[8]CHAN OF BOOL A:
PROC branch (CHAN OF INT req, Lreq, Rreq, CHAN of BOOL
ans, Lans, Rans)
- body of PROC
PROC leaf (CHAN OF INT req, CHAN of BOOL ans)
- body of PROC
PROC User.Interface (CHAN OF INT out, CHAN of BOOL
in)
- body of some appropriate user interface process
    PAR
      branch(C[1],C[2],C[3],A[1],A[2],A[3])
      branch(C[2],C[4],C[5],A[2],A[4],A[5])
      branch(C[3],C[6],C[7],A[3],A[6],A[7])
      PAR i = 4 FOR 4
        leaf(C[i],A[i])
      User.Interface(C[1],A[1])
```

A concurrent program in OCCAM is configured as a set of processes communicating via channels. A process receives some input data (in the form of *channel ? data*) from one of its associated channels, then outputs some output data to one of its associated channels (in the form of *channel ! data*). The OCCAM is a block-structured language. A block process is a specification terminated by a colon ':') followed by a process; a process can be a primitive process (STOP, SKIP, assignment, input or output); a composite process obtained by gluing together several simpler processes with a constructor; or a block process.

Any variable *v* declared in the form of CHAN OF *protocol v* designates a channel whose behavior follows the protocol *protocol* specified in the declaration. In Example 5.6 the protocol *INT* specifies that each time exactly an integer is deposited on the channel and each time exactly an integer is retrieved from the channel when a rendezvous occurs between two communicating processes. The keywords WHILE, SEQ and PAR are constructors. Following the keyword SEQ, a number of processes can be specified; these are executed in the sequence they are specified. On the other hand, following the keyword PAR, a number of processes can be specified; these can be executed in parallel. The meaning of the WHILE constructor should be obvious: If the associated condition is true, then the following process should be executed. The statement PAR *i = 4* FOR *4* instantiates a *replicator;* it means that for the variable *i* with the initial value 4, the following process is executed in parallel for each increment of *i* (up to 4).

The actual OCCAM language is of course more complicated than Example 5.6. For example OCCAM allows the programmer to associate a priority with a process so that when a group of processes are executed in parallel, processes with higher priorities are executed first. In addition the programmer can allocate some processes to a specific processor to optimize performance. Interested readers are referred to Refs. 24 and 25 for details.

PROBLEMS

1. Write a C++ program to simulate the behavior of a combinational circuit that consists of a network of two-input, one-output logic gates. Your program should interact with the user to enter network components and the initial value associated with each input port. The program then computes the value that should appear at each output port according to gate functionalities.

Your program should prompt the user to enter the following:

- Gate types.
- Gate names: e.g., *x1, x2, y1*.

- Connections between gates in the form of *gate—name.terminal—name:* It is assumed that each gate has three terminals: *in1, in2,* and *out.* If the user enters *x1.in1 = x2.out,* this means input terminal *in1* of Gate *x1* is connected to the output terminal *out* of Gate *x2.*

If *in* 1 or *in* 2 of a gate remains unconnected, it is assumed to be an input port of the network. Similarly if *out* of a gate remains unconnected, it is assumed to be an output port of the network. Once the user enters the network, create a combinational circuit tree such that inputs applied at the input ports propagate through the circuit and produce outputs at the output ports. Now ask the user to enter input port values, then compute and print out values presented at output ports.

2. For the robot/inserting-machine problem in Chapter 4, sketch a CSP program that solves the problem.

3. A c++ does not provide constructs for processes; therefore it is not appropriate for concurrent programming. Based on your knowledge of CSP, sketch possible extensions to c++ so that it can be used for concurrent programming.

4. Implement the object-oriented solution described in Example 4.3 using c++.

5. Implement the object-oriented solution described in Example 4.3 using the extended c++ language developed in Problem 5.3. Compare this program to the program developed in Problem 5.4.

6. Implement the object-oriented solution developed in Problem 4.8 for the ray-tracing algorithm using c++.

7. Implement the object-oriented solution developed in Problem 4.8 for the ray-tracing algorithm using the extended c++ language developed in Problem 5.3. Compare this program to the program developed in Problem 5.6.

8. The SMALLTALK is not only a language but also a system. Discuss possible approaches to make UNIX/c++ an object-oriented system/language.

9. What is the output from the following c++ program?

```
class X {
  protected:
```

```
      int a;
   public:
      void make_a(int i) { a = i;};
      X(int);
}
class Y {
   protected:
      int b;
   public:
      void make_b(int i) { b = j;}
      Y(int);
}
class Z : public X, public Y {
   protected:
      int c;
   public:
      int make_ab(void) { return a * b;};
      Z(int,int);
}
X::X(int i) { a = i; cout << "initializing X to" << a;}
Y::Y(int j) { b = j; cout << "initializing Y to" << b;}
Z::Z(int i,int j): X(i),Y(j) { c = i*j; cout << "ini-
tializing Z to" << c;}
   main(void)
   {
      Z r(10,20);
      cout < make_ab();
      return 0;
   }
```

10. Using c++ define a base class *shape* and three derived classes: *line, triangle,* and *rectangle;* all should share the same set of interface functions, where *n, e, s, w, ne, se, sw,* and *nw* are defined as shown below for the smallest rectangle that contains the shape:

(a) *draw( ):* Draws the object on screen.
(b) *move(int,int):* Moves the object, where the first argument designates the offset along the *x*-axis and the second argument designates the offset along the *y*-axis.
(c) *north( ):* Returns the point *n*.
(d) *south( ):* Returns the point *s*.
(d) *west( ):* Returns the point *w*.

(e) *east( ):* Returns the point *e*.

(f) *neast( ):* Returns the point *ne*.

(g) *seast( ):* Returns the point *se*.

(h) *nwest( ):* Returns the point *nw*.

(i) *swest( ):* Returns the point *sw*.

The preceeding definitions should be made so that the code makes sense. You should also show output produced by the program.

REFERENCES

1. Agha, G. *Actors: A model of concurrent computation in distributed systems* (MIT Press, Cambridge, MA, 1986).
2. Meyer, B. *Object-Oriented Software Construction* (Prentice-Hall, Englewood, N.J., 1988).
3. Wegner, P. *ACM SIGPLAN Notices* (June 1990).
4. Stroustrup, B. *The C++ programming language,* 2d ed. (Addison Wesley, Reading, MA., 1991).
5. Goldberg, A., and Robson, D. *Smalltalk-80: the language and its implementation* (Addision Wesley, Reading, MA, 1983).
6. Goldberg, A., and Deutsch, L. P. *Byte* **16**:8, 108–115 (Aug. 1991).
7. LaLonde, W. R., and Pugh, J. R. *Inside Smalltalk,* vols. 1 & 2 (Prentice-Hall, Englewood, NJ, 1990).
8. Hu D. *Object-oriented environment in C++* (Management Information Source, Portland, OR, 1990).
9. Kaehler, T., and Patterson, D. *A Taste of Smalltalk* (Norton, New York, 1986).
10. Chin, R. S., and Chanson, S. T. *ACM Computing Surveys* **23**:1, 91–124 (Mar. 1991).
11. Strom, R. E., and Yemini, S. "NIL: an integrated language and system for distributed programming." *Proc., SIGPLAN '83 Symposium on Programming Language Issues in Software Systems* (1983), pp. 73–82.
12. Hoare, C. A. R. *ACM* **21**:8, 666–677 (Aug. 1978).
13. Shapiro, E., and Takeuchi, A. *New Generation Computing* **1**:1, 25–48 (1983).
14. Saloma, R., Liu, W., and Gyurcsik, R. S. "Software experience with concurrent C and LISP in a distributed system" *Proc., ACM 16th Annual Computer Science Conference* (1988), pp. 329–34.
15. Bal, H. E., Steiner, J. G., and Tanenbaum, A. S. *ACM Computing Surveys* **21**.3 (Sept. 1989) 261–322.
16. Ahuja, S., Carriero, N., and Gelenter, D. *IEEE Computer* **19.8**, 26–34 (Aug. 1986).
17. Schlichting, R. D., Andrews, G. R., Hutchinson, N. C., Olsson, R. A., and Peterson, L. L. *Lecture Notes in Computer Science* (*International Workshop, Kaiserlautern, F.R.G., Sept., 1987*) (G. Goos and J. Hertmanis, eds.) (Springer-Verlag, New York, 1988), 271–291.
18. Jul, E., Levy, H., Hutchinson, N., and Black, A. *ACM Transactions on Computer Systems* **6**:1, 109–135 (Feb. 1988).
19. Yokote, Y., and Tokoro, M. "Experience and evolution of concurrent Smalltalk." *Proc., OOPSLA* (New York, 1987), pp. 406–15.
20. Yonezawa, A., and Tokoro, M. In *Object-oriented concurrent programming* (Yonezawa and Tokoro, eds.) (MIT Press, Cambridge, MA, 1987), pp. 55–84.
21. Chandra, R., Gupta, A., and Hennessy, J. "COOL: a language for parallel programming." *Proc., Second Workshop on Programming Languages and Compilers for Parallel Computing,* IEEE Computer Press (1989).

22. Wyatt, B. B., Kavi, K., and Hufnagel, S. *IEEE Software* **9**:6, 56–66 (Nov. 1992).
23. Hull, M. E. C., and McKeag, R. M. *ACM Transactions on Programming Languages and Systems* **6.2,** 175–191 (Apr. 1984).
24. Burns, A. *Programming in Occam 2* (Addision Wesley, Reading, MA, 1988).
25. Wexler, J. *Concurrent programming in OCCAM 2* (Ellis Horwood, New York, 1989).

Programming Tools

Programming can be made easier if aided by certain tools, ranging from interactive program development to software libraries. Reusable library modules have proved to be useful in many aspects of programming, such as graphic user interface and network programming. Such libraries usually provide a much simpler (abstract) view of some tedious tasks through high-level subroutines. Chapter 6 describes the basic ideas behind some programming tools available for Windows[1] programming (Section 6.1), X-Window programming (Section 6.2), and UNIX network programming (Section 6.3). A simple project illustrates object-oriented Window programming with the library functions available in Object Windows.[2] The same project also summarizes features provided in an interactive programming environment IDE that supports TURBO c++ programming. The choices made were arbitrary; our intent is to show how reusable libraries facilitate programming and to illustrate some desired features of an IDE.

6.1. OBJECT-ORIENTED PROGRAMMING FOR WINDOWS

The three major aspects of object-oriented programming (i.e., encapsulation, inheritance, and polymorphism) as implemented in c++ makes it particularly suitable for Windows programming. A Windows system contains a set of objects. For example the main window is considered an object; similarly the help menu that pops up is considered an object. Each object has data members (such as the box itself, the border, the caption, etc.) and member functions, such as close, minimize, and maximize). These objects need a way of communicating with each other. In other words when the user selects the menu bar for help, the menu bar help window should open. A message-sending/processing scheme is needed. Once developed this makes any application self-sustaining. For example suppose we want to define an item on a list. The list is an object with data and member functions. We can define a function called *add* that is executed if *Menu|add* is selected. *Menu|add* has a message, which we can call *add_message*. So we can execute *add* if we receive *add_message*. This is a trivial example, but it shows the effectiveness of object-oriented programming for Windows applications.

6.1.1. Simple Project

This sample program entails building two functions: *Choices* and *Forms*. *Choices* opens a menu with items that are passed as parameters to it. The user selects an item from the menu that returns the index of the item selected. The index refers to the place of the selected item on the list. *Forms* takes as parameters an array with a list of items; each item has a label (i.e., name), a type, a length, and a value. The function opens a form window with an edit window for each item. The user is allowed to go to any field to change the value of the field or to select OK to close the window. The user can also select CANCEL, in which case the function returns zero. If OK is selected, a type check is performed to ensure that the new value (if any) for each item is consistent with the type. If it is, the window closes and the function and returns 1. Otherwise an error message appears, and the user cannot exit unless CANCEL is selected (in this case the function returns 0).

The program is divided into six parts, each with a relevant functional synopsis. There are three items in the main window menu bar: *Store, Display,* and *Help.* There are three subitems under *Store: Choices, Forms,* and *Exit;* there are two subitems under *Display: Choices* and *Forms;* there is only one item under *Help: Help.* The actions associated with these items follow:

- *Store|Choices:* Store the array to be passed to the *Choices* function.

- *Store|Forms:* Store the array to be passed to the *Forms* function.

- *Store|Exit:* Exit from the program.

- *Display|Choices:* Execute the *Choices* function.

- *Display|Forms:* Execute the *Forms* function.

- *Help|Help:* Display the *Help* menu.

6.1.1.1. Store|Choices

This item accepts inputs from the user, then stores the inputs in the array *Items_Choices.* When selected a dialog box appears on the screen asking the user to enter command line arguments for the *Choices* function. Elements of the array are entered in the form of:

```
string string . . . string
```

A string is defined as a letter of the alphabet followed by any combination of alphanumeric characters. Once the command line arguments are entered and the user selects OK, a check is made to see if the line entered is syntactically correct. If it is, the message is sent that the input is vaild and stored; otherwise an error message is sent. An example of a correct command is

```
aaa bbb cde ff12 gg
```

The array *Items—Choices* stores the following:

```
Items_Choices [0] <= aaa
Items_Choices[1] <= bbb
Items_Choices[2] <= cde
Items_Choices[3] <= ff12
Items_Choices[4] <= gg
```

6.1.1.2. Store|Forms

This item accepts inputs from the user, then stores these in the array *Items —Forms*. When selected a dialog box appears on the screen asking the user to enter command line arguments for the *Forms* function. Each element of the array (called a field) is entered in the form of

```
⟨name⟩⟨type⟩⟨length⟩⟨old_value⟩
```

where ⟨*name*⟩ is defined as a letter of the alphabet followed by any combination of alphanumeric characters; ⟨*type*⟩ is either int, float, or string; ⟨*length*⟩ is an integer designating the length of the associated field; and ⟨*old_value*⟩ is any-old value for the field. If the field does not have any-old value, an asterisk is used. Once command line arguments are entered and the user selects OK, a check is made to see if the line entered is syntactically correct and the values entered are consistent with their associated types. If they are, a message is sent that the input is vaild and stored; otherwise an error message is sent. An example of a correct command is

```
a int 5 5 b string 10 mygod ccc float 10 5.5
```

The array *Items—Choices* stores the following:

```
Items_Forms[0][0] <= a
Items_Forms[0][1] <= int
Items_Forms[0][2] <= 5
Items_Forms[0][3] <= 5
Items_Forms[1][0] <= b
```

```
Items_Forms[1][1] <= string
Items_Forms[1][2] <= 10
Items_Forms[1][3] <= mygod
Items_Forms[2][0] <= ccc
Items_Forms[2][1] <= float
Items_Forms[2][2] <= 10
Items_Forms[2][3] <= 5.5
```

6.1.1.3. Store|Exit

This item opens a window to confirm the user's action. If the action is confirmed, the application is terminated; otherwise the program continues.

6.1.1.4. Display|Choices

When selected, this item executes the *Choices* function, which is an integer type. If the array *Items_Choices* does not contain a element, an error message appears. Otherwise a menu of array elements and two buttons: INDEX and CANCEL are created in a window. The user can select any item on the list in two ways—by double clicking on an item in the menu, which closes the window; the function then returns the index of the selected item. The second way is by single clicking on the item, then selecting INDEX. If the user selects CANCEL, the window closes and 0 is returned as the function value.

6.1.1.5. Display|Forms

When selected this item executes the *Forms* function, which is an integer type. If the array *Items_Forms* does not contain a element, an error message appears. Otherwise a menu of array elements and two buttons: INDEX and CANCEL are created in a window. Each item is display as a field with a label and a box whose length is defined and contains the old value of the field (empty if none). The user can move to any field to enter its new value; the user then selects OK. The new value of the ith field (if any) is stored in *Items_Forms*[i][4]. If no new value is entered for the ith field and it did not have an old value, an asterisk is stored in *Items_Forms*[i][4]. If every thing is fine after type checking, the function returns 1. If there is a type mismatch or CANCEL is selected, an error message appears (in the case of a type mismatch), and the function returns 0. Furthermore if CANCEL is selected, all changes entered are invalidated. Again the user can select any item on the list in two ways—by double click on a menu item, which closes the window; the function then returns the index of the selected item. The second way is by a single clicking on an item, then selecting INDEX. If the user selects CANCEL, the window closes and 0 is returned as the function value.

6.1.1.6. Help|Help

This item displays a list box, a display window, and two buttons: HELP and CANCEL. The user can access help for an item on the list by doubly clicking on the item. The display window displays help text about the item selected. The same effect can be achieved by clicking on the desired item, then selecting HELP. Selecting CANCEL closes the Help window. Unlike *Choices* and *Forms* windows, *Help* windows can be active while the user is executing other commands. Help windows are referred to as *modeless*; other windows are referred to as *modal*.

6.1.2. Object Windows

ObjectWindows is an object-oriented library that uses the advantages of object-oriented programming to make programming Windows applications, especially the user interface, easier.[2] Similar facilities are provided by Microsoft's Visual C++ in its Foundation Class library. ObjectWindows defines all major window elements with well-stated behaviors, attributes, and data. It provides three major features: encapsulation of window information, abstraction of many window functions, and an automatic message response scheme.

In Object Windows encapsulation of window information is provided for major window elements. These elements are usually standard in any code for programming Windows. Be defining these the application programmer can spend more time figuring out the logistics of the application rather than coding standardized and repetitive classes. On the other hand, with a member function that abstracts a called window's function, programming becomes a lot easier. There are approximately 600 window functions, most of which (but not all) are abstracted. ObjectWindows also provides automatic message response. Windows require its applications to respond to Windows messages that it receives. With traditional Windows programming in c, a switch statement responds to all possible messages that can be sent to an object. With ObjectWindows however, Windows messages are handled by object member function calls. A member function can be defined for each message to be handled. Once a message is received, the appropriate function is called. This makes the code shorter than in traditional programming.

As a simple example, consider an application that requires a function creating a window, then hangs until some input is received from the window. ObjectWindows has a predefined class called *TDialog* designed specially for this purpose. In a similar way, basic window classes and objects that appear in them (such as list boxes, edit windows, static text, etc.) are provided in ObjectWindows.

The following sections summarize some important facilities provided by ObjectWindows to implement the simple project.

6.1.2.1. Modal and Modeless Windows

There is an important distinction between modal and modeless windows when programming with ObjectWindows. A modal window hangs the parent window until some user input is received; on receiving the input, the modal window returns control to the parent window. A modeless window exists along with the parent window, so the user can switch between them at will. For the simple project previously discussed, the *Choices* window and the *Forms* window are implemented as modal windows, but the Help window is implemented as a modeless window. Note that when the user exits the application, a modeless window closes automatically along with the main window. The code for creating a modal window is much different from that for creating a modeless window. In ObjectWindows a typical type of modal windows is dialog box.

6.1.2.2. Applications Main Program

All ObjectWindows applications contain a main program that controls the application. For almost all applications using ObjectWindows, the main program contains the following lines of code:

```
Int PASCAL WinMain (handle hInstance, HANDLE hPrev-
Instance,LPSTR lpCmdLine, int nCmdShow)
{ TAppExample AppExample("Application Example",
hInstance,hPrevInstance, lpCmdLine,nCmdShow);
  AppExample.Run();
  return AppExample.Status;
}
```

The first line of code calls the constructor of the class *TAppExample*, a subclass of the ObjectWindows class *TApplication*, to construct an application object, called *AppExample* in the preceding. The second statement calls a member function *Run* of the object *AppExample*. Internally the function calls another function *AppExample.InitApplication* to initialize the first instance of the object *AppExample*. *AppExample.Run()* then calls the function *InitMainWindow*, which creates and initializes the main window of the application. This function is usually redefined for each application by the user. Finally *AppExample.Run()* calls the function *MainWindow.MessageLoop()* to process messages to and from the application. The last statement returns the final state of the application: 0 to successfully close the application. Any nonzero value represents an error condition. The class *TAppExample* can be defined as follows:

```
class TAppExample: public TApplication
{
  TAppExample(LPSTR AName, Handle hInstance, HAN-
DLE hPrevInstance, LPSTR lpCmdLine, int nCmdShow):
TApplication (AName, hInstance, hPrevInstance,
lpCmdLine, nCmdShow){};
  virtual void InitMainWindow();
}
```

The member function *InitMainWindow()* can be defined as follows:

```
void TAppExample::InitMainWindow()
{
  MainWindow = new TMainWindow(NULL, "MainWindow of
Application");
}
```

During initialization of the application, *InitMainWindow* is executed and creates the desired main window for the application.

6.1.2.3. Resource File

A resource refers to any Windows interface element, such as a regular window, an edit window, a dialog box, or a button, etc. Each application usually has a resource file, which defines the main window menu bar. Additional resources, such as dialog boxes, can be included as well. The resource file for the sample program (see Section 6.1.3) resembles the following:

```
COMMANDS MENU
BEGIN
  POPUP "&Store"
  BEGIN
    MENUITEM "&Choices", CM_CHOICES
    MENUITEM "&Forms", CM_FORMS
    MENUITEM "&Escape", CM_ESCAPE
    MENUITEM "&Exit", CM_EXIT
  END
  POPUP "&Display"
  BEGIN
```

```
    MENUITEM "&Choices", CM_DISCHOICES
    MENUITEM "&FORMS", CM_DISFORMS
    MENUITEM "&Escape", CM_DISESCAPE
  END
  POPUP "&Help"
  BEGIN
    MENUITEM "&Help", CM_HELP
  END
END
FORM3 DIALOG LOADONCALL MOVEABLE DISCARDABLE 10,
10, 100, 100
STYLE     WS_CAPTION|WS_SYSMENU|DS_MODALFRAME|WS
_POPUP
BEGIN
END
FORM2 DIALOG LOADONCALL, MOVEABLE DISCARDABLE 10,
10, 100, 100
STYLE     WS_CAPTION|WS_SYSMENU|DS_MODALFRAME|WS
_POPUP
BEGIN
END
FORM1 DIALOG LOADONCALL MOVEABLE DISCARDABLE 100,
100, 300, 200
STYLE     WS_CAPTION|WS_SYSMENU|DS_MODALFRAME|WS
_POPUP
BEGIN
END
```

The resource file defines the main window menu bar and the two dialog boxes used for the *Choices* and *Forms* functions. Each resource in the resource file has a unique identifier, somewhat like a handle. In the main program, a programmer can access a resource of the resource file by using the associated resource identifier. For instance as seen from the source (see Section 6.1.3), the identifier COMMANDS is used as the sole argument of the statement

```
AssignMenu("COMMANDS");
```

in the constructor of the class *TMyWindow*. With this the resource identified by COMMANDS is bound to be the menu of the application. Similarly the resource FORM1 is bound to be the dialog box in the following call:

```
GetModule()->ExecDialog(new TFormWindow(this,
"FORM1",items,count);
```

The resource file is compiled separately, and it is bound to the main program at link time. ObjectWindows provides an interactive user interface to define resources in a resource file, although it can be written as a file by the user. ObjectWindows is basically a library of some base classes that can be reused by application programs. The following list summarizes some base classes used in the sample program in Section 6.1.3.

TApplication: Defines the basic structure and behavior of all ObjectWindows applications. All ObjectWindows applications must contain a derived class of *TApplication.*

TWindowsObject: Defines basic structure and behavior of all ObjectWindows interface objects, such as windows and dialog boxes. Member functions of this class create interface objects, handle messages, and destroy interface objects.

TWindow: Is a subclass of the class *TWindowsObject,* and it provides fundamental window features. A *TWindow* object can be used as the main window for an application or as a pop-up window.

TDialog: Is the base class for modal and modeless dialog boxes. For each dialog box, there must exist a resource definition in the resource file describing its controls, which include buttons, list boxes, edit windows, etc. Member functions of this class handle message responses between a dialog box and its controls.

TListBox: Defines the structure and behavior of list boxes (or choice boxes).

TEdit: Defines the structure and behavior of an edit window, which includes a text editor. There are two basic types of edit control: single line and multiline.

TButton: Defines the structure and behavior of a push button. There are two types of push buttons: default and regular. A default button performs the default action of a window; i.e., if the keyboard is enabled, a return should be synonymous to selecting the default button. A regular button has no default action.

TStatic: Defines graphics or text that can be displayed in a window. Static controls are not selected or modified by the user. In our example it is ideal for the label of a field of a *Forms* window. There is no need to access a static control and therefore no need to have a unique ID for a static object.

6.1.3. Sample Program

Figure 6.1 (see pages 164–180) shows a sample program that creates an interactive user interface in Windows. The program basically creates three classes: one for the main window (*TMyWindow*), one for *Choices* (*TFormWindow*), and one for *Forms* (*TForm2Window*).

6.1.3.1. TFormWindow

This is a derived class of the ObjectWindows class *TDialog*. It is defined in the resource file with the resource ID Form1. There are two types of dialog boxes: modal and modeless. The program declares the dialog box of a *TForm-Window* to be modal so that the calling function waits for user input. *TFormWindow*'s constructor creates an instance of *TListBox* called *ListBox*. The constructor of the class *TListBox* takes as parameters a pointer (which is *this*), a unique ID (which is FORM1), the *x*-coordinate, the *y*-coordinate, the width, and the height. Position is stated relative to the class *TFormWindow*. To handle list box messages, a member function *HandleListBoxMsg* is defined. It is invoked whenever a list box is selected, and its execution is automatic due to ObjectWindows automatic message-item processing facility. The following code shows how a member function is declared for this purpose:

```
virtual void HandleListBoxMsg (RTMEssage Msg)
    = [ID_FIRST + ID_LISTBOX];
```

Other member functions of this class include OK and *HandleButton2Msg*. OK handles the *OK* button when selected, and *HandleButton2Msg* handles the *CANCEL* button when selected. The *TDialog* class has its own *OK* function, and this class overloads it. *HandleButton2Msg* simply closes the window and sets the global *Choices_return* to 0. The *Setup Window* function overloads the function from its parent class and puts all items in the list box from the array and sizes the window using the *MoveWindow* function. Note that an array is passed from outside of a class to the class through its constructor.

6.1.3.2. TForm2Window

This class is also derived from *TDialog* and it is modal. In the constructor of this class, width, height, the *x*-coordinate and the *y*-coordinate are calculated using information from the array and an integer count passed to the constructor. A label and an edit window are placed in a *TForm2Window* by creating a *Tstatic* object and a *Tedit* object, respectively. Each edit window must have a unique identifier, so an integer *BASE_EDIT* is defined to represent the identifier of the first edit box. Once the first edit window is placed, the integer is incremented for every edit window placed. On the other hand, a *TStatic* object does not need an identifier, since we never have to select or modify static text. The constructor of *Tedit* takes as parameters a pointer to the parent (which is *this*), the ID (of the object), the default text, the *x*-coordinate, the *y*-coordinate (with respect to the *TForm2Window*), the length, height, maximal number of characters allowed in the window, and a Boolean value (when FALSE it designates a single-line edit window). The constructor of *TStatic* takes as parameters a pointer to the parent (which is *this*), the ID (which is don't care, −1), the text, the *x*-coordinate, the *y*-coordinate (with respect to the *TForm2Window*), length, height, and maximal number of characters allowed in the window. In this class a function OK is needed to overload the *Tdialog::OK* function to do type checking. If no type checking error occurs, the function in turn calls *TDialog::OK*, which in turn closes the window. Otherwise it closes the window and does not allow *TDialog::OK* to return *IDOK* to the calling function.

6.1.3.3. TMyWindow

This class is derived from the class *TWindow* of ObjectWindows. The *WinMain* function initializes the application to point to a *TMyWindow* object. The constructor of this class assigns the resource COMMANDS to this window and does some additional initializations. The function *Choices_store* is executed whenever the user selects *Store|Choices*. The function is declared as follows:

```
virtual void Choices_store (RTMessage Msg)
    = [CM_FIRST + CM_CHOICES];
```

where *CM_CHOICES* is the ID of the menu item *Choices* under the group item *Store*.

The following function opens up a standard input dialog box:

```
GetApplication()->ExecDialog(new     TInputDialog
(this,"Command Line:", "Command Line", InputText,
sizeofInputText));
```

This function opens up a single-line dialog box and stores whatever is entered in *InputText*. If there are no syntactic errors, the Boolean variable *Choices_filled* is made true; otherwise it remains false. The function *Forms_store* works in a similar way. The function *Choices_display* is the action corresponding to the menu item *Display|Choices*. It creates a *TFormWindow* object using the *Exec-Dialog* function with the identifier FORM1. The program hangs until input is received from the user. If the returned value of the *ExecDialog* function is IDOK (which is handled by *Tdialog::OK*), the function copies from the global transfer integer *Choice_return*, then returns this value; otherwise it returns 0. The function *Display_Forms* works similarly except that an array is copied. Finally the function *CanClose* is overloaded from the class *TWindow*. It returns true if the user selects *YES* in the message box asking to confirm the exit request. This function is called before the *TMyWindow* is closed. If the return value is true, the window is closed and the reverse, otherwise.

6.1.3.4. TMyApp

This class is derived from the ObjectWindows class *TApplication*. It has a member function called *InitMainWindow* that sets the data member *MainWindow* to point to a *TMyWindow* object.

6.2. IDE—AN INTERACTIVE PROGRAMMING ENVIRONMENT

The TURBO c++ IDE provides an editor, a compiler, and a debugger. The editor lets the user create or modify a program. The compiler converts a program into instructions. The debugger helps the programmer identify parts of a program that do not work correctly. The integrated environment consists of three parts:

- *Windows:* Display information on the screen.

- *Pull-down Menus:* Provide commands for manipulating a program.

- *Status line:* Displays options available to the programmer.

The following summarizes the menu items that can be chosen in IDE:

6.2.1. File Menu

- *Open:* Opens an existing file.

- *New:* Opens a new edit window with the default name of NONAMExx.C, where xx is a number from 00–99.

- *Save:* Saves the file in the active edit window in the current directory.

- *Save As . . . :* Saves (copies) the current file under a different filename, in a different directory, or on a different drive.

- *Save All:* Saves the contents of all modified files.

- *Change Dir . . . . :* Lets the programmer choose a different directory or a different drive.

- *Print:* Prints the entire file in the active edit window to the printer.

- *Get Info . . . :* Displays a box containing information about the current file.

- *DOS Shell:* Takes the programmer to DOS. To return to IDE, the programmer simply types *exit,* then selects Return.

- *Quit:* Terminates IDE.

6.2.2. Edit Menu

The Edit menu contains the following commands for editing files:

- *Restore Line:* Restores the last line changed or deleted.

- *Cut:* Cuts selected text. Text can be selected by clicking the left mouse button at the beginning of the text, dragging the mouse until the desired text is highlighted, then releasing the mouse button. A selected text can be pasted anywhere using the paste option.

- *Copy:* Works the same way as *Cut* except that *Copy* does not delete text from its original position. However the selected text can be pasted anywhere in the file.

- *Paste:* Puts previously selected text into the window (at the position of the cursor).

- *Copy Example:* Copies preselected text blocks from the Help window to the clipboard.

- *Clear:* Works like *Cut* except it does not paste selected text (i.e., it fully deletes selected text).

6.2.3. Compile Menu

The *Compile* menu contains the following commands for compiling programs:

- *Compile to OBJ:* Creates an .OBJ object file.

- *Make EXE File:* Creates an executable .EXE file, using the name of the current file or the name of the project file specified with the *Project* menu's *Open* command. In the process of making an executable .EXE file, TURBO C++ also creates an .OBJ file.

- *Link EXE File:* Takes the current .OBJ and .LIB files and links them to produce an executable file.

• *Build All:* Rebuilds all the files in a project regardless of their date.

• *Remove Messages:* Clears any messages in the Message window.

6.2.4. Debug Menu

The *Debug* menu lets the programmer to debug a Turbo C++ program:

• *Inspect:* Allows the programmer to examine and modify the contents of a data element, such as character, pointer, array, function, class or structure.

• *Evaluate/Modify:* Allows the programmer to examine and modify the value of a variable.

• *Call stack:* Lists the sequence of functions called by a program.

• *Watches:* Displays a pop-up menu of four watch point commands:

—*Add Watch:* Lets the programmer examine the content of a variable while running a program with the TURBO C++ integrated debugger.
—*Delete Watch:* Removes displayed watch points created with the *Add Watch* command.
—*Edit Watch:* Allows the programmer to edit a watch point created with the *Add Watch* command.
—*Remove All Watches:* Removes all watch points created by the *Add Watch* command.

• *Toggle Breakpoint:* Allows the programmer to set a breakpoint or remove an existing one. A *breakpoint* is a line in a program where the program stops running until the programmer gives the command to continue (through *Step* or *Run*).

6.2.5. Run Menu

The *Run* menu provides the following options:

• *Trace Into:* It runs the program line by line. When the debugger reaches a function call, the debugger displays the lines of the called function. Upon exiting the function, the debugger again goes back to the main program.

• *Step Over:* This command runs the program line by line just like the *Trace into* command. The difference is that when the debugger reaches a function call, it does not display the lines of the called function.

• *Breakpoints:* It display a list of all breakpoints, their line numbers, and their conditions. This command lets the programmer quickly view and delete any breakpoints set in a program.

6.2.6. Search Menu

The *Search* menu helps in searching for specific text, function declaration, and errors in a program.

- *Find:* Displays a dialog box that provides several search criteria:

    —*Case Sensitive:* Differentiates between uppercase and lowercase letters.
    —*Whole Words only:* Searches for strings separated by punctuations or spaces on both sides.
    —*Regular Expression:* Recognizes GREP-like wild cards in a search string.
    —*Origin:* Determines the starting point for search—from the cursor position or the beginning/end of a file.
    —*Direction:* Determines the direction of the search from the origin selected.
    —*Scope:* Determines whether to search selected text in a file or the entire directory.

- *Replace:* Displays a dialog box that lets the programmer search and replace text within a file. The replace dialog box contains the same options as the *Find* Dialog box, with an additional command line to write/search for the text that replaces the original text.

- *Search Again:* Repeats the last *Find* or *Replace* command with the same settings.

- *Go to Line Number:* Prompts the programmer to enter the line number to view and displays it.

- *Previous Error:* Displays the line in a program that contains the previous error or warning message. This command works only if the *Message* window contains messages.

- *Next Error:* Displays the line in a program that contains the next error or warning message. This command works only if the Message window contains messages.

- *Locate Function:* Lets the programmer find the name of a function. This command is available while only using the integrated TURBO c++ debugger.

6.2.7. Option Menu

The option menu contains commands for changing the settings of the TURBO
c++ integrated development environment.

- *Full Menu Option:* Determines the complete TURBO c++ menus or displays only a partial set.

- *Compiler:* Consists of suboptions about how TURBO c++ creates optimized code from a program.

- *Transfer:* Allows programs to be added or deleted from the System menu.

- *Make:* Lets the user specify conditions that stop project making.

- *Linker:* Lets the programmer define how TURBO c++ links together .OBJ
  files in a project.

- *Debugger:* Lets the user define how the integrated debugger works.

- *Directories:* Specifies in which directories TURBO c++ can find include
  and library files; also lets the user specify in which directory to save
  program files.

- *Environment:* Displays a pop-up menu to specify the appearance of TURBO
  c++ integrated environment, how the integrated debugger behaves, when
  TURBO c++ automatically saves files, how the editor works, and how a
  mouse works with TURBO c++.

- *Save:* Saves any option set so TURBO c++ automatically uses them the
  next time TURBO c++ is run.

6.2.8. Project Menu

The *Project* menu contains six commands for managing projects. A project
is simply a collection of separate files that work together to realize a single
program.

- *Open Project:* Creates a new project or loads an existing one; also creates
  some files that contain information needed to create an executable .EXE
  program file.

- *Close Project:* Closes the current project.

- *Add Item:* Allows a file to be added to a project.

- *Delete Item:* Allows a file to be deleted from a project.

- *Local Options:* Display an *Override Options* dialog box that defines options for a project. The available options are

—*Overlay this module:* Makes selected project items as overlay files.

—*Exclude Debug information:* Makes smaller .EXE files at the expense of removing debug information. (Without debugging information, the user cannot examine how a file works with the TURBO c++ integrated debugger.)

—*Exclude From Link:* Prevents a file from being linked to create an .EXE executable file.

—*Include files:* Lists include files that the current project file uses.

6.2.9. Window Menu

The *Window* menu contains commands for changing the appearance of the TURBO c++ integrated development environment windows.

- *Size/Move:* Lets the user change the size and position of a window.

- *Zoom:* Resizes the current window to fill the entire screen. Reselecting this option restores the window to its original size.

- *Tile:* Displays all windows so they fit on the screen; i.e., no windows overlaps another window.

- *Cascade:* Displays windows so they overlap one another.

- *Next:* Makes another window active. (If there is more than one window on the screen, then Next flips from one window to another, making the other one active.)

- *Close:* Removes the active window from the screen.

- *Message:* Opens the Message window (i.e., the window where commands, such as compiling, linking, etc., are displayed at the time TURBO c++ performs respective jobs). If the Message window is already open, this command activates the message window.

- *Output:* Opens a window that shows program output.

- *Watch:* Opens a Watch window and makes it active; this window displays variables and their values.

- *User Screen:* Displays a full screen of the program's output.

- *Project:* Lists all files in the current project.

- *List:* Displays all files currently open.

- *Project Notes:* Lets the programmer write information about each project.

- *Register:* Displays CPU registers and their contents to help the user debug a program.

6.3. X-WINDOW PROGRAMMING

The X is a windowing and graphics system designed to operate over a network.[3] Therefore the system always involves at least two parts: a client and a server talking to each other over a communications channel. They communicate using the X protocol, which defines a compact way of describing window operations, graphics operations, and events (button selections, operations completed, etc.).

A *client* is an applications program anywhere on the network that makes requests to the *server* to do something on the screen. The client is programmed using XLIB,[4] a low-level C language programming interface to X services. The XLIB converts XLIB library calls into X protocol requests to the server.

The server controls the display of the particular terminal; therefore its code is written by the specific manufacturer of the graphics hardware. Thus servers appear as black boxes to users and X programmers, allowing any machine communicating with the X protocol to connect to the network.

The X *toolkit*[5] is a higher level subroutine library that implements such user interface operations as menus or scrollbars (commonly known as *widgets*) using XLIB. The standard toolkit distributed with X is the *Xt* toolkit. A toolkit is essentially a much simpler interface for programming X; it insulates the programmer from the details of, say, creating a window or resizing a window. Widget sets are collections of widgets, and these provide the most common windowing operations with a certain look and feel specific to the vendor. For example two popular widget sets, Open Software Foundation's Motif[6] and Sun Microsystem's Open Look,[7,8] are two different widget sets designed to work with Xt. They differ in how their windows look, their scroll bars operate, fonts change, etc. Toolkit intrinsics facilitate new widget creation.

Before getting into XLIB programming, there are certain things to know about X-Windows system architecture:

- X is a windowing system for bit-mapped color, gray-scale, and monochrome graphic displays. A display is any number of screens, a keyboard, and a mouse.

- X is a network-oriented windowing system. Client applications can run on many different machines by sending requests to the server display and receiving events (keyboard, mouse, etc.) from the server. The server therefore is the middle man between user programs and the local system. Since clients can run on other machines across a network, distributed processing can be performed, helping to balance system loads.

- A separate program controls the screen layout, appearance, etc. It is called the window manager. The window manager is also written with XLIB, and it has special privileges for controlling windows appearing on the user's screen. Clients or applications must cooperate with the window manager and its window layout policy by indicating how they want their windows displayed. The X does not require a particular type of window manager, thus allowing the market to decide what the standard window interface should be. This enables better designs than present ones to become available.

- There is a major difference in programming X and in programming UNIX or DOS: Event-driven programming allows the user to tell the program or client what to do. For example in UNIX, when a program wants to obtain an input from the user, it must poll for input using a function to obtain characters. Alternatively in X functions for receiving events (keypress, mouse input, reexposing a hidden portion of a window) are used to cause the program to branch accordingly. Numerous events of many different types are placed in a queue, which is usually processed in first in, first out order. Event-driven programming is a natural form of programming for any mouse-based windowing system.

- The X is extensible: Separate code on the same level as XLIB subroutines define a method for adding new extensions, such as displaying PostScript. This is necessary to ensure that third-party and software vendors do not have to modify existing core XLIB subroutines to add a new extension; they merely have to add new code accordingly.[4]

The first thing to do to use XLIB is to include ⟨*X11/Xlib.h*⟩. The following program shows an X application that connects to the server, creates a window, makes it visible, sleeps for 10 seconds, and exits.

```
#include⟨stdio.h⟩
#include⟨stdlib.h⟩
#include⟨X11/Xlib.h⟩
main()
{
  Display *mydisplay;
  Window mywindow;
  int myscreen;
  unsigned long myforeground, mybackground;
```

```
    /* connect to the server */
    mydisplay = XOpenDisplay("");
    if(mydisplay == NULL){
      fprintf(stderr, "cannot connect to server0);
      exit(EXIT_FAILURE);
    }
    /* get a screen */
    myscreen = DefaultScreen (mydisplay);
    /* look up "black" and "white" */
    mybackground = WhitePixel (mydisplay,myscreen);
    myforeground = BlackPixel (mydisplay,myscreen);
    /* create a window at (100,50), width 350, height
250 */
    mywindow = XCreateSimpleWindow (mydisplay, De-
faultRootWindow
      (mydisplay), 100, 50, 350, 250, 2, myforeground,
mybackground);
    if(mywindow == NULL){
    fprintf (stderr,Rcannot open window0); exit (EXIT
_FAILURE);
    }
    /* pop this window up on the screen */
    XMapRaised (mydisplay,mywindow);
    XFlust (mydisplay);
    sleep (10);
    exit (EXIT_SUCCESS);
}
```

To compile the program, it must be linked with the X library using the -1 option at the end of the command line:

```
cc -o p7-1 p7-1.c -1X11
```

In the preceding program, *XOpenDisplay* opens a connection to the X server that controls a display. The NULL string passed to it means that the DISPLAY variable in the user's environment is used by default. *Mydisplay* is a pointer to a *Display* structure defined in ⟨*X11/Xlib.h*⟩. This structure defines the place where all subsequent X requests are sent. *XOpenDisplay* returns NULL if the function cannot be performed (*Xlib* routines generally return 0 if there is an error). The macro *DefaultScreen* returns an integer that represents the default screen for the user's server (*Xlib* subroutine names begin with uppercase X while macros do not). The macros *WhitePixel* and *BlackPixel* obtain values for white and black on the monitor screen. This is a good programming practice for ensuring total portability, because we cannot assume that black is 0 and white is 1 (on color screens it may be different). The function *XCreateSimpleWindow* is called with the format:

```
Window *XCreateSimpleWindow (Display *display,
Window window,
int ulx, int uly, int width, int height, int
borderwidth, int foregroundcolor, int background-
color)
```

where *display* is the server on which the window is to be created, *window* is the parent window, *ulx* and *uly* are the position of the upper left-hand corner of the window, the rest is self-explanatory. This function does the bulk of the work of creating a window. The macro, *DefaultRootWindow* returns the root window of the server (the parent of the new window). Note that an entire hierarchy of windows can be defined. Once a window is created, it still must be displayed or mapped. *XMapRaised* makes the window visible on the display and causes it to appear on top of existing windows or to be moved to the front. When *XFlush* is called, it causes queued requests to be sent to the server. The following program makes use of the window created in the preceding program and incorporates mouse events:

```
#include ⟨stdio.h⟩
#include ⟨stdlib.h⟩
#include ⟨X11/Xlib.h⟩
main()
{
  Display *mydisplay;
  Window mywindow;
  int myscreen;
  unsigned long myforeground, mybackground;
  XEvent myevent;
  KeySym mykey;
  int i;
  char text[10];
  int doneflag = 0;
  /* connect to the server */
  mydisplay = XOpenDisplay("");
  if (mydisplay == NULL){
    fprintf (stderr, "cannot connect to server0);
    exit (EXIT_FAILURE);
```

```
      }
      /* get a screen */
      myscreen = DefaultScreen (mydisplay);
      /* look up "black" and "white" */
      mybackground = WhitePixel (mydisplay,myscreen);
      myforeground = BlackPixel (mydisplay,myscreen);
      /* create a window at (100,50), width 350, height
250 */
      mywindow = XCreateSimpleWindow (mydisplay,
      DefaultRootWindow(mydisplay),
      100, 50, 350, 250, 2, myforeground, mybackground);
      if (mywindow == NULL){
       fprintf (stderr, "cannot open window0);
       exit (EXIT_FAILURE);
      }
      /* ask to receive Expose, ButtonPress, and Key-
Press events */
      XSelectInput (mydisplay, mywindow, ButtonPress-
Mask|KeyPressMask
        |ExposureMask);
      /* pop this window up on the screen */
      XMapRaised (mydisplay, mywindow);
      /* the event loop */
      while (!doneflag){
        /* get the next event in the event queue */
        XNextEvent (mydisplay, &myevent);
        switch (myevent.type){
          case ButtonPress:
          /* user pressed a pointer button */ /* draw the
rectangle */
          XDrawRectangle (mydisplay, mywindow,
          Default(mydisplay,myscreen),
          myevent.xbutton.x,myevent.xbutton.y,50,50);
          /* move the cursor relative (50,50) */
          XWarpPointer(mydisplay, None, None, 0, 0, 0,
0, 50, 50);
          break;
          case KeyPress:
          /* user pressed a key, see if it's a "q" */
          i = XLookupString (&myevent, text, 10, &mykey,
0);
          if (i == 1 && *text == "q")
            doneflag = 1;
```

```
    break
    case Expose:
      /* ignore Expose events */
      break;
  }
}
/* exit gracefully */
XDestroyWindow (mydisplay, mywindow);
XCloseDisplay (mydisplay);
  exit (EXIT_SUCCESS);
}
```

In the preceding program, the *XSelectInput* function requests notification of a mask specifying the events to receive. The program asks to receive *Expose* (the event the window appears on the screen or whenever a part of the window is obscured and subsequently exposed), *ButtonPress* (the event the mouse button is selected), and *KeyPress* (the event a key is selected from the keyboard) events. Incidentally mask constants are all defined in *Xlib.h*. The event loop is entered when *XNextEvent* is called to flush the event request queue, then return the next event. The *XNextEvent* function takes two arguments, a display and a pointer to an *XEvent* union. The *XEvent* union is a combination of all different event structures, one for each event type. In this program the *XExposeEvent* structure is used in this union. The type entry in the *XEvent* union specifies the event type returned by *XNextEvent*. The program then switches on *myevent.type* to determine which of the three event types has occurred. If a mouse button was selected, a rectangle is drawn with the function *XDrawRectangle,* which requires the following format:

```
XDrawRectangle (Display *display, Window window, GC
gc, int ulx, int uly, int width, int height)
```

where *gc* is a graphics context (or *GC,* discussed later), *ulx* and *uly* are the upper left-hand corner of the rectangle in the window's coordinate system. For this program the default *GC* is used by calling the macro *DefaultGC*. After the rectangle is drawn, the cursor is moved to the right-hand corner of the rectangle by a call to *XWarpPointer* with the following format:

```
XWarpPointer (int *display, Window source, Window
destination, int
    ulx, int width, int height, int x, int y)
```

If a source window is given, then the integer parameters specify a rectangular region that the cursor must be in for the move to take place; if a destination window is given, *x* and *y* specify the destination position relative to the origin of that window. If *None* is specified as the source, the rectangle is ignored and the cursor is moved. If *None* is specified as the destination, *x* and *y* specify offsets from the current cursor position. Since *None* is specified for both the source and destination windows, the cursor is moved down and over 50 pixels from its present position (the width and height of the rectangle that is drawn). If the event is a key selection, the program checks to see if *q* were selected, which would cause the program to exit the event loop and terminate. To enter the string, the program uses *XLookupString*, which looks up keyboard event information in the *XEvent* union, then returns the correct mapping for the key selected. Its format is

```
int XLookupString (XEvent *event, char *text, int
length, KeySym *key, XComposeStatus *compose)
```

where *event* is a pointer to the *XEvent* structure returned from the *XNextEvent* that received the key selection event; *text* is a pointer to a buffer where a string version of the key is placed; *length* is the size of the buffer; *key* is a pointer to a *KeySym* structure where information about special keys being selected, such as shift and control keys, is placed, and *compose* is a pointer to an *XComposeStatus* structure that is presently unused but will someday allow programmers to process multikey sequences entered with a *Compose* key. If the event is an *Expose* event, nothing is done. Normally, the code here is used to redraw the just exposed portion of the window. Saving the coordinates of all drawn rectangles and redrawing them when an *Expose* event occurs accomplish this.

All X-drawing routines use a value called a *graphics context* (GC) to specify many variables to a graphics request. These include such values as line width and style, color, font, clipping window, etc. The GCs provide an efficient means of communicating graphics parameters to the server. By specifying a GC, the user does not have to specify a bewildering array of information to every drawing routine. If the server is capable of caching several GCs, a client can switch between GCs quickly, allowing the program for example to draw dotted, dashed, and solid lines without sending line style changes with every draw request.[3]

Having gone through the basic steps required to set up a program using XLIB, it is clear that an application of XLIB can still be tedious. This is why widget sets were created in Motif, as illustrated in the following program:

```
/* hello.c--
Initialize the toolkit using an application context
and a toplevel
shell widget, then create a pushbutton that says
Hello using the
```

```
R4 varangs interface. */
#include ⟨Xm/Xm.h⟩
#include⟨Xm/PushB.h⟩
main(argc,argv)
char *argv[];
{
  Widget toplevel,button;
  XtAppContext app;
  void i_was_pushed();
  XmString label;
  toplevel = XtVaAppInitialize (&app, "Hello",
NULL, 0, &argc, argv,
    NULL,NULL);
  label = XmStringCreateSimple("Push here to say
hello");
  button = XtVaCreateManagedWidget("pushme",xm-
PushButtonWidgetClass,
  toplevel, XmNLabelString, label, NULL);
  XmStringFree (label);
  XtAddCallback(button,XmNactivateCallback, i
_was _pushed, NULL);
  XtRealizeWidget(toplevel);
  XtAppMainLoop(app);
}
void i_was_pushed(w,client_data,cbs)
Widget w;
XtPointer client_data;
XmPushButtonCallbackStruct *cbs;
{
  printf("Hello Yourself!");
}
```

The preceding program produces a Motif-style push button with the label, "push here to say hello." Before widgets are created, the toolkit (*Xt*) must be initialized by using *XtVaAppInitialize*(). The widget returned by this function is a *shell* widget. When other widgets are created, these will be children of this top-most widget. The first argument to *XtVaAppInitialize* is the application context address. This is a structure that lets *Xt* manage *Xt* internal data associated with the application. The second argument is the application's class name. It is used in a resource database allowing specification of values that apply to all instances of an application, widget, or resource. The third and fourth parameters allow the user to specify an array of command line arguments defined for the program. In the preceding NULL and 0 are provided as parameters. The fifth and sixth arguments contain the value and the count of command line arguments. The seventh argument is usually a pointer to a list of fallback resources for the top-level widget. If the app-defaults file is not installed, fallback resources protect the program from crashing. If they are installed then this argument is ignored.

The call:

```
button   =   XtVaCreateManagedWidget(RpushmeS,xm-
PushButtonWidgetClass,
    toplevel, XmNLabelString, label, NULL);
```

creates a button as a child of the Shell window. The first argument, pushme, is the name of the widget in the resource database, so all subsequent calls to change this widget's resource refer to the widget's name as in *hello.pushme.foreground: blue*. This command changes the color of the button label in *Hello.c*. The second argument is the widget class type to be created. The third argument is the parent. The rest of the arguments are a variable length list of resource settings. Each resource name begins with the prefix *XmN* and identifies the resource as being Motif related. Many different types of resources can be specified, such as width, height, and label of the push button. If they are not specified, then default values are used. Resources are set not only during the creation of widgets, but the routine *XtVaSetValues* overrides any values the widget was initialized with.

Any widget expecting to call an application function for the purpose of, say, passing control from the widget to the application program must define one or more call-back resources. One common way of connecting an application function to a call-back resource is by calling *XtAddCallBack*(), as shown in the preceding program. The first argument is the widget in which the callback is to be installed, in this case, button. The second argument is the name of the resource, and the third argument is a pointer to the call-back function. The fourth argument is the data to be passed to the application when called, and these are usually pointers to data structures. Right now widgets exist only as data structures on the client side. *XtRealizeWidget(toplevel)* creates its windoiw. After this call widgets are fully instantiated. Finally *XtAppMainLoop(app)* gives control of the application to *Xt*, which sends information about events to the widgets, which in turn pass the information to the application with callbacks. Unlike traditional UNIX or DOS programming, the code here is idle until summoned by user-generated events.[6]

6.4. UNIX NETWORK PROGRAMMING

In structured programming global variables and parameter passing pass data between modules. All modules have something in common; that is, they are all part of the same program. However modules of the same program are not executed concurrently, which makes it easy for any module to access the same data without problems. Thus there are no instances of two modules trying to change the same data at the same time, whether it is in RAM or on disk.

Interprocess programming is not so simple. First of all to write programs that act between processes, a suitable operating system, such as UNIX, must be used. Such operating systems as MS-DOS or CP/M do not support multitasking and therefore do not support interprocess programming. There are also many more problems involved with running a time-shared, multitasking system. Two processes may want to access the same file at the same time, for example, one file accessed by two text editors. This problem can be solved by using file locking. A message may want to be passed between a process and a related (child) process. For this a *pipe* between the two processes can be created. To communicate between two processes on different computers on the same network, a *socket* may be used. These and other aspects of interprocess communication are discussed in this section, as well as servers and clients.

6.4.1. Simple Interprocess Communication

6.4.1.1. File Locking

A lock on a file prevents some other processes from accessing that file:

```
lockf(char *filename, intLOCKING_MODE, long size):
```

where LOCK_MODE can be either one of the following: LOCK_SH (shared lock; only a certain group of processes can work on the locked file), LOCK_EX (exclusive lock; only one process can use the file), or LOCK_UN (unlock the file).

6.4.1.2. Pipes

A *pipe* functions as an intermediate buffer to pass information between a parent process and a child process. The pipe is a unidirectional, first in, first out queue between two related processes. How these processes are actually implemented depends on the operating system. The comparison to an actual liquid-carrying pipe works well. The stream of liquid that passes through a pipe is the data stream. The first drops of liquid (data) that enter the pipe are the first drops to come out the other end. Liquid (data) flows in one direction. A longer pipe can hold more liquid. (UNIX pipes are of variable length; that is, the buffer (pipe) can vary in size.) There are two ends to a pipe: one end that the stream enters (*write* end) and the other end that the stream exits (*read* end).

The C function call to create a pipe is

```
int pipe (int *filedes)
```

where *filedes* points to an array that contains the following: *filedes* [0] is the file descriptor for the read end to the pipe, and *filedes* [1] is the file descriptor for the write end of the pipe. The file descriptor is just a way of referencing the pipe. It refers to the buffer that the operating system set up to be the pipe. To write a string *string* of size *size* (in terms of bytes) to the pipe *filedes* [1] (put data into), the following function should be called:

```
void write (filedes[1], int *string, int size)
```

To fill a string *string* of size *size* (in terms of bytes) from the pipe *filedes* [0] (read data from) the following function should be called:

```
int read (filedes[0], int *buffer, int size)
```

This functions returns a negative value if there is an error. The following function closes either the write end or the rear end of a pipe:

```
void close (filedes[⟨0 or 1⟩])
```

A pipe is useless if it is used in only one process; that is, if the read end and the write end can be accessed by only one program. On the other hand, a pipe cannot be set up between two arbitrary processes. A pipe must be established between two related processes: a child and its parent. The steps involved to create a pipe are

1. The parent invokes the pipe function and obtains the file descriptors.

2. The parent creates a copy of itself (creates a child).

3. The parent closes the read end of the pipe.

4. The child closes the write end of the pipe.

5. A unidirectional pipe is now created from the parent to the child.

When a child is created by its parent, all files opened by the parent are also open to the child, and all variables have the same values, including file descriptors for the pipe. If a pipe has to be created in the opposite direction, the parent closes the write end, and the child closes the read end. Bidirectional pipes can be implemented by using two pipes.

6.4.1.3. FIFO (First in, First out) Structures

A UNIX FIFO structure is almost identical to a pipe except that processes acting on the FIFO are not required to be related. A FIFO can be thought of as a named pipe, with the name being how an arbitrary process accesses the buffer. The name is a UNIX pathname. The following function creates a FIFO:

```
void mknod (char *pathname, int mode, int dev)
```

where *pathname* is just a UNIX pathname, *mode* specifies read and write permissions for the FIFO, and *dev* is ignored when creating a FIFO. To read from or write to a FIFO, the following function can be used:

```
int open (char *pathname, int mode)
```

where *pathname* is the UNIX pathname specifying the pipe, *mode* is either 0 for reading or 1 for writing. This function returns the file descriptor of the FIFO.

6.4.2. Network Interprocess Programming

Up to now we have discussed communication between processes on the same computer. Now we consider processes at different sites. There are naturally additional complications when programming on a network. More things must be specified, since more things must be known about processes that are communicating. When a pipe is created, it is necessary to know is where the read end and the write end are. For a FIFO we must give the buffer a name, since the two processes working on it do not have a parent–child relationship and therefore do not have all opened files in common. For internetwork programming, even more needs to be specified. First a local address must be specified. This is the unique number of each computer connected to the network. The Internet standard requires only 4 bytes, while the XNS standard requires 10 bytes. This way when a packet is sent over the network, the receiver knows who sent it. Second a local process must be specified. The local process identification is necessary because sometimes the superuser, group, or the authority of a specific user is required to access a resource on a foreign system. Third a foreign address must be specified to route data sent over the network correctly. Finally a foreign process must be specified. This process is the server, which returns data requested by a client. A server is specified when a client connects with a serving computer. The client–server relationship is important. It is obvious that a process cannot create a child process on another computer on the same network. The parent–child relationship implies that all open files are shared, and the relationship is basically symmetrical. This is not the case in network programming. A local process that needs something done by a foreign process is the client. The foreign process that does the work and returns the data requested is the server; this is a one-sided relationship. A client initiates a request, then receives data from the server, and uses it. The server waits for a client to request its services, does the work, then waits for the next client.

A *socket* is the name used for a connection between two processes over a network. It is opened like a FIFO, and the function for creating the socket returns a file descriptor, as does the function call for a FIFO. Unlike a FIFO or a pipe, the connection is bidirectional.

The following function opens a socket:

```
int socket (int family, int type, int protocol)
```

where *family* is one of the constants defined in the *socket.h* header file. This function lets the operating system know what protocol to use when talking on the network. The protocols are

- *AF_UNIX:* UNIX internal protocols
- *AF_INET:* Internet protocols
- *AF_NS:* Xerox NS protocols
- *AF_IMPLINK:* IMP link layer protocol (for intelligent packet switching network connections)

This family of protocols is network dependent. UNIX internal protocols are used to create pipes and FIFOs. The Internet protocol is used for most LANs and WANs; it is the most widely used protocol for networking. Xerox NS protocol is specific to that vendor, and it is used with its network hardware. The parameter *type* is used to specify the type of connection with the server. For simplicity only two types of sockets are discussed here:

- *SOCK_STREAM:* Sets up a stream-type socket.
- *SOCK_DATAGRAM:* Sets up a datagram socket (connectionless).

A stream socket is much like a FIFO: A connection between two processes remains connected until either the server or the client breaks the connection. A datagram socket does not make a connection—it only sends and receives data across the network. The difference between the two is that a stream socket does not have to specify a foreign address and foreign process each time it is used. On the other hand, a datagram socket allows a process to communicate with many other foreign processes at the same time. The function *socket( )* returns a socket descriptor, a value used for future references to the socket. The protocol and the type of connection are specified in the socket function call. The local process, the local address, the foreign process, and the foreign address remain to be specified. To do this other functions must be called. The following function binds a name to an unnamed socket:

```
int bind (int sockfd, struct sockaddr *myaddr, int
addrlen)
```

where *sockfd* is the socket descriptor returned by a previous call to *socket()*, *myaddr* is a pointer to the following structure that is passed to the function. The structure looks like the following:

```
struct sockaddr {
  unsigned short sa_family; /* address family:AF
_xxx value */
  char sa_data[14]; /* up to 14 bytes of protocol-
specific address */
```

For example if the *sa—family* is *AF—INET*, *sa—data* is a 4-byte number. This number is found by logging into the system and entering the command *hostid*. The parameter *addrlen* is the size of the address structure. The function returns a value less than 0 if there is an error condition.

After *bind()* is called, the local process and local address are specified. Since the data needed to specify the local process changes from one invocation to the next, the *bind()* function knows what process it is in and passes this information to the foreign process when it is needed. All that is left to do now is to specify the foreign address. The foreign process is determined by the server. For a stream socket, a connection is created by:

```
int connect (int sockfd, struct sockaddr *servaddr,
int addrlen)
```

where *sockfd* is the value returned by the socket system call, *servaddr* is a pointer to a structure that contains address information for the foreign computer; the structure is of the same type as in *bind()*. As before *addrlen* is the size of the address structure.

To pass data through a connection-oriented socket, two functions are used, one to send data and one to receive

```
int send (int sockfd, char *buff, int nbytes, int
flags)
int recv (int sockfd, char *buff, int nbytes, int
flags)
```

In the preceding functions, *sockfd* is the socket file descriptor, *buff* is a pointer to the buffer being sent (or the buffer received data enters), *nbytes* is the number of bytes in the buffer, and *flags* is usually zero (it is used only for more advanced socket programming and is not discussed here). The server process creates a socket and binds an address to that socket, just as a client does. The difference is that the server is not connected to anything: It waits for a client process to connect to it. Therefore instead of invoking the *connect()* function, the server listens at the socket:

```
int listen (int sockfd, int backlog)
```

where *sockfd* is the socket file descriptor. This function tells the server which socket to listen to. The parameter *backlog* specifies the number of additional server requests that can be queued by the serving system while it is waiting for the *accept*() system call to be invoked. A server first connects with a client, then accepts [*accept*()] the client, and creates a child server to handle backlogged clients waiting to access the server. Backlogs occur during the period when a client is accepted [*accept*()] and a new server is being created.

Now the server hears a client knocking and lets it in:

```
int accept (int sockfd, struct sockaddr *peer, int
*addrlen)
```

where *sockfd* is the socket descriptor on the foreign system that the server was listening [*listen*()] to, *peer* is a pointer to a function that obtains the address and process information about the client process, and on return contains the size (in bytes) of the *sockaddr* structure. The pointer returns a new socket descriptor. The original file descriptor is used by the child process to service the connection, and the new file descriptor is used by the parent to service new clients. If there is an error, the file descriptor returns a negative value. When a client is accepted [*accept*()], the foreign process is determined.

Connectionless clients do not invoke *connect*(), so they do not have a specified foreign address to send [*send*()] to or receive [*recv*()] from a socket. Instead functions specify the data to be sent (what) and the foreign address (where). Since the foreign address is specified at every I/O function invocation a connection does not have to be maintained. These functions are self-explanatory, since they are similar to functions used for connection-oriented transfer.

```
int sendto(int sockfd, char *buffer, int nbytes, int
flags, struct sockaddr *to, int addrlen)
int recvfrom(int sockfd, char *buffer, int nbytes,
int flags, struct sockaddr *from, int addrlen)
```

Example 6.1. (Ref. 9) Ping is a standard routine for determining if the computer at the address specified at the command line is connected to the network. Ping sends a datagram to the foreign computer, then waits for a reply. If it obtains a reply, Ping prints a message indicating that the foreign address is connected to the network. Some implementations also indicate how long the datagram took to make the round trip. Example 6.1 shows how the previously discussed functions can be used to implement Ping. Note: Although Ping uses the syntax of c, it is really no better than pseudocode.

```
/*Ping client routine ping (hostname)*/
main (hostname)
{
struct protoent *protoptr;
struct sockaddr *myaddr,*servaddr; /* structure
defined above */
char buffer[30]="This is a test string",recv-
buffer[30]="";
int  sockfd,i,bufsize,  MAX_WAIT=(some  large
number, about 3 seconds worth);
/* this function searches the file /etc/proto-
cols
for the specified name, and returns a pointer
to the structure that contains the protocol num-
ber.
'udp' stands for unix datagram protocol.
*/
/* make socket */
   protoptr=getprotobyname("udp");
   sockfd=socket(AF_INET,SOCK
_DATAGRAM,protoptr->proto);
/* make and give values to socket address struc-
ture */
/* hostid() is a system call that returns the lo-
cal address */
   myaddr=(struct   sockaddr   *)malloc(sizeof-
(struct sockaddr));
   myaddr->family=AF_INET;
   strcpy(myaddr->sa_addr,hostid());
/* bind address to socket */
   bind(sockfd,myaddr,strlen(myaddr->sa
_addr));
/* get address of foreign host (ping server) */
   servaddr=gethostbyname(hostname);
/* send the test buffer */
   sendto(sockfd,buffer,strlen(buffer),0,-
strlen(servaddr->sa_addr));
```

```
/* wait for the packet to echo */
   for(i=0;i<=MAX_WAIT && bufsize=0;i++)
   recvfrom(sockfd,recvbuffer,strlen(buffer),0,
      servaddr,strlen(servaddr->sa_addr));
   if (!strcmp(buffer,recvbuffer)
      printf("Host %s is alive.",hostname);
   else printf("Host %s does not respond.",host-
name);
   close (sockfd);
   }
   /*Ping server routine.*/
   main()
   {
   struct protoent *protoptr;
   struct sockaddr *myaddr, *clientaddr;
   char buffer[30];
   int sockfd,int backlog;
   /* make socket */
      sockfd=socket(AF_INET,SOCK
_DATAGRAM,protoptr->proto);
   /* make and give values to socket address struc-
ture */
   /* hostid() is a system call that returns the lo-
cal address */
   myaddr=(struct    sockaddr    *)malloc(sizeof-
(struct sockaddr));
   myaddr->family=AF_INET;
   strcpy(myaddr->sa_addr,hostid());
   /* bind address to socket */
   bind(sockfd,myaddr,strlen(myaddr->sa
_addr));
   /* process waits for a client */
   listen(sockfd,backlog);
   /* accepts the client and gets its address */
   accept(sockfd,clientaddr,strlen(client-
addr->sa_addr));
   /* this function, omitted, will create a child
process to handle the client, while the server will
restart and wait for a new ping client.
   */
create_child();
```

```
/* the child will then do the following: */
/* receive the string from the client */
  recvfrom(sockfd,buffer,30,0,clientaddr,
strlen(clientaddr->sa_addr));
/* and send it back */
sendto(sockfd,buffer,strlen(buffer),0,clientaddr,
strlen(clientaddr->sa_addr));
close(sockfd);
}
```

PROBLEMS

1. Modify the function *forms* of the sample program so that the user can specify the position of each item in the window.

2. Extend the sample program with the function *check_box*, which realizes multiple choices. The function should take an array of strings as the input, create a window, create a check box for each string, and display the check box/string pairs in one or two columns (depending on the maximal length of the strings and the width of the window). The window should contain two buttons: *OK* and *CANCEL*. The user selects strings of interest by pressing the mouse button. Once all choices are made, the user selects the OK button, the function returns the indices of the strings checked, and returns 1 as its value. The user can select *CANCEL* any time and the function returns −1 as its value.

3. Repeat Problem 6.2 except create a button for each input string so that the user selects buttons.

4. Combine the two functions *forms* and *buttons* into one function *forms _and_buttons* to contain string entries and choice buttons in one window. Specify the interface to the function clearly.

5. The network programming tool discussed in Chapter 6 is not object-oriented. Sketch an approach that provides an object-oriented tool for UNIX network programming. (*Hint:* Can you provide an object model for network aspects of UNIX?)

```
#include "sheu_par.h"
#include <edit.h>
#include <button.h>
#include "hwind.h"
#include <ctype.h>
#include <string.h>
#include <owl.h>
#include <dialog.h>
#include <listbox.h>
#include <inputdia.h>
```

/**** Forms_transfer is the array used
to transfer the changes from
the form to the main window.
When the user makes a change to
a field in a form, the array
that stores item characteristics
should be updated to reflect the
change. As can be seen, the
array is globally defined. ****/

```
char Forms_transfer [16][5][33];

int Forms_return;
```

/**** This is a global integer and is
set in the Choices window. The
user clicks on an item in the menu
and this int value is set to
the index of the selected item.
The main window function Choices
then returns this value. ****/

```
int Choices_return;
```

/**** This is the declaration of the
class derived from TApplication.
All applications need to have
such a class with the member function InitMainWindow which sets up
the main window of the
application. ****/

```
class TMyApp : public TApplication
{
public:
TMyApp(LPSTR AName, HANDLE hInstance,
  HANDLE hPrevInstance, LPSTR lpCmdLine,
  int nCmdShow) :
  TApplication(AName, hInstance,
  hPrevInstance, lpCmdLine, nCmdShow) { };
  virtual void InitMainWindow();
};
```

/**** This is the class for the window
that is created when the Forms
function is executed. We will
comment specific parts of the class
itself and also its member functions.
The class is based on the
ObjectWindows class TDialog and
sets up a modal dialog box that

hangs the calling function until
user input is received and the
box ix closed.   ****/

```
class TForm2Window : public TDialog
{
public:
char Items_store[16][5][33];
int count_store;
```

/**** Edit is an array of pointers
to TEdit, an ObjectWindows class
that sets up an edit box. ****/

```
PTEdit Edit[16];
```

/**** Static is an array of pointers
to TStatic, and ObjectWindows
class that displays text on the
screen, text that is not modified
by the user. This is used for the
labels of each of the fields.****/

```
PTStatic Static[16];
```

/**** Height and width refer to
the Forms window ****/

```
int height, width;
```

/**** This is the constructor to
the TForm2Window class. It takes
as arguments, the parent window,
the name, the passed array, and
the number of items, count.
In addition to the above a string
is also passed that will be the
caption to the dialog box. This
is "ATitle." ****/

```
TForm2Window(PTWindowsObject AParent,
  LPSTR name, LPSTR ATitle, char
  Items_input[16][5][33], int
  count_input);
```

/**** This is an overloaded function.
It is defined in TDialog and redefined here. It is executed
right after the constructor of
the class is invoked. ****/

```
virtual void SetupWindow();
```

/**** The function Ok is also an
overloaded operator which is
redefined in this derived class.
It gets executed when the OK button
of dialog box is pressed. ****/

```
virtual void Ok(RTMessage Msg)
= [ID_FIRST + IDOK];
```

Figure 6.1. Program listing.

```
/**** The function HandleButton2Msg
gets executed when the CANCEL button
is pressed. ****/

virtual void HandleButton2Msg(RTMessage
   Msg)
= [ID_FIRST + ID_BUTTON4];
private:

/**** These are private functions of
the class and check for integer,
string and float values and using
these check for valid values. ****/

BOOL is_int(char temp[33]);
BOOL is_float(char temp[33]);
BOOL is_string(char temp[33]);
BOOL is_value(char item[33], char temp[33]);
};

/**** The function is_int checks a
string to see whether it is integer. ****/

BOOL TForm2Window::is_int(char temp[33])
{
 if (!strcmp(temp, " ")) return TRUE;
 if (!isdigit(temp[0])) return FALSE;
 for(int i=0; i<strlen(temp); i++)
 { if (!isdigit(temp[i]))  return FALSE;
 }
 return TRUE;
}

/**** The function is_float checks whether
a string qualifies for float. ****/

BOOL TForm2Window::is_float(char temp[33])
{
 if (!strcmp(temp, " ")) return TRUE;
 BOOL dec = FALSE;
 for(int i=0; i<strlen(temp); i++)
 { if (!isdigit(temp[i]) &&
      !((temp[i] == '.') &&
        (dec == FALSE)))
   { return FALSE;
   }
   if (temp[i] == '.') dec = TRUE;
 }
 return TRUE;
}

/**** The function is_string checks to
see if argument is a valid string. ****/

BOOL TForm2Window::is_string(char temp[33])
{
 if (!strcmp(temp, " ")) return TRUE;
 if (isalpha(temp[0]))
 { for(int i=0; i<strlen(temp); i++)
   { if (!isalpha(temp[i]) &&
        !isdigit(temp[i]) &&
        !ispunct(temp[i]))
```

```
   return FALSE;
   }
   return TRUE;
 }
 else
 { return FALSE;}
}

/**** The function is_value takes
two arguments, the first being the type
and the second being the input value.
If the type specified is
consistent with the value the function
returns true, else returns false. ****/

BOOL TForm2Window::is_value(char
         item[33], char temp[33])
{
 if (!strcmp(item, "int"))
 { if (is_int(temp)) return TRUE;
 }
 if (!strcmp(item, "float"))
 { if (is_float(temp)) return TRUE;
 }
 if (!strcmp(item, "string"))
 { if (is_string(temp)) return TRUE;
 }
 return FALSE;
}

/**** This is the constructor for
the TForm2Window. The special thing to
notice here is that it accepts an array
and an integer count. It
copies the passed array to its own data
member array and works on
this copy of the passed array. As we'll
see later, when the array
if updated it is sent to a global transfer
array and taken by the
array passed to the Forms function.****/

TForm2Window::TForm2Window(PTWindowsObject
   AParent, LPSTR name, LPSTR ATitle,
   char Items_input[16][5][33],
   int count_input)
      : TDialog(AParent, name)
{
 int use_len;
 int num_lines, x_position, y_position;
 int size[17];
 width = 0;
 height = 0;
 BOOL sec_column[17];
 int offset, max_edit;
 BOOL one_col;
 int row_size;
 row_size = 0;
 int max_1, max_2, max_3;

 /**** Copies passed int into its own
 data member count_store. ****/
```

Figure 6.1. Continued.

```
count_store = count_input;
char temp[16][33];

/**** Copies passed array into its
own data member Items_store. ****/

for (int i=0; i<count_store; i++)
{ strcpy(Items_store[i][0],
                Items_input[i][0]);
  strcpy(Items_store[i][1],
                Items_input[i][1]);
  strcpy(Items_store[i][2],
                Items_input[i][2]);
  if (!strcmp(Items_input[i][3], "*"))
  { strcpy(Items_store[i][3], " ");
  }
  else
  { strcpy(Items_store[i][3],
                Items_input[i][3]);
  }
  if (!strcmp(Items_input[i][4], "*"))
  { strcpy(Items_store[i][4], " ");
  }
  else
  { strcpy(Items_store[i][4],
                Items_input[i][4]);
  }
}

/****Items_store now have the passed array
If wanted length is more than 32,
it cuts to 32.    ****/

for (int h=0; h<count_store; h++)
{ if ((atoi(Items_store[h][2])) > 32)
  { strcpy(Items_store[h][2], "32");
  }
}

/**** The array temp is what will be shown
in the edit boxes in
the Form window.  If there's no new value,
we take the old
value, else we take the new value. ****/

for (int p=0; p<count_store; p++)
{
  if (strcmp(Items_store[p][4], " "))
      strcpy(temp[p], Items_store[p][4]);
  else
      strcpy(temp[p], Items_store[p][3]);
}

/**** The rest of the code determines
   the width, height, and the
   position of the Form window and
   also of the edit boxes and
   static labels in the window.
   Basically we determine the
   position of each item before
   actually placing.  The convention
   used is that if there is only one
```

```
   column, align edit boxes to
   the left, else align them to the
   right.  It should be noted
   that this scheme is implemented with
   the knowledge that the
   average label length equals the
   average edit length.    ****/

for (p=0; p<count_store;p++)
{ size[p] = (atoi(Items_store[p][2])*8)
  + (strlen(Items_store[p][0])*8) + 21;
}
for (p=count_store; p<17; p++)
{
  size[p] = 0;
}
sec_column[0] = FALSE;
for (p=1; p<count_store;p++)
{ if ((sec_column[p-1] == FALSE) &&
    (size[p-1] < 265) && (size[p] < 265))
    sec_column[p] = TRUE;
  else
    sec_column[p] = FALSE;
}
for (p=count_store; p<17; p++)
{
  sec_column[p] = FALSE;
}
one_col =TRUE;
for (p=0; p<count_store; p++)
{
  if (sec_column[p] == TRUE)
        one_col = FALSE;
}
max_edit = 0;
for (p=0; p<count_store; p++)
{
  if ((sec_column[p] == FALSE)
    && (atoi(Items_store[p][2]) >
    atoi(Items_store[max_edit][2])))
    max_edit = p;
}
max_1 = 0;
max_2 = 0;
max_3 = 0;
for (p=0; p<count_store; p++)
  if ((sec_column[p] == FALSE) &&
    (sec_column[p+1] == TRUE) &&
    (size[p] > max_1))
    max_1 = size[p];
  else if ((sec_column[p] == FALSE) &&
    (sec_column[p+1] == FALSE) &&
    (size[p] > max_3))
    max_3 = size[p];
  else if ((sec_column[p] == TRUE) &&
    (size[p] > max_2))
    max_2 = size[p];
if ((max_3 + 20) > (max_1 + max_2 + 30))
    row_size = max_3 + 20;
else row_size = max_1 + max_2 + 30;
if (row_size < 154)
    offset = (154 - row_size)/2;
```

Figure 6.1. Continued.

```
else offset = 0;
y_position = 8;
num_lines = 0;
for (p=0; p< count_store;p++)
{
  if ((sec_column[p] == FALSE) &&
      (sec_column[p+1] == TRUE))
  {
    Static[p] = new TStatic(this, -1,
      Items_store[p][0], 10 + offset,
      y_position,
      strlen(Items_store[p][0])*8 +8,
      19, 21);
    Edit[p] = new TEdit(this, BASE_EDIT + p,
      temp[p], (max_1 + 10) -
      (atoi(Items_store[p][2])*8) - 8 +
      offset, y_position,
      atoi(Items_store[p][2])*8 + 8,
      19, 33, FALSE);
  }
  else if ((sec_column[p] == FALSE) &&
           (sec_column[p+1] == FALSE))
  {
    if (size[p] <= max_1)
      x_position =
      (max_1 + 10) -
      (atoi(Items_store[p][2])*8) - 8;
    else if ((one_col == TRUE) &&
             (strlen(Items_store[p][0]) <=
             strlen(Items_store[max_edit][0])))
      x_position = row_size -
      (atoi(Items_store[max_edit][2])*8) - 18;
    else
      x_position = row_size -
      (atoi(Items_store[p][2])*8) - 18;
    Static[p] = new TStatic(this, -1,
      Items_store[p][0], 10 + offset,
      y_position, strlen(Items_store[p][0])*8
      +8, 19, 21);
    Edit[p] = new TEdit(this, BASE_EDIT + p,
      temp[p], x_position + offset, y_position,
      atoi(Items_store[p][2])*8 + 8, 19, 33,
      FALSE);
    y_position = y_position + 22;
    num_lines++;
  }
  else if (sec_column[p] == TRUE)
  {
    Static[p] = new TStatic(this, -1,
      Items_store[p][0], max_1 + 20 + offset,
      y_position, strlen(Items_store[p][0])*8
      + 8, 19, 21);
    Edit[p] = new TEdit(this, BASE_EDIT + p,
      temp[p], row_size -
      (atoi(Items_store[p][2])*8)
      - 18 + offset, y_position,
      atoi(Items_store[p][2])*8 + 8, 19,
      33, FALSE);
    y_position = y_position + 22;
    num_lines++;
  }
}
```

```
if ( row_size < 154) width = 154;
else width = row_size;
height = (num_lines * 22) + 76;
new TButton(this, IDOK, "Ok", 0,
  height - 60, width/2, 30, TRUE);
new TButton(this, ID_BUTTON4, "Cancel",
  width/2, height -60, width/2, 30, FALSE);

/**** This sets ATitle to the caption of the
  dialog box.  It is predefined. ****/

TDialog::SetCaption(ATitle);
}

/**** The function Ok is excuted when the
  user presses OK in the Form
  window.  In a for loop each edit window
  is looked at, and if a change
  is made, it is checked for validity and
  then stored.  If it is an
  value, an error message is popped and the
  window is closed.  If
  change is valid, it is recorded and the
  window is closed after
  looking at all the edit fields in the window.
  ****/

void TForm2Window::Ok(RTMessage Msg)
{
  char TheText[33];
  char new_temp[33];
  for (int i=0; i<count_store; i++)
  {

    /**** This gets the text from the
      specified edit window.    ****/
    Edit[i]->GetText(TheText, sizeof(TheText));
    /**** The next batch of lines copy
      the gotten text into the dataj
      member array.  ****/
    if (!strcmp(Items_store[i][3], TheText) &&
        !strcmp(Items_store[i][4], " "))
      { strcpy(Items_store[i][4], " ");
      }
    else if (!strcmp(Items_store[i][4], TheText))
      { strcpy(Items_store[i][3],
          Items_store[i][4]);
        strcpy(Items_store[i][4], " ");
      }
    else
      { if (is_value(Items_store[i][1],
                 TheText))
        { if (!strcmp(Items_store[i][4], " "))
            strcpy(Items_store[i][4], TheText);
          else
          { strcpy(Items_store[i][3],
              Items_store[i][4]);
            strcpy(Items_store[i][4], TheText);
          }
        }
        else
        { MessageBox(HWindow, "You have entered
```

Figure 6.1. Continued.

```
            a bad items value.0ress OK to
            cancel application.", "ERROR!!",
            MB_OK | MB_ICONHAND);
      Forms_return = 0;
      CloseWindow();
      return;
    }
  }
}
for (i=0; i<count_store; i++)
{  if (strlen(Items_store[i][3]) >
          atoi(Items_store[i][2]))
   { strcpy(new_temp, Items_store[i][3]);
     for (int j=0; j<atoi(Items_store[i][2]);
          j++)
     Items_store[i][3][j] =
     new_temp[strlen(new_temp) -
     atoi(Items_store[i][2]) + j];
     Items_store[i][3][atoi(Items_store[i][2])]
     = ' ';
   }
}
 for (i=0; i<count_store; i++)
{  if (strlen(Items_store[i][4]) >
          atoi(Items_store[i][2]))
   { strcpy(new_temp, Items_store[i][4]);
     for(int j=0; j<atoi(Items_store[i][2]);
          j++)
     Items_store[i][4][j] =
     new_temp[strlen(new_temp)
     - atoi(Items_store[i][2]) + j];
     Items_store[i][4][atoi(Items_store[i][2])]
     = ' ';
   }
}

for (i=0; i<count_store; i++)
{ strcpy(Forms_transfer[i][0],
              Items_store[i][0]);
  strcpy(Forms_transfer[i][1],
              Items_store[i][1]);
  strcpy(Forms_transfer[i][2],
              Items_store[i][2]);
  strcpy(Forms_transfer[i][3],
              Items_store[i][3]);
  strcpy(Forms_transfer[i][4],
              Items_store[i][4]);
}
Forms_return = 1;
TDialog::Ok(Msg);
}

/**** If CANCEL is pressed this function
is executed. It merely closes the window.
****/
void TForm2Window::HandleButton2Msg(RTMessage)
{
  Forms_return = 0;
  CloseWindow();
}
```

```
/**** After the constructor this function,
     SetupWindow is executed. It
     performs the usual dialog box setup
     and then resizes the window to
     the position, height, and width determined
     in the constructor.
     MoveWindow takes as arguments, the handle
     of the window to resize,
     the new x coordinate, y coordinate, width
     and height. ****/

void TForm2Window::SetupWindow()
{
  TDialog::SetupWindow();
  MoveWindow(this->HWindow,
     317 - width/2, 250 - height/2,
     width+10, height, TRUE);
  HANDLE hEditFont;
  HANDLE hStaticFont;
  LOGFONT LogFont;

/**** This is the font for the edit boxes
     in the dialog box. A fixed
     width font is used to insure control
     over number of characters in
     view in the edit box. ****/

  memset(&LogFont, 0, sizeof(LOGFONT));
  LogFont.lfHeight = 10;
  LogFont.lfWidth = 10;
  LogFont.lfPitchAndFamily = FF_MODERN;
  lstrcpy(LogFont.lfFaceName, "Courier 10");
  hEditFont = CreateFontIndirect(&LogFont);

/**** This is the font for the label in the
     dialog box. The only difference
     is that there is some extra weight put
     on it for emphasis.        ****/

  memset(&LogFont, 0, sizeof(LOGFONT));
  LogFont.lfHeight = 10;
  LogFont.lfWidth = 10;
  LogFont.lfWeight = 200;
  LogFont.lfPitchAndFamily = FF_MODERN;
  lstrcpy(LogFont.lfFaceName, "Courier 10");
  hStaticFont = CreateFontIndirect(&LogFont);

  for (int i=0; i<count_store; i++)
    SendMessage(Edit[i]->HWindow, WM_SETFONT,
       hEditFont, TRUE);

  for (i=0; i<count_store; i++)
    SendMessage(Static[i]->HWindow, WM_SETFONT,
       hStaticFont, TRUE);
}

/**** This is the class definition for the
     third window type, exactly like
     the TForm2Window class with the exception
     of having a third button
     labeled ESCAPE which when pressed returns
```

Figure 6.1. Continued.

a -1. It gets executed
when the Escape function is used. ****/

```
class TForm3Window : public TDialog
{
public:
char EItems_store[16][5][33];
int Ecount_store;
```

/**** EEdit[16] is an array of pointers
to TEdit, an ObjectWindows class
that sets up an edit box. ****/

```
PTEdit EEdit[16];
```

/**** EStatic[16] is an array of pointers
to TStatic, and ObjectWindows
class that displays text on the screen,
text that is not modified
by the user. This is used for the labels
of each of the fields. ****/

```
PTStatic EStatic[16];
```

/**** Height and width refer to the Forms
window. ****/

```
int Eheight, Ewidth;
```

/**** This is the constructor for the
TForm3Window class. It takes as
arguments, the parent window, the name,
the passed array, and
the number of items, count.
In addition it takes the caption string,
ATitle. ****/

```
TForm3Window(PTWindowsObject AParent,
LPSTR name, LPSTR ATitle,
char Items_input[16][5][33],
int count_input);
```

/**** This is an overloaded function. It is
defined in TDialog and redefined
here. It is executed right after the
constructor of the
class is invoked. ****/

```
virtual void SetupWindow();
```

/**** The function Ok is also an overloaded
operator which is redefined
in this derived class. It gets executed
when the OK button of the
dialog box is pressed. ****/

```
virtual void Ok(RTMessage Msg)
= [ID_FIRST + IDOK];
```

/**** The function HandleButton2Msg gets
executed when the CANCEL button
is pressed. ****/

```
virtual void Cancel(RTMessage Msg)
= [ID_FIRST + IDCANCEL];
```

/**** The function HandleButton3Msg gets
executed when the ESCAPE button
is pressed. ****/

```
virtual void HandleButton3Msg(RTMessage Msg)
= [ID_FIRST + ID_BUTTON4];
private:
```

/**** These are private functions of the
class and check for integer,
string and float values and using
these check for valid values. ****/

```
BOOL is_int(char temp[33]);
BOOL is_float(char temp[33]);
BOOL is_string(char temp[33]);
BOOL is_value(char item[33], char temp[33]);
};
```

/**** The function is_int checks a
string to see whether it is
an integer. ****/

```
BOOL TForm3Window::is_int(char temp[33])
{
if (!strcmp(temp, " ")) return TRUE;
if (!isdigit(temp[0])) return FALSE;
for(int i=0; i<strlen(temp); i++)
  if (!isdigit(temp[i]))  return FALSE;
return TRUE;
}
```

/**** The function is_float checks whether
a string qualifies for float. ****/

```
BOOL TForm3Window::is_float(char temp[33])
{
if (!strcmp(temp, " ")) return TRUE;
BOOL dec = FALSE;
for(int i=0; i<strlen(temp); i++)
{ if (!isdigit(temp[i]) && !((temp[i] == '.') && (dec == FALSE)))
  return FALSE;
  if (temp[i] == '.') dec = TRUE;
}
return TRUE;
}
```

/**** The function is_string checks to see
if argument is a valid string. ****/

```
BOOL TForm3Window::is_string(char temp[33])
{
if (!strcmp(temp, " ")) return TRUE;
if (isalpha(temp[0]))
{ for(int i=0; i<strlen(temp); i++)
  if (!isalpha(temp[i]) &&
    !isdigit(temp[i]) &&
    !ispunct(temp[i]))
    return FALSE;
```

Figure 6.1. Continued.

```
      return TRUE;
   }
   else
      return FALSE;
}

/**** The function is_value takes two
      arguments, the first being the type
      and the second being the input value.
      If the type specified is
      consistent with the value the function
      returns true, else returns false. ****/

BOOL TForm3Window::is_value(char item[33],
   char temp[33])
{
   if (!strcmp(item, "int"))
      if (is_int(temp)) return TRUE;
   if (!strcmp(item, "float"))
      if (is_float(temp)) return TRUE;
   if (!strcmp(item, "string"))
      if (is_string(temp)) return TRUE;
   return FALSE;
}

TForm3Window::TForm3Window(PTWindowsObject AParent,
   LPSTR name, LPSTR ATitle,
   char Items_input[16][5][33], int count_input)
      : TDialog(AParent, name)
{
   int use_len;
   int num_lines, x_position, y_position;
   int size[17];
   BOOL sec_column[17];
   BOOL one_col;
   int max_edit;
   int max_1, max_2, max_3;
   int row_size;
   Ewidth = 0;
   Eheight = 0;
   int offset;

   /**** Copies passed int into its own
         data member Ecount_store. ****/

   Ecount_store = count_input;
   char temp[16][33];

   /**** Copies passed array into its own
         data member EItems_store. ****/

   for (int i=0; i<Ecount_store; i++)
   { strcpy(EItems_store[i][0],
            Items_input[i][0]);
     strcpy(EItems_store[i][1],
            Items_input[i][1]);
     strcpy(EItems_store[i][2],
            Items_input[i][2]);
     if (!strcmp(Items_input[i][3], "*"))
        strcpy(EItems_store[i][3], " ");
     else
        strcpy(EItems_store[i][3],
```

```
            Items_input[i][3]);
     if (!strcmp(Items_input[i][4], "*"))
        strcpy(EItems_store[i][4], " ");
     else
        strcpy(EItems_store[i][4],
               Items_input[i][4]);
   }

   /**** EItems_store now have the passed
         array. If the wanted length is more
         than 32, it cuts to 32.   ****/

   for (int h=0; h<Ecount_store; h++)
      if ((atoi(EItems_store[h][2])) > 32)
         strcpy(EItems_store[h][2], "32");

   /**** The array temp is what will be shown
         in the edit boxes in
         the Form window. If there's no new
         value, we take the old
         value, else we take the new value. ****/

   for (int p=0; p<Ecount_store; p++)
      if (strcmp(EItems_store[p][4], " "))
         strcpy(temp[p], EItems_store[p][4]);
      else
         strcpy(temp[p], EItems_store[p][3]);

   /**** The rest of the code determines the
         width, height, and the
         position of the Form window and also
         of the edit boxes and
         static labels in the window.
         This implements the new placing scheme
         where position of all
         items is decided before actually placing.
         If there is only one
         column, then edit fields are aligned left,
         else they are aligned right.  ****/

   for (p=0; p<Ecount_store;p++)
      size[p] = (atoi(EItems_store[p][2])*8)
         + (strlen(EItems_store[p][0])*8) + 21;
   for (p=Ecount_store; p<17; p++)
      size[p] = 0;
   sec_column[0] = FALSE;
   for (p=1; p<Ecount_store;p++)
      if ((sec_column[p-1] == FALSE) &&
          (size[p-1] < 265) && (size[p] < 265))
         sec_column[p] = TRUE;
      else
         sec_column[p] = FALSE;
   for (p=Ecount_store; p<17; p++)
      sec_column[p] = FALSE;
   one_col =TRUE;
   for (p=0; p<Ecount_store; p++)
      if (sec_column[p] == TRUE) one_col = FALSE;
   max_edit = 0;
   for (p=0; p<Ecount_store; p++)
      if ((sec_column[p] == FALSE) &&
          (atoi(EItems_store[p][2]) >
           atoi(EItems_store[max_edit][2])))
```

Figure 6.1. Continued.

```
   max_edit = p;
max_1 = 0;
max_2 = 0;
max_3 = 0;
for (p=0; p<Ecount_store; p++)
 if ((sec_column[p] == FALSE) &&
     (sec_column[p+1] == TRUE) &&
     (size[p] > max_1))
    max_1 = size[p];
 else if ((sec_column[p] == FALSE) &&
     (sec_column[p+1] == FALSE) &&
     (size[p] > max_3))
    max_3 = size[p];
 else if ((sec_column[p] == TRUE) &&
     (size[p] > max_2))
    max_2 = size[p];
if ((max_3 + 20) > (max_1 + max_2 + 30))
   row_size = max_3 + 20;
else row_size = max_1 + max_2 + 30;
if (row_size < 184)
   offset = (184 - row_size)/2;
else offset = 0;
y_position = 8;
num_lines = 0;
for (p=0; p< Ecount_store;p++)
{
 if ((sec_column[p] == FALSE) &&
     (sec_column[p+1] == TRUE))
 {
  EStatic[p] = new TStatic(this, -1,
      EItems_store[p][0], 10 + offset,
      y_position, strlen(EItems_store[p][0])*8
      +8, 19, 21);
  EEdit[p] = new TEdit(this, BASE_EDIT + p,
      temp[p], (max_1 + 10) -
      (atoi(EItems_store[p][2])*8) - 8 +
      offset, y_position,
      atoi(EItems_store[p][2])*8 + 8,
      19, 33, FALSE);
 }
 else if ((sec_column[p] == FALSE) &&
     (sec_column[p+1] == FALSE))
 {
  if ((p == (Ecount_store -1)) &&
     ( size[p] < max_1))
    x_position = (max_1 + 10) -
        toi(EItems_store[p][2])*8) - 8;
  else if ((one_col == TRUE) &&
     (strlen(EItems_store[p][0]) <
       strlen(EItems_store[max_edit][0])))
    x_position = row_size -
       (atoi(EItems_store[max_edit][2])*8) - 18;
  else
    x_position = row_size -
       (atoi(EItems_store[p][2])*8) - 18;
  EStatic[p] = new TStatic(this, -1,
      EItems_store[p][0], 10 + offset,
      y_position, strlen(EItems_store[p][0])*8 +
      19, 21);
  EEdit[p] = new TEdit(this, BASE_EDIT + p,
      temp[p], x_position + offset, y_position,
      atoi(EItems_store[p][2])*8 + 8, 19,
```

```
      33, FALSE);
  y_position = y_position + 22;
  num_lines++;
 }
 else if (sec_column[p] == TRUE)
 {
  EStatic[p] = new TStatic(this, -1,
      EItems_store[p][0], max_1 + 20 + offset,
      y_position, strlen(EItems_store[p][0])*8 + 8,
      19, 21);
  EEdit[p] = new TEdit(this, BASE_EDIT + p, temp[p],
      row_size - (atoi(EItems_store[p][2])*8) - 18 i
      + offset, y_position,
      atoi(EItems_store[p][2])*8 + 8, 19, 33, FALSE);
  y_position = y_position + 22;
  num_lines++;
 }
}

if (row_size < 184) Ewidth = 184;
else Ewidth = row_size;
Eheight = (num_lines * 22) + 76;

new TButton(this, IDOK, "Ok", 0, Eheight - 60,
    Ewidth/3, 30, TRUE);
new TButton(this, IDCANCEL, "Cancel", Ewidth/3,
    Eheight -60, Ewidth/3, 30, FALSE);

/**** This is the third button, the Escape button
    which when pressed returns -1 *****/

new TButton(this, ID_BUTTON4, "Escape", 2*Ewidth/3,
    Eheight -60, Ewidth/3, 30, FALSE);

/**** Makes ATitle the caption of the
    dialog box.  ****/

TDialog::SetCaption(ATitle);
}

void TForm3Window::Ok(RTMessage Msg)
{
  char TheText[33];
  char new_temp[33];
  for (int i=0; i<Ecount_store; i++)
  {
    /**** This gets the text from the specified
        edit window.     ****/

    EEdit[i]->GetText(TheText, sizeof(TheText));

    /**** The next batch of lines copy the
        gotten text into the data
        member array.    ****/

    if (!strcmp(EItems_store[i][3], TheText) &&
        !strcmp(EItems_store[i][4], " "))
        strcpy(EItems_store[i][4], " ");
    else if (!strcmp(EItems_store[i][4], TheText))
    { strcpy(EItems_store[i][3],
            EItems_store[i][4]);
        strcpy(EItems_store[i][4], " ");
```

Figure 6.1. Continued.

```
        }
  else
  {  if (is_value(EItems_store[i][1], TheText))
       if (!strcmp(EItems_store[i][4], " "))
         strcpy(EItems_store[i][4], TheText);
       else
       {
         strcpy(EItems_store[i][3],
              EItems_store[i][4]);
         strcpy(EItems_store[i][4], TheText);
       }
     else
       MessageBox(HWindow,
         "You have entered a bad items
         value.0ress OK to cancel application.",
         "ERROR!!", MB_OK | MB_ICONHAND);
       Forms_return = 0;
       CloseWindow();
       return;
     }
  }
}
for (i=0; i<Ecount_store; i++)
{  if (strlen(EItems_store[i][3]) >
       atoi(EItems_store[i][2]))
   {  strcpy(new_temp, EItems_store[i][3]);
     for (int j=0; j<atoi(EItems_store[i][2]);
          j++)
     EItems_store[i][3][j] =
       new_temp[strlen(new_temp) -
       atoi(EItems_store[i][2]) + j];
     EItems_store[i][3][atoi(EItems_store[i][2])]
       = ' ';
   }
}
for (i=0; i<Ecount_store; i++)
  if (strlen(EItems_store[i][4]) >
      atoi(EItems_store[i][2]))
  {  strcpy(new_temp, EItems_store[i][4]);
    for(int j=0; j<atoi(EItems_store[i][2]); j++)
    EItems_store[i][4][j] =
      new_temp[strlen(new_temp) -
      atoi(EItems_store[i][2]) + j];
    EItems_store[i][4][atoi(EItems_store[i][2])]
      = ' ';
  }

for (i=0; i<Ecount_store; i++)
{  strcpy(Forms_transfer[i][0], EItems_store[i][0]);
  strcpy(Forms_transfer[i][1], EItems_store[i][1]);
  strcpy(Forms_transfer[i][2], EItems_store[i][2]);
  strcpy(Forms_transfer[i][3], EItems_store[i][3]);
  strcpy(Forms_transfer[i][4], EItems_store[i][4]);
}
Forms_return = 1;
TDialog::Ok(Msg);
}

/**** If CANCEL is pressed this function
      is executed. It merely closes
      window. ****/
```

```
void TForm3Window::Cancel(RTMessage Msg)
{
  TDialog::Cancel(Msg);
}

/**** This is the function for the new
      button in the Escape window.
      It imitates cancel except that
      it returns a -1. ****/

void TForm3Window::HandleButton3Msg(RTMessage)
{
  Forms_return = 0;
  CloseWindow(ID_BUTTON4);
}

/**** After the constructor this function,
      SetupWindow is executed. It
      performs the usual dialog box setup a
      nd then resizes the window to
      the position, height and width
      determined in the constructor. ****/

/**** MoveWindow takes as arguments,
      the handle of the window to resize,
      the new x coordinate, y coordinate,
      width and height.          ****/

void TForm3Window::SetupWindow()
{
  TDialog::SetupWindow();
  MoveWindow(this->HWindow,
    317 - Ewidth/2, 250 - Eheight/2,
    Ewidth+10, Eheight, TRUE);
  HANDLE hEEditFont;
  HANDLE hEStaticFont;
  LOGFONT ELogFont;

/**** This is the font for the edit fields.
      It is a fixed width Courier
      with width of 10.   ****/

  memset(&ELogFont, 0, sizeof(LOGFONT));
  ELogFont.lfHeight = 10;
  ELogFont.lfWidth = 10;
  ELogFont.lfPitchAndFamily = FF_MODERN;
  lstrcpy(ELogFont.lfFaceName, "Courier 10");
  hEEditFont = CreateFontIndirect(&ELogFont);

/**** This is the font for the labels,
      again Courier. The only difference
      is that there is a little extra weight
      put on it.         ****/

  memset(&ELogFont, 0, sizeof(LOGFONT));
  ELogFont.lfHeight = 10;
  ELogFont.lfWidth = 10;
  ELogFont.lfWeight = 200;
  ELogFont.lfPitchAndFamily = FF_MODERN;
  lstrcpy(ELogFont.lfFaceName, "Courier 10");
  hEStaticFont = CreateFontIndirect(&ELogFont);
```

Figure 6.1. Continued.

```
for (int i=0; i<Ecount_store; i++)                    {
  SendMessage(EEdit[i]->HWindow, WM_SETFONT,  DisableAutoCreate();
        hEEditFont, TRUE);
                                              /**** Creates an instance of TListBox with
  for (i=0; i<Ecount_store; i++)                    the position of the listbox
    SendMessage(EStatic[i]->HWindow, WM_SETFONT,  determined by the last four parameters
        hEStaticFont, TRUE);                  passed to the new statement. ****/
}
                                              ListBox = new TListBox(this, ID_LISTBOX,
/**** This is the definition of a class to          20, 20, 180, 80);
      represent the Choices window
      that is opened when the Choices function is  /**** This basically says that do not put
      called. ****/                                into alphabetical order.   ****/

_CLASSDEF (TFormWindow)                        ListBox->Attr.Style &= ~LBS_SORT;
class TFormWindow : public TDialog
{                                                 /**** Creating instances of two buttons,
public:                                                 Index and Cancel.       ****/
char Items_stored[32][33];
int count_stored;                              new TButton(this, IDOK, "Index", 0, 142,
                                                    150, 30, TRUE);
  /**** Declaration of ListBox as a pointer    new TButton(this, ID_BUTTON2, "Cancel",
      to class TListBox, and ObjectWindows          150, 142, 150, 30, FALSE);
      class that builds a list box. ****/      count_stored = count_input;

PTListBox ListBox;                                /**** Copies passed array into its
                                                        own data member.      ****/
  /**** Constructor to the class, takes parent,
      name, passed array, and int count. ****/ for (int i=0; i<count_stored; i++)
                                               { strcpy(Items_stored[i], Items_input[i]);}
TFormWindow(PTWindowsObject AParent,           TDialog::SetCaption(ATitle);
        LPSTR name, LPSTR ATitle,              }
        char Items_input[32][33],
        int count_input);                      /**** This function gets executed right after
  /**** This function is executed right after        the constructor and sets
      the constructor to the class. ****/            up the dialog box with the list box and
                                                     adds the items in the passed
virtual void SetupWindow();                          array into the listbox.  Then it positions
                                                     the window using the
  /**** This function handles double clicks on       MoveWindow function. ****/
      an item in the listbox.    ****/
                                               void TFormWindow::SetupWindow()
virtual void HandleListMsg(RTMessage Msg)      {
= [ID_FIRST + ID_LISTBOX];                       TDialog::SetupWindow();
                                                 ListBox->ClearList();
  /**** This function handles pressing the       for (int i=0; i<count_stored; i++)
      INDEX button on the Choices window. ****/  { ListBox->AddString(Items_stored[i]);}
                                                 MoveWindow(this->HWindow, 100, 100, 300,
virtual void Ok(RTMessage Msg)                       200, TRUE);
= [ID_FIRST + IDOK];                           }
                                               /**** This function gets executed when the
  /**** This function handles pressing the           list box item is double clicked
      CANCEL button on the Choices window. ****/      and basically takes the item, finds
                                                     the items index in the list,
virtual void HandleButton2Msg(RTMessage Msg)         and places it in Choices_return and
= [ID_FIRST + ID_BUTTON2];                           closes the window. ****/
};
  /** Constructor to the class TFormWindow **/  void TFormWindow:: HandleListMsg(RTMessage Msg)
TFormWindow::TFormWindow(PTWindowsObject AParent,  {
    LPSTR name, LPSTR ATitle,                  char my_string[30];
    char Items_input[32][33], int count_input) :  if (Msg.LP.Hi == LBN_DBLCLK)
TDialog(AParent, name)                         {
```

Figure 6.1. Continued.

```
    itoa(ListBox->GetSelIndex() + 1, my_string,
            10);
    MessageBox(HWindow, my_string,
            "Index Number =", MB_OK);
    Choices_return = ListBox->GetSelIndex() + 1;
    TDialog::Ok(Msg);
    }
}

/**** If Index is pressed the selected item in
    the list has its index
    value placed in Choices_return and the
    window is closed.   ****/

void TFormWindow:: Ok(RTMessage Msg)
{
  char my_string[30];
  itoa(ListBox->GetSelIndex() + 1, my_string, 10);
  MessageBox(HWindow, my_string, "Index Number =",
        MB_OK);
  Choices_return = ListBox->GetSelIndex() + 1;
  TDialog::Ok(Msg);
}

/**** If Cancel is pressed the window is merely
    closed.  ****/

void TFormWindow::HandleButton2Msg(RTMessage)
{
  Choices_return = 0;
  CloseWindow();
}

/**** Class TMyWindow is the main window of
    the application.  It is very
    important to understand this class and
    its member functions.  ****/

_CLASSDEF(TMyWindow)
class TMyWindow : public TWindow
{
public:
  char Items_Forms[16][5][33];
  char Items_Choices[32][33];
  char Items_Escape[16][5][33];
  BOOL Choices_filled;
  BOOL Forms_filled;
  BOOL Escape_filled;
  int Choices_count;
  int Forms_count;
  int Escape_count;

/**** Constructor to the class.  ****/

TMyWindow(PTWindowsObject AParent, LPSTR ATitle)

/**** The function CanClose() is checks to
    see if it returns TRUE
    before the actual closing action
    can be executed.  ****/

virtual BOOL CanClose();
```

```
/**** This function gets executed when
    Store | Choices is clicked. ****/

virtual void Choices_store(RTMessage Msg)
= [CM_FIRST + CM_CHOICES];

/**** This function gets executed when
    Store | Forms is clicked.  ****/

virtual void Forms_store(RTMessage Msg)
= [CM_FIRST + CM_FORMS];

/**** New function to store the
    Escape array. ****/

virtual void Escape_store(RTMessage Msg)
= [CM_FIRST + CM_ESCAPE];

/**** This function gets executed when
    Display | Forms is clicked.  ****/

virtual void Forms_display(RTMessage Msg)
= [CM_FIRST + CM_DISFORMS];

/**** This function gets executed when
    Display | Choices is clicked.  ****/

virtual void Choices_display(RTMessage Msg)
= [CM_FIRST + CM_DISCHOICES];

/**** New function to display the
    Escape window. ****/

virtual void Escape_display(RTMessage Msg)
= [CM_FIRST + CM_DISESCAPE];

/**** This is the function Choices, the
    main part of the program.  ****/

virtual int Choices(char items[32][33],
            int count, char box_name[20]);

/**** This is the function Forms, the
    main part of the program.   ****/

virtual int Forms(char items[16][5][33],
            int count, char box_name[20]);
virtual int Escape(char items[16][5][33],
            int count, char box_name[20]);

/**** This function gets executed when
    Help | Help is clicked.   ****/

virtual void Help(RTMessage Msg)
= [CM_FIRST + CM_HELP];
private:

/**** These are private functions and are
    quite self-explanatory.  ****/

BOOL is_name(char temp[33]);
BOOL is_type(char temp[33]);
```

Figure 6.1. Continued.

```
BOOL is_len(char temp[33]);
BOOL is_value(char item[33], char temp[33]);
BOOL is_float(char temp[33]);
BOOL is_int(char temp[33]);
BOOL is_string(char temp[33]);
};

/**** This is the constructor of the main
      window.  It assigns the menu
      defined in the resource file to this
      window.  It also sets initial
      variables. ****/

TMyWindow::TMyWindow(PTWindowsObject AParent,
                     LPSTR ATitle)
    : TWindow(AParent, ATitle)
{
  AssignMenu("COMMANDS");
  Choices_filled = FALSE;
  Forms_filled = FALSE;
  Escape_filled = FALSE;
  Choices_count = 0;
  Forms_count = 0;
  Escape_count = 0;
}
/**** This is an overloaded function of class
      TWindow on which TMyWindow
      is based.  Before exiting, the user is
      now asked if he wants to
      leave.  If yes is clicked, the application
      is closed, else left open. ****/

BOOL TMyWindow::CanClose()
{
  char ii[16][5][33];
  for (int i=0; i<16;i++)
  {
    ii[i][0][0] = ' ';
    strcat(ii[i][0],
          "aaaaaaaaaaaaaaaaaaaaaaaaaaaaaaaa");
    ii[i][1][0] = ' ';
    strcat(ii[i][1],"string");
    ii[i][2][0] = ' ';
    strcat(ii[i][2],"32");
    ii[i][3][0] = ' ';
    strcat(ii[i][3],"*");
    ii[i][4][0] = ' ';
    strcat(ii[i][4],"*");

  }
  Forms(ii,16,"yes");
  return MessageBox(HWindow,
      "Do you really want to exit?", "EXIT",
      MB_YESNO | MB_ICONQUESTION) == IDYES;
}

/**** Checks to see if argument is integer. ****/

BOOL TMyWindow::is_int(char temp[33])
{
  if (!strcmp(temp, "*")) return TRUE;
  if (!isdigit(temp[0])) return FALSE;
```

```
  for(int i=0; i<strlen(temp); i++)
  { if (!isdigit(temp[i])) return FALSE;
  }
  return TRUE;
}

/**** Checks to see if argument is floating ****/

BOOL TMyWindow::is_float(char temp[33])
{
  BOOL dec = FALSE;
  if (!strcmp(temp, "*")) return TRUE;
  for(int i=0; i<strlen(temp); i++)
  { if (!isdigit(temp[i]) &&
        !((temp[i] == '.') &&
          (dec == FALSE)))
      return FALSE;
    if (temp[i] == '.') dec = TRUE;
  }
  return TRUE;
}

/**** Checks to see if argument is string. ****/

BOOL TMyWindow::is_string(char temp[33])
{
  if (!strcmp(temp, "*")) return TRUE;
  if (isalpha(temp[0]))
  { for(int i=0; i<strlen(temp); i++)
    if (!isalpha(temp[i]) && !isdigit(temp[i])
        && !ispunct(temp[i]))
      return FALSE;
    return TRUE;
  }
  else
    return FALSE;
}

/**** Checks to see if argument is a valid name. ****/

BOOL TMyWindow::is_name(char temp[33])
{ if (isalpha(temp[0]) && (strlen(temp) == 1))
    return TRUE;
  if (isalpha(temp[0]))
  { for(int i=0; i<strlen(temp); i++)
    if (!isalpha(temp[i]) && !isdigit(temp[i])
        && !ispunct(temp[i]))
      return FALSE;
    return TRUE;
  }
  else
    return FALSE;
}
/**** Checks to see if argument is a valid type
      (int, float, or string) ****/

BOOL TMyWindow::is_type(char temp[33])
{
  if (strcmp(temp,"int") && strcmp(temp,"float")
      && strcmp(temp,"string"))
    return FALSE;
```

Figure 6.1. Continued.

```
return TRUE;
}

/**** Checks to see whether argument is a
     valid length.    ****/

BOOL TMyWindow::is_len(char temp[33])
{
 if (!isdigit(temp[0])) return FALSE;
 for(int i=0; i<strlen(temp); i++)
  if (!isdigit(temp[i])) return FALSE;
 if (atoi(temp) == 0) return FALSE;
 return TRUE;
}

/**** Checks to see if the second argument
     is a valid value for the type
     in the first argument. ****/

BOOL TMyWindow::is_value(char item[33],
                         char temp[33])
{
 if (!strcmp(item, "int"))
  if (is_int(temp)) return TRUE;
 if (!strcmp(item, "float"))
  if (is_float(temp)) return TRUE;
 if (!strcmp(item, "string"))
  if (is_string(temp)) return TRUE;
 return FALSE;
}

/**** This function opens up a standard input
     dialog box and puts the
     user input into a long string . Then
     through the use of strtok
     function the long string is tokenized
     and placed in an array.
     Finally a check is done to see the
     validity of the input. If
     this input is valid the boolean
     Forms_filled is made true and a
     message is diplayed saying the array
     is stored. If the input has
     some error in it, an error message is
     popped and the array is not
     stored, this Forms_filled is false. ****/

void TMyWindow::Forms_store(RTMessage)
{
 int counter;
 char InputText[1000];
 char *p;
 char temp[33];
 int len;
 int looper;
 strcpy(InputText, " ");
 if (GetApplication()->ExecDialog
   (new TInputDialog(this, "Command line:",
    "Command line:", InputText,
     sizeof InputText)) == IDOK)
  {   if (!strcmp(InputText, " ")) return;
     strcpy(Items_Forms[0][0],
```

```
     strtok(InputText, ", "));
 counter = 1;
 while (((p = strtok(NULL, ", ")) != NULL)
        && (counter < 64))
 {
   strcpy(Items_Forms[(counter -
     (counter%4))/4][(counter%4)], p);
   counter++;
 }
 if (counter%4 == 0) looper = counter/4;
 else
 {
   looper = ((counter - (counter%4))/4) + 1;
   MessageBox(HWindow, "Inv. # of Args",
        "Not Stored", MB_OK);
   Forms_filled = FALSE;
   return;
 }
 for(int j=0; j<looper; j++)
 {  if(!is_name(Items_Forms[j][0]))
    {
      MessageBox(HWindow, "Invalid item name",
           "Not Stored", MB_OK);
      Forms_filled = FALSE;
      return;
    }
    if(!is_type(Items_Forms[j][1]))
    {
      MessageBox(HWindow, "Invalid item type",
           "Not Stored", MB_OK);
      Forms_filled = FALSE;
      return;
    }
    if(!is_len(Items_Forms[j][2]))
    {
      MessageBox(HWindow, "Invalid item length",
           "Not Stored", MB_OK);
      Forms_filled = FALSE;
      return;
    }
    if(!is_value(Items_Forms[j][1],
              Items_Forms[j][3]))
    {
      MessageBox(HWindow, "Invalid item value",
           "Not Stored", MB_OK);
      Forms_filled = FALSE;
      return;
    }
 }
 for (int i=0; i<looper; i++)
 {
   if (strlen(Items_Forms[i][0]) > 32)
   {
     MessageBox(HWindow,
        "Name cannot exceed 32",
        "Not Stored", MB_OK);
     Forms_filled = FALSE;
     return;
   }
   if (strlen(Items_Forms[i][3]) > 32)
   {
     MessageBox(HWindow,
```

Figure 6.1. Continued.

```
                    "Value cannot exceed 32",              (new TInputDialog(this, "Command line:",
                    "Not Stored", MB_OK);                      "Command line:", InputText,
                 Forms_filled = FALSE;                         sizeof InputText)) == IDOK)
                 return;                                  {  if (!strcmp(InputText, " ")) return;
              }                                               strcpy(Items_Escape[0][0],
           }                                                     strtok(InputText, ", "));
           for (i=0; i<looper; i++)                           counter = 1;
           {  if (strlen(Items_Forms[i][3]) >                 while (((p = strtok(NULL, ", ")) != NULL)
                    atoi(Items_Forms[i][2]))                      && (counter < 64))
              {  strcpy(temp, Items_Forms[i][3]);            {
                 len = strlen(Items_Forms[i][3]);              strcpy(Items_Escape[(counter -
                 for(int k=0;                                    (counter%4))/4][(counter%4)], p);
                    k<atoi(Items_Forms[i][2]); k++)            counter++;
                 Items_Forms[i][3][k] =                      }
                    temp[len -                               if (counter%4 == 0) looper = counter/4;
                    atoi(Items_Forms[i][2]) + k];            else
                 Items_Forms[i][3]                           {
                    [atoi(Items_Forms[i][2])] = ' ';           looper = ((counter - (counter%4))/4) + 1;
              }                                                MessageBox(HWindow,
           }                                                     "Inv. # of Args", "Not Stored", MB_OK);
           for (i=0; i<looper; i++)                            Escape_filled = FALSE;
              strcpy(Items_Forms[i][4], "*");                  return;
           Forms_filled = TRUE;                              }
           Forms_count = looper;                             for(int j=0; j<looper; j++)
           for (i=looper; i<16; i++)                         {  if(!is_name(Items_Escape[j][0]))
           {  strcpy(Items_Forms[i][0], " ");                   {
              strcpy(Items_Forms[i][1], " ");                      MessageBox(HWindow,
              strcpy(Items_Forms[i][2], " ");                         "Invalid item name",
              strcpy(Items_Forms[i][3], " ");                         "Not Stored", MB_OK);
              strcpy(Items_Forms[i][4], " ");                      Escape_filled = FALSE;
           }                                                       return;
           MessageBox(HWindow, "Array stored",                  }
              "Message", MB_OK);                                if(!is_type(Items_Escape[j][1]))
        }                                                      {
    }                                                              MessageBox(HWindow,
                                                                      "Invalid item type",
/**** This function opens up a standard input                         "Not Stored", MB_OK);
   dialog box and puts the                                         Escape_filled = FALSE;
   user input into a long string . Then                            return;
   through the use of strtok                                    }
   function the long string is tokenized                        if(!is_len(Items_Escape[j][2]))
   and placed in an array.                                      {
   Finally a check is done to see the                               MessageBox(HWindow,
   validity of the input. If                                          "Invalid item length",
   this input is valid the boolean Escape_filled                       "Not Stored", MB_OK);
   is made true and a                                              Escape_filled = FALSE;
   message is diplayed saying the array is stored.                  return;
   If the input has                                              }
   some error in it, an error message is popped                  if (!is_value(Items_Escape[j][1],
   and the array is not                                              Items_Escape[j][3]))
   stored, this Escape_filled is false. ****/                   {
                                                                   MessageBox(HWindow,
void TMyWindow::Escape_store(RTMessage)                               "Invalid item value",
{                                                                     "Not Stored", MB_OK);
   int counter;                                                    Escape_filled = FALSE;
   char InputText[1000];                                          return;
   char *p;                                                     }
   char temp[33];                                             }
   int len;                                                   for (int i=0; i<looper; i++)
   int looper;                                                {
   strcpy(InputText, " ");                                       if (strlen(Items_Escape[i][0]) > 32)
   if (GetApplication()->ExecDialog                               {
```

Figure 6.1. Continued.

```
      MessageBox(HWindow,
        "Name cannot exceed 32",
        "Not Stored", MB_OK);
      Escape_filled = FALSE;
      return;
    }
    if (strlen(Items_Escape[i][3]) > 32)
    {
      MessageBox(HWindow,
        "Value cannot exceed 32",
        "Not Stored", MB_OK);
      Escape_filled = FALSE;
      return;
    }

  }
  for (i=0; i<looper; i++)
  { if (strlen(Items_Escape[i][3]) >
      atoi(Items_Escape[i][2]))
    { strcpy(temp, Items_Escape[i][3]);
      len = strlen(Items_Escape[i][3]);
      for(int k=0;
        k<atoi(Items_Escape[i][2]); k++)
        Items_Escape[i][3][k] =
        temp[len - atoi(Items_Escape[i][2])
        + k];
        Items_Escape[i][3]
        [atoi(Items_Escape[i][2])] = ' ';
    }

  }
  Escape_filled = TRUE;
  Escape_count = looper;
  for (i=looper; i<16; i++)
  { strcpy(Items_Escape[i][0], " ");
    strcpy(Items_Escape[i][1], " ");
    strcpy(Items_Escape[i][2], " ");
    strcpy(Items_Escape[i][3], " ");
    strcpy(Items_Escape[i][4], " ");

  }
  for (i=0; i<looper; i++)
  {
    strcpy(Items_Escape[i][4], "*");

  }
  MessageBox(HWindow,
    "Array stored", "Message", MB_OK);
  }
}
```

/**** This function's job is to store the
   Choices array. It opens up a
   standard dialog box an places the user
   input into a long string.
   Through the use of the strtok function
   the string is tokenized and
   placed in an array. A validity check
   is done. If the input is
   valid, Choices _filled is made true
   and a message is popped saying
   the array is stored. If the input has
   some sort of error, an error
   message is popped and Choices_filled
   is false. ****/

```
void TMyWindow::Choices_store(RTMessage)
{
  int counter;
  char InputText[200];
  char *p;
  strcpy(InputText, " ");
  if (GetApplication()->
    ExecDialog(new TInputDialog
    (this, "Command line:", "Command line:",
    InputText, sizeof InputText)) == IDOK)
    { if (!strcmp(InputText, " ")) return;
      strcpy(Items_Choices[0],
        strtok(InputText, ", "));
      counter = 1;
      while(((p = strtok(NULL, ", ")) != NULL)
        && (counter < 32))
      {
        strcpy(Items_Choices[counter], p);
        counter++;
      }
      for (int i=0; i<counter; i++)
      {
        if (!is_name(Items_Choices[i]))
        { MessageBox(HWindow,
          "Invalid argument",
          "Not Stored", MB_OK);
          Choices_filled = FALSE;
          return;
        }
      }
      Choices_filled = TRUE;
      Choices_count = counter;
      MessageBox(HWindow,
        "Array stored.", "Message", MB_OK);
    }
}
```

/**** This function displays the Forms window.
   It checks to see if the
   array is filled. If it is, it called
   the Forms function, else it
   returns a message saying that the array
   is not filled.   ****/

```
void TMyWindow::Forms_display(RTMessage)
{
  int b;
  if (Forms_filled)
    b = Forms(Items_Forms,
      Forms_count, "Form Window Test");
  else
    MessageBox(HWindow,
      "Array not filled.", "ERROR", MB_OK);
}
```

/**** This function displays the Escape window.
   It checks to see if the
   array is filled. If it is, it called
   the Escape function, else it
   returns a message saying that the array
   is not filled. ****/

Figure 6.1. Continued.

```
void TMyWindow::Escape_display(RTMessage)
{
 int b;
 if (Escape_filled)
   b = Escape(Items_Escape,
       Escape_count, "Escape Window Test");
 else
 MessageBox(HWindow,
     "Array not filled.", "ERROR", MB_OK);
}

/**** This function displays the Choices
    window.  It checks to see if
    the Chocies array is filled.  If
    it is, it calls the Choices function
    else it returns a message saying that
    the array is not filled. ****/

void TMyWindow::Choices_display(RTMessage)
{
 int b;
 if (Choices_filled)
   b = Choices(Items_Choices,
       Choices_count, "TestTitle");
 else
   MessageBox(HWindow,
     "Array not stored.", "ERROR", MB_OK);
}

/**** This the main Choices function.
    It displays the Choices window
    and if the user clicks Index,
    returns the index of the selected
    item.  If Index is not pressed,
    it return a simple 0.    ****/

int TMyWindow::Choices(char items[32][33],
    int count, char box_name[20])
{
 if (GetModule()->ExecDialog
   ( new TFormWindow(this, "FORM1",
     box_name, items, count)) == IDOK )
     {
     MessageBox(HWindow,
       "return is 1", "Message", MB_OK);
     return Choices_return;
     }
 else
     return 0;
}

/**** This is the main Forms function.
    It displays a Forms window and
    if an OK is received from the window,
    it copies from the global
    transfer buffer to its own array.
    This is to account for changes
    to the fields in the form window.
    If OK is no received, a 0 is
    returned.  If OK is received, a 1 is
    returned. ****/
```

```
int TMyWindow::Forms(char items[16][5][33],
    int count, char box_name[20])
{
 if(GetModule()->ExecDialog
   ( new TForm2Window(this, "FORM2",
     box_name, items, count)) == IDOK )
   { MessageBox(HWindow, "return is 1",
       "Message", MB_OK);
     for(int i=0; i<count; i++)
     { if (!strcmp
         (Forms_transfer[i][4], " "))
         strcpy(items[i][4], "*");
       else
         strcpy(items[i][4],
           Forms_transfer[i][4]);
       if (!strcmp
         (Forms_transfer[i][3], " "))
         strcpy(items[i][3], "*");
       else
         strcpy(items[i][3], Forms_transfer[i][3]);
     }
     return 1;
   }
 else
     return 0;
}

/**** This is the main Escape function.
    It opens up a dialog box, a if OK
    is pressed, returns 1.  If CANCEL
    is pressed it returns 0.  If Escape
    is pressed, it returns a -1.  This
    third button is the only difference
    between the Form Window and the
    Escape Window.     ****/

int TMyWindow::Escape(char items[16][5][33],
    int count, char box_name[20])
{
  switch(GetModule()->ExecDialog
   ( new TForm3Window(this, "FORM3",
     box_name, items, count))) {
 case(IDOK):
   MessageBox(HWindow,
     "return is 1", "Message", MB_OK);
     for(int i=0; i<count; i++)
     { if (!strcmp(Forms_transfer[i][4], " "))
         strcpy(items[i][4], "*");
       else
         strcpy(items[i][4],
           Forms_transfer[i][4]);
       if (!strcmp(Forms_transfer[i][3], " "))
         strcpy(items[i][3], "*");
       else
         strcpy(items[i][3],
           Forms_transfer[i][3]);
     }
     return 1;
 case(IDCANCEL):
   MessageBox(HWindow, "ESCAPE",
     " return is 0", MB_OK);
     return 0;
```

Figure 6.1. Continued.

```
            default:
              MessageBox(HWindow, "ESCAPE",
                "return is -1", MB_OK);
              return -1;
          }
        }

        /**** This is the help function, and makes
              the help window on the screen.
              The help window is defined in
              hwind.cpp .              ****/

        void TMyWindow::Help(RTMessage)
        {
        PTWindow HelpWindow;
        HelpWindow = new THelpWindow(this);
        GetApplication()->MakeWindow(HelpWindow);
        }

        /**** This function is necessary for all
              applications and basically tells
              what the main window is. In this
              case our main window is TMyWindow
              and thus we assign is as such.  ****/

        void TMyApp::InitMainWindow()
        {
          MainWindow = new TMyWindow(NULL, Name);
        }

        /**** This is common to all applications. ****/

        int PASCAL WinMain(HANDLE hInstance,
           HANDLE hPrevInstance, LPSTR lpCmdLine,
           int nCmdShow)
        {
          TMyApp MyApp("SAMPLE PROJECT",
            hInstance, hPrevInstance, lpCmdLine, nCmdShow);
          MyApp.Run();
          return MyApp.Status;
        }
```

Figure 6.1. Continued.

REFERENCES

1. *Microsoft Windows, User's Guide* (Microsoft, 1990).
2. *ObjectWindows, Programmer's Manual* (Borland Int., 1991).
3. Scheifler, R. W., and Gettys, J. *X window system, the complete reference to Xlib, X Protocol, ICCCM, XLFD* (Digital Press, 1992).
4. Nye, A. *Xlib programming manual* (O'Reilly, Sebastopol, CA., 1990).
5. Nye, A., and O'Reilly, T. *X Toolkit intrinsics programming manual* (O'Reilly, Sebastopol, CA., 1990).
6. Heller, D. *Motif programming manual* (O'Reilly, Sebastopol, CA., 1990).
7. Sun Microsystems, Inc. *OPEN LOOK graphical user interface application style guide* (Addison-Wesley, Reading, MA, 1990).
8. Sun Microsystems, Inc. *OPEN LOOK graphical user interface functional specification* (Addison-Wesley, Reading, MA, 1990).
9. Stevens, W. R., *UNIX network programming* (Prentice-Hall, Englewood Cliffs, NJ, 1990).

7

Declarative Programming

A program is declarative if it requires little specification about control; instead it specifies as much as possible what to compute. The most ambitious objective of declarative programming is to derive computations from requirements specifications automatically in every domain. A more conservative goal of declarative programming is to make programming a simple task so that only the key portion of a program must be figured out by the programmer and most low-level details can be completed by the programming system automatically. Such objectives have been successfully accomplished in many well-defined domains. Chapter 7 first discusses a number of very high level programming languages that provide the programmer with additional tools to simplify manipulations of complex data structures (Sections 7.1–7.2). Section 7.3 discusses a logic programming language, PROLOG. Section 7.4 discusses the concept of declarative programming in database systems—a well-defined yet powerful domain that covers a large number of applications.

A logic programming language, such as PROLOG, is considered declarative because a logic program is treated as a goal to be proved by a mechanical theorem-proving process. Compared with first-order logic (see Section 3.1), logic programming is more restrictive in terms of the notations allowed (e.g., the use of negation is strictly restricted). This implies that the programmer sometimes has to implement some search procedure explicitly. A logic programming language may be considered a formal requirements specification language for simple problems; however since it would require some specification of control for complicated problems, we discuss it here rather than in Chapter 3. Automatic programming for general domains is discussed in Chapter 8.

7.1. VERY HIGH LEVEL PROGRAMMING

Ideally the term declarative program refers to a program that says *what* is to be accomplished by the program, rather than *how* it is to be accomplished. Therefore a program is declarative if it is only a specification. Due to practical constraints (see Chapter 8), declarative programs may also exist in the form of *very high level programs* in a *very high level programming language*. A language

is a very high level programming language if it extends a high-level programming language with some additional constructs so that the user's intentions can
easily be expressed. An example of such languages is SETL, a language that
mainly extends ALGOL with the notion of sets and tuples (which are ordered
sets).[1] A set can be specified by enumeration (e.g., $\{1,2,3\}$) or by using a general
set former construction $\{x \in s | C(x)\}$ [which constructs a subset from a set s with
those elements x in s satisfying the Boolean condition $C(x)$]). In SETL sets can be
manipulated by ordinary set-oriented operations, such as union, intersect, and
difference. SETL also allows quantified expressions to be written over sets, such
as $\exists x \in s | C(x)$ and $\forall x \in s | C(x)$, where s is a set and $C(x)$ is a Boolean
expression.

> **Example 7.1.** (Ref. 2) This example illustrates that with the additional
> set-oriented constructs available in SETL, a program computing the
> shortest path between two vertices in a graph can be expressed in a very
> concise and readable form.
>
> ```
> read(graph,cost,x,y); // graph is a map from a
>                               node to its successors
>         // cost is an integer map from two nodes
>         // x is the source
>         // y is the destination
> prev := {}; // initialization
> val := {};
> val(x) := 0;
> newnodes := {x};
> (while newnodes != {})
>   select n from newnodes;
>   (∀m ∈ graph{n}) // for each of its successors
>     newval := val (n) + cost (n,m);
>     if val (m) =om or val(m) > newval then
>         // om is a special symbol
>         // that designates an undefined
>         // value
>       val(m) := newval;
>       prev(m) := n;
>       if m != y then
>         newnodes with := m;
>           // add m to newnodes
>       end if;
>     end if;
>   end ∀
> end while;
> ```

```
if val(y) = om then
    print("y is not reachable from x");
  else
    path := [y];  // build the path backwards
    z := y;
    (while (z := prev(z)) != om)
      path with := z;
    end while;
              // the following reverses the re-
              versed path
    path := [path(#path + 1 -i):i := 1 ...
#path]; // # takes the cardinality
    print(path);
  end if;
  end program MINPATH;
```

In addition to SETL, a number of other very high level programming languages have been proposed. A partial list includes GIST,[3] V,[4] BAGL,[5] and GAMMA.[6] An important issue related to almost all very high level languages is *data structure selection*. For example in SETL, the notions of set and tuple are provided without implementation. The choice of the most appropriate and efficient implementation for sets and tuples in a program can be done automatically. For example Ref. 2 proposes choosing to implement some *base* sets of a program as hash tables, then implementing sets that can be derived from base sets from the base tables automatically. Data flow analysis is proposed to determine base sets for a program. Some other optimization ideas are reported in Ref. 7. The success of very high level programming languages in some special domains are given in Ref. 8.

7.2. OBJECT-ORIENTED DECLARATIVE PROGRAMMING

The concept of declarative programming is incorporated into object-oriented database programming languages in Ref. 9. A number of object-oriented database systems extend c++ with the concept of set and persistent object. In the following we extend c++ to include some high-level constructs that can be used to access sets of objects. We assume that all objects are programming objects (i.e., not persistent objects) and all sets are ordered.

Set Classes: Given a class of α, the class of all possible ordered sets that can be derived from instances of α is declared as:

```
class set_of_α {
  . . .
  //methods
  . . .
}
```

The following declaration defines a set *a* of class α:

```
set_of_α a;
```

Set Projection: Given a set or an object *a* of class α, the following notation designates the projection of *a* on attributes *A* 1, . . . , *An:*

$$a_{A 1, \ldots, An}$$

Head and Tail: The function *head*() applied to an ordered set returns the first element of the set; the function *tail*() returns the remainder of the set. The symbol *NIL* designates the empty set.

Universal Quantifier: A variable in a logical expression can be universally quantified by the quantifier:

```
(forall ⟨variable_id⟩ in ⟨set_id⟩)
```

Existential Quantifier: A variable in a logical expression can be existentially quantified by the quantifier:

```
(exist ⟨variable_id⟩ in ⟨set_id⟩)
```

Membership: The following function returns 1 if ⟨*variable_id*⟩ is an element of ⟨*set_id*⟩:

```
⟨set_id⟩:member(⟨variable_id⟩);
```

The following functions/statements can be used to access the elements in a set:

- ⟨set_id⟩:insert(⟨variable_id⟩);

- ⟨set_id⟩:delete(⟨variable_id⟩);

- (foreach ⟨variable_id⟩ in ⟨set_id⟩) statement;

Example 7.2. Assume the following declarations:

```
class rectangle {
  public:
    vertex a,b,c,d;
    int intersect(rectangle r); /*test if two
rectangles intersect*/
```

```
    int size(); //returns the size of a rectangle
        void plot(); //plot a rectangle
        //others
        . . . .
};
class vertex {
  public:
    float x,y;
    //others
    . . .
};
class block {
  //attributes
  void plot(); //plot a block
    . . . .
};
class on_top {
  public:
    block top,bottom;
    //others
    . . .
};
class set_of_block {. . .};
class set_of_on_top {. . .};
class set_of_rectangle sr;
set_of_block sb;
set_of_on_top sot;
set_of_rectangle sr;
op_top a;
rectangle s,t,u;
```

The following are some example statements that access objects associatively:

```
/*plot pairs of rectangles of sr which intersect
each other*/
    (foreach t in sr)
      (foreach u in sr)
        if (t.intersect(u) == 1) {t.plot(); u.plot();
}
    //plot the smallest rectangle in sr
    (foreach t in sr)
      if !((exist s in sr) (s.size() > t.size()))
t.plot();
```

```
//plot each block which does not support any other
block
     (foreach b in sb)
       if !((exist a in sot) (a.bottom == b)) b.plot();
```

Object-oriented declarative programming, as briefly described in the preceding, may make a program less sensitive to changes, as Example 7.3 illustrates.

Example 7.3. Consider the simple scenario consisting of three surface
ships: one carrier and two cruisers. The three ships move from the base
to a battle zone. On the way and before the attack begins, each ship is
responsible for any threat detected, and any ship must clear the threat.
Once all ships reach the battle zone, they should attack the target together. The following c++ program employs inheritance, function overriding, and set-oriented constructs to implement this scenario:

```
class surface_ship {
  coordinate position;
  double speed;
  double bearing;
  set_of_weapon weapons;
    . . . .
  void surface_ship(void);
  int transit (float speed, set_of_segment
path);
  virtual int attack (target target);
  virtual int clear_threat (threat threat);
  virtual threat detect_threat (void); /* it re-
turns a threat if detected*/
        // it returns NULL otherwise.
    . . . .
  class carrier : surface_ship {
  set_of_aircraft aircraft;
    . . . .
  void carrier(void);
  int attack (target target);
  int clear_threat (threat threat);
  threat detect_threat(void);
  int launch_aircraft (. . . .);
  int recover_aircraft (. . . .);
  }
  class cruiser : surface_ship {
  // cruiser specific attributes;
```

. . . .
```
    void cruiser(void);
    int attack (target target);
    threat detect_threat(void);
    int clear_threat (threat threat);
    int launch_missile(. . . .);
}
class target {. . . .}
class threat {. . . .}
void main()
{
int clock = 0;   // the global clock
threat threat;   // intended to be a variable
carrier carrier(. . . .); /* create and initial-
ize carrier*/
    cruiser cruiser1(. . .), cruiser2(. . .);
                    /* create and initialize two
                    cruisers*/
    surface_ship ship, ship1, ship2; /* intended to
be a variable*/
    set_of_surface_ship task_force;
    task_force.insert(carrier); /* create the task
force*/
    task_force.insert(cruiser1);
    task_force.insert(cruiser2);
    while (exist ship in task_force) (ship.status
!= "arrived")
            // as long as not all the ships have arrived
    {
      clock++;
      (forall ship in task_force)
        if (ship.status != "arrived")
        {
            ship.transit(. . . .); // move
            if ((threat = = ship.detect_threat()) !=
NULL)
            ship.clear_threat(threat);
              // if a threat is detected by a ship
            have that ship clear the threat with its
own way*/
        }
    }
```

```
(forall ship in task_force) ship.attack_target-
(target);
    // attack the target
}
```

A c program can be written for the same purpose:

```
struct carrier {
  coordinate position;
  double speed;
  double bearing;
  weapon *weapons;
  aircraft *aircraft;
  . . . .
}
int carrier_transit (carrier carrier, float
speed, segment *path);
int carrier_attack (carrier carrier, target
target);
int carrier_clear_threat (carrier carrier,
threat threat);
struct threat carrier_detect_threat(void);
int carrier_launch_aircraft (. . . .);
int carrier_recover_aircraft (. . . .);
struct cruiser {
  coordinate position;
  double speed;
  double bearing;
  weapon *weapons;
  . . . .
}
int cruiser_transit (cruiser cruiser, float
speed, segment *path);
int cruiser_attack (cruiser cruiser, target
target);
int cruiser_clear_threat (cruiser cruiser,
threat threat);
struct threat cruiser_detect_threat(void);
int cruiser_launch_missile (. . . .);
struct target {. . . .}
struct threat {. . . .}
void main()
{
threat threat;  /* intended to be a variable */
```

```
carrier carrier;   /* create and initialize carrier
*/
    cruiser cruiser1, cruiser2;
                    /* create and initialize two
                    cruisers */
    int clock = 0;
    while ((carrier.status != "arrived")||(cruiser-
1.status != "arrived")
      ||(cruiser2.status != "arrived"))
    {
      clock++
    /* move the ships */
    if(carrier.status != "arrived")
        cruiser_transit(cruiser1, . . . .);
    if (cruiser2.status != "arrived")
        cruiser_transit(cruiser2, . . . .);
    /* detect and clear threats */
    if ((threat = carrier_detect_threat(carrier))
!= NULL)
        carrier_clear_threat(carrier,threat);
    if((threat         =         cruiser_detect
_threat(cruiser1)) != NULL)
        cruiser_clear_threat(cruiser1,threat);
    if ((threat = cruiser_detect_threat(cruiser
2)) != NULL)
        cruiser_clear_threat(cruiser2,threat);
    }
    /* attack the target */
    carrier_attack_target(carrier,target);
    cruiser_attack_target(cruiser1,target);
    cruiser_attack_target(cruiser2.target);
    }
```

We note that the c++ program is much cleaner and easier to understand; furthermore the program is much less sensitive to changes. For example if a new cruiser is added to the task force, only one line of code (i.e., *task_force.insert(cruiser3)*) has to be added to the program, while a global change has to be made to the c program. This results not only from using set-oriented constructs but also from the function-overriding mechanism. In addition the function *transit* is common to different types of surface ships in the c++ program; it is inherited from the class *surface_ship* by any subclass. Any change to be made to *transit* requires only one place to be changed. This is not true for the c program. The property of being less sensitive to changes may be regarded as a form of reusability—most of the software can be reused when the software evolves.

7.3. LOGIC PROGRAMMING—PROLOG

Logic-programming languages are programming languages based on logic. PROLOG[10] may be the most popular; it is based on first-order logic, but unlike resolution-based, refutational theorem proving, a theorem in PROLOG is proved backward, i.e., from goals to supporting facts. It is generally agreed that backward, or *deductive*, theorem proving is more efficient than refutational theorem proving, since it is guided by goals. However the axioms of a deductive theorem-proving system are restricted to *Horn* clauses (i.e., clauses that have at most one unnegated literal). PROLOG was designed to be declarative in the sense that programs are considered as theorems to be proved. Therefore a considerable amount of programming detail is eliminated with an automatic theorem prover.

In brief a PROLOG program consists of a set of *procedures,* where each procedure forms the definition of a certain *predicate*, and it is presented as a sequence of *clauses* of the form:

$$P \text{ :- } Q1, Q2, \ldots, Qn.$$

where each Qi, $1 \le i \le n$, is a predicate. The preceding clause is interpreted as:

$$P \text{ is true if } Q1 \text{ is true, } Q2 \text{ is true, } \ldots, \text{ and } Qn \text{ is true}$$

A clause of the form P. is simply interpreted as *P is true.* The P and Qs are called *goals* or *procedure calls;* each goal or procedure call consists of a predicate applied to some arguments.

Example 7.4. The following procedure defines the predicate *american:*

```
american(america).
american(X) :- partof(X,Y), american(Y).
```

The clauses can be interpreted as *American is American; for any X and Y, X is American if X is a part of Y and Y is American.*

The arguments of a predicate are called *terms;* a term can be a constant, a variable, or a structure. A variable by convention starts with a capital letter. A structure consists of a *functor* with a set of terms as its arguments; it is analogous to a record in conventional programming languages. For example, the structure *vertex* (2,3) designates a point with coordinates 2 and 3.

A PROLOG program is evaluated interactively by issuing a question, which is a clause without a left-hand side. Answers to the question can be either true or false (if there is no variable in the question) or any set of values that *instantiate* variables in the question so that the question clause is evaluated to true with the instantiations. For example the question:

?- partof(X,america)

is interpreted as *is X a part of America?* The question is answered by finding alternative values of *X*s that are part of America from the program. Specifically a value *a* can instantiate *X* if there exists a clause *partof(a,america)*. The clause *partof(a,america)* is evaluated as false if there is no clause *partof(a,america)* in the procedure. In general to find instances of the variables of a goal predicate in a question, PROLOG first matches the goal predicate with the left-hand side of some clause. If a match can be found (i.e., if the clause can be unified by the goal predicate), the right-hand side of the clause is evaluated. Goals are evaluated from left to right, and clauses are matched in the order they appear in the procedure.

If a match is found in the procedure, instantiations found should be propagated as goals that have not been evaluated. In other words if an instantiation *a* for a variable *X* is found in the match, *a* should be substituted for all instances of *X* in goals that have not been evaluated, thus making those goals more specific.

If no match can be found in the procedure, PROLOG *backtracks* to the most recently evaluated goal to try to find an alternative match. PROLOG allows a list (sequence) of objects to be used as a term; a list consists of two variables [*X*|*L*] (the head and the tail, separated by |) on a sequence of constants separated by commas (e.g., [*a, b, c*]) or a mix of variables and constants (e.g., [*a, b*|*L*]). PROLOG provides a number of *procedural predicates*, which are predicates whose true/false values are evaluated directly by the system, but not by matching. A simple example of such predicates is, say, *multiply*. The predicate takes three terms as its arguments; it is true if the result of multiplying the first and second arguments is the third argument. For example *multiply(2,3,6)* is true. If any arguments are variables, PROLOG produces different sets of instantiations such that the predicate can be evaluated as true. For instance given the predicate *multiply(A,B,6)*, variables *A* and *B* can be instantiated to (1,6), (6,1), (2,3), (3,2), respectively. Note that functions are not allowed to be a term in PROLOG, since functions can be well implemented as procedural predicates.

Example 7.5. Assume that the database of a PROLOG program has the following facts about the major cities in California and New Jersey:

```
american(united_states).
partof(california,united_states).
partof(los_angles,california).
```

partof(san_francisco,california).
partof(new_jersey,united_states).
partof(newark,new_jersey)
distance(los_angeles,san_francisco,360)
distance(san_francisco,los_angeles,360)
distance(los_angeles,newark,4300).
distance(newark,los_angeles,4300).
distance(san_francisco,newark,4300).
distance(newark,san_francisco,4300).

Also assume that the program contains the following rules:

american(X) :- partof(X,Y), american(Y).

Now consider the question of retrieving all pairs of U.S. (American) cities whose distances are less than or equal to 400 miles:

?- american(X),american(Y),distance(X,Y,D),D<=400.

The execution profile for the preceding query is shown in the table below. Note that a goal that is not defined in the database [e.g., *distance(newark,newark,D)*] is evaluated as false.

american(X)	american(Y)	distance(X,Y,D)	D <= 400
united_states	united_states	F	
united_states	los_angeles	F	
united_states	san_francisco	F	
united_states	newark	F	
united_states	F		
los_angeles	united_states	F	
los_angeles	los_angeles	F	
los_angeles	san_francisco	360	T
los_angeles	newark	4300	F
los_angeles	F		
san_francisco	united_states	F	
san_francisco	los_angeles	360	T
san_francisco	san_francisco	—	
san_francisco	newark	4300	F
san_francisco	F		
newark	united_states	—	
newark	los_angeles	4300	F
newark	san_francisco	4300	F
newark	newark	—	
newark	F		
F			

Example 7.6. The following PROLOG program defines the predicate *dot(A,B,P)*, which computes the inner product *P* of two vectors **A** and **B**. The inner product of two vectors $(a1, \ldots, an)$ and $(b1, \ldots, bn)$ is defined to be the value of $a1b1 + a2b2 + \ldots + an\, bn$.

R1: dot([A1],[B1],P) :- P is A1*B1.
R2: dot([A1|A2],[B1|B2],P) :- P1 is A1*B1, dot(A2,B2,P2), P is P1 + P2.

In the preceding a clause of the form *A is B*C* means the value of *B*C* is assigned to *A*, and a clause of the form *A is B + C* means the value of *B + C* is assigned to *A*. Now consider the goal *dot([3,2,1],[1,2,3])*. The goal is first matched by *R2* (since the head of *R1*, in which the first two arguments are single-element lists, cannot be matched by the goal), thus instantiating *A1* to 3, *B1* to 1, *A2* to [2,1], *B2* to [2,3]:

R21 dot([3|[2,1]],[1|[2,3]],P) :- P1 is 3*1,dot([2,1],[2,3],P2), P is P1 + P2.

The first subgoal *P1 is 3*1* can be evaluated as true directly by PROLOG; thus *P1* is instantiated to 3. The second subgoal *dot([2,1], [3,2],P2)* is matched by *R2* (*R1* cannot match because the first two arguments of the subgoal are not single-element lists), thus instantiating *A1* to 2, *B1* to 2, *A2* to [1], *B2* to [3]:

R22 dot([2|[1]],[2|[3]],P) :- P1 is 2*2, dot([1],[3],P2), P is P1 + P2.

The *P1* can be instantiated directly to 4. The subgoal *dot([1],[3],P2)* can now be matched by *R1*:

R23 dot([1],[3],P) :- P is 1*3.

Therefor the variable *P* in *R23*, which is the variable *P2* in *R22*, is evaluated to 3. *R22* becomes

R22 dot([2|[1]],[2|[3]],P) :- P1 is 2*2, dot([1],[3],3), P is 4 + 3.

The variable *P* is *R22*, which is the variable *P2* in *R21*, is now instantiated to 7. *R21* becomes

R21 dot([3|[2,1]],[1|[2,3]],P) :- P1 is 3*1, dot([2,1],[2,3],7), P is 3 + 7.

Consequently the *P* in *R21* is evaluated to 10, which is the final answer.

7.4. COMPOSE—AN OBJECT-ORIENTED DATABASE ENVIRONMENT

The object-oriented paradigm in database technology is based on the following concepts: class, complex object (aggregation), encapsulation, inheritance, message, and object identity. An *object-oriented database* management system (OODBMS) uses two techniques for performance. Instead of using foreign keys (i.e., those attributes whose values are the keys of other records from other tables) OODBMSs employ embedded pointers to establish data relationships, and rather than assembling aggregates in an ad hoc fashion, they preassemble all composite objects. Current commercial vendor products differ in many ways (e.g., system architecture; defining, storing and manipulating objects; supporting object-oriented paradigm; query language; and other fundamental database technology, such as indexing, clustering, concurrency control and recovery); see Refs. 9, and 11 for a comprehensive survey.

This section first introduces the essences of a relational query language, then it discusses an object-oriented database system that provides a declarative query language. A survey of object-oriented query languages that have been proposed is found in Ref. 12.

7.4.1. Relational Query Languages

A relational database consists of a number of tables (relations); a table consists of a number of rows (tuples), each tuple consists of a number of columns (attributes), and the value of each attribute is defined by a domain (type). In a simplified version of a relational query language (QUEL),[13] a query is presented in the following form without losing generality:

```
variable-specifier
. . .
variable-specifier
command
[where qualification]
```

A variable specifier declares a tuple variable:

```
range of ⟨variable-id⟩ is ⟨relation-id⟩
```

A variable declared in this form is called a *range variable* whose domain is ⟨*relation-id*⟩. Any attribute of the tuple variable is referenced by ⟨*variable-name*⟩.⟨*attribute-name*⟩.

A command is composed of the name of the command and its associated arguments; an argument can be a constant, a range variable, or an attribute of a range variable. The command can be one of the following:

- *retrieve(argument . . . argument):* Retrieves values of the arguments, where each argument is an arithmetic expression defined recursively as follows:
    —An attribute of a variable whose domain is *integer* or *float* is an arithmetic expression.
    —An integer constant or a float constant is an arithmetic expression.
    —If a and b are arithmetic expressions, then $a + b$, $a - b$, $a * b$, and a/b are arithmetic expressions.
    —If a is an arithmetic expression then (a) is an expression.

In the preceding we assume that type conversions and operator precedences are handled/defined in the same way as in c.

- *append:⟨relation-id⟩* (⟨*variable-id*⟩): Appends the value of the variable ⟨*variable-id*⟩ to the relation whose name is ⟨*relation-id*⟩.

- *delete:⟨relation-id⟩*(⟨*variable-id*⟩): Deletes any tuple whose value matches the instantiated value of the variable ⟨*variable-id*⟩.

- *replace:⟨relation-id⟩* (⟨*variable-id1*⟩,⟨*variable-id2*⟩): Replaces any tuple whose value matches the value of the first variable with the value of the second variable in the relation ⟨*relation-id*⟩.

- *quit:* Terminates the execution of the query interpreter.

A *qualification* is defined recursively as follows:

- A constant, an attribute of a variable, or an arithmetic expression is a term. A string constant is expressed in the form of string.

- A comparison between two terms is a qualification; it is expressed as (*term op term*), where *op* can be $==$, $\neq$, $<$, $>$, $\leq$, or $\geq$.

- An assignment operation between two terms is a qualification; it is expressed as (*term = term*) (i.e., the value of the second term is assigned to the first term). An assignment is always evaluated as true.

- If a and b are qualifications, then (*a and b*) and (*a or b*) are qualifications.

As an example, assume the following relations are defined.

7.4.1.1. Schema Definitions

In the following, each tuple in the class *emp* has the following attributes: *name* (a character string of length 12), *age* (an integer of length 3), *salary* (a floating point number of length 10), *dname* (a character string of length 10 designating the name of the department in which the employee works), and *manager* (a character string of length 12 designating the name of the manager for which the employee works). Among these the attribute *name* is chosen as the key attribute. The other relations are self-explanatory.

1. define relation emp (name:string:l2,age:int:3, salary:float:10, dname:string:10, manager:string:l2) key:name go
2. define relation dept (dname:string:10,floor:int:2,sales:int:12) key:dname go
3. define relation sball (ename:string:12,position:string:12) go

7.4.1.2. Sample Data

emp

name	age	salary	dname	manager
mike	29	150000.00	shoe	enda
sally	42	87750.00	toy	ted
georgia	25	10000.00	—	—
ted	0	26157.80	toy	melcom
enda	25	20000.00	shoe	malcom
malcom	50	280000.00	admin	—

dept

dname	floor	sales
shoe	1	2500
toy	2	1500
admin	5	0

sball

ename	position
mike	pitcher
ted	shortstop
georgia	centerfield
georgia	pitcher

The following are examples of some queries that may be made to the database.

7.4.1.3. Example Queries

- Find the yearly salary and daily salary for Mike.

```
range of t is emp
retrieve (t.salary,t.salary/12,t.salary/250)
where (t.name == "mike") go
```

- Find the age of the pitchers on the softball team.

```
range of s is sball
range of e is emp
retrieve (e.age)
where (s.position == "pitcher") and (e.name == s.en-
ame) go
```

- Find the names of the employees who work on the first floor.

```
range of d is dept
range of e is emp
retrieve (e.name)
where (e.name == d.dname) and (d.floor == 1) go
```

- Find the floors that shortstops work on.

```
range of d is dept
range of e is emp
range of s is sball
retrieve (e.name,d.floor)
where d.dname == e.dname) and (e.name == s.ename) and
(s.position == "shortstop") go
```

- Find all employees who are paid more than their managers.

```
range of t is emp
range of e is emp
retrieve (e.name)
where (t.name == e.manager) and (e.salary > t.salary)
go
```

- Append an employee to the class *emp*. The name of the employee is *tom*, the age of *tom* is 29, his salary is 37,000.00, his department is *shoe*, and his manager is Mike.

```
range of t is emp
```

```
   append:emp(t)
   where (t.name = "tom") and (t.age = 29) and fas(t.sal-
ary = 37000.00)
   and (t.dname = "shoe") and (t.manager = "mike")) go
```

- Append all employees who work in the administration department to the softball relation, and the position they play is pitcher.

```
range of t is emp
range of s is sball
append:sball(s)
where (t.dname == "admin") and (t.name == s.name) and
("pitcher" == s.position) go
```

- Fire Georgia.

```
range of e is emp
delete:emp(s)
where (e.name == "georgia") go
```

- Give a 15% raise to Mike.

```
range of t is emp
range s is emp
replace:emp(t,s)
where (t.name == "mike") and (s.salary = t.salary *
1.15) and (s.name =
t.name) and (s.dname = t.dname) and (s.age = t.age) and
(s.manager = t.manager) go
```

7.4.2. COMPOSE

Unlike a relational database, where all information has to be stored and accessed as tables, an object-oriented database system can support an object-oriented application system directly and effectively by allowing objects to be stored and accessed as a set of interconnected records. Consequently accessing a complex object is accomplished in an object-oriented database without joining several tables as a relational database requires. This capability has proved to be useful in such complex applications as CAD, CAM, and CASE.

In addition to the features just discussed, the COMPOSE object-oriented database[14] provides the following capabilities:

- In COMPOSE objects can be selectively retrieved based on some conditions. Unlike conventional databases where conditions are restricted to simple comparisons (such as $=$, $<$, $>$), a condition in COMPOSE can be any logical property of an object or among a set of objects. Such conditions can be defined by the user and added to the environment any time.

- In conventional databases only a few operations (such as append, delete, or print) can be applied to objects (tuples). In COMPOSE however any user-defined operations can be applied to objects. As conditions, such operations can be added to the environment dynamically. This is particularly important for multimedia applications: Drivers for different media can be included as operations (conditions) dynamically to present objects in different forms (such as voice, graphics, and images).

Consider a set of object classes and a set of objects in these classes. The following is a summary of the COMPOSE facilities for specifying queries, integrity constraints, triggers, and views.

7.4.2.1. Queries

A COMPOSE query is presented in the following form, which retrieves all possible instantiations (for the variables declared) that satisfy the qualifications and apply the identified operation to the qualified objects.

```
variable-specifier
. . . /* declare the variables to be used by the query
*/
variable-specifier
command /* retrieval/storage operation based upon
some conditions */
[where logical_expression]
```

A variable specifier takes the following form:

1. range of ⟨variable-id⟩ is ⟨class-id⟩
2. var ⟨variable-id⟩ is ⟨class-id⟩

If a ⟨*class-id*⟩ is used, a variable declared in Form (1) is called a *range variable;* a variable declared in Form (2) is called a *temporary variable.* Either way a *variable* ⟨*variable-id*⟩ is declared with domain ⟨*class-id*⟩. In general all possible values of a range variable are enumerated in the query evaluation process, whereas temporary variables are typically used to store results produced by some functions. Any attribute ⟨*attribute-id*⟩ of a variable ⟨*variable-id*⟩ can be accessed by ⟨*variable-id*⟩.⟨*attribute-id*⟩. If the attribute itself is another object, access to any of its attributes (say, ⟨*attribute-id'*⟩ is accomplished via the path ⟨*variable-id*⟩.⟨*attribute-id*⟩.⟨*attribute-id'*⟩. The same rule can be applied as long as an attribute (of an object) is an object.

A command is composed of the name of the command and its associated arguments (a constant, a range or temporary variable, or an attribute path). A command can be one of the following:

- *retrieve(argument, . . . , argument):* Retrieves the values of the arguments; a constant cannot be used.

- *append:⟨class-id⟩(⟨variable-id⟩):* Appends the value of variable ⟨*variable-id*⟩ to class ⟨*class-id*⟩; ⟨*variable-id*⟩ must be a temporary variable.

- *delete:⟨class-id⟩(⟨variable-id⟩):* Deletes any object from class ⟨*class-id*⟩ whose value matches the value of variable ⟨*variable-id*⟩; ⟨*variable-id*⟩ is a range variable.

- *replace:⟨class-id⟩ (⟨variable-id1⟩,⟨variable-id2⟩):* Replaces any object whose value matches the value of the first variable with the value of the second variable in class ⟨*class-id*⟩; the second variable must be a temporary variable, and the first variable must be a range variable.

- Any function call with its arguments.

Logical_expression is any c++ logical expression.

> **Example 7.7.** Assume that two objects classes are defined: *vertex* and *rect*. Each *rect* object is defined in terms of four vertices, and each *vertex* object is characterized by its two coordinates:
>
> ```
> class vertex {key char *vid; int x,y}
> class rect {key char *rid; vertex vi,vii,viii,viv}
> ```
>
> where the keyword *key* precedes the attribute that is the key of a class. Further assume that he following functions are defined:
>
> - *int rect::contain (rect p):* Returns 1 if the target object (i.e., *self*) contains the argument rectangle *p* and returns 0 otherwise.
> - *int rect::size (void):* Returns the size of the target object.
>
> Based on the preceding, the following query retrieves rectangles contained in Rectangle C with sizes greater than 4.
>
> ```
> range of t is rect
> range of s is rect
> var temp is int
>
> retrieve (s.rid)
> ```

```
where (t.name == "C") && t.contain(s) && ((temp =
s.size) > 4)
```

If this query were expressed in QUEL (relational), it would be much lengthier and require specific knowledge about how to perform the query:

```
range of r is rectangle
range of s is rectangle
range of r1 is vertex
range of r2 is vertex
range of r3 is vertex
range of r4 is vertex
range of s1 is vertex
range of s2 is vertex
range of s3 is vertex
range of s4 is vertex
retrieve(r.name)
where
s.name = "C" and
s.vertex1 = s1.name and s.vertex2 = s2.name and
s.vertex3 = s3.name and
s.vertex4 = s4.name and r.vertex1 = r1.name and
r.vertex2 = r2.name and
r.vertex3 = r3.name and r.vertex4 = r4.name and
((r2.x - r1.x) * (r2.y - r3.y) > 4) and
r1.x > s1.x and r1.y < s1.y and r2.x > s2.x and
r2.y < s2.6 and
r3.x > s3.x and r3.y < s3.y and r4.x > s4.x and
r4.y < s4.y
```

7.4.2.2. Integrity Constraints

An integrity constraint in COMPOSE is specified as:

```
variable-specifier
. . .
variable-specifier
logical_expression => logical_expression
```

An integrity constraint presented in the preceding form asserts that all possible instantiations (for the variables declared) that satisfy the logical expression on the left-hand side of => must satisfy the logical expression on the right-hand side as well.

7.4.2.3. Triggers

A trigger in COMPOSE is specified as:

```
variable-specifier
. . .
variable-specifier
logical_expression => Operations
```

A trigger presented in this form asserts that for all possible instantiations (for variables declared) that satisfy the logical expression, the associated operation is performed.

7.4.2.4. Views

The command to create a view is

```
create view ⟨class-id⟩:⟨variable-id⟩ (⟨attribute-
id⟩:⟨class-id⟩[width], . . . ,
⟨attribute-id⟩:⟨class-id⟩[width]) body
```

where *body* is in the form of:

```
variable-specifier
. . .
variable-specifier
logical_expression
```

As in queries, variables are classified as range variables and temporary variables, which can be declared in an arbitrary order. The format for a variable specifier is the same as that for queries. Let us assume that a view is declared in the following form:

```
create view ⟨class-id⟩ : ⟨variable-id⟩
range of ⟨variable-id-1⟩ is ⟨class-id-1⟩
. . .
range of ⟨variable-id-k⟩ is ⟨class-id-k⟩
var ⟨variable-id-(k + 1)⟩ is ⟨class-id-(k + 1)⟩
. . .
var ⟨variable-id-(k + r)⟩ is ⟨class-id-(k + r)⟩
logical_expression
```

The semantics of the preceding definition follows:

```
⟨variable-id⟩ is in ⟨class-id⟩ IF
for every ⟨variable-id-1⟩ in ⟨class-id-1⟩
. . .
for every ⟨variable-id-k⟩ in ⟨class-id-k⟩)
there exists a ⟨variable-id-(k + 1)⟩ in ⟨class-id-(k
+ 1)⟩
. . .
there exists a ⟨variable-id-(k + r)⟩ in ⟨class-id-(k
+ r)⟩
SUCH THAT
logical_expression is true.
```

Example 7.8. In control theory a linear system is an automaton characterized by a set of inputs, states, and outputs. The system takes the inputs, adjusts the states, and produces the outputs. The system is linear because subsequent states can be computed as a linear function (by means of a state transition matrix) of its current states and the inputs. Consequently the class *linear_system* is characterized by the following attributes: *id, state_transition_matrix, input_matrix* and *output _matrix*. In control theory a linear system can often be visualized as a block diagram that consists of a box designating the system, a set of input wires, output wires, and feedback wires that carry some weights whose values are determined by the state transition matrix.

To produce a block diagram of each linear system object, the following view *linear_system$_g$* can be defined:

```
/* produce a geometric object */
create view linear_system_g s (id:string,
b:block_diagram)
range of t is linear_system
sas(t.id,s.id) and c_transform(t,s.b)
```

where *c_transform (t,s.b)* is a method for generating a block diagram object *t.b* (which consists of a set of block and arc objects in symbolic form) from a linear system object *s*.

To display a linear system (or a set of linear systems) represented as a block diagram based on some properties of the block diagram, the following query can be used

```
var w is window
range of s is linear_system_g
```

```
display_view(s,w)
where
qualifications for s and w
```

where *display_view(s,w)* draws the view for block diagram *s* into a window *w*. Figure 7.1 shows an example. The transformation from a linear system into a block diagram is transparent, so the user assumes that the view actually exists. If the user is aware of the existence of the transformation procedure and wants to display a linear system (or a set of linear systems) based on some of its generic properties, the following query is valid as well:

```
var w is window
range of t is linear_system
var s is block_diagram
display_view(s,w)
where
c_transform(t,s) and qualifications for t and w
```

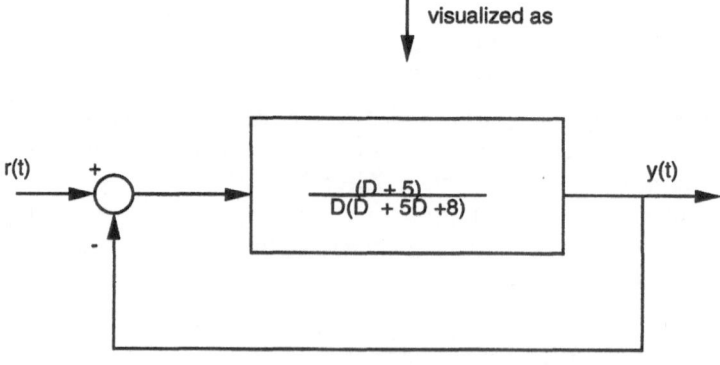

Figure 7.1. Visualization of a linear system.

PROBLEMS

1. Design a COMPOSE database that supports graphical applications. For example the database can contain a number of geometric types (e.g., circle, triangle, square) and a number of methods associated with geometric types (e.g., intersect, tangent). Write at least three queries that contain some methods for the database.

2. Design a COMPOSE database that supports multimedia applications. For example the database can contain a number of media types (e.g., image and voice) and a number of methods associated with such types (e.g., play, record, display). Write at least three queries that contain some methods for the database.

3. For the geometric types defined in Problem 1, write a simple c++ program that solves the three queries developed for that problem using the set constructs described in Section 7.2.

4. For the multimedia types defined in Problem 1, write a simple c++ program that solves the three queries developed for that problem using the set constructs described in Section 7.2.

5. Based on the answers to Problems 3 and 4, compare the solutions implemented as methods and as programs. Is it true that any object-oriented query can be answered by a program? If yes, what are the disadvantages associated with this approach?

6. Rewrite the SETL program in Example 7.1 in c++ with the set-oriented constructs as described in Section 7.2.

7. Enumerate changes that can be made to the scenario in Example 7.3 and discuss the impact created by each possible change to the c++ program given. Do the same for the c program given.

8. Combine extensions made to c++ in this chapter and Problem 5.3. Revise the c++ program in Example 4.3 and discuss the advantages of the extensions.

9. Consider the framework of a deductive database discussed in Section 3.2. Discuss the possibility of a declarative concurrent-programming system so that concurrent programs are written without communication/synchronization details. (*Hint:* Can communication/synchronization requirements be specified as constraints?)

10. Define a predicate, *equal_ab(L)*, in PROLOG, where *equal_a_b(L)* is true if *L* contains an equal number of *a* and *b*.

11. Define a predicate, *min(L,M)*, in PROLOG, where *min(L,M)* is true if *M* is the smallest element of the list *L*.

REFERENCES

1. Kennedy, K., and Schwartz, J. *Computers and Mathematics with Applications* **1**, 97–119 (1975).
2. Schonberg, E., Schwartz, J., and Sharir, M. *ACM Transactions on Programming Languages and Systems* **3**:2, 126–143 (Apr. 1981).
3. Feather, M. S., and London, P. E. *Science of Computer Programming* **2**, 91–131 (1982).
4. Green, C., and Westfold, S. *Machine Intelligence* **10**, 339–359 (1982).
5. Cooke, D. E., "An executable high-level language based upon multisets" (Dept. of Computer Science, University of Texas at El Paso, 1994).
6. Banatre, J. P., and Le Matayer, D. *Communications of ACM* **36-1**, 98–111 (Jan. 1993).
7. Freudenberger, S., Schwartz, J., and Sharir, M. *ACM Transactions on Programming Languages and Systems* **5**:1, 26–45 (1983).
8. Cheng, T., Lock, E., and Prywes, N. *IEEE Transactions on Software Engineering* **10**:5, 552–563 (Sept. 1984).
9. *Communications of the ACM,* **34**:10, Oct. 1991.
10. Warren, D. H. D., Pereira, L. M., and Pereira, F. "PROLOG—the language and its implementation compared with LISP." *Symposium on AI and Programming Languages, ACM SIGPLAN* **12**:8 (1977) 109–115.
11. Everest, G. C., and Hanna, M. S. "Survey of object-oriented database management systems," Carlson School of Management, University of Minnesota, Minneapolis, 1992).
12. Bertino, E., Negri, M., Pelagatti, G., and Sbattella, L. *IEEE Transactions on Data and Knowledge Engineering* **4.3**, 223–237 (June 1992).
13. Stonebraker, M., Wong, E., Kreps, P., and Held, G. D. *ACM Transactions on Database Systems* **1**:3, 189–222 (Sept. 1976).
14. Sheu, P.C.-Y., *COMPOSE user's guide* (Visual/Interactive Data Engineering Laboratory, University of California, Irvine, CA, 1996).

Automatic Program Synthesis and Reuse

Given a requirements specification, the goal of automatic program synthesis is to derive, or synthesize, an executable program whose functionalities meet the specification. If we are willing to sacrifice performance, a requirements specification may already be executable. For example a requirements specification in first-order logic can be proved by a theorem prover given a standard set of axioms of mathematics, where the proof procedure essentially constructs a program. However this process could be very inefficient. Automatic program synthesis with reasonable efficiency has been the core of software engineering for a long time.[1,2] Unfortunately most of the approaches proposed are restrictive because they work only for small examples. The major difficulty of program synthesis lies in the fact that it has to derive the control structure of a program—hopefully efficient—a task that is difficult even for a programmer.

Existing approaches to automatic program synthesis are classified as deductive synthesis (Section 8.1) or program transformation (Section 8.2). In a deductive program synthesis system, program functionalities are first specified in logic. A proof is then attempted from the input specifications to the required output specifications, based on some available axioms. If such a proof exists, a program can then be built based on the proof process. In a program transformation system, a very high-level and possibly inefficient program specification is transformed with a set of transformation rules into a more efficient executable program.

An area closely related to automatic programming is software reuse. Chapter 8 also presents the idea of program abstraction (Section 8.3), which employs highly parametrized program templates that can be instantiated from applications, and an approach applicable to instantiating abstract algorithms automatically (Section 8.4).

8.1. DEDUCTIVE PROGRAM SYNTHESIS

In a deductive program synthesis system, program functionality can be expressed in the following form:

program_name(X) <- find Y such that q(X,Y) where p (X)

where $p(X)$ asserts the properties of the input variable X (this can be extended to a set of variables) and $q(X,Y)$ asserts the properties of the output variable Y this can be extended to a set of output variables) and its relationship with X. Examples 8.1 and 8.2 are taken from Ref. 3.

Example 8.1. The following assertions specify a program that computes the square root of a nonnegative integer:

```
sqrt(N) <= find Z such that
    integer(Z) and Z² ≤ N ≤ (Z + 1)²
    where integer(N) and 0 ≤ N
```

Example 8.2. The following assertions specify a program that sorts a list:

```
sort(L) <= find Z such that
    ordered(Z) and permutation(L,Z)
    where islist(L)
```

Now given a specification

program_name(X) <- find Y such that q(X,Y) where p(X)

the deductive synthesis system tries to establish a proof for the theorem

$$(\forall X)(\exists Y)(p(X) \rightarrow q(X,Y))$$

The proof of the theorem must be constructive; i.e., it must show how to obtain the output(s) from the input(s). To do this various rules can be expressed and used to guide the proof process. Reference 3 uses a basic structure called *sequent,* which is a table consisting of multiple records of the form:

[assertions: . . . ; goals: . . . ; outputs: . . .]

We call each of these records a sequent record. It consists of three logical sentences: assertions, goals, and outputs. Consider a sequent consisting of the following records:

```
[assertions: A1(a,X); goals: null; outputs: t1(a,X)]
 . . .
[assertions: Am(a,X); goals: null; outputs: tm(a,X)]
[assertions: null; goals: G1(a,X); outputs: t1(a,X)]
 . . .
```

```
[assertions:null;goals:Gn(a,X);outputs:tn(a,X)]
```

The following is its semantics:

```
if for all X, A1(a,X) and
  . . .
  for all X, Am(a,X) then
    for some X, G1(a,X) or
    . . .
    for some X, Gn(a,X)
```

Initially the system has one sequent record for the program to be constructed: The assertion is $p(X)$, the goal is $q(X,Y)$, and the output is Y and some generic sequents common to all programs. As the proof proceeds, additional sequents are produced based on some rules. Since the objective is to prove that *assertions -> goals* (i.e., *~assertions $\bigvee$ goals*), this process continues until a sequent record whose *goals* attribute becomes true or whose *assertions* attribute becomes false. At this point the *outputs* attribute becomes the program. The following sections summarize rules that can be applied to produce new sequents. The logical foundation of such rules can be found in Ref. 3.

8.1.1. Splitting Rules

- *And-Split Rule:* A sequent record of the form [*assertions: F and G; goals: null; outputs: t*] can produce two sequents (or be split into two sequents): [*assertions: F; goals: null; outputs: t*] and [*assertions: G; goals: null; outputs: t*]

- *Or-Split Rule:* A sequent record of the form [*assertions: F or G; goals: null; outputs: t*] can produce two sequents (or be split into two sequents): [*assertions: null; goals: F; outputs: t*] and [*assertions: null; goals: G; outputs: t*]

- *If-Split Rule:* A sequent record of the form [*assertions: null; goals: if F then G; outputs: t*] can produce two sequents (or be split into two sequents): [*assertions: F; goals: null; outputs: t*] and [*assertions: null; goals: G, outputs: t*]

8.1.2. Transformation Rules

Transformation rules are presented in the form of:

$$r => s \text{ if } P$$

which means an occurrence of the logical expression r can be replaced by an equivalent expression s provided that the condition P is true. For example the following rule:

$$X + 0 => X \text{ if number(X)}$$

states that any occurrence of the expression $X + 0$ can be replaced by the expression X if X is a number. The general forms of the sequents that can be produced from a transformation rule are the following:

- A sequent record of the form: [*assertions: F; goals: null; outputs: t*] can produce the following sequent record (or be transformed into the following sequent record) from the transformation rule $r => s$ *if P*: [*assertions: if Pθ then Fθ(r$\theta \leftarrow$ sθ); goals: null; outputs: tθ*], where the notation $F\theta(r\theta \leftarrow s\theta)$ *stands for "Apply the unifier θ to F and replace all instances of r θ with s θ."*

- A sequent record of the form: [*assertions: null; goals: F; outputs: t*] can produce the following sequent record (or be transformed into the following sequent record) from the transformation rule $r => s$ *if P*: [*assertions:null; goals: Pθ and Fθ(r$\theta \leftarrow$ sθ); outputs: tθ*].

8.1.3. Resolution Rules

Assuming that (1) the sequent record contains two assertions and/or goals F and G, (2) P_1 and P_2 are subsentences of F and G, respectively, not within the scope of any quantifier, and (3) there exists a unifier θ for P_1 and P_2 so that $P_1\theta$ and $P_2\theta$ are identical, the following rules hold:

- *The AA-Resolution Rule:* Two sequents of the form: [*assertions: F; goals: null; outputs: null*] and [*assertions: G; goals: null; outputs: null*] can be resolved and produces the new sequent record: [*assertions: Fθ(P$_1$ $\theta \leftarrow$ true) or Gθ(P$_2$ $\theta \leftarrow$ false); goals: null; outputs: null*].

- *The GG-Resolution Rule:* Two sequents of the form: [*assertions: null; goals: F; outputs: null*] and [*assertions: null; goals: G; outputs: null*] can be resolved and produces the new sequent record: [*assertions: null; goals: Fθ(P$_1$ $\theta \leftarrow$ true) and Gθ(P$_2$ $\theta \leftarrow$ false); outputs: null*].

- *The GA-Resolution Rule:* Two sequents of the form: [*assertions: null; goals: F; outputs: null*] and [*assertions: G; goals: null; outputs: null*] can be resolved and produces the new sequent record: [*assertions: null; goals: Fθ(P$_1$ $\theta \leftarrow$ true) and not(Gθ(P$_2$ $\theta \leftarrow$ false)); outputs: null*].

- *The AG-Resolution Rule:* Two sequents of the form: [*assertions: F; goals: null; outputs: null*] and [*assertions: null; goals: G; outputs: null*] can be resolved and produces the new sequent record: [*assertions: null; goals: not(F θ(P_1 θ ← true)) and G θ(P_2 θ ← false); outputs: null*].

For the preceding rules if only F or G has an output expression t, then the new sequent record has $t\ \theta$ as its output expression. If F has t_1 as its output expression and G has t_2 as its output expression, then the new sequent record has *if $P_1\ \theta$ then $r_1\ \theta$ else $t_2\ \theta$* as its output expression.

8.1.4. Induction Hypothesis

Given the sequent record: [*assertions: p(A); goals: r(A,Z); outputs: Z*], a new assertion, namely, the induction hypothesis, can always be added: [*assertions: if $U <w\ a$ then if $p(U)$ then $r(U,f(U))$; goals: null; outputs: null*], where $<w$ is any ordering relation that is well defined.

Example 8.3, given in Ref. 3, illustrates the program synthesis process.

Example 8.3. Consider the problem of constructing two programs *div(I,J)* and *rem(I,J)* which finds the integer quotient of dividing a nonnegative integer *I* by a positive integer *J*. A specification for the problem can be established as:

```
(div(I,J),rem(I,J)) <= find (Y,Z) such that
        I = YJ + Z and 0 ≤ Z and Z < J
        where 0 ≤ I and 0 < J
```

The two programs can be derived as follows:

1. Establish initial sequents:

   [assertions: 0 ≤ I and 0 < J; goals; null; outputs: null] (#1)
   [assertions: null; goals: I = YJ + Z and 0 ≤ Z and Z < J; outputs: (div(I,J) = Y, rem(I,J) = Z)] (#2)

2. Assume the following generic sequents:

   [assertions: U = U; goals: null; outputs: null] (#3)
   [assertions: U ≤ V or V < U; goals: null; outputs: null] (#4)

3. Apply the *And-Split* rule to #1 to obtain

   [assertions: 0 ≤ I; goals: null; outputs: null] (#5)
   [assertions: 0 < J; goals: null; outputs: null] (#6)

4. Assume the following transformation rules (TR3) are available:

   0V => 0 (TR#1)
   (U + 1)V => <+ V (TR#2)
   0 + V => V (TR#3)

5. Apply TR#1 to *YJ* in #2 with the unifier: $\theta = (0/Y,J/Z)$ produces the following sequent record:

   [assertions: null; goals: I = 0 + Z and 0 ≤ Z and Z < J; outputs: (div(I,J) = 0, rem(I,J) = Z)] (#7)

6. Apply TR#3 to #7 to obtain

   [assertions: null; goals: I = Z and 0 ≤ Z and Z < J; outputs: (div(I,J) = 0, rem(I,J) = Z)] (#8)

7. Apply the *GA-Resolution Rule* to #8 and #3 with $\theta = (I/U,I/Z)$, $P_1 = (I = Z)$, and $P_2 = (U = U)$, the following sequent record can be produced

   [assertions: null; goals: 0 ≤ I and I < J; outputs: (div(I,J) = 0, rem(I,J) = I)]
   (#9)

8. Apply the *GA-Resolution Rule* to #9 and #5 with θ being the identity unification and $P_1 = P_2 = (0 ≤ I)$, the following sequent record can be produced

   [assertions: null; goals: I < J; outputs: (div(I,J) = 0, rem(I,J) = I)] (#10)

9. Apply TR#2 to #2 with $\theta = ((Y_1 + 1)/Y,Y_1/U,J/V)$, the following can be obtained

   [assertions: null; goals: I = Y$_1$J + J + Z and 0 ≤ Z and Z < J; outputs: (div(I,J) = Y$_1$ + I, rem(I,J) = Z)] (#11)

10. Assume the following transformation rule is available:

    U = V + W => U − V = W (TR#4)

11. Apply TR#4 to #11 to produce

    [assertions: null; goals: I − J = Y$_1$J + Z and 0 ≤ Z and Z < J; outputs: (div(I,J) = Y$_1$ + 1, rem(I,J) = Z)] (#12)

12. Form the following induction hypothesis based on #2:

    [assertions: if (U_1,U_2) <w (I,J) then if $0 \leq U_1$ and $0 <$ U_2 then $U_1 = div(U_1,U_2)$ U_2 + $rem(U_1,U_2)$ and $0 \leq$ $rem(U_1,U_2)$ and $rem(U_1,U_2) < U_2$] (#13)

13. Apply the *GA-Resolution Rule* to #12 and #13, with $\theta = (I - J/U_1, J/U_2, div(I - J,J)/Y_1, rem(I - J,J)/Z)$, P_1 being $(I - J = Y_1J + Z$ and $0 \leq Z$ and $Z < J)$, and P_2 being $(U_1 = div(U_1,U_2)$ U_2 + $rem(U_1,U_2)$ and $0 \leq rem(U_1,U_2)$ and $rem(U_1,U_2) < U_2)$, the following can be obtained

    [assertions: null; goals: true and not (if $(I - J,J)$ <w (I,J) then if $0 \leq I - J$ and $0 < J$ then false; outputs: $(div(I,J) = div(I - J,J) + 1$, $rem(I,J) = rem(I - J,J)$] (#14)

14. Reduce #14 to the following by the fact that *not(P -> R))* is equivalent to *P and Q and not(R)*:

    [assertions: null; goals: $(I - J,J)$ <w (I,J) and $0 \leq I - J$ and $0 < J$; outputs: $(div(I,J) = div(I - J,J) + I$, $rem(I,J) = rem(I - J,J)$] (#15)

15. Assume the following transformation rule is available:

    (U_1,U_2) <w (V_1,V_2) => true if $U_1 < V_1$ and $0 \leq U_1$ and $0 \leq V_1$ (TR#5)

16. Apply TR#5 to #15 to produce the following:

    [assertions: null; goals: $(I - J,J) < (I,J)$ and $0 \leq I - J$ and $0 \leq I$ and $0 \leq I - J$ and $0 < J$; outputs: $(div(I,J) = div(I - J,J) + 1$, $rem(I,J) = rem(I - J,J)$] (#16)

17. Apply transformation rules and the *GA-Resolution Rule* with #5, #6 and #16 to produce

    [assertions: null; goals: $J \leq I$; outputs: $(div(I,J) = div(I - J,J) + 1$, $rem(I,J) = rem(I - J,J)$] (#17)

18. Apply the *GA-Resolution Rule* to #4 and #17 to obtain

    [assertions: null; goals: not$(I < J)$; outputs: $(div(I,J) = div(I - J,J) + 1$, $rem(I,J) = rem(I-J,J)$] (#18)

19. Apply the *GG-Resolution Rule* to #18 and #10:

    [assertions: null; goals: true; outputs: $(div(I,J) = $ if $I < J$

then 0 else div(I − J,J) + 1, rem(I,J) = if I < J then I else rem(I − J,J)] (#19)

which is the programs sought. Note that conditions are added to the outputs, since both $10 and $18 have output expressions.

Other work on deductive program synthesis is found in Ref. 4. The approach in Example 8.3 attempts to compose a program, based on some available algorithms, with a theorem-proving process. A more drastic approach is to develop a new algorithm completely from scratch.[5,6] Reference 6 proposes a top-down approach for automatic algorithm design based on the divide-and-conquer principle. A divide-and-conquer algorithm can be expressed in its generic form as:

```
f:X = if
  Primitive:X -> Directly_Solve:X;
  ~Primitive:X -> Compose·(id × f)·Decompose:X
fi
```

where f is the function to be designed, *Primitive* stands for a logical function on the inputs variable X, *id* is the identity function that returns whatever is input, and *Compose* and *Decompose* are functions to be determined. (However the function *Decompose* should decompose the input set into smaller subsets, and *Compose* should merge partial answers obtained from solving those subsets). The notion $F{:}X$ is the same as the notation $F(X)$, i.e., applying the function F to the variable X; and the notion $G \times H$ is defined by $G \times H{:}\langle x,y \rangle = \langle G{:}x, H{:}y \rangle$. Finally the notion $G \cdot H$, called the *composition* of G and H, designates the function resulting from applying G to the result of applying H to its argument. Note that we use a variable notation for the functions *Compose, Decompose, Directly_Solve*, and *Primitive;* this means they are themselves variables and their values need to be determined.

As a simple instance of the generic divide-and-conquer algorithm, consider the specification for the algorithm *min* that computes the smallest element from an integer list:

$$\text{min:X = Z such that X} \neq \text{nil -> Z} \in \text{bag:X and Z} \leq \text{bag:X}$$
$$\text{where integer\_list:X = true}$$

Now let *min* be a function that computes the smallest element from an integer list, *min2* a function that computes the smaller element from its two arguments, *rest* a function that removes the first element from its input (list) and returns the remaining list, *first* returns the first element from its input list, and *first_rest:L = $\langle$first:L,rest:L$\rangle$*. Using the following substitutions:

```
~rest/Primitive
first/Directly_Solve
min2/Compose
first_rest/Decompose
```

The generic algorithm becomes

```
min:X = if
  rest:X -> first:X;
  ~rest:X -> min2·(id × min)·first_rest:X
  fi
```

This is a beautiful recursive algorithm that computes the smallest element from an integer list.

The approach proposed in Ref. 6 accomplishes the preceding task as follows.

1. The algorithm chooses a good function to decompose a list; the function *first_rest* naturally stands out.

2. The function *~rest* is chosen to be *Primitive*, since *first_rest* has to return a value to *min* (which is *rest:X*) so that the input specification $X \neq nil$ is satisfied and the else branch of *min* can be meaningfully executed.

3. The algorithm introduces the following new variables:

```
first_rest:X₀ = ⟨X₁,X₂⟩
Id:X₁ = Z₁
min:X₂ = Z₂
Compose:⟨Z₁,Z₂⟩ = Z₀
```

$$\text{first\_rest}:X_0 = \langle X_1, X_2 \rangle$$
$$\text{Id}:X_1 = Z_1$$
$$\text{min}:X_2 = Z_2$$
$$\text{Compose}:\langle Z_1, Z_2 \rangle = Z_0$$

4. The algorithm tries to verify that the output (which is Z_0) of the composite function call

```
Compose · (id × min) · first_rest:X₀
```

and the input to *min* (which is X_0) satisfies the specification of *min*. Obviously this attempt fails, since *Compose* is not known. However the algorithm can derive the output condition for *Compose* during the verification process.

5. Specifically assuming the following are true:

$$\text{first\_rest}:X_0 = \langle X_1, X_2 \rangle \ (\text{i.e.,} \ X_1 = \text{first}:X_0 \ \text{and} \ X_2 = \text{rest}:X_0)$$

$$\text{id}:X_1 = Z_1 \ (\text{i.e.,} \ X_1 = Z_1)$$
$$\text{min}:X_2 = Z_2 \ (\text{i.e.,} \ Z_2 \in \text{bag}:X_2 \ \text{and} \ Z_2 \leq \text{bag}:X_2)$$

the algorithm tries to verify the following specification for *min:*

$$Z_0 \in \text{bag}:X_0 \ \text{and} \ Z_0 \leq \text{bag}:X_0$$

6. The process of deriving output conditions for *Compose* proceeds from the theorem (i.e., the preceding specification) to be proved. First $Z_0 \in bag:X_0$ if $Z_0 = first:X_0$ or $Z_0 \in rest:X_0$. In other words $Z_0 \in bag:X_0$ if $Z_0 = Z_1$ or $Z_0 \in Z_2$ by definition. This means if we can prove that $Z_0 = X_1$ or $Z_0 = X_2$ (note that this is a stronger condition), then we can prove $Z_0 \in bag:X_0$. Now $Z_0 \leq bag:X_0$ if $Z_0 \leq first:X_0$ and $Z_0 \leq bag \cdot rest:X_0$. In other words $Z_0 \leq bag:X_0$ if $Z_0 \leq X_1$ and $Z_0 \leq bag:X_2$ by definition. Also by definition $X_1 = Z_1$ and $Z_2 \leq bag:X_2$. This means that if $Z_0 \leq Z_1$ and $Z_0 \leq Z_2$, then we can prove $Z_0 \leq bag:X_0$.

7. In summary if we have

$$(Z_0 = Z_1 \text{ or } Z_0 = Z_2) \qquad (Z_0 \leq Z_1 \text{ and } Z_0 \leq Z_2)$$

then the specification for *min* can be verified. This can easily be accomplished if we set the preceding conditions to be the output conditions for *Compose*! Thus the following specification can be written

```
Compose:⟨Z₁,Z₂⟩ = Z₀
such that (Z₀ = Z₁ or Z₀ = Z₂) and
  (Z₀ ≤ Z₁ and Z₀ ≤ Z₂)
where integer:Z₁ = true and integer:Z₂ = true
```

A similar approach can be followed to find that the operator *first* satisfies the output conditions of *Directly_Solve*. From the preceding, if a simple algorithm for *min2* can be derived, and it is relatively straightforward according to Ref. 6, the task of designing a divide-and-conquer algorithm for finding the smallest element of an integer list can be accomplished.

8.2. TRANSFORMATIONAL PROGRAM SYNTHESIS

Program transformation includes predefined transformations (e.g., rewriting rules) and program constructions from a high-level specifications to a low-level executable form. As an example of the semantic transformation approach, assuming that associated with an object class *synchronous_cell*, we have an efficient algorithm called *G:shortpath (A,B,P,R)*, which asserts the existence of a path P of length less than or equal to R between two vertices A and B in a circuit G. The property of *shortpath* can be expressed by rewriting a rule of the form LHS $<=$ RHS, which says the clause RHS can be replaced by the clause LHS in a specification (presented in PROLOG syntax).

Rule 1:
G:shortpath(A,B,P,R) $<=$ G:path(A,B,P), G:length(P,L), L $\leq$ R

Finding an electrical path that does not pass through a specific terminal is equivalent to finding a path in a modified circuit that excludes the undesirable terminal from the original circuit. This information can be described as rewriting Rule 2:

Rule 2:
G:remove(C,G'), G':path(A,B,P) <= G:path(A,B,P), ~G:member(C,P)

where *G:remove(C,G')* is a method for removing a terminal *C* from a circuit *G* and the resulting circuit is *G'*.

With the preceding a logic program:

g:path(a,b,P), ~g:member(c,P), g:length(P,L), L ≤ R

can be transformed into the following equivalent program by rewriting Rule 2:

g:remove(c,G'), G':path(a,b,P), G':length(P,L), L ≤ R

The transformed program can be transformed again by rewriting Rule 1:

g:remove(c,G'), G':shortpath(a,b,P,R)

The resulting program is much more efficient than the original program! Note that applying rewritten rules in the transformation process preserves the correctness of the program, i.e., given the same set of inputs, the same set of outputs is produced. Criteria for correctness preservation in a program transformation system are discussed in Ref. 7. A survey of program transformation approaches is found in Refs. 8 and 9.

The program to be transformed is usually written in a *wide-spectrum* language, which contains a mixture of low-level procedures and high-level specifications.[10,11] Existing transformation systems can be further divided into two classes: those that perform transformations automatically[12–15] and those guided by users.[16,17]

One of the major problems with existing automatic program transformation systems is that most of them try to transform a program from scratch; consequently the lack of driving force in a design process can lead only to limited successes in practical applications. Even though some search approaches, based on cost functions, have been employed, global strategies have yet to be integrated effectively.[18]

8.3. PROGRAM ABSTRACTION AND INSTANTIATION

Software reuse is closely related to automatic programming. In Chapter 6 we discussed some programming tools that provide a rich set of generic algorithms from which new applications can easily be built. This feature is particularly enforced in such object-oriented programming languages as c++. In addition to the mechanism that supports inheritance, c++ also supports the concept of *templates*—highly abstract classes for which even the types of some members can be parameterized.

> **Example 8.4.** (Ref. 19) The following is a c++ template that declares a parameterized class *vector*. Note that the type of the attribute *v* is a parameter.

```
template⟨class T⟩ class vector{
  T *v;
  int sz;
public:
  vector (int s);
  T& operator[] (int i);
  int size(void);
  void sort (Vector⟨T⟩ &v)
}
void template⟨class T⟩::sort (Vector⟨T⟩ &v)
{
  unsigned n = v.size();
  int i,j:
  T temp;
  for (i = 0; i < n-1; i++)
  for (j = n-1; i < j; j--)
  {
    if (v[j] < v[j-1])//the operator < has to be
//overloaded for T
    temp = v[j];
    v[j] = v[j-1];
    v[j-1] = temp;
  }
}
```

The concept of parameterizing a type is significant in software reuse, since a template can be written for many possible instantiations. A template function, such as the function *sort* in Example 8.4, is a typical example of the *program schemata* discussed in,[20] which goes beyond templates by attempting to automate the process of abstracting several algorithms similar in structure into an abstract algorithm. For example the following two algorithms P_1 and P_2 can be abstracted to the program schema R based on an analogy with mappings[20]:

```
0 => k <= b
n => lamda <= c
≤ => α <= ≥
z => β <= B[p]
A => δ <= B
where
P₁: begin comment minimum-value program
  type n,i ∈ N, z ∈ R, A ∈ [0:n] -> R
  B₂: assert true
  (z,i) := (A[0],0)
  loop L₂: assert z ≤ A[0:i], z ∈ A[0:i]
    until i = n
    i := i + 1
    if A[i] < z then z := A[i] fi
    repeat
E₂: assert z ≤ A[0:n], z ∈ A[0:n]
end
P₂: begin comment maximum-position program
  type b,c,p,j ∈ Z, B ∈ [b:c] -> σ*
  B₂: assert b ≤ c
  (p,j) := (c,c)
  loop L₂: assert B[p] ≥ B[j:c], p ∈ [j:c]
    until j ≠ b
    j := j - 1
    if B[j] < B[p] then p := j fi
    repeat
  E₂: assert B[p] ≤ B[b:c], p ∈ [b:c]
end
R: begin comment maximum-position program
  type i,k,lamda ∈ Z, β ∈ T,
    δ ∈ [k:lamda] -> T, α ∈ T × T -> B
  B₂: assert k ≤ lamda, α(u,u),
    α(w,u) ∧ ~α(w,u) -> α(v,u)
    (β,i) := (δ(k),k)
  loop L₂: assert α(β,δk:i])
      assert β ∈ δ[k:i])
    until i = lamda
    i := i + 1
if ~α(β,δ[i]) then β = δ[i] fi
  repeat
  E₂: assert α(β,δ[k:lamda]),
      assert β ∈ δ[k:lamda]
end
```

The reverse of the program abstraction program is called the *program instantiation problem*. An abstract program schema can be instantiated by substituting the symbols used. For example with the set of substitutions π, the program schema R can be instantiated to the program P_3:

```
π:
  k => 1
  lamda => 100
  α(β,δ[u]) => odd(u) -> f(m) ≤ f(u)
P₃: begin comment function minimum program
  type i,m ∈ N, f ∈ N -> R
  B₂: assert true
  (m,i) := (1,1)
  loop L₂: assert (∀ ∈ [1:i])(odd(u) -> f(m) ≤ f(u))
    until i = 100
    i := i + 1
    if odd(i) ∧ f(m) > f(i) then m := i fi
    repeat
  E₂: assert(∀ ∈ [1:100])(odd(u) -> f(m) ≤ f(u))
  end
```

8.4. AUTOMATIC SOFTWARE REUSE

Software reuse has been a major objective of modern programming systems.[21-23] Research on software reuse has focused primarily on building software libraries so that library modules can be reused either directly[24-26] or through some transformations.[14,15]

A critical problem associated with software reuse is that given the specifications of two problems, how does a developer determine if the solution (program) for one can be instantiated and reused to solve the second. This problem is quite practical and severe. For example a Smalltalk programmer must select the best program from 5000 messages (or 249 classes) without semantic-based tools, guided only by very thick manuals. Obviously a programmer cannot keep all the classes and their message protocols in mind. Most solutions to this problem are based on some form, indices, or catalogs.[27,28] However, these are not fully automatic.

A simple solution to the problem of mapping abstract algorithms to application algorithms automatically follows:

- Construct abstract object classes and their associated methods at the object level.

- Compare the application with the abstract classes and their associated methods; if a match can be identified, instantiate those abstract algorithms whose functionalities can be matched.

We consider a library of algorithms to be a collection of useful methods presented in an object-oriented logic system as described in Chapter 3. To be instantiated by most applications these algorithms should be as abstract as possible. As an example we define the abstract class *w_graph* (weighted_graph) and some methods that implement efficient graph-based algorithms as follows*:

```
class(node)
class(edge,v1:node,v2:node,w:float)
class(w_graph,ns:set_of_node,es:set_of_edge)
w_graph:method(w_path,P:set_of
_edge,A:node,B:node,W:float)
-------------------------------------------------
G.w_path(P,A,B,W) <- (∃ E)
member_of(E,G.es), (E.v1 = A), (E.v2 = B), (P =
[E]), (W = E.w).
G.w_path(P,A,B,W) <- (∃ E)(∃ P 1)(∃ W1)
member_of(E,G.es), (E.v1 = A), set_of_edge(P1),
float(W1),
G:w_path(P1,E.v2,B,W1), (W = E.w + W1), (P = [E|P1])
G.shortest_path(P:set_of
_edge,A:node,B:node,W:float) <-
G:w_path(P,A,B,W),
~((∃ P1)(∃ W1) set_of_flight(P1),
float(W1), G:w_path(P1,A,B,W1), (W1 < W)))
```

If we compare the functionality of the method *shortest_path* and the functionality of the method *cheapest_connection* described in Chapter 3 (p. 44), we find that the following terms syntactically correspond to each other:

vertex(V)	*city(C)*
edge(E)	*flight(F)*
w_graph(G)	*airline(A)*
G.path(P,A,B,W)	*A.connection(C,S,T,F)*
G.shortest	*A.cheapest*
_path(P,A,B,W)	*_connection(C,S,T,F)*

---

*In the remainder of Chapter 8, for clarity we use the notation *c:m(p1:d1, . . . , pn:dn)* in place of *c:m(p1, . . . , pn)* when the functionality of the method is given.

In conventional unification algorithms, two predicates with different predicate heads cannot be unified. However we know that the *shortest_path* algorithm in class *w_graph* can be used to find for instance the cheapest connection in the class *airline* by properly instantiating the variables in the *shortest_path* algorithm with those in the airline reservation system. This is an example of matching with analogy[4,29]; to perform this we need an *analogical* unification process. This can be accomplished by extending the object unification algorithm to include second order. However a second-order unification algorithm considers only the number of arguments when two predicates are matched; as a consequence some random substitutions may be produced. For example consider two predicates *is_equal _set(S_1,S_2)* and *is_equal_tuple(T_1,T_2)*, where the former is true if two sets S_1 and S_2 are equal and the latter is true if two tuples T_1 and T_2 are equal. According to the analogical unification algorithm, they can be unified. However since the argument domains for the two predicates are different, an algorithm testing for set equality is fundamentally different from that for tuples.

To solve problems with second-order unification, a little more thought suggests that the match between an application program and an abstract program should be done with theorem proving. This implies that we should parameterize the structure of an abstract class and present it as a derived class. The concept of parrameterization is similar to that of templates in c++. However to instantiate a template in c++, the programmer has to be aware of its existence. Declaring a template as a derived class can eliminate such a need, so that the association between an application and a template can be established and transparent to the programmer. With such we can establish the following principles:

If P -> Q, then P can be used to solve Q.
If P <-> Q, then P can be used to solve Q, and vice versa.

Example 8.5. As an example we can write the abstract class *w_graph* as follows:

```
class(w_graph,NS:set_of_X,ES:set_of_Y)
instance_of(GNS,FS,graph) <-
    instance_of(G.NS,set_of_X),    instance_of
(G.ES,set_of_Y),
    attribute(Y,A,X), attribute(Y,B,X), attri-
bute(Y,C,float).
    w_graph:method(w_path,P:set_of_Y,S:X,
T:X,W:float,L:int)
-----------------------------------------------
    G.w_path(P,S,T,W,L) <-
      (∃ E) (∃ A) (∃ B) (∃ C)
```

```
member_of(E,G.ES), (E.A = S), (E.B = T),
   (P = [E]), (W = E.C), (L = 1).
G.w_path(P,S,T,W,L) <-
   (∃ E) (∃ A) (∃ B) (∃ C) (∃ P 1)(∃ W 1)(∃ L 1)
   set_of_edge(P1), integer(L1), float(W1),
   member_of(E,G.ES), (E.A = S),
   G.w_path(P1,E.B,T,W1,L1), (P = [E|P1]),
   (W = E.C + W1), (L = L1 + 1).
G.shortest_path(P,S,T,W,L) <-
   G.w_path(P,S,T,W,L),
   ~((∃ P 1)(∃ W 1) set_of_edge(P1), float(W1),
   G.w_path(P1,S,T,W1,L), (W1 < W))
```

To make the example more interesting, let us assume that a connection between two cities is restricted to either one or two flight segments. In addition we assume that *connection* is interested only in computing the fare for a connection between two cities. Note that with this, the number of arguments associated with the predicates *w_path* and *connection* are different.

```
class(city,state:string)
class(flight,source:city,destination:    city,
fare: float)
class(airline,cs:set_of_city,fs:set_of
_flight)
airline:method(connection,C:set_of_flight,
S:city,T:city,Fare:float)
--------------------------------------------------
A.connection(C,S,T,Fare) <- (∃ F)
   member_of(F,A.fs), (F.source = S), (F.desti-
nation = T),
   (C = [F]), (Fare = F.fare).
A.connection(C,S,T,Fare) <- (∃ H) (∃ F)
   member_of(F,A.fs), (F.source = S),
   member_of(H,A.fs), (H.source = F.destina-
tion),
   (H.destination = T), (Fare = F.fare + H.fare).
A.cheapest_fare(S,T,Fare) <-
   A.connection(C,S,T,Fare),
   ~(∃ C 1) (∃ F) set_of_flight(C1), float(F),
   A.connection(C1,S,T,F), (F < Fare)).
```

The *shortest_path* can be used to solve the problem of *cheapest_fare:*

1. The object $A_{cs,fs}$ forms a *w_graph* object. This can be proved by the following substitutions:

```
A.fs/G.ES
A.cs/G.NS
city/X
flight/Y
source/A
destination/B
fare/C
Acs,fs/G
```

Since

```
airline(A) ->
set_of_flight(A.fs),
set_of_city(A.cs)
```

the following can be established at schema level [Recall that whenever an assertion *instance_of(a,b)* is made in *Ls*, the assertion *b(a)* is made in L_0 and vice versa]:

```
instance_of(A.fs,set_of_flight),
instance_of(A.cs,set_of_flight)
```

Consequently

```
airline(A), attribute(flight,source,city),
attribute(flight,destination,city),     attri-
bute(flight,fare,float) ->
w_graph(Acs,fs)
```

2. The predicates *w_path* and *shortest_path* can be instantiated according to the preceding instantiations:

```
Acs,fs.w_path(P,S,T,W,L) <-
(∃E) member_of(E,A.fs), (E.source = S), (E.des-
tination = T),
    (P = [E]), (W = E.fare), (L = 1).
Acs,fs.w_path(P,S,T,W,L) <-
    (∃E) (∃P1) (∃L1) (∃W1)
    member_of(E,A.fs), (E.source = S),
    A.w_path(P1,E.destination,T,W1,L1),    (P =
[E|P1]),
```

```
set_of_edge(P1), float(W1), integer(L1),
   (W = E.fare + W1), (L = L1 + 1).
```
$A_{cs,fs}$.shortest_path(P,S,T,W,LL) <-
    $A_{cs,fs}$.w_path(P,S,T,W,L), (L <= LL)
    ~((∃ P 1) (∃ L 1) (∃ W 1)
    set_of_edge(P1), float(W1), integer(L1),
    $A_{cs,fs}$.w_path(P1,S,T,W1,L1), (L1 <= LL), (W1 <

W))

3. It can then be proved that

A.connection(C,S,T,Fare)   -> $A_{cs,fs}$.w_path
(P,S,T,W,1)

with the following set of substitutions from the first law associated with *A:connection:*

```
S/S
T/T
F/E
C/P
Fare/W
```

It can also be proved that

A.connection(C,S,T,Fare)   -> $A_{cs,fs}$.w_path
(P,S,T,W,2)

with the following set of substitutions from the second law associated with *A.connection:*

```
S/S
T/T
F/E
[H]/P1
H.Fare/W1
Fare/W
1/L1
2/1
```

4. Similarly it can be proved that

$A_{cs,fs}$.w_path(P,S,T,W,1)   ->   A.connection(C,
S,T,Fare)

with the following set of substitutions in the first law associated with *A.connection:*

```
S/S
```

```
T/T
E/F
P/C
W/Fare
```

And it can be proved that

$A_{cs,fs}$.w_path(P,S,T,W,2) -> A.connection
(C,S,T,Fare)

with the following set of substitutions in the second law associated with *A:connection:*

```
S/S
T/T
E/F
P1/[H]
W1/H.Fare
W/Fare
```

5. Based on Steps 2 and 3 and Section 3.1, we conclude that

A.connection(C,S,T,Fare) <-> $A_{cs,fs}$.w
_path(P,S,T,W,1) ‖
$A_{cs,fs}$.w_path(P,S,T,W,2)

Subsequently the following can be concluded

$A_{cs,fs}$.shortest_path(P,S,T,W,2) <-> A.cheap-
est_fare(C,S,T,F)

This is because

A.connection(C,S,T,Fare) <-> $A_{cs,fs}$.w_path(P,
S,T,W,L), (L <= 2)

Example 8.6. As another example consider the following two versions of *sort*. Note that syntactically they look quite different.

Version 1

```
set_of_integer:method(sort,B:set_of
_integer)
------------------------------------------------
A.sort(B) <- A.permutation(B), B.sorted().
[].sorted().
[H|T].sorted() <- ~((∃ X) member_of(X,T), (X <
H)), T.sorted().
```

Version 2

```
set_of_integer:method(sort,B:set_of
_integer)
set_of_integer:method(sorted',B:set_of
_integer)
-----------------------------------------------
A.sort(C) <- A.permutation(B), B.sorted'(C).
[].sorted'().
[H|T].sorted'() <- [H|T].sorted_1(0).
[H|T].sorted_1(N) <- (N <= H), T.sorted_1(H).
```

It can be proved by induction that *[H|T].sorted() -> [H|T].sorted _1(0)* and therefore *[H|T].sorted() -> [H|T].sorted'(0)* as follows:

1. It is trivial that *[].sorted() -< [].sorted_1(0)*.
2. Assume that *[H|T].sorted() -> [H|T].sorted_1(0)* (the Hypothesis). Now the following can be proved

```
[H'|[H|T]].sorted()  ->  ~((∃ X) member_of(X,
[H|T])), (X <= H')),
    [H|T].sorted().
```

From our hypothesis, the preceding statement, and since *[H|T].sorted_1(N) -> (N <= H), T.sorted_1(H):*

```
[H'|[H|T]].sorted()
-> (H >= H'), [H|T].sorted().
-> (H >= H'), [H|T].sorted_1(0).
-> (H >= H'), (0 < H), T.sorted_1(H).
-> (0 < H), (H >= H'), T.sorted_1(H).
-> (0 < H), [H|T].sorted_1(H').
-> (0 < H), [H|T].sorted_1(H').
-> [H'|[H|T]].sorted_1(0).
```

Similarly we can prove that *[H|T].sorted'() -> [H|T].sorted(0)* and conclude that *[H|T].sorted'() <-> [H|T].sorted(0)*.

PROBLEMS

1. Extend the c++ class declaration language so that a class declaration includes functional specifications. To do this consider incorporating the set constructs described in Section 7.2.

2. Derive a transformation mechanism that can be used to transform a c++ class declaration into an object-oriented logic system.

3. Using either the extended c++ class declaration language or an object-oriented logic system to declare the abstract class *integer_set* and the functional specification for a set-oriented method *find_minimum,* which finds the minimal member in an integer set.

4. Based on Problem 3 and declarations for the class *flight* and the class *airline* as described in Section 8.4, write a specification for the method *find_cheapest,* which finds the cheapest fare among all direct flights between two cities for one airline. Prove or disprove that the method *find_cheapest* can be solved by *find_minimum.*

REFERENCES

1. Balzer, R. *IEEE Transactions on Software Engineering* **SE-11:**11, 1257–1268 (Nov. 1985).
2. Barstow, D. "Artificial intelligence and software engineering." *Proc. of 9th International Conference on Software Engineering* (1987), pp. 200–211.
3. Manna, Z., and Waldinger, R. *ACM Transactions on Programming Languages and Systems* **2.1,** 90–121 (1980).
4. Dershowitz, N. In *Machine learning: An artificial intelligence approach,* vol. 2 (Michalski, R., Carbonell, J., and Mitchell, T., eds.) (Morgan Kaufmann, San Mateo, CA, 1986), pp. 395–423.
5. Barstow, D. In *Machine intelligence,* vol. 10 (Hayes, I. E., Michie, D., and Pao, Y-H., eds.) (Wiley, New York, 1982).
6. Smith, D. R. *Artificial Intelligence* **27:**1, 43–96 (1985).
7. Broy, M., and Pepper, P. *IEEE Transactions on Software Engineering* **7:**1, 14–22 (Jan. 1981).
8. Feather, M. Survey and classification of some program transformation approaches and techniques." *Working Conference on Program Specification and Transformation* (Tolz, Federal Republic of Germany, Apr. 1986).
9. Partsch, H., and Steinbruggen, R. *ACM Computing Surveys* **15:**3, 199–236 (Sept. 1983).
10. Bauer, F., Bray, M., Gnatz, R., Hesse, W., Krieg-Bruckner, B., Partsch, H., Pepper, P., and Wossner, H. *ACM SIGPLAN Notices* **13:**12, 15–24 (1978).
11. Smith, D., Kotik, G., and Westfold, S. *IEEE Transactions on Software Engineering* **SE-11:**11, 1278–1295 (Nov. 1985).
12. Manna, Z., and Waldinger, R. *IEEE Transactions in Software Engineering* **SE-5:**4, 294–328 (July 1979).
13. Pressburger, T., and Smith, D. In *Software engineering environments* (Brereton, P., ed.) (Ellis Horwood, England, 1988).
14. Boyle, J., and Muralidharan, M. *IEEE Transactions on Software Engineering* **SE-10:**5, 574–588 (Sept. 1984).
15. Cheatham, T. *IEEE Transactions on Software Engineering* **SE-10:**5, 589–594 (Sept. 1984).
16. CIP Language Group. *Lecture notes in computer science, vol. 1: Munich project CIP* (Spring-Verlag, New York, 1984).

17. Bauer, F., Moller, B., Partsch, H., and Pepper, P. *IEEE Transactions on Software Engineering* **15**:2, 165–180 (Feb. 1989).
18. Schach, S. R. *Software engineering* (Aksen, Homewood, IL, 1990).
19. Stroustrup, B. *C++ programming language,* 2d ed. (Addison Wesley, Reading, MA, 1991).
20. Dershowitz, N. *ACM Transactions on Programming Languages and Systems* **7**:3 (July 1985) 446–477.
21. Meyer, B. *IEEE Software*, 50–64 (Mar. 1987).
22. Prieto-Diaz, R., and Freeman, P. *IEEE Software* 4, 6 (Jan. 1987).
23. Biggerstaff, T. J., and Perlis, A. J., eds. *IEEE Transactions on Software Engineering* **SE-10**:5 (Sept. 1984) 474–477.
24. Burton, B., Aragon, R. W., Bailey, S., Koehler, K. D., and Mayes, L. A. *IEEE Software* **4**:4, 25 (July 1987).
25. Estublier, B. "Experience with a database of programs. *Second Software Engineering Symposium on Practical Software Development Environments* (Palo Alto, CA, Dec. 1986), pp. 84–91.
26. Kaiser, G. E., and Garian, D. *IEEE Software,* **4**:3, 17–24 (July 1987).
27. Wood, M., and Sommerville, I. In *Software Engineering Environments* (Brereton, P., ed. (Ellis Horwood, England, 1988).
28. Dillistone, B. In *Software engineering environments* (Brereton, P., ed.) (Ellis Horwood, England, 1988).
29. Nishida, F., Takamatsu, S., Fujita, Y., and Tani, T. *IEEE Transactions on Software Engineering* **17**:9, 853–871 (Sept. 1991).

Program Verification and Testing

Once a program is written, its correctness with respect to the specification has to be verified or validated. The theory of program verification stems from the desire to prove formally that a program is correct, based on written code and requirements specification. In general two approaches are proposed for formal program verification—one based on theorem proving and one based on symbolic execution.

If formal program verification cannot be performed, the program can be tested by test cases, so that the program's outputs are compared to expected outputs. There are in general two approaches to testing: *black box* and *white box*. Black box testing involves looking at the application as if it were a box whose internal workings are hidden from the outside world. It involves applying input commands to the program, after which the program's response is checked against the software specifications. In essence this type of testing attempts to simulate the activities of an actual system user.

White box testing on the other hand assumes that the internal structure of the program is known, so testing is performed against the structure. Approaches to white box testing fall into two categories: one based on structural coverage (*structural testing*) and one based on potential errors (*error-based testing*). Structural testing techniques assure that certain structural coverage, such as all possible paths in a program, are tested at least once with appropriate test cases. Error-based testing techniques focus on three major types of errors that may occur in a program: *missing path errors, computational errors,* and *domain errors*. Missing path errors occur when some conditional branches are accidentally omitted from the program. Computational errors result when incorrect computations, such as multiplication, are mistakenly replaced by an addition. A domain error occurs if some condition in an IF statement is incorrect, such as a < operator, is mistakenly replaced by a > operator. Unfortunately no testing strategy so far proposed can cover all three types of errors. For example missing path errors and domain errors clearly cannot be detected by a testing strategy derived simply from the paths in a program.

Chapter 9 first discusses the basic approaches to formal program verification (Section 9.1). Subsequently it introduces the primary approaches to program testing: black box testing (Section 9.2), structural testing (Section 9.3), and error-based testing (Section 9.4). Section 9.5 overviews approaches to automatic test case generation. Section 9.6 discusses problems and some possible solutions to test and debug distributed programs. Finally, Section 9.7 discusses some metrics and techniques for measuring the quality of a software system.

9.1. FORMAL PROGRAM VERIFICATION

Given a program, its functional specification can be verified with an automatic theorem prover. An acceptable approach to formal program verification involves associating an assertion to each arc in a flowchart such that if the assertion P associated with the entrance arc of an action π is true before π is executed, then the assertion R associated with the exit arc of π is true after π is executed. The theorem prover can proceed statement by statement to verify that the assertion at the output arc of each statement is true according to the assertion at the input arc. The theorem prover can also proceed backward.

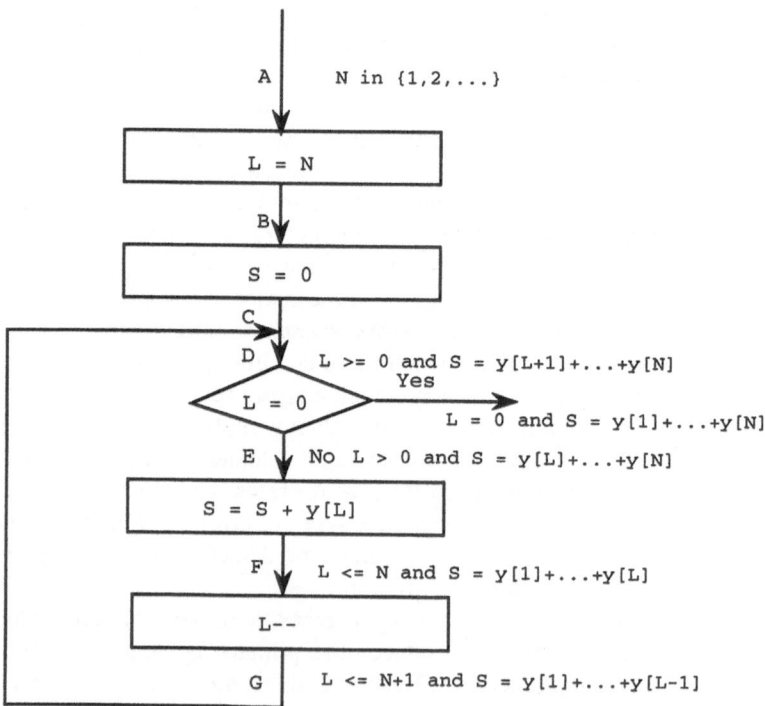

Figure 9.1. A flowchart. Reprinted with permission from Ref. 1. (c) 1991, Aksen Associates.

Example 9.1. (Ref. 1) Consider the following program segment:

```
L = N;
S = 0;
while (L >= 0) {
    S = S + y[L];
    L--;
}
```

The preceding flowchart shows a set of assertions associated with the program statements; these assertions can be proved as follows:

1. The assertion at point *A* corresponds to the initial state of the program segment.
2. The assertions at points *B* and *C* are trivial, since they are directly produced by corresponding statements.
3. The assertion presented at point *D* is a loop invariant. This can be proved by induction as follows:

Base: $L = 1, N > 1 => L \le N + 1, S = 0$
Hypothesis: $L = L0, 1 \le L0 \le N + 1 => L0 \le N + 1, S = y[1] + \ldots + y[L0 - 1]$
 Proof: At H: $L0 = N + 1, S = y[1] + \ldots + y[N]$, based on Hypothesis and $L0 > N$
 At E: $L0 \le N, S = y[1] + \ldots + y[L0 - 1]$, based on Hypothesis and $L0 < N$
 At F: $L0 \le N, S = y[1] + \ldots + y[L0]$, based on E and $S = S + y[L0]$
 At G: $L0 \le N + 1, S = y[1] + \ldots + y[L0 - 1]$, based on F and $L0 = L0 + 1$

The program should terminate properly, since *L0* is incremented during each loop, and it is bound by $N + 1$.

Another approach to formal verification, referred to as *symbolic execution* in the literature, first assumes a symbol value for each variable in a program. These values then designate the *state* of the program. Subsequently program statements are executed in sequence, and the state of the program changes according to decisions made and actions taken along the path traversed. Then this approach tries to prove that the output specification is indeed satisfied along each possible path that could be executed by the program. Example 9.2 illustrates this approach.

Example 9.2. (Ref. 2) Consider the following program segment that sets a variable *x* to its absolute value:

```
if (x < 0) x = -x;
```

Assume the precondition for the program segment is

    x == y

Also assume that the postcondition (i.e., the condition to be verified) for the program segment is

    (x > 0) && ((y == x)‖(y == −x))

To start symbolic execution, the initial state is set to:

    {x is X, y is Y}

where X and Y are two symbolic constants. Substituting these into the program precondition, the initial path condition is $\{(X == Y)\}$. There are only two paths in the program, depending on whether X is negative or positive. Assuming X is negative, the assumption is added to the path condition and it becomes

    state = {x is X, y is Y}, path condition = (X == Y)
    && (X < 0)

Next the statement $x = -x$ is executed, thus changing the state and path condition to:

    state = {x is −X, y is Y}, path condition = (X ==
    Y) && (X < 0)

Now the state can be substituted into the postcondition to obtain

    (−X > 0) && ((Y == X)‖(Y == −X))

which is apparently true based on the path condition. On the other hand, if the other path is followed [i.e., if $(x < 0)$ is false], the state remains unchanged, but the path condition becomes

    path condition = (X == Y) && ~(X < 0)

Based on the state, i.e., $\{x$ is X, y is $Y\}$, the postcondition becomes

    (X > = 0) && ((Y == X)‖(Y == −X))

which is again true based on the path condition. At this point, both paths have been verified and therefore the program is proved correct.

Although formal verification works on simple programs, it suffers from the complexity encountered in most theorem-proving systems. Approaches have been proposed to reduce the size of search space; these include using domain knowledge and allowing human interactions. Surveys of existing work on program verification are found in Refs. 3–5. Due to its cost, formal verification has been employed for only small and highly critical programs, such as communication protocols[6,7] and reusable data-type verifications.[8]

9.2. BLACK BOX TESTING

In general black box testing can be performed simply by taking all possible combinations of input variables. It is however clear that this approach is impractical. Therefore the idea of *boundary value analysis* was proposed, based on the observation that a number of *equivalence classes* of inputs can be established, so that as long as one test case of an equivalence class works properly, it is likely that other cases of the same class also work properly. It is not uncommon to find that such equivalence classes can be formed by first splitting the domain and its complement of each input variable into a number of subranges followed by taking the Cartesian product of such subranges. Experience has also shown that if a test case is chosen to be on or to one side of the boundary of an equivalence class, the chance of detecting a fault is usually higher.

Unfortunately there are no universal rules for dividing an input variable into subranges, the rules-of-thumb are

- If the domain of an input variable x is (R_1, R_2), five subranges can be formed: $x < R_1$, $x = R_1$, $R_1 < x < R_2$, $x = R_2$ and $x > R_2$.

- If the domain of an input variable x is a set A, two subranges can be formed: A and $\sim A$ (i.e., the complement of A).

9.3. STRUCTURAL TESTING

Structural testing is a type of white box testing whose test cases are derived from the structure of a program. The following strategies have been suggested.

Statement Coverage: Requires a set of test cases to be run so that every statement of the program is correctly executed.

Branch Coverage: Requires a set of test cases to be run so that every branch of the program is tested as least once; some variations are discussed in Ref. 9.

Path Coverage: Requires a set of test cases to be run so that every path of the program is tested.[10] Since the number of paths could explode exponentially, a number of approaches can be taken:

- *Boundary interior path testing*[11]: Groups of paths are formed so that paths in the same group differ only in the number of times they iterate on some loops. Two classes of paths in the same group are then considered for each loop: Those entering the loop but not iterating it (boundary tests) and those iterating the loop at least once (interior tests).

Among the boundary tests, those following different paths are chosen to execute; among the interior tests, those following different paths during the first iteration are chosen to execute.

- *Structural path testing*[12]: Similar to boundary interior path testing. Groups of paths are formed and executed according to the same criteria. Subsequently paths in the same group that do not iterate more than k times, where k is usually a small number, are executed.
- *Linear code sequence and jump*[13]: Tests each linear code sequence and jump (LCSAJ), where an LCSAJ is a sequence of consecutive statements, starting at an entry point or after a jump and terminating at a jump or an exit point.
- *2-dr interaction testing*[14]: This approach and the following are based on data flow analysis. A *2-dr interaction* is defined as a path that begins with the definition of a variable and ends at a use (reference) to the variable; the variable is not redefined along the path. This approach requires all 2-dr interactions to be tested.
- *data flow testing strategies*[15]: A distinction is made between a variable used in a computation (c-use) and a variable used in a predicate (p-use). The six strategy class members are
  - *All-uses strategy:* Each interaction between a p-use or a c-use and its definition is tested.
  - *All-defs strategy:* Each interaction between a definition and a c-use or a p-use is tested.
  - *All-p-uses strategy:* Each interaction between a definition and a p-use is tested.
  - *All-c-uses/some-p-uses strategy:* Each interaction between a definition and a c-use is tested; some interactions between a definition and a p-use are tested.
  - *All-p-uses/some-c-uses strategy:* Each interaction between a definition and a p-use is tested; some interactions between a definition and a c-use are tested.
  - *All-du-paths strategy:* Each interaction between a p-use or a c-use and a definition that reaches it is tested along all cycle-free paths.

References 16–18 compare the preceding strategies. A more detailed discussion of testing techniques are found in Refs. 19 and 20. As discussed earlier, any structural testing strategy is insufficient for detecting domain errors or missing path errors.

Example 9.3. The following program was used to compute the grades for a class of students:

```
#include <stdio.h>
#define NO_GRADES 12
#define NO_STUDENTS 250
#define NO_RANGE 7
struct student_record {
  char name[20];
  char ssn[10];
  int score[NO_GRADES];
  float avg;
  int section;
  char grade[3];
} students[NO_STUDENTS];

char letter[NO_RANGE][2] = {"A","A-","B+",
"B","B-","C+","C"};
float weight[NO_GRADES] = {0.02727,0.02727,
0.02727,0.02727,0.02727,0.02727,0.02727,0.02727,
0.02727,0.02727,0.3,0.4};
float cut_off[NO_RANGE] = {90.0, 80.0, 70.0,
60.0, 50.0, 40.0, 30.0};
int bucket[NO_RANGE + 1];

main()
{
  FILE *fp;
  char number[10];
  char number[100], fname[100];
  int student_count,score,count_nz,i,j;
  float sum, sum1, avg;

  /*** Initialization ******/
  for (i = 0; i < NO_RANGE +1; i++) bucket[i]
= 0;
  for (i = 0; i < NO_STUDENTS; i++)
  {
    for (j = 0; j < NO_GRADES; j++)
    students[i].score[j] = 0;
    students[i].avg = 0;
    students[i].section = 0;
  }
  count_nz = 0;
  sum = 0;
  i = 0;
```

```
/***** Read student data *****/
fp = fopen("roster","r");
while (fscanf(fp,"%s %s %d",students[i].ssn,
students[i].name, &(students[i].section)) != EOF)
i++;
fclose(fp);
student_count = i;   /**** student count
******/
for (i = 0; i < student_count; i++) /***** for
each student ****/
{
    for (j = 0; j < NO_GRADES; j++) /***** for
each homework***/
    {
        fname[0] = ' '; /**** compose the name of
the score file ***/
        strcat(fname,"hw/");
        sprintf(number,"%d",j + 1);
        strcat(fname,number);
        strcat(fname,"/");
        strcat(fname,"xgrade.");
        sprintf(number,        "%d",         stu-
dents[i].section);
        strcat(fname,number);
          /***** obtain grade with a linear search
****/
        fp = fopen(fname,"r");
        if(fp == NULL)
          printf("ERROR   OPENING   GRADE   FILE
%s!0,fname);
        while   (fscanf(fp,"%s%s%d",ssn,student,
&score) != EOF)
        {
            if(strcmp(ssn,students[i].ssn) == 0)
            {
              students[i].score[j] = score;
              break;
            }
        }
        fclose(fp);
    }
```

```
        /***** calculate the average for the student
*****/
        sum1 = 0;
        for (j = 0; j < NO_GRADES; j++) sum1 +=
(students[i].score[j]) * weight[j];
        students[i].avg = sum1;
          /**** if the student got 0 in final ****/
        if((students[i].score[NO_GRADES - 1] == 0)
&& (students[i].avg != 0))
        {
          strcat(students[i].grade,"F");
          (bucket[7])++;
        }
        else
        {
          count_nz++; /**** count_nz keep track of
                            #students who
                            got non-zeros in final
                            *****/
        sum = sum + sum1; /*** update total sum
****/
            /****** compute letter grade ****/
          if(sum1 >= cut_off[0])
          {
            strcat(students[i].grade,"A+");
            (bucket[0])++;
          }
          for (j = 1; j < NO_RANGE; j++)
          if((sum1 >= cut_off[j]) && (sum1 < cut
_off[j - 1]))
          {
          strcat(students[i].grade,letter[j]);
          (bucket[j])++;
          }
          if (sum1 < cut_off[NO_RANGE])
          {
          strcat(students[i].grade,"F");
          (bucket[7])++;
          }
        }
    }
```

```
fp = fopen("fscore","w");
    for (i= 0; i < student_count; i++)
    {
      if (students[i].avg != 0)
      {
      fprintf(fp, "%9s %15s %d",students[i].ssn,
students[i].name,students[i].section);
      for (j = 0; j < NO_GRADES; j++)fprintf(fp,"
%d3",students[i].score[j]);
      }
    }
    fclose(fp);
    avg = sum/count_nz;
    printf(" = = = = = = = = = = = = = = = = = = = =
= 0);
    printf("THE NUMBER OF STUDENTS IS %d0,count
_nz);
    printf("THE AVERAGE IS %f0,avg);
    printf("0);
    printf("# students who get A+: %d0,bucket[0]);
    for (j = 1); j < NO_RANGE - 1; j++)
      printf("# students who get %s: %d0,letter[j
- 1],bucket[j]);
    printf("# students who get F: %d0,bucket[NO
_RANGE - 1]);
    }
```

The flowchart for the program follows.

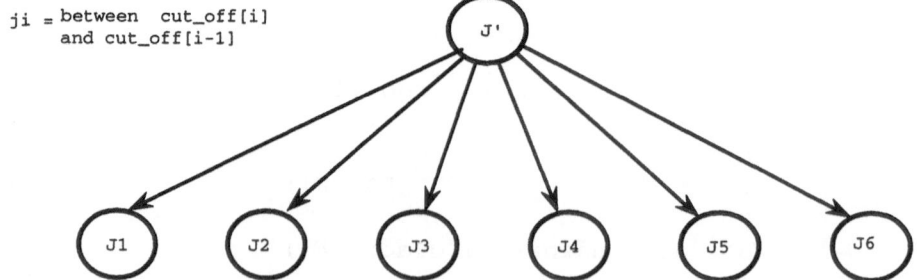

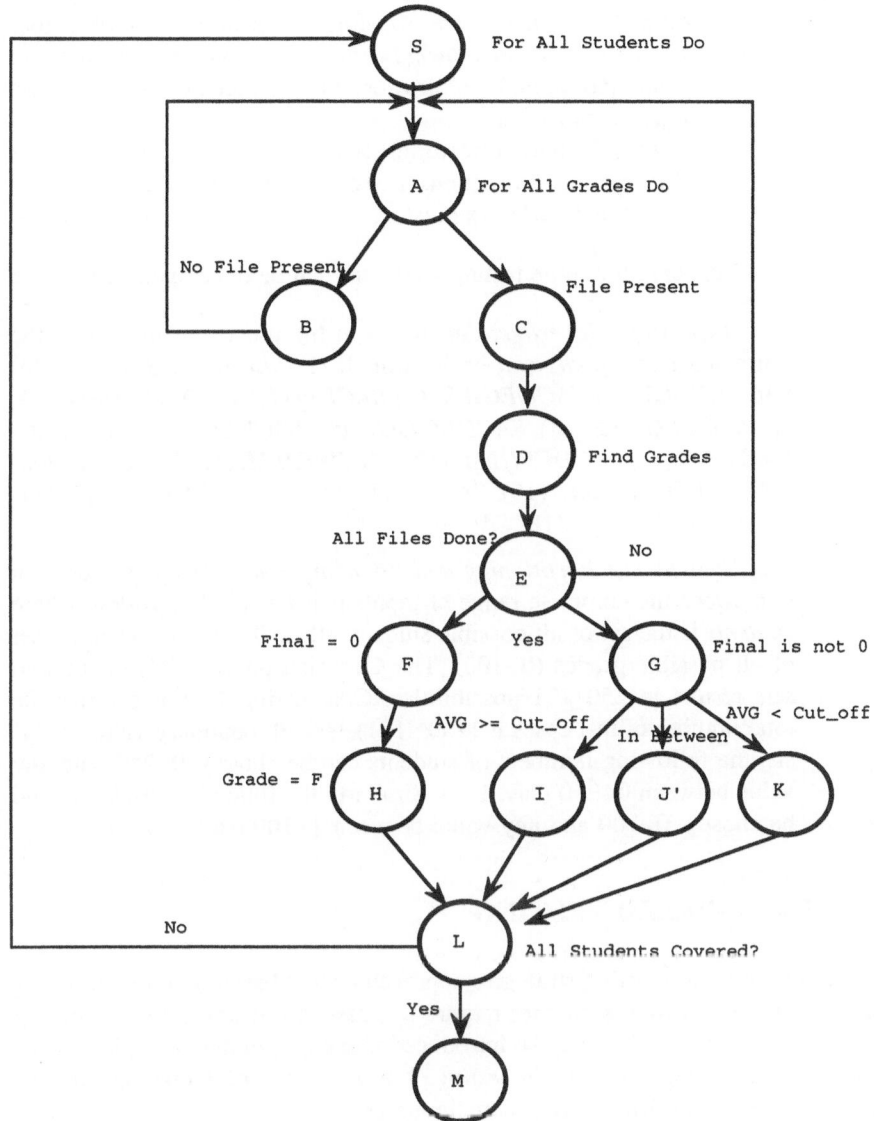

In order to develop test data, the following directories/files need to be created

- Roster file with each student's social security number, name and lecture section.
- hw directory with 1,2 . . . . 12 directories under it, where each

directory *hw/i*, $1 \le i \le 10$, stores the scores of the *i*th home-work; the directory *hw/11* stores the scores of the midterm examination; and the directory *hw/12* stores the scores of the final examination.
- In each of these directories, two files: *xgrade.1* and *xgrade.2* (for two lecture sections 1 and 2, respectively).
- Each file *xgrade.xxx* must have student's ssn, name, and score.

Test data for some testing strategies can be developed as follows:

Basic Path Coverage: As shown in the preceding flowchart, the following *basic paths* can be identified: (1) *SABA*, (2) *SACDEA*, (3) *SACDEFHLS*, (4) *SACDEGILS*, (5) *SACDEGJ₁LS*, (6) *SACDEGJ₂LS*, (7) *SACDEGJ₃LS*, (8) *SACDEGJ₄LS*, (9) *SACDEGJ₅LS*, (10) *SAC-DEGJ₆LS*, (11) *SACDEFHLM*, (12) *SACDEGILM*, (13) *SACDEGJ₁LM*, (14) *SACDEGJ₂LM*, (15) *SACDEGJ₃LM*, (16) *SACDEGJ₄LM*, (17) *SACDEGJ₅LM*, and (18) *SACDEGJ₆LM*.

Equivalence Partitioning and Boundary Value Analysis: For each homework the complete range of inputs is $|students| \times |grades|$, where *students* is the set of all possible students (0–250) and *grades* is the set of all possible grades (0–100). The Cartesian product ($\times$) of the two sets results in 250*101 possibilities. Considering 12 homeworks, the total number of test cases is (250* 101).[12] With boundary value analysis, the following numbers of students can be chosen: 0, 250, and any value between 0–250 (say, 125). Similarly the following grades should be chosen: 0, 100 and any value between 1–100 (say, 50).

9.4. ERROR-BASED TESTING

While structural testing strategies approach testing based on program structures, error-based testing strategies require test cases to be developed according to the type(s) of errors that may be introduced into a program. One typical error-based testing strategy is *domain testing*.[21] It is a type of white box testing designed specifically for locating domain errors.

A domain is simply a set of defined inputs that cause a certain program control flow to occur. A unique program path and a unique program control flow correspond to each domain. In the domain-testing method, the domain itself sets up the simulation input for each path to be tested. All control is performed through a combination of predicates, also known as the path condition. These consist of Boolean operators (such as AND and OR) and relational comparisons (such as $>$, $<$, $\le$, $\ge$, $=$, and $\ne$). These predicates can easily be found in any program inside of an IF THEN ELSE construct. The THEN clause constitutes one possible path, and the ELSE clause specifies another. For example consider the following program segment[21]:

```
[1]: scanf("%d%d",&i,&j);
[2]: if (i <= j + 1) k = i + j - 1;
[3]: else k = 2i + 1;
[4]: if (k >= i + 1) n = i + 1;
[5]: else n = j - 1;
[6]: if (i == 5) m = 2n + k;
[7]: else m = n + 2k - 1;
[8]: printf("%d",m);
```

The first path flow decision to be made is in Statement 2, *if* $<= j + 1$. There is only one path interpretation of this predicate, since both i and j are input variables read in from the user. Therefore Statement 2 is executed depending on the values of i and j. The second path flow decision in Statement 4, *if* $k >= i + 1$, has two interpretations because k is not an input variable but receives its value from the previous path control block. If $i <= j + 1$ in Statement 2 is true, then Statement 4 is interpreted as *if* $i + j - 1 >= i + 1$ (to simplify $j >= 2$). Otherwise if $i <= j + 1$ in Statement 2 is false, then Statement 4 is interpreted as *if* $2i + 1 >= i + 1$ (to simplify $i >= 0$).

Since the domain is a set of inputs, there is some definition about how the domain appears in relation to the whole set of real numbers. We assume that all variable types, including integers, strings, characters, etc., can be described or converted into floating point numbers. Therefore every domain has its own border segments, which in turn are determined by the domain and the types of operator used. For example a closed border segment is determined by an equality operator ($==$), a less than or equal to operator ($<=$), or a greater than or equal to operator ($>=$). An open border segment is determined by a nonequality operator ($\neq$), a less than operator ($<$), or a greater than operator ($>$).

One of the first assumptions in the domain-testing process is to consider only linear predicates. This makes the testing process easier to understand and much simpler to implement. Another assumption is to ignore the phenomenon known as *coincidental correctness*. This occurs when an incorrect input set coincidentally makes its way through the program control path to produce the correct output. The number of test points situated in the domain however can be determined by the tester. Usually it is preferable to have more test points placed near or precisely on the domain border itself, since these areas are more prone to domain errors. Other assumptions to make the domain-testing process more efficient involve excluding loops (or loops with indefinite iteration), subroutines, functions, and arrays. Of course these are common in everyday practice; in this discussion they would complicate the central idea behind domain testing.

To understand the domain and the input set that it contains graphically, a diagram called the *input-space-partitioning structure* was devised. The number of input variables in a program determines the dimensionality of the structure. For instance a program with one variable defines the structure of a single number line. Two variables define a planar structure; three variables define a solid structure. As the number of variables increases, the complexity of the input space also increases. For simplicity let us envision a two-variable, two-dimensional graph. Predicates involving the inequalities describe a plane, where the edges represent the boundaries of the domain. An equality predicate can simply be described as the domain of a single line. To explain a nonequality predicate, two domains are required. Instead of presenting the predicate as $x \neq y$, two predicates $x < y$ and $x > y$ achieve the same representation and easily divide the original domain in half. For example Figure 9.2 shows a two-dimensional input space based on the simple program described earlier in this section. In Figure 9.2. eight regions are identified, and each region is labeled with three letters $C_1 C_2 C_3$, where C_i, $1 \le i \le 3$, is T if the *i*th condition is true and E otherwise.

Note that the paths EET and TET are not possible due to the logic of the program. As mentioned previously, Statement 2, *if* $i <= j + 1$, has only one interpretation. Therefore its visual representation on the structure is a single line dividing the space into two exclusive domains (shown as the solid diagonal border I across the entire space). Since Statement 4, $k >= i + 1$, had two interpretations, its visual representation is two discontinuous lines (II and III in Figure 9.2) breaking up the domain space. Statement 6, *if* $i == 5$, has only one interpretation. Since an equality operator is used within the predicate, the visual representation of the domain is the single line IV in Figure 9.2.

When the program itself is considered, it is necessary to establish the errors types that can occur within it. A program can be simply considered as consisting of two parts: A set of domains, one for each possible flow path, and a set of assignments for each of the domains. Therefore the entire program is the set of domain/assignment pairs that make up its flow path from beginning to end. From this description of a program, three general types of changes can be made due to errors uncovered during domain testing. The first is a *domain boundary modification,* which occurs when the domain of the domain/assignment pair is altered for

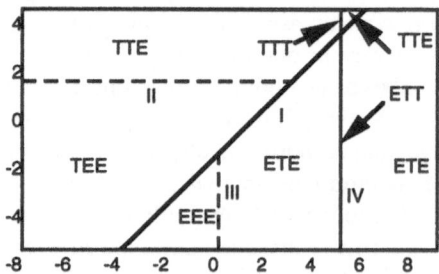

Figure 9.2. Input space domain test points. Reprinted with permission from Ref. 21. © 1980, IEEE.

correct output. The second is a *domain computation modification*, which occurs when the group of assignments of the domain/assignment pair is changed. The third is a *missing path modification*, which occurs when a new domain is created as a subset of the original domain (from the domain/assignment pair).

In general it is best to use domain boundary modification rather than domain computation modification, since it is simpler to change a predicate operator, such as switching a less than operator to a greater than operator, than change the functions that refer to an incorrect operator. Therefore using a particular type of modification can simplify the correction process and make the testing procedure more efficient. For example in our sample program segment, assume there is an error in Statement 4, *if k >= i + 1*. If we use domain boundary modification, this condition statement is changed to *if k < i + 1*. However if we use domain computation modification, Statement 4 is not changed but assignment Statements 4 and 5 are switched, so that Statement 4 becomes *n = j − 1* and Statement 5 becomes *n = i + 1*.

Because most domain errors occur near or actually on the domain border, it is crucial for test points needed in checking the domain to lie in these designated areas. An *on* test point is a point on the domain border itself. An *off* test point does not exist on the domain border but rather at some small distance *e* from the border segment. By shifting the border segment, then checking to see if the wrong flow path is taken by a certain domain, we can detect domain errors. For example in Figure 9.3(a), A and B show correct results, since they are in Domain 1.

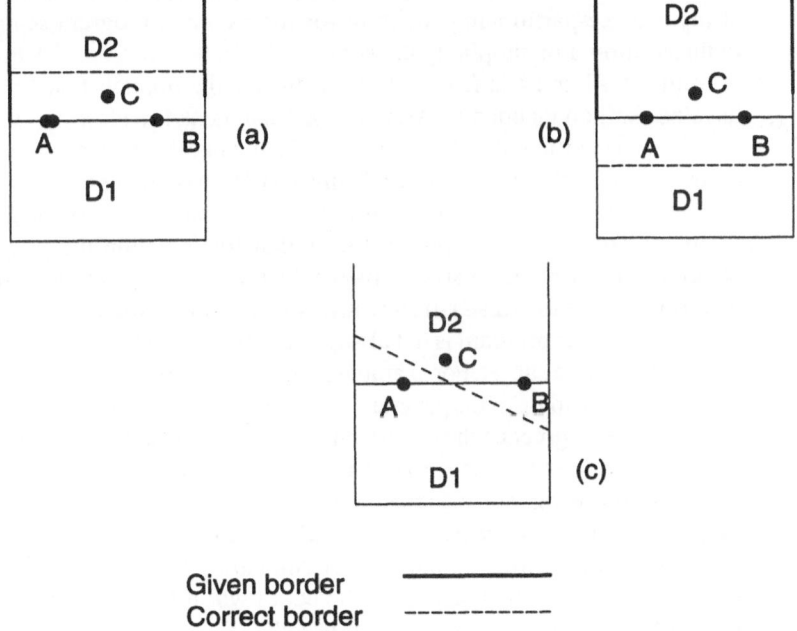

Given border ———————
Correct border - - - - - - - -

Figure 9.3. Three types of border errors. Reprinted with permission from Ref. 21. © 1980, IEEE.

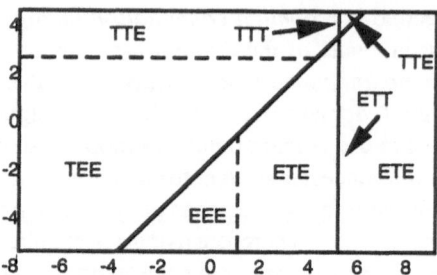

Figure 9.4. Correct input space for a domain error. Reprinted with permission from Ref. 21. © 1980, IEEE.

But as the border segment passes point C, an incorrect output results, since Point C should be inside Domain 1, and not in Domain 2. In Figure 9.3(b) Point C is correctly in Domain 2, yet Points A and B show incorrect outputs when the border passes the correct border segment, thereby placing them inside Domain 1 (the incorrect domain). A third type of shifting combines both Figures 9.3(a) and (b). This is realized in Figure 9.3(c), where Points A and C are now in their proper domain, but as the shifting takes place, Point B results in an error by indicating a diagonal (not horizontal) domain border segment.

> **Example 9.4.** (Ref. 21) Consider two input variables, a two-dimensional input-space-partitioning structure for the example program segment in this section. For simplicity the structure has a bounded space where J is from -5–5 and I is from -8–8. In theory the domain field should have no limit on its bounds. Assume that Statement 4 reads $k >= i + 2$.
>
> To select efficient test data points, it is first necessary to examine the input space partitioning structure (Figure 9.4). We would like to select a set of data points such that each path is taken in the control flow of the given program. There are three IF-THEN-ELSE constructs within the program creating three Boolean variable path selectors ranging in values from ELSE/ELSE/ELSE to THEN/THEN/THEN. Note that the domain of the paths needed to test the program is not always the complete set of possible path values but rather a subset. For example the paths TET and EET can never be achieved by the logic of the program itself. Since the three predicates form closed border segments, the on test data points reside on the segment, and the off test points are placed at some distance e near the segment.
>
> The following tables depict the test data selected (for i and j), their outputs, the appropriate path taken, and expected outputs. If a domain error exists, the correct output (predetermined by the programmer who knows the correct functionality of the code) will differ from the output gained through the current program tested.

on Test Data Points

I	J	K	L	M	PATH	K(correct)	L(correct)	M(correct)
5	4	8	6	20	TTT	8	6	20
×3	2	4	4	11	TTE	4	1	8
0	-1	-2	-2	-7	TEE	-2	-2	-7
5	2	11	6	23	ETT	11	6	23
×0	-3	1	1	2	ETE	1	-4	-3
-2	-4	-3	-5	-12	EEE	-3	-5	-12

off Test Data Points

I	J	K	L	M	PATH	K(correct)	L(correct)	M(correct)	PATH(correct)
-.2	-4	0.6	-5	-4.8	EEE	0.6	-5	-4.8	EEE
×.2	-4	1.4	1.2	3	ETE	1.4	-5	-3.2	EEE
×-2	2.2	-.8	-1	-3.6	TTE	-0.8	1.2	-1.4	TEE
-2	1.8	-1.2	.8	-2.6	TEE	-1.2	0.8	-2.6	TEE

These points are not the only data that could be used: There could be a large set of test data points depending on the testers' style. In fact the off test points in this simple example are not even needed to solve the domain error, since the on points have already detected the problem and the error was only a horizontal and vertical shift in the boundary segments. These tables provide only a guideline for selecting the testers' input data. Since on test points remain on the border segment while it is being shifted, there is no change in the path when an error is detected, so a table column for this trait is not necessary. However when dealing with off points, which do not reside on the border segment, a shift in the border segment may put these points inside a new and different domain. If there is a difference in the points domain from the current program and the correct program, an error has occurred and the boundary segment must be shifted to its proper position. Only when no differences are detected in the current and correct program can we say that domain boundary segments are correct.

Looking back at the example, once the on/off testing points are put on the input space structure, shifting border segments reveals an inconsistency in the correctness of the output. Since k originally had two interpretations, both dashed segments must be modified. Figure 9.3 shows domain boundary placements due to domain boundary modification.

Another error-based testing strategy is *mutation testing*.[22] Mutation testing assumes that if a program is not correct, it is almost correct; that is if a program is not correct, then it is a *mutant* of a correct program—it differs from a correct program only by containing such simple errors as an correct variable in an assignment statement, an extra loop bound, etc. A mutation-testing process therefore subjects a program to a sequence of mutation transformations to produce a number of mutants that differ from the original program slightly. Consider a program P and a mutant of P, say, P'. Let A_{tP} be the result of applying a test case t to P, and let $A_{tP'}$ be the result of applying t to P'. If A_{tP} is not correct but $A_{tP'}$ is, this indicates a mutation error (i.e., an error resulting from a mutation transformation) occurred and can be identified. The goal of mutation testing is therefore to construct a set of test cases that differentiate as many mutation errors as possible.

Example 9.5. (Ref. 23) Consider the following program:

```
int max(int m, int n)
{
  int max;
  max = m;
  // % max = n;
  // % max = abs(m);
```

```
   if (n > m) max = n;
   // % if (n < m) max = n;
   // % if (n >= m) max = n;
   return max;
}
```

In this program a statement commented out and preceded by a % is a mutation of the statement preceding it. Consequently four possible mutants can be obtained from the original program. The mutational error obtained from the last mutation [i.e., *if (n >= m) max = n*] cannot be detected, since it produces the same result as the original program.

9.5. AUTOMATIC TEST CASE GENERATION

This method can make the testing process more effective. Some testing approaches described in the previous sections, such as mutation testing, are systematic and can readily be automated. Traditionally three types of test data generators have been proposed: *data specification systems, random test data generators*, and *pathwise test data generators*. A data specification system allows the programmer to specify properties of the test data; the system then generates test data from the specifications. Random test generators select random values from possible input domains. Pathwise test data generators consist of four basic operations: program graph construction, path selection, symbolic execution, and test data generation. The symbolic executor accepts symbolic values for some inputs and algebraically manipulates these symbols according to expressions in which they appear. These tools perform operations as if the program were executing. Output values are symbolic expressions that are functions of input symbolic variables. Example 9.6 illustrates the use of symbolic execution for test case generation.

Example 9.6. (Ref. 24) Consider the following program:

```
void main(void)
{
  float a,b,c,x;
  scanf("%f%f",&b,&c);
  a = b + c;
  x = a * c;
  if (a <= x) {statement _I}
  else if ((b >= 1)||(b <= -1))
    {statement _II}
    else {statement _III}
}
```

Assume that symbolic constants *B* and *C* are read and assigned to *b* and *c*, respectively. Symbolic path expressions for paths leading to the execution of *statement_I*, *statement_II*, and *statement_III* are obtained as follows:

statement_I: (B + C) ≤ (B + C)*C
statement_II: ((B + C) > (B + C)*C) && ((B ≥ 1) ‖ (B ≤ −1))
statement_III: ((B + C) > (B + C)*C) && (−1 < B < 1)

Domains of input data corresponding to different paths can be derived accordingly (see "Problems").

One problem with test case generation as just described is that it uses symbolic values in place of variables. Normally this works, but problems may arise when using arrays. The index of an array may depend on input values, in which case the value of the array cannot be evaluated beforehand. Reference 25 describes a dynamic test generator that generates test data by data flow analysis, actual execution of the program, and function minimization. The process takes a program and the testing criteria as input and generates test data as output. First it analyzes the program, using the testing criteria to determine which paths to test. It then executes with sample input the program to traverse a specific path. When an undesired branch occurs, the branch predicate *E1 op E2* is transformed into a real-valued function *F rel 0*, based on the following transformations:

Branch Predicate	F	Relation
E1 > E2	E2 − E1	<
E1 >= E2	E2 − E1	<=
E1 < E2	E1 − E2	<
E1 <= E2	E1 − E2	<=
E1 == E2	abs(E1 − E2)	==
E1 != E2	abs(E1 − E2)	!=

The test process then alters the input values to minimize *F*. When *F* is negative, the program takes the correct branch. The test process must rerun the entire program however to assure that the change in input values does not cause an improper branch to be taken. The search procedure is a blind search operating on one input variable at a time in the order that it is input into the program. The first step applied to the variable is an exploratory search. This is a small alteration in either direction to see which direction minimizes *F* the most. The program is executed with the new input variable and if the program reaches the present branch successfully, then the new value of *F* is tested. If *F* has improved, then a larger jump is made. This process continues until either *F* becomes negative or reaches a minimum positive value. If *F* does become negative, then a successful set has been found and the program continues execution to the next branch. If *F* is still positive at this point, then a new exploratory search is made to see if further improvement is possible with this input variable. If not, the program continues by testing the next input variable.

The problem with this method is that it can be very slow, especially if the best variable to change is at the end of the input list. An improvement can be made by using an heuristic search based on data flow analysis. The data flow influence network discussed in Ref. 26 was used to determine which input variables have the most influence on the branch function *F*. These variables are tested first instead of in the rigid order imposed by the blind search just described. This can greatly speed up the process of evaluating the branch function, which is the most time-consuming part of the process.[25]

9.6. TESTING AND DEBUGGING DISTRIBUTED PROGRAMS

A traditional way of testing and debugging a program is to execute it with input, then compare test results with the expected result. If the result differs from the expected value, then the program is executed again with the same test input to replay the erroneous execution and collect debugging information. After corrections the same procedure is repeated again, and the program is checked for further errors. This testing and debugging approach is called *cyclical debugging*.[27] Unfortunately it does not work satisfactorily for concurrent programs. Testing and debugging a concurrent program is more complex because of the following[28]:

- Probe effect
- Nonrepeatability
- Lack of a synchronized global clock

The term probe effect refers to the fact that analyzing a system changes its behavior, so the same result may not be obtained again. Moreover for some distributed programs, different executions using the same inputs may produce a totally different set of outputs. In other words the program cannot necessarily repeat. In addition the absence of a synchronized global clock makes it difficult to determine the precise order of events occurring in a distributed environment. The probe effect and unpredictable results are also referred to as nondeterministic behavior in concurrent programs. One way of finding errors in a nondeterministic program is to execute deterministic sequences of synchronization commands within the program.[29-31]

Concurrent programs written as large-grain parallel computation units (for example those written in CSP or ADA) have motivated debuggers to shift to structural testing from a flowchart model of the system.[31] In this flowchart each node represents a statement or a collection of sequential statements that are executed as a block. The flow of control from one block to the next is represented by an edge. Nodes with multiple exiting edges represent a branch predicate. The debugger who chooses to employ this tool may use one of various forms of control-flow- and data-flow-testing strategies, which we discuss later. Three examples of control-flow-testing strategies are path testing, branch testing, and statement testing. An example of data flow testing is all definition use paths (all DU paths).

These strategies are defined with respect to the flowchart of a concurrent program, which we call a collection of *concurrency states*. In a flowchart program logic defines paths that may occur during execution, since not all flowchart paths correspond to executable sequences of statements. Testing strategies previously introduced use the following definitions: *H(s)* is the complete concurrency history and *E* is the set of all pairs *(C,C')*, where *C* and *C'* are concurrency states and *C'* is directly reachable from *C*.

The *all concurrency paths* criterion is the most impractical among concurrency flowchart-testing methods, since it requires every path be covered by the test set, which is infinite for a nontrivial concurrent system. The *all proper concurrency histories* criterion tests all paths of a finite length without duplications, and it may be the most thorough approach that is realistically possible. A weaker but more practical approach is the *all edges between cc states*, which includes every edge in the concurrency flowchart that transfers control from one node to its successor. The all cc states criterion simply includes every node in the flowchart.

> **Example 9.7.** (Ref. 31) Consider the CSP program that solves the dining philosopher problem described in Section 5.5 (for simplicity, only two philosophers are assumed):
>
> ```
> PHIL1 = *[. . during his/her lifetime -> THINK;
>    room!enter();
>    fork((i + 1)mod 5)!pickup();
>    fork(i)!pickup();
>    EAT;
>    fork((i + 1)mod 5)!putdown();
>    fork(i)!putdown();
>    room!exit()]
> PHIL2 = *[. . during his/her lifetime -> THINK;
>    room!enter();
>    fork(i)!pickup();
>    fork((i + 1)mod5)!pickup();
> ```

```
    EAT;
    fork(i)!putdown();
    fork((i + 1)mod 5)!putdown();
    room!exit()]
    FORK  =  *[phil(i)?pickup()  ->  phil(i)?put-
down();
        *phil((i - 1)mod 5)?pickup()  ->  phil((i -
1)mod 5)?putdown();]
    ROOM  =  *[(i|0.  . 4)phil(i)?enter  ->  (i|0.
. 4)phil(i)?exit]
```

This CSP program with five philosophers generates 11 flowcharts, one for each philosopher, each fork, and the main program itself. For simplicity we limit our program to two philosophers, which results in only five concurrency flowcharts.[32] A concurrency state table is generated by identifying the next possible concurrency states from both the preceding code and the five flowcharts, each of which represents an individually operating process (see the table that follows). Our next step is to create the concurrency flowchart between the previously defined concurrency states, as shown in Figure 9.5.

State No.	Fork (1)	Fork (2)	Philos (1)	Philos (2)	Next State
1	up	up	fork1.up	fork2.up	2,8
2	down	up	fork2.up	fork2.up	3,7
3	down	down	fork1.down	fork2.up	4
4	up	down	fork2.down	fork2.up	5
5	up	up	fork1.up	fork2.up	6,13
6	down	up	fork2.up	fork2.up	3,7
7	down	down	fork2.up	fork1.up	
8	up	down	fork1.up	fork2.up	7,9
9	down	down	fork1.up	fork2.down	10
10	down	up	fork1.up	fork1.down	11
11	up	up	fork1.up	fork2.up	12,17
12	up	down	fork1.up	fork1.up	7,9
13	up	down	fork1.up	fork1.up	7,14
14	down	down	fork1.up	fork2.down	15
15	down	up	fork1.up	fork1.down	16
16	up	up	fork1.up	fork2.up	13,17
17	down	up	fork2.up	fork2.up	7,18
18	down	down	fork1.down	fork2.up	19
19	up	down	fork2.down	fork2.up	16

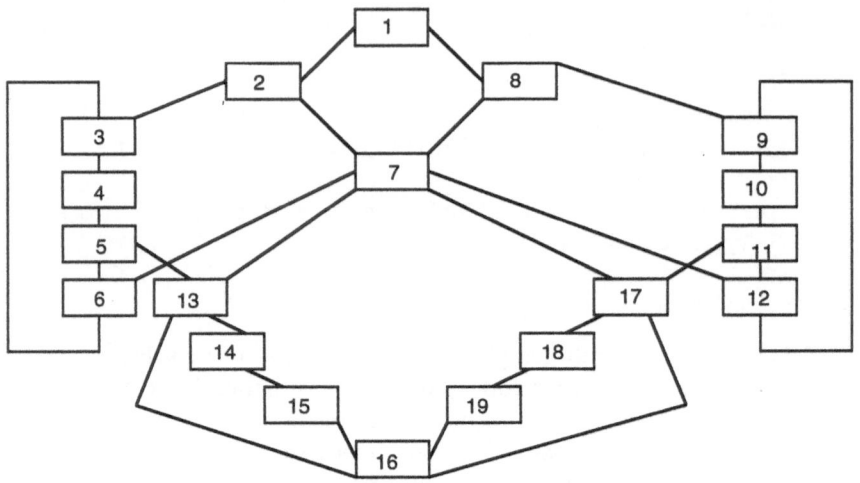

Figure 9.5. A concurrency graph.

Now we apply some testing criteria to the concurrency flowchart of the two dining philosophers. The following path sets are defined: Pa = the set of all paths through the graph, Ph = the set of all paths satisfying the all proper cc histories criterion, Pe = the set all sets of paths satisfying the all edges between cc states criterion, and Pcc = the set of all sets of paths satisfying the all cc states criterion. The Pa is defined as the set of all paths through the concurrency flowchart; it may include infinite paths, such as $(1, 2, 3, 4, 5, 6, 3, 4, 5, 6, 3 \ldots)$. The Ph is defined as the set of finite-length paths through the flowchart that are valid for the program. An example path for Ph is $(1, 2, 3, 4, 5, 6, 7)$. Two example paths for Pe are $(5, 6, 7)$ and $(1, 2, 3, 4, 5)$, which are significant because they are not members of Ph; i.e., these two paths are not possible flows of execution for the code. An example path for Pcc is $(6, 3)$, which covers testing both Nodes 3 and 6 but not a proper concurrency flowchart history.

A program's suitability for static concurrency analysis can be determined by estimating the state space explosion problem. This problem occurs due to the large number of interprocess interactions, concurrency flowchart edges, and atomic events. The size of the concurrency flowchart for an application can be calculated via Taylor's algorithm such that the number of unique concurrency states is approximately equal to $(n/t)(t/2)$, where n is the total number of state nodes in all tasks, t is the total number of tasks in the system, and n/t is the average number of state nodes per task.[32] There is software available to generate and analyze the concurrency flowchart based on the criteria a debugger wishes to use. The CATS is an example of a tool suite automating the processes of building the concurrency flowchart and its related histories.[31] Obviously the more paths included by the criteria selected, the longer to process the flowchart. For an idea of just how fast the concurrency flowchart grows with the size of the system under test, if we adhered to our original code with five philosophers, the concurrency flowchart would consist of 1653 nodes and 6130 edges.

Some useful techniques to be employed to simply the test procedure follow:

- *Reduced Concurrency Graphs:* If a flowgraph can be converted into a reduced form, then testing becomes simpler. For example all delay statements can be neglected if they do not affect the order of task interactions; a rendezvous can be represented by two nodes instead of three.

- *Path Steering:* A concurrent program may produce different outputs based on the same input because the scheduler steered from one state to different successor states. If there are two or more possible successor states, and the scheduler selects the next state arbitrarily, this makes the task of debugging difficult. To avoid this situation, it is desirable to have a controllable scheduler to allows the user to choose a specific rendezvous to be followed.

See Refs. 28, 33, and 34 for a more detailed discussion of testing and debugging concurrent programs.

9.7. ANALYSIS TOOLS AND SOFTWARE METRICS

Even if it is determined that a program meets specifications, it is desirable to analyze the quality of the program so that further improvements can be made. Section 9.7 describes some basic approaches to system analysis. See Ref. 35 for discussion of CASE analysis tools.

9.7.1. Static Analysis Tools

These tools analyze characteristics obtained from a program structure without executing the program. Statically analyzing programs may include any or all of the functions listed below:

- *Code Auditing:* Examines source code to determine whether or not specified programming practices and rules have been followed. This can include syntax rules, proper use of portable language subsets, and use of a standard coding format.

- *Consistency Checking:* Determines whether or not units of program text are consistent in that they use uniform notation or terminology and are consistent with a specification.

- *Cross Referencing:* Relates entities by logical names, for example functions called by each function, variables used in a function.

- *Interface Analysis:* Checks interfaces between program modules for consistency and adherence to a set of predefined rules; an example is checking parameters passed between functions.

- *Data Flow Analysis:* Determines constraints that can be placed on data values at various points of execution in the source program.

- *Error Checking:* Determines discrepancies in the code, such as misspelled keywords; uninitialized variables; variables set, but not used; isolated code segments.

- *Type Analysis:* Checks data names against their types.

- *Unit Analysis:* Determines if units or physical dimensions attributed to an object are correctly defined and consistently used.

Many static analysis tools are available. In UNIX for example *Cscope* maintains a symbol cross-reference table that is updated as files are changed. Since UNIX C compilers do not provide thorough checking, a valuable static analysis tool known as *lint* is extremely helpful in ensuring the quality of the source code. It reports many useful things to the programmer, such as syntax errors the compiler would have found; functions without a return value; function declarations and calls with incorrect number or type of arguments; variables declared, but not used; unreachable program statements; ill-advisable automatic-type conversions. Another useful static analysis tool in UNIX is *cia*. One type of information that *cia* captures is the calling relationship among functions. It stores its information in a relational database that can be accessed by using its reporting tools or other database tools. By using graphic tools with *cia*'s reporting tools, a graph can be generated to describe the calling relationship among functions. The *cia* also has many other uses, such as program version comparison; i.e., two versions of a program can be compared by looking at differences between their *cia* databases. This tool also helps search for reusable code, because it provides information about functions commonly used in the source code.

9.7.2. Dynamic Analysis Tools

These tools collect information from an executing program. They can perform one or more of the following operations:

- *Coverage Analysis:* Records the amount and type of coverage achieved by a set of test cases. Coverage is the percentage of code actually tested by a specific test set. The type of coverage can be branch coverage, statement coverage, path coverage, etc.

- *Tracing:* Traces the historical record of program execution. Tracing can be further divided into path flow tracing, breakpoint flow, logic flow tracing, and data flow tracing.

- *Tuning:* Determines which part of a program has been executed the most; the number of times a statement is executed; the initial, final, and average value of a variable, the number of times a condition of a branch is true.

- *Timing:* Reports the actual CPU time associated with a program or its paths.

- *Resource Utilization:* Analyzes resources unused by the program.

- *Integrity Checking:* Similar to integrity constraint checking. It is also useful in detecting data flow anomalies.

- *Constraint Evaluation:* Includes generating and/or solving path input or output constraints to determine test inputs or prove that a program is correct.

Some dynamic analysis tools available in UNIX include the following:

- *lprof:* An assembler instrumentation tool to determine how many times each line of code in a file is executed. It is used to measure statement coverage.

- *nvcc (new verifier for C code):* Inserts instrumentation code into a c or c++ source file. Instrumentation code generates coverage information.

9.7.3. Software Metrics

Most hardware benchmarks attempt to measure the performance of various central-processing units (CPUs). *Software metrics* are benchmarks that attempt to assess software systems objectively. In general metrics assess software based on a number of characteristics of interest to developers, namely, clarity, reliability, maintainability, and efficiency. Using software metrics does not require reading source code, yet such metrics provide a rapid way of assessing software of arbitrary length. However like hardware benchmarks, these metrics do not always accurately reflect real-world performance. The following list summarizes some popular software metrics.[36,37]

McCabe Complexity Metric: Measures the complexity of the program's control structure. It is usually denoted as *MC* and determined by the expression $M = \#$ of decisions $+ 1$.

Halstead Program Length Metric: Estimates program length. Three equations are generally used: $N = N_1 + N_2$, where N_1 is the total number of operators in the program and N_2 is the total number of operands; $N_H = N_1 \log_2 (N_1) + N_2 \log_2 (N_2)$; and $N_J = \log_2 (N_1!) + \log_2 (N_2!)$, which is supposedly a more accurate estimate of *N*.

Program Bandwidth: Average nesting level of the program. A straight-line program has bandwidth 1; a program with many nested loops has a higher bandwidth number. A formula for bandwidth is $BW = (i * L(i))/(number\ of\ nodes\ in\ the\ program\ control\ graph)$, where *L(i)* is the number of nodes at level *i*.

Other metrics include such basic and simple metrics as number of lines, number of characters, and number of comments. A variety of tools are available to measure such software metrics. For example DATRIX[38] allows the user to choose which metrics to use and the valid ranges of values for the metrics. It supports the following steps for software evaluation based on metric measurements:

- *Project Analysis:* Runs the project through the DATRIX analyzer. DATRIX outputs metric values for each function.

- *Metric Distributions:* Examines the metric value for each function, then calculates the usual range of values for the project. It then identifies any function with out-of-range values.

- *Percentile Profile:* Shows the number of functions falling within the selected range of metric values. All functions with unusual metric values are identified and listed.

- *Normality Profile:* Usually a grouping of individual metrics to form a composite metric. For instance average bandwidth, number of loops, and McCabe's complexity metric an be combined into a quality factor called *testability.*

- *Function Interrelationships:* A call graph of total calls to a function versus total calls from the function versus the frequency count.

Reference 39 contains other software metric surveys.

PROBLEMS

1. Identify a set of paths for the program given in Example 9.3 based on: (a) statement coverage and (b) branch coverage.

2. Prepare test data for the program given in Example 9.3 based on the set of paths identified in this example and the two sets of paths identified in Problem 1.

3. Prepare test data for the program given in Example 9.3 based on boundary value analysis.

4. For the program in Section 9.4, assume Statement 6 reads ($i \neq 5$). Develop ON/OFF data points to detect the fault.

5. Based on Example 9.6, draw a two-dimensional structure (taking B and C as the axes) that shows the domains of input data leading to the execution of Statements I, II, and III.

6. Consider the following code fragment:

```
c = 0;
f = c;
while (c < N) {
  c++
  f = f * c;
}
```

Sketch a proof for the fragment and verify that it correctly computes $N!$ if $N \in \{1, 2, 3, \ldots\}$.

7. Discuss if testing can be facilitated by an object-oriented paradigm. For example is test case generation easier if classes of test cases can be developed? Is a c++ program easier to test than an equivalent C program?

REFERENCES

1. Schach, S. R. *Software engineering* (Aksen, IRWIN, Homewood, IL, 1991).
2. Dannenberg, R. B., and Ernst, G. W. *IEEE Transactions on Software Engineering* **SE-8:**1, 43–52 (Jan. 1982).
3. Boyle, R., and Moore, J. *Journal of Automated Reasoning* **1:**1, 17–22 (1985).
4. *Proceedings of VERshop III, A Formal Verification Workshop, 18–21 Feb. 1985.* ACM Software Engineering Notes Special Issue **10:**4 (Aug. 1985).
5. Wallce, D. R., and Fuji, R. U. *IEEE Software* **6:**3, 10–17 (May 1989).
6. Sunshine, C., Thompson, D., Erickson, R., Gerhart, S., and Schwabe, D. *IEEE Transactions on Software Engineering* **8:**5, 460–489 (Sept. 1982).
7. Good, D. I. *Philos. Trans. Royal Society of London* **312,** 389–409 (1984).
8. Gerhart, S., *et al.* In *Information processing* (Lavington, ed.) (North Holland, 1980).
9. Tai, K. C. *ACM Software Engineering Notes* **14:**2, 58–61 (Apr. 1989).
10. McCabe, T. *IEEE Transactions on Software Engineering* **SE-2:**4, 308–320 (Dec. 1976).

11. Howden, W. E. *IEEE Transactions on Computer* **24**:5, 554–559 (May 1975).
12. Howden, W. E. Symbolic testing—design techniques, costs, and effectiveness. NTIS PB-268518, May 1977.
13. Woodward, M. R., Hedley, D., and Hennell, M. A. *IEEE Transactions on Software Engineering* **SE-6**:5, 278–286 (May 1980).
14. Ntafos, S. C. *IEEE Transactions on Software Engineering* **SE-10**:6, 795–803 (Nov. 1984).
15. Rapps, S., and Weyuker, E. J. *IEEE Transactions on Software Engineering* **SE-11**:4, 367–375 (Apr. 1985).
16. Frankl, P. G., and Weyuker, E. J. *IEEE Transactions on Software Engineering* **SE-14**:10, 1483–1498 (Oct. 1988).
17. Ntafos, S. C. *IEEE Transactions on Software Engineering* **SE-14**:6, 868–874 (June 1988).
18. Basili, V. R., and Selby, R. W. *IEEE Transactions on Software Engineering* **SE-13**:12, 1278–1296 (Dec. 1988).
19. Beizer, B. *Software testing techniques* (Van Nostrand Reinhold, New York 1990).
20. Gelperin, D., and Hetzel, B. *Communication of ACM*, **31**:6, 687–695 (June 1988).
21. White, L. J., and Cohen, E. I. *IEEE Transactions on Software Engineering* **SE-6**:5, 247–257 (May 1980).
22. DeMillo, R. A. *Software testing and evaluation* (Benjamin/Cummings, Menlo Park, CA, 1987).
23. DeMillo, R., and Offut, A. J. *IEEE Transactions on Software Engineering* **SE-17**:9, 900–910 (Sept. 1991).
24. Fairley, R. E. *Software engineering concepts* (McGraw-Hill, New York, 1985).
25. Korel, B. *IEEE Transactions on Software Engineering* **SE-16**:8, 870–879 (Aug. 1990).
26. Korel, B., *Information Processing Letters* **24**, 102–107 (Jan. 1987).
27. Lutz, M. *IEEE Software*, **7**:5, 53–57 (May 1990).
28. McDowell, C. E., and Helmbold, D. P. *ACM Computing Surveys* **21**:4 593–618 (Dec. 1989).
29. Carver, R. H., and Tai, K. C. *IEEE Software* **8**:2, 66–74 (Mar. 1991).
30. Katz, S., and Peled, D. *Distributed Computing* **6**:2, 107–120 (1992).
31. Tai, K. C., Carver, R. H., and Obaid, E. E. *IEEE Transactions on Software Engineering* **TSE-17**:1, 45–62 (Jan. 1991).
32. Taylor, R. N., Levine, D. L., and Kelly, C. D. *IEEE Transactions on Software Engineering* **TSE-18**:3, 206–215 (Mar. 1992).
33. Cheung, W. H., Black, J. P., and Manning, E. *IEEE Software*, **7**:1, 106–115 (Jan. 1990).
34. Wing, J. M., and Gong, C. *Journal of Parallel and Distributed Computing* **17**:1, 164–182 (1993).
35. Oman, P. W. *IEEE Software* **7**:3, 37–43 (May 1990).
36. Lind, R. K., and Vairavan, K. *IEEE Transactions on Software Engineering* **SE-16**:3, 373–388 (Apr. 1990).
37. Cote, V., Bourque, P., Oligny, S., and Rivard, N. *Journal of Systems and Software* **8**:2, 121–131 (Mar. 1988).
38. Robillard, P. N., Coupal, D., and Coallier, F. *Software—Practice and Experience* **21**:5, 507 (May 1991).
39. Waguespack, L. J., and Badlani, S. *ACM Software Engineering Notes* **12**:4, 52–71 (Oct. 1987).

Software Maintenance

Programming is both a tedious and sensitive task. During the development of large programs, coordination can make the problem even worse. A useful programming environment eases the task by automating many of the programmer's routine operations. Such assistance includes automatic configuration management and version management. Chapter 10 describes approaches to software maintenance, emphasizing applications of database technologies to managing programming objects at various levels of abstraction.

Chapter 10 first introduces the different components of software maintenance (Section 10.1), then overviews some existing approaches using database techniques to support software maintenance (Section 10.2). Sections 10.3 and 10.4 discuss the use of the COMPOSE object-oriented database (see Section 7.4) for software maintenance. In particular Section 10.3 explores various programming objects in c++ that can be involved in queries, integrity constraints, and triggers. Section 10.4 discusses integrity constraints and triggers in incremental testing and integrity control. Section 10.5 discusses reverse engineering and design recovery techniques that can be applied to identify various components of a software system and to create representations of the system with a higher level of abstraction.

10.1. COMPONENTS OF SOFTWARE MAINTENANCE

The term *software maintenance* can be used in a broad sense to cover all aspects of programming as a software system evolves.[1] A more specific definition of software maintenance includes two major components: automatic configuration management and version management. Both components handle changes made to a software system; consequently the term *change management* is frequently used to cover that aspect in both components.

10.1.1. Configuration Management

A large-scale software system is comprised of many distinct components. To assure optimal product performance, these components must be arranged in such a way that changes to the system (or system evolution) can be monitored and do not affect the reliability, integrity, or correctness of that software system. Configuration management (CM) is formally defined as "the discipline of developing uniform descriptions of a complex product at discrete points in its life cycle with a view to systematically controlling the manner in which the product evolves."[2] Software configuration management (SCM) is the application of CM rules and regulations to software systems.

It is very important to realize the differences between software system configuration and maintenance and hardware system configuration and maintenance. Certain principles can be applied to hardware systems but cannot be carried over to software systems without being modified. In general a hardware system is well-defined and often is not modified after creation. However because software systems readily allow modification and are logically more complex, they are not so concretely defined at the beginning.

10.1.2. Version Management

A version can be a *revision* or a *variation* of a programming object. A revision of a programming object is a new programming object obtained by revising the old one to improve its performance. Consequently only one revision survives. A variation of a programming object is usually obtained from the object because of a different operating requirement. Therefore potentially different variations of an object can coexist at the same time. Versions may be defined among different projects, different programs, different segments, and different functions. Different versions of a program object may be similar in structure with possibly minor differences. Consequently it is desirable that whenever one version is changed, and the change is made to a common version among different versions, the other versions are changed accordingly.

10.2. DATABASE AND SOFTWARE MAINTENANCE

One system whose goal is to control the process of managing different components of a software system is the Evolution Support Environment (ESE) system.[3] Supporting software evolution involves minimizing the effort required to develop a new version from existing versions. The ESE system helps software evolution by maintaining an integrated database on information about software configuration, life cycle configuration, and version control. Another aim of the ESE system is to understand the structure and function of a large evolving system. Hence it is "important to store relationships among software objects, such as specifications, code and test cases . . . "[3]

This system also provides mechanisms for organizing a program into subsystems, layers, and modules. Some of the features offered in this system are traceability across the software life cycle, configuration management using a modular organization of resources, and version support at the systems level. Traceability is referred to as the capability to access objects based on their attributes or relationships with other objects. This task lasts throughout the entire life cycle of the product, including requirement specifications, design specifications, coding, and testing of the software product. Traceability helps assure that the software system satisfies user requirements. However there may be difficulties in dealing with changes to the original specifications. The ESE system uses the entity relationship model to organize objects and provide traceability among them. A modular approach to resource organization is undertaken because groups of software components can be similar and compose layers in a hierarchically designed system. The ESE system also provides the capability of dealing with different versions of the modules or groups of modules.

The ESE system has the following layers: the ESE kernel, the software libraries layer, and the applications layer. The ESE kernel provides mechanisms for creating, deleting, modifying software objects, and maintaining relations between them. The software libraries layer uses the kernel to organize objects of different types into a library structure. The applications layer provides various facilities to the user, for example algorithms that use link information to go from one object to its related object. This layer may also use facilities provided by other software tools, such as the C Information Abstract system,[4] which is discussed in detail later. This system automatically derives some of the configuration information useful in deriving the ESE system from C source programs.

Another project that applies database techniques to software and software environments is Cactis, which encompasses the "design, coding, and debugging of computer programs, as well as the creation, maintenance, and reuse of modules and versions."[5] The data model used in Cactis includes powerful type constructors necessary when modeling such objects as programs and program versions. There are many forms of derived data in a software environment, and the Cactis database management system is unique in its ability to represent and maintain derived data in a time- and space-efficient fashion.

A software environment must support detailed data about each module and statements for optimizing code within a compiler. A database can simplify this task by allowing a program to be viewed as a number of data objects. The Cactis system is also able to control program recompilation based on last modification times and mutual dependencies. This is similar to the make capability in UNIX and other environments. The proper application of the recompilation utility ensures that inconsistencies between parts (or modules) of a software system do not occur.

The general goal of Cactis is to centralize all database functionality of a software environment, thus minimizing the effort needed to construct environments and allowing the efficient design, use, reuse and maintenance of software. A Cactis database is viewed as a collection of objects. Attached to each data object is a group of data values called attributes. The type of the object determines the set of attributes attached to it. Types of objects can be modified dynamically without affecting related objects. The Cactis data model also allows some local behavior: Individual objects can respond to changes elsewhere in the database. This behavior characterizes the Cactis data model as an object-oriented model.

Version control is accomplished in the Cactis data-modeling system by grouping sets of modules together and allowing only groups of modules to be checked out, modified, and checked in as a new version. In this system subsequent versions of a program are not explicitly stored but rather derived from a current version by applying some delta mechanism. Hence only this delta mechanism has to be stored and applied to the program when necessary. In this way it is very easy to retrieve older versions of the program.

The Source Code Control system (SCCS) is a software tool developed to help programmers control changes to source code.[6] This particular system takes a formal approach to the mechanisms of version control as discussed earlier. This system was an early attempt at maintaining the integrity of a software system when changes were made to different modules in the system. The main features of SCCS are storage, protection, identification, and documentation. All versions of a module are stored together in the same file. A programmer may not have access to certain modules or certain versions of modules. Access to modules is allowed only through SCCS. The system automatically stamps modules with the version number and time. Documentation of who made the change as well as what the change was and where it was made is automatically performed. As in the Cactis model, each change made to a file is stored as a discrete delta. To produce the current version of the program, deltas are applied in a chronological sequence. Deltas may be optional, which means they can be applied only when the user passes a designated flag. Deltas may also include or exclude the application of other deltas. The ideas presented in this system have been used in more complex systems, such as Cactis.

The C Information Abstraction system (CIA) analyzes the structure of c programs, extracts relational information from the programs, then stores this information in a database. After a program's structural information is executed and stored in a database, programmers can invoke relational queries to analyze different aspects of the software. The database stores only pointers to the source text. A database query operation and a source file access operation are sufficient to retrieve the full text of any software object. The CIA can be used to study the following aspects of program structures:

- *Subsystems:* Identify self-contained components in a large system. This reachable set (closure) can be computed by tracing all reference relationships.

- *Layering:* Topologically sorts different combinations of reference relationships. Two layering strategies are type-layering structure and file-layering structure.

- *Dead Code:* Detects unused code in a software system.

- *Coupling:* Analyzes the binding strength between pairs of software objects. Two functions are considered to be strongly coupled if they share many references to the same objects. In general binding strength values can be used to cluster functions to reduce cross coupling between modules. This approach has the advantage of localizing the impact of each change in the software system.

In CIA a c program is viewed as a collection of global objects that can be referred to across function boundaries. Each object has a set of attributes. Two objects may have a reference relationship between them; for example if *A* refers to *B*, *A* cannot be compiled and executed without the definition of *B*. In database terms this relationship is called referential integrity. Applying techniques developed in the CIA system to achieve the preceding goals facilitates automating the use and maintenance of software systems. When this is accomplished, the net cost of maintaining a software system may be drastically reduced.

References 7–11 present other work on applying database techniques to software maintenance. See Refs. 12–15 for a general discussion of software maintenance and maintenance tools.

10.3. PROGRAMMING OBJECT BASES

The term programming object base is used in Ref. 16 to signify the use of an object base, such as COMPOSE (see Section 7.4), for programming. The term object base is used instead of object-oriented database because the structures of programming objects as well as the behavior of programming objects (i.e., methods, programs, and processes) are understood and managed by the object base management system. In addition unlike systems described in Section 10.2, programming objects at different levels of abstraction (down to the level of variables and statements) are targeted in such an environment. This section describes the major features of a programming object base.

Files in COMPOSE are recognized as file objects. The concept of directory is realized by classifying files into ordinary files and directory files, where a directory file object is a set of files among which some can be directories. Therefore the file system is recognized as a directory object, where each file is identified by its (absolute) path in the file system. Each file object is characterized by a set of attributes and operations that can be applied to files. Since an object can be a set whose elements cannot be predetermined, sets and object attributes are treated differently in the environment. The notation *object.attribute* is used exclusively to identify an attribute of an object, and the notation *object/attribute* is used exclusively to identify an element of a set object. For example assume *file _system* is the file system installed for the environment. The size of a file *lisa* in the directory *john* of the directory *mary* of *file _system* can be identified as:

```
file_system/mary/john/lisa.size
```

However the total amount of memory used by *file _system* can be identified as:

```
file_system.total_memory
```

Programming objects at different levels of abstraction are organized hierarchically. For example a c++ project consists of a set of modules. A module consists of a set of classes and globals. A class consists of a set of variables and functions. A function consists of a set of variables and statements. A statement can be an assignment statement, an if statement, etc. The following summarizes the set of programming classes.

```
CPP_Project
{
set_of_Module_Type  Module;
        // each source file in project
Proj_DateTime_Type  Proj_DateTime;
        // time of last update
}

Module_Type
{
Module_DateTime_Type Module_DateTime;
        // time of last update
Module_Name_Type Module_Name;
        // name of source file
set_of_Global_Include_Type Global_Inc;
        //Global includes
set_of_Global_Define_Type Global_Def;
        // Global defines
set_of_Class_Type Class;
set_of_Class_Type Model;
```

```
set_of_Function_Type    Global_Func;
        // Global functions
set_of_Variable_Type Global_Var;
        // Global variables
}
Global_Include_Type
{
set_of_Module_Type Include_File;
        // list of include files
}
Global_Define_Type
{
Define_Macro_Type Define_Macro;
Define_Expr_Type Define_Expr;
}
Class_Type
{
set_of_Class_Type Parent_Class;
        // name of parent class
set_of_Function_Type Local_Func;
        // Local functions
set_of_Variable_Type Local_Var;
        // Local variables
}
Function_Type
{
Name_Of_Variable Type_Of_Func;
set_of_Variable_Type Argument_List;
        // List of arg's
set_of_Variable_Type Variable;
        // List of local variables
set_of_Statement_Type Statement;
}
Variable_Type
{
Type_Of_Variable Var_Type;
        // int, float, double, etc.
Name_Of_Variable Var_Name;
        // actual variable name
Init_Type Var_Init; // initialization value
```

```
}

Assignment_Type : Statement_Type
{
Name_Of_Variable Var_Name;
Expression_Type Assigned_Expression;
}

Switch_Type : Statement_Type
{
Name_Of_Variable Switch_Var; // name of var
set_of_Switch_Block_Type Switch_Block;
}

Switch_Block_Type
{
Switch_Block_Constant Switch_Constant;
Block_Type Switch_Block_Statements;
}

If_Type : Statement_Type
{
Condition_Type If_Condition;
Block_Type If_Block;
}

While_Type : Statement_Type
{
Condition_Type While_Condition;
Block_Type While_Block;
}

DoWhile_Type : Statement_Type
{
Condition_Type DoWhile_Condition;
Block_Type DoWhile_Block;
}

For_Type : Statement_Type
{
Statement_Type Init_Statement
Condition_Type Term_Cond; // Term. condition
Statement_Type Increment_Statement;
        // Incr. Statement
```

```
Block_Type For_Block;
}

Block_Type : Statement_Type
{
set_of_Statement_Type Block_Statement;
        // set of statements
}

Condition_Type
{
Expression_Type Expr;
}

Expression_Type
{
Constant_Type Constant; // any constant
Name_Of_Variable Variable; // any variable
Expression_Type Left_Expression;
Operator_Type Operator;
Expression_Type Right_Expression;
}
```

Turning to object classes, the following sections show some examples of COMPOSE facilities that can be applied for software maintenance (See Section 7.4 for details about COMPOSE):

10.3.1. Queries

The following query retrieves the names of all global include files, module names, and function types for all modules whose date/time stamp is after 10:30 AM on February 28, 1993:

```
range of MOD1 is Module_Type
range of FUNC is Function_Type
range of GLOBINC is Global_Include_Type
retrieve ( GLOBINC.Include_File,
  MOD1.Module_Name,
  FUNC.Type_Of_Func )
where MOD1.Global_Func.contains(FUNC) and
```

```
MOD1.Global_Inc.contains(GLOBINC) and
MOD1.Module_DateTime > "199302281030AM"
```

10.3.2. Integrity Constraints

The following integrity constraint asserts that a variable called Tel_String is always of the type string (for any module):

```
range of VAR is Variable_Type
VAR.Var_Name = "Tel_String" => VAR.Var_Type =
"string"
```

As another example, the following constraint asserts that all modules with a global macro definition of TREW1, must have its value set to 123L. This ensures that the same global defined in different source files has the same value. This constraint is checked whenever the value of any global define of this variable is modified or a new global define for this variable is added.

```
range of MOD1 is Module_Type
range of GLDEF is Global_Define_Type
MOD1.Global_Def.contains(GLDEF) and
GLDEF.Define_Macro == "TREW1" =>
GLDEF.Define_Expr == "123L"
```

10.3.3. Triggers

The following trigger implements *make:*

```
range of PROJ is CPP_Project
range of MOD is Module_Type
Proj.Module.contains(MOD) and (PROJ.Proj_DateTime
< MOD.Module_DateTime)
=> MOD.compile(), Proj.link(), (PROJ.Project_
DateTime = get_time())
```

10.3.4. Views

The following version transformation query transforms a module called TRTEXT.CPP such that if there is a global function of the type int and a global variable of the type string, then the attribute Class replaces the attribute Model in the definition of the module. This is an example of how a more complex query performs a realistic transformation of a module into another version. Similarly a countertransformation can be applied to transform a later version of a programming object into an earlier version. In this simple case, all that has to be modified in the countertransformation is the order of the variables in the *replace()* operation.

```
Module_Type Module :=
  range of MOD1 is Module_Type
  range of GLVAR is Variable_Type
  range of FUNC is Function_Type
  replace:Module_Type(MOD1.Class,MOD1.Model)
  where (MOD1.Module_Name == "TRTEXT.CPP" and
MOD1.Global_Func.contains(FUNC) and
MOD1.Global_Var.contains(GLVAR) and
    (GLVAR.Var_Type == "string") and
    (FUNC.Type_Of_Func == "int")
```

10.4. PROGRAM MANAGEMENT

A c++ program or function in COMPOSE is converted into and stored as a production system. This is accomplished by first transforming the module into a flowchart, labeling each node with a special state variable α, then converting the labeled flowchart into production rules.[17] As discussed in Section 10.3, COMPOSE manages programming objects based on integrity constraints and triggers. It further combines testing and maintenance on executable programming objects, such as programs and functions, so that the validity of a test case is determined not only by its expected functionality (as in most systems) but also by the constraints asserted on valid states, which are assigned incrementally from changes made at the statement level.

10.4.1. Incremental Testing

Given a test case a, assuming the testing strategy is path coverage (see Section 9.3), consider a flowchart P. The execution profile of a can be recorded and stored as a sequence of nodes (in the flowchart). Test case profiles can be used to support incremental testing, which means some test cases remain valid after changes are made to a program or function.

10.4.1.1. Adding and Deleting an Operation Node

Adding a node a between two existing nodes b and c of P invalidates those test cases whose profiles include b and c. The same set of test cases is invalidated when deleting a node a between two nodes b and c of P.

10.4.1.2. Adding and Deleting an Arc

Adding an arc between two existing nodes b and c of P invalidates those test cases whose profiles include b. The same set of test cases is invalidated when deleting an arc a between two nodes b and c of P.

A finer approach may avoid excluding some test cases even though they contain b and/or c as just described: Consider a program P expressed as a production system as described earlier. Assume P consists of a set of variables V_P, a set of input objects I_P, and a set of output objects O_P. Let v_0 represent values for the variables of P initially. Let t be a test case and the execution profile for t is the sequence $EP_{P_t} = \langle (v_1, r_1, v_1'), \ldots, (v_n, r_n, v_n') \rangle$, where each r_i, $1 \leq i \leq n$, is a production executed on behalf of t; v_i are values of the variables of P before r_i is executed; and $v_{i'}$ are values of the variables of P after r_i is executed.

Based on these assumptions, we say there is *data dependency* between an output object x and a production r_j, $1 \leq j \leq n$ (or x *depends on* r_j) if the action part of r_j modifies the value of x. We say there is *control dependency* between two productions r_j and r_k, where $k < j$ (or r_j *depends on* r_k) if the condition part of r_j references a variable x and x is modified in r_k. The *accumulated set of modifiers* of a production r_j is defined to be the set of productions $\{r_k\}$, where $k < j$ and r_j depends on r_k. Based on the preceding, productions are added and deleted as described in the sections that follow.

10.4.1.2.a. Deleting a Production. Consider a production r to be deleted. If r does not belong to EP_{P_t}, t remains a test case. If r belongs to EP_{P_t}, assume that the index for r in EP_{P_t} is i. If no output variable depends on r and r_i does not belong to the accumulated set of modifiers for any particular production r_k, where $1 \leq i < k$, and the condition part of r_{i+1} remains to be true after r_{i-1} is executed, assuming the value assigned to α in r_i is assigned to α in r_{i-1}, then t remains a test case. Otherwise t is invalidated.

10.4.1.2.b. Adding a Production. Consider a production r to be added. Assume that the node corresponding to r is to be added between two nodes a and b in the flowchart and the productions corresponding to a and b are r_a and r_b, respectively. If EP_{P_t} does not include r_a, then t remains a test case, since no path can reach the node corresponding to r without going through a. If EP_{P_t} does include r_a and if the condition part of r is not true after r_a is executed, t remains a test case, since a must correspond to a test statement (e.g., if, switch). Now let us consider the case when EP_{P_t} includes r_a and r is enabled. If no output variable exists that depends on r and r does not belong to the accumulated set of modifiers for any particular production r_k, where $1 \leq i < k$, and r_b can be enabled by r after the value assigned to α in r_a is assigned to α in r, then t remains a test case. Otherwise t is invalidated.

10.4.2. Integrity Control

Given a program or a function P, let the set $state_P$ store the set of tuples (t, v), where v is a possible instantiation of V_P (i.e., the set of variables of P described earlier) obtained according to a valid test case t. Let the set $trans_P$ store the set of tuples $\langle t, v, r, v' \rangle$, where t is a valid test case and $\langle v, r, v' \rangle$ is a member of EP_{P_t}. Assume the four components of each element of $trans_P$ are accessed as *test _case*, *current _state*, *production*, and *next _state*, respectively; and assume the two components of each element of $state_P$ are accessed as *test _case* and *state*, respectively. Some fundamental properties of P can be defined in terms of integrity constraints and verified by the set of reachable states according to the test cases performed. For example the property *proper termination* can be defined as at least one member of FS_P, which designates the set of final states, should be in $trans_P$ (*current _state* $= s_0$). An application-dependent constraint can be asserted in terms of a logical liveness property and/or a logical reachability property, which are defined in the following:

- *Logical Liveness:* Given a logical expression E over the current state, next state, and/or production, the set $\sigma_E(trans_P)$ is not empty. This guarantees that states satisfying E are active states, where σ designates the relational select operator.

- *Logical Reachability:* Given a logical expression E over the states, the set $\sigma_E(state_P)$ is not empty. This guarantees that states satisfying E are reachable from the initial state.

For instance the constraint that an application cannot terminate with a file, say, a, open can be stated as an integrity constraint:

```
state_p(S)∧trans_p(R)∧(R.current_state = S) →
~S.state/a.isopen().
```

Clearly integrity constraints asserted over valid states can be verified incrementally. Given P, $trans_P$ and $state_P$, consider a change made to P at statement level. The following can be computed

- $\delta+_{trans}$: Designates which objects should be added to $trans_P$ due to the change.

- $\delta-_{trans}$: Designates which objects should be removed from $trans_P$ due to the change.

- $\delta+_{state}$: Designates which objects should be added to $state_P$ due to the change.

- $\delta-_{state}$: Designates which objects should be removed from $state_P$ due to the change.

An integrity constraint is presented as:

$$P_1 \wedge \ldots \wedge P_k \rightarrow Q$$

where the predicate symbol of P_i, $1 \le i \le k$, is either $trans_P$, $\sim trans_P$, $state_P$, or $\sim state_P$ can be converted into:

$$T_1 \wedge \ldots \wedge T_k \rightarrow Q$$

according to the following rules:

- If the predicate symbol of P_i, $1 \le i \le k$, is $trans_P$, then T_i has $\delta+_{trans}$ as the predicate symbol with the same set of arguments.

- If the predicate symbol of P_i, $1 \le i \le k$, is $\sim trans_P$, then T_i has $\delta-_{trans}$ as the predicate symbol with the same set of arguments.

- If the predicate symbol of P_i, $1 \le i \le k$, is $state_P$, then T_i has $\delta+_{state}$ as the predicate symbol with the same set of arguments.

- If the predicate symbol of P_i, $1 \le i \le k$, is $\sim state_P$, then T_i has $\delta-_{state}$ as the predicate symbol with the same set of arguments.

10.5. REVERSE ENGINEERING AND DESIGN RECOVERY

Numerous advances in the field of software engineering led to the development of increasingly large scale software systems. Maintenance costs associated with these systems have correspondingly risen as well. These exorbitant costs spurred the innovation of many procedures to simplify the maintenance process. These innovations include reverse engineering and design recovery. Reverse engineering approaches the understanding of a software system from various design perspectives, which means that the system can be more easily altered and maintained.

Before discussing the concepts of reverse engineering and design recovery, some key concepts of software development are defined.

- *Subject System:* Actual code or set of programs to be analyzed. The subject system is not confined to programming code; it can also refer to data files, signal interfaces, etc.

- *Life Cycle* of Software: Set of phases that software usually proceeds through during development. These phases can be separated into three distinct stages: requirements, design, and implementation.

- *Levels of Abstraction:* Classify the transition from general concepts to implementation details. Higher abstraction levels are associated with early stages in the life cycle, while lower abstraction levels are identified with later stages.

According to Ref. 18, "Reverse engineering is the process of analyzing a subject system to: (1) identify the system's components and their interrelationships, and (2) create representations of the system in another form or at a higher level of abstraction." Design recovery is generally regarded as a subset of reverse engineering. In design recovery design concepts are recovered from the subject system and presented using various representations, such as data flow, control flow, and module structure. According to Ref. 19, "Design recovery must reproduce all of the information required for a person to fully understand what a program does, how it does it, why it does it, and so forth."

The first step in reverse engineering is to analyze the subject system for objects to store in a domain model. The domain model is "a knowledge base of expectations expressed as patterns of program structures, problem domain structures, language structures, naming conventions, and so forth, which provide frameworks for the interpretation of the code."[19] In other words the domain model stores various data structures, module structures, variable specifications, and informal information in object-oriented classes. Instances of these classes are then identified in the subject system code. In general informal information is not related to the structure of a system; rather it refers to semantic information encoded by the software engineer. Informal information greatly aids in understanding the subject system; therefore it is part of the domain model.

Once various structures, variables, and informal information have been stored in object-oriented classes, interrelationships and connections must be identified. Each instance of these classes has two important properties: structural patterns and associative connections. Structural patterns are used to produce relationships between objects that operate on the same data structure or within some module structure. Associative connections are formed using natural language associations and informal information. These connections take advantage of fuzzy relationships ignored by structural patterns. Reverse engineering produces relationships among different structures within a software system. These relationships can then be examined to produce a variety of displays, including program flow, program structure, program description, module breakdown, and formal specifications.

According to Ref. 19, the design recovery process can be separated into three steps:

1. *Support program understanding for maintenance:* The analyst searches the system for recognizable organizational structures and design concepts. This part of design recovery requires reverse engineering. The

reverse engineering process extracts conceptual abstractions and presents them using informal diagrams, flow of control, and design rationale. Conceptual abstractions are the "semantically rich natural-language abstractions . . . that represent the essential concept underlying the module." Once this step in design recovery is accomplished, increased understanding from the additional design information simplifies software system maintenance.

2. *Support population of reuse and recovery libraries:* Once design concepts are recovered from the subject system, they can be factored into smaller, more independent design aspects. These design aspects are then added to a component library for reuse. The more independent a design aspect is, the more likely it can be reused in similar components from other systems. Thus future software systems can easily be developed from existing system designs.

3. *Apply results of design recovery:* New systems are produced from reuse library designs best fitted to the particular applications.

With these three steps, design concepts are detected in existing software, gathered into libraries, then implemented in suitable new software systems.

Most reverse engineering systems and tools have similar architectures. Figure 10.1 shows various components in reverse engineering systems. Reverse engineering systems analyze a software system by passing it through a parser/analyzer to extract structures and designs. These structures are then stored in an information base. This information base consists of a complex interrelationship scheme of numerous data structures, module structures, and other objects. The objects are then examined by a variety of composers to produce diverse views of the software system. Depending on how the composers traverse the relationships in the information base, views can be composed of program flow, program control, design rationale, informal relations, etc. The following sections discuss some existing tools.

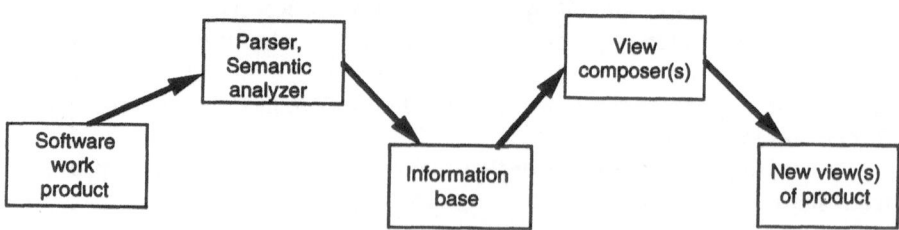

Figure 10.1. Model of reverse engineering systems. Reprinted with permission from Ref. 18, © 1990, IEEE.

10.5.1. Desire Version 1.0

The system[19] is comprised of three parts: a parser, a set of post-processing functions, and a PlaneText hypertext system. The parser takes C code from a software system as input, then parses it into trees. Informal information, such as variable names, comments, and other semantic clues are preserved separately. Postprocessors are then invoked to store the information recovered from the parse trees. Postprocessors construct a dictionary to preserve information about functions, data items, informal information, and relationships between them. Function information includes the location of these functions within system files. Information on data items consists of their definitions, where they are defined, and where they are used. Informal information is associated with corresponding functions or data items it describes. Relationships stored between these functions and data items consist of calls, uses, and dependencies.

Once all information is stored in the dictionary, the PlaneText processor takes control to compute a hypertext web of nodes and links. Separate views are displayed using a browser to exhibit some views and suppress others. For example if the programmer wishes to view function calls, PlaneText displays the functions involved and the lattice of calling relationships; however other information, such as data items and files is not displayed.

Different views supported by Desire Version 1.0 are defined by a set of prolog queries. These queries answer questions at different structural levels, including what functions call function x or what functions defined in File *A* call a function defined in File *B*. Queries can also answer questions relating to function types, such as what functions appear to be utility functions. The visual interface of Desire Version 1.0 is relatively simple and straightforward. When the user enters a query in the prolog interaction window, the system highlights all functions, data items, or files in the PlaneText web that satisfy the query.

Desire Version 1.0 takes advantage of informal semantic information within a software system. It implements the domain model using a set of CLOS classes, which are specially suited for storing semantic information and using informal patterns as entities in the dictionary. By using informal information, Desire Version 1.0 provides a more detailed and complete description of the software system.

10.5.2. MicroScope

MicroScope[20] is designed to analyze programs written in COMMON LISP and COMMON OBJECTS. It is essentially a reverse-engineering system because it offers utilities to analyze program code and retrieve design information. The knowledge base of MicroScope spans data flow, control flow, cross-reference, and display strategies. Since MicroScope runs in a programming environment, it also offers debugging strategies and execution history in addition to normal reverse-engineering strategies.

Tools offered by MicroScope allows programmers to evaluate a program structure at different detail levels. A programmer can also preview the effects certain changes produce on other modules. In addition MicroScope allows the programmer to monitor program execution to locate run-time errors. Various MicroScope features that make it an attractive system:

- MicroScope supports views of a program's structure at different abstraction levels. This allows the programmer to focus on modules of interest within a graphical representation of the program's structure.

- When altering a function or variable, a programmer must evaluate effects of the proposed change on other structures within the program. This evaluation is referred to as impact analysis. MicroScope browsers display areas in a program affected by a change in the present source code.

- MicroScope also associates annotations to each structure analyzed. These annotations contain information on source code, documentation, variable declarations, function calls, design specifications, etc. These annotations are indeed objects within the domain model. Annotations are analogous to nodes within a hypertext system. MicroScope displays different views of a program with any desired annotations. This can include such items as the number of times a function is called, the calling function, the variables altered in a specific function, etc.

- Program slices allow the programmer to use flow analysis to observe specific statements within a program that lead to certain variable values. Program slices help determine for example which statements were involved in resetting the value of I to null.

In summary reverse engineering can be applied to any software system for maintenance as well as development purposes. This is accomplished by simplifying the understanding of the software system. Although this is the main goal of reverse engineering, Ref. 19 points out alternative objectives:

- Simplifying and managing the excessive size and complexity of certain software systems. Reverse engineering provides various tools for examining the subject system and analyzing design methods.

- Producing various views and perspectives. Graphical representation is a key method of displaying results in reverse engineering.

- Recover lost information through design recovery.

- Assisting the search for existing software that is aptly suited for re-usability.

PROBLEMS

1. Assert the following as integrity constraints in a program object base:
(a) A program should start and terminate in the same directory.
(b) All files should be closed before termination.

2. Assert the following as triggers in a program object base:
(a) When a version of a programming object is changed, all other versions are automatically changed.
(b) Close any open files before termination.

3. Modify the incremental-testing approach described in Section 10.3.4 assuming branch coverage is the testing strategy.

4. Modify the incremental-testing approach described in Section 10.3.4 assuming statement coverage is the testing strategy.

5. Is the incremental-testing approach described in Section 10.3.4 sufficient and necessary? If yes, why? If not, why not?

6. Is the incremental change management approach described in Section 10.3.3 sufficient and necessary? If yes, why? If not, why not?

7. Is it possible to run a programming object base as a shell in UNIX? If yes, what problems may arise? If not, why not?

8. Define a view in a program object base that removes all #*include* ⟨*malloc.h*⟩ from each module of a project (i.e., given a project, the corresponding view removes all such declarations).

REFERENCES

1. Schneidewind, N. F. *IEEE Transactions on Software Engineering* **SE-13**:3, 303–310 (Mar. 1987).
2. Narayanaswamy, K., and Scacchi, W. *IEEE Transactions on Software Engineering* **SE-13**:3, 324–334. (Mar. 1987).
3. Ramamoorthy, C. V., Usuda, Y., Prakash, A., and Tsai, W. T. *IEEE Transactions on Software Engineering* **SE-16**:11, 1225–1234 (Nov. 1990).

4. Chen, Y.-F., Nishimoto, M. Y., and Ramamoorthy, C. V. *IEEE Transactions on Software Engineering* **SE-16:**3, 325–334 (Mar. 1990).
5. Hudson, S., and King, R. *IEEE Transactions on Software Engineering* **SE-14:**6, 709–719 (June 1988).
6. Rockhind, M. *IEEE Transactions on Software Engineering* **SE-1:**4, 364–370 (Dec. 1975).
7. Adams, E., Honda, M., and Miller, T. "Object management in a CASE environment." *Proc. of the 11th International Conference on Software Engineering* (Pittsburg, May 1989), pp. 154–63.
8. Estublier, B. "Experience with a data base of programs." *Second Software Engineering Symposium on Practical Software Development Environments* (Palo Alto, CA, Dec. 1986), pp. 84–91.
9. Penedo, M. "Prototyping a project master database for software engineering environments." *Second Software Engineering Symposium on Practical Software Development Environments* (Palo Alto, CA, Dec. 1986), pp. 1–11.
10. Dillistone, B. In *Software Engineering Environments* (Brereton, P., ed.) (Ellis Horwood, England, 1988).
11. *Proc. of the Second Workshop on Configuration Management* (ACM, Princeton, NJ, Oct. 1989).
12. Oman, P. *IEEE Software* **7:**3, 59–65 (May 1990).
13. Rombach, H. D. *IEEE Transactions on Software Engineering* **SE-13:**3, 344–354 (Mar. 1987).
14. Osborne, W. M., and Chikofsky, E. J. *IEEE Software* **7:**2, 10–11 (Jan. 1990).
15. Su, S. Y. W., and Shyy, Y. In *Advanced Database Systems* (N. Adam and B. Bhargava, eds.) (Springer-Verlag, New York, 1993) pp. 105–26.
16. Sheu, P. C.-Y., and Peterson, L. J. In *Advanced Database Systems* (N. Adam and B. Bhargava, eds.) (Springer-Verlag, New York, 1993), pp. 65–86.
17. Sheu, P. C.-Y. "Concurrent production systems." *Proc. of 1985 Hawaii International Conference on System Science* (Jan. 1985).
18. Chikofsky, E. J., and Cross, J. H. *IEEE Software,* **7:**1, 13–17 (Jan. 1990).
19. Biggerstaff, T. J. *IEEE Computer* **22:**7, 36–49 (July 1989).
20. Ambras, J., and O'Day, V. *IEEE Software* **5:**3, 50–58 (May 1988).

Advanced Programming Environments

In Chapter 5 some basic facilities provided by a conventional programming environment were discussed. Chapter 11 discusses some advanced concepts related to the programming environment that were explored in the past. These include knowledge-based programming environments (Section 11.1), visual programming environments (Section 11.2), distributed programming environments (Section 11.3), programming environments that support concurrent engineering (Section 11.4), and component software (Section 11.5).

11.1. KNOWLEDGE-BASED PROGRAMMING ENVIRONMENTS

Artificial intelligence integrated within software engineering is a major and active research commitment to enhance software productivity. This development is important because it both aids the software engineer and increases program reliability. By developing a knowledge-based software engineering environment (KBSEE), an expert system can increase productivity and assist all areas of the software development process. For a KBSEE to be effective, it must also be comprehensible and supply tools to assist all areas of software development. A KBSEE differs from conventional software engineering environments in that is created to change specifications to produce efficient implementations. Recent systems use such models as rules, logic, and object-oriented programming as opposed to procedural. The key to these systems lies in the fact that the amount of aid an environment provides is proportional to the level of intelligence and comprehensibility it carries. This intelligence is related to how the knowledge base is implemented and how system components interact with each other. This section briefly summarizes features of two KBSEE environments.

11.1.1. KBEmacs

The MIT began research into knowledge-based techniques to support software engineering in the mid-1970s. The result was a project called the Programmer's Apprentice (PA).[1] The focus was to develop ways of automating tasks used by software engineers. In the process a knowledge-based demonstration system, called the Knowledge-Based Editor in Emacs (KBEmacs), was developed.[2] Though not ideal it displayed most of the capabilities of the PA. The KBEmacs acts as an editor programming assistant by making programming smoother for an expert programmer. It makes it possible to create programs out of algorithmic fragments, to define new fragments and to intermix a knowledge-based editor with syntax-based programming. It also aids in program documentation.

One of the ideas of the PA is to have a division of labor and shared knowledge; in KBEmacs shared knowledge takes the form of *clichis*—a vocabulary of relevant intermediate and high-level algorithmic concepts. The basic ideas of clichis are assumed to be shared with the programmer and the KBEmacs library. The KBEmacs uses these clichis to form programs and program segments to aid the programmer. The following is an example of a clichi that compares two numbers, then returns a Boolean value that states whether or not the numbers differ by less than a given epsilon.[2]

```
clichi EEQUALITY_WITHIN_EPSILON is
  primary roles X, Y;
  described roles X, Y, EPSILON;
  comment "determines whether { the x } and { the y }
    differ by less than { the epsilon }";
  constraints
    DEFAULT ({ the epsilon }, 0.00001);
  end constraints;
begin
  return abs({ the input x} − { the input y}) < { the
epsilon};
end EQUALITY_WITHIN_EPSILON;
```

The programmer accesses this clichi when communicating with KBEmacs by a phrase similar to *an equality_within_epsilon of A and B*.

Referring to the concept of the assistant and the expert, it is common for an expert to give orders to an assistant requesting completion of certain tasks. An example may be to: "Define a simple report program UNIT_REPAIR_REPORT. Enumerate the chain of repairs associated with a unit record, printing each one. Query the user for the key (UNIT_KEY) of the unit record to start from. Print the title 'Report of Repairs on Unit' & UNIT_KEY. Do not print a summary."[2] This request assumes that the expert and assistant share a good deal of knowledge. For example the request assumes the assistant knows what simple report, enumerate the chain, and query the user for the key all mean. In this way KBEmacs clichis serve as a medium of assumed knowledge between the user and the knowledge base.

Similar to the preceding request, knowledge-based commands of KBEmacs allow the user to prompt a request that usually takes the form ⟨verb⟩ followed by ⟨noun phrases⟩. For instance if the user wants to construct a program UNIT _REPAIR_REPORT, the programmer uses a knowledge-based command define in a statement such as, Define a simple_report program UNIT_REPAIR _REPORT. The KBEmacs interprets this statement as Define a program UNIT _REPAIR_REPORT by using the clichi *simple_report*. The KBEmacs communicates results by placing an instance of simple_report in the editor buffer and directly modifying it. In this way the programmer is able to adjust and edit the program normally after the change is completed. The KBEmacs also keeps track of information about the program, such as clichis and clichi constraints to update variable limits later and maintain consistency that the expert may overlook. The KBEmacs has other features, such as automatic documentation; however, since it is still primitive in development, it displays only a small portion of the Programmer's Assistant capabilities.

11.1.2. CHI

The CHI, developed at Kestrel Institute,[3] resulted in a compiler that was self-reliant or bootstrapped due to its ability to refine itself from very high level specifications. The compiler of CHI allows programs to be written in a very high level language and in terms of sets and maps; afterward a program can be compiled into bit vector, list, or hash table representations. These transformations are done in a wide-spectrum language called V. The transformation of one level of code into another is embedded in transformation rules. These rules are kept within a knowledge base of descriptions called DKB, and they carry the single design decision to translate one level of code into another.

From the DKB compilers in the system create default implementations. From a list developed by the system, the user selects a set of transformation rules to develop an efficient implementation. The DKB stores enough information about the process to allow the user to backtrack to select alternative implementation routes. Throughout this process the DKB continues to interact with the user and evolve. In this way as abstract solution to a problem is found, the system creates various branches or paths from the original specification in an attempt to refine it. One of the purposes of the DKB is to maintain a collection of distinct mappings, called properties, defined on objects. The objects represent the relationship between other objects and the objects' internal attributes. An example object describing the V expression 3 * S has the following format:

```
⟨object 495⟩
   instance-of: ⟨generic-object member-op⟩
   element-expr: ⟨object 902⟩ (literal-integer)
   set-expr: ⟨object 113⟩ (variable)
```

Object 495 has three properties: *instance-of*, *element-expr*, and *set-expr*. It is an instance of some generic object *member-op* that evaluates an object of the class *literal-integer* to object 902 (which describes 3), then evaluates an object of the class *variable* to the object 113(S). The DKB has a kernel of special objects called *generic objects* that map uniquely to each construct of the V language. Each CHI object must be an instance of one and only one generic object. A generic object describes certain properties inherent in that instance. Two main properties are generic properties and print forms. Generic properties (P) describes the standard properties applicable to instances of object P. Likewise print forms (P) describes the syntax of an instance of object P. The DKB also develops a way of storing all contexts or states of the knowledge base in a tree. In this way backtracking is simplified when exploring alternative implementations.

The CHI uses V because it is able to represent descriptions at all levels of program synthesis from very high to low; this is a valuable feature, since CHI is used by itself. The V has four components: The procedural component is used to develop target programs or initial code. This component looks similar to PASCAL and may also include first-order logic constructs. Another component describes objects of the DKB in V expressions; values of object properties can be accessed at this level. The other two are components that support compilers in translating V expressions.

11.2. VISUAL PROGRAMMING ENVIRONMENTS

Visual programming refers to using visual techniques—diagrams, freehand sketches, icons, or graphical manipulations—to ease various programming activities, such as design, editing, coding, documenting, and debugging. When the syntax of a programming language includes such expressions, it is called a visual programming language (VPL). On the other hand, a visual programming environment (VPE) provides visual facilities to work with a (visual or textual) programming language.

Visual programming languages are available in different forms. Some visual languages provide a set of graphical user interface (GUI) building blocks so that the user creates the GUI by using and connecting these building blocks. Typically the behaviors (semantics) of such building blocks are implemented in a textual programming language; examples include HyperCard (semantic language: HyperTalk) and Visual Basic (semantic language: Basic). A more uniform approach to visual programming requires program semantics to be visually specified. One typical paradigm uses data flow diagrams: Programs are constructed in terms of a set of data flow diagrams, then automatically transformed into textual forms. Some visual languages are constraint-based; i.e., a program is constructed by establishing a set of constraints presented in some graphical form.

Many visual languages resemble logic programming; i.e., a program is built by establishing a set of rules, but the building is done visually. For example in ThinkPad,[4] objects and data structures can be presented/created graphically and a rule (constraint) can be established by connecting various objects, which may be constants, variables, or predicates. ThinkPad is also an instance of *programming by demonstration,* which allows a program to be built automatically from the demonstrations given by the programmer (for example a binary tree insertion program can be built by showing how a node is inserted graphically). Yet another type of visual languages is *form-based,* where a program is built by constructing and completing various forms (possibly using variables and subforms). This type of visual language can be regarded as extensions of *spreadsheet programming*; it has proved useful in larger domains than spreedsheet programming (e.g., constructing and manipulating matrices). Examples of such languages include Show-and-Tell,[5] Forms,[6] and Form/Formula.[7]

Similar to VPL, VPEs have been presented in various forms.[8] The simplest ones provide a visual interface that includes windows and views (view refers to a particular aspect of a program that can be shown graphically, such as data flow diagrams, entity relationship diagrams, and flow charts). Smalltalk is a typical window-based programming environment. A typical programming environment that provides the user with multiple views of a program is Pecan.[9] Some VPEs support vsual editing; this includes syntax-directed editing (e.g., the Cornell Program Synthesizer)[10] and specification-directed editing, which allows rules in addition to syntax to be imposed on program structures. An example of specification-directed editor is Use.It.[11] More recent VPEs provide object-oriented libraries and extensive tools (e.g., drawing tools, configurations, versions) to help the user create application specific programs; examples of such environments include Agentsheets[12] and VPE.[13]

The domain of VPEs has also been extended to provide *program visualization,*[14] which allows the state of a program (code, data, and control state) and the behavior of the program (or state transitions, execution history) to be visualized. Compared with traditional VPEs, program visualization systems emphasize the dynamics of a program and the ease of visualizing such dynamics from an observer's point of view; therefore a program's visual presentation may be animated or in other ways unrelated to the program's textual contents (or structure). For example a program that implements the quicksort algorithm may be visualized as a set of vertical bars (showing the data state) and a set of data swaps (shown as a sequence of ball pairs connected by a horizontal link). A partial list of program visualization systems includes Tango,[15] Pavane,[16] and Zeus.[17]

It has been widely accepted that the world of computing is strongly driven toward the "point and click" visual programming paradigm. Despite of its many successes, applications of visual programming for large scale problems requires additional work to be done. In Reference 18, issues pertaining to the "scaling-up" problem was pointed out; these include static representation, effective use of screen real estate, documentation, procedural abstraction, interactive visual data abstraction, type checking, efficiency, and persistence.

11.3. DISTRIBUTED OBJECT-ORIENTED PROGRAMMING SYSTEMS

A Distributed Object-Oriented Programming system enables independent workstations or personal computers to operate as a decentralized network environment through object-oriented programming. Object-oriented programming systems provide objects with the ability to execute concurrently on separate processors while allowing the user to maintain an independent workstation environment. Therefore if a workstation malfunctions, the entire network is not affected. Distributed object-oriented systems are very useful for creating networks with dissimilar equipment.[19] A distributed system acts as an operating system to manage object behavior and communication. Examples of object control are synchronization, object interaction, resource management, and security.

It is important for a distributed system to manage object behavior correctly. The operating system must monitor and maintain execution to maximize system speed and data validity. Some important properties of a distributed system according to Ref. 19 are

- *Atomicity:* Actions within the system are either completed fully or terminated in such a way that all changes made by an object are undone. The action must either commit or abort. If the action is successful, it commits. The system then performs actions to make these changes permanent. If the action faults, it aborts. The system then undoes modifications made by that action to prevent invalid partial states from remaining within the system.

- *Serializability:* The system provides for efficient concurrent execution to maximize performance. Scheduling effects of this concurrent execution should be the same as for a sequential one.

- *Permanence:* If an object action is completed successfully, the effects remain intact.

An important control tactic is synchronization, which prevents object operations from conflicting with one another. It is important for serializability to be sustained. A partial state of one object must be protected from the actions of another object. There are many schemes for synchronization, but most fall under the following two schemes[20]:

- *Pessimistic:* Action is taken to prevent conflicts. In the event that an object conflicts with another, the conflicting object is halted until the other object is completed. The commit procedure of the other object is a signal to the conflicting object procedure to proceed.

- *Optimistic:* Action is taken to test objects to see if they interfere with each other. An object is executed and examined to verify that it does not alter data formed from another object. If the object fails the test, it is aborted; otherwise it is executed. This increases concurrency, since objects are not halted. Since there must be several copies of the object to test it, this increases overhead and decreases the system's free memory space.

The system must support request handling in some manner. If the passive object model is used, the direct invocation method is used. In this method patron processes are relocated from object to object whenever an invocation is made. The patron process carries messages and parameters within it to the serving object and back. The active object model uses the message-passing method. In this method the parameters are bundled within the invocation itself and sent to the receiving object. The receiving object then accepts the invocation and unbundles it to process the request.

Security is required to prevent unauthorized clients from accessing objects. One common security method is the capability scheme.[21] A key or capability that holds information about the object name and access rights to it is used to access objects. When an object makes a request, the key is sent as one of the parameters to the serving object. There can be many keys, all with various access rights. Another method is the control procedure.[22] A control procedure to make sure the client's access rights are valid is set up for all object requests. If the check fails, the procedure terminates the request. The advantages of this method is its flexibility, since the scheme can be altered to offer a variety of security algorithms.

Resource management is another essential tool. In the event of workstation failure, adequate secondary storage resources should be available. The system holds one copy of the object in volatile memory for execution, and another copy is maintained on secondary storage in case of failure. Every time an object action commits, the secondary storage is updated with new information. If an object is needed for recovery, it is easily recopied to memory. The system also manages processor scheduling. Schemes are used to maximize throughput and make object communication more efficient. Processes are usually sent to lightly loaded processors to reduce waiting. Another effort is required to make sure objects that make requests are on nearby processors; this reduces time spent waiting for invocations.

The following distributed object-oriented programming systems have successfully been used:

Amoeba[23]: A research project directed by A. Tanenbaum beginning in 1985 at Urije Universiteit in Amsterdam on a distributed operating system with use of object orientation. Amoeba generally operates with large-grain objects using the fixed-type active object model. It uses both pessimistic and optimistic schemes and incorporates the capability scheme for security. Requests are handled by the message-passing method. The processor scheduler uses a pool to optimize idle processor usage.

Argus[24]: A distributed system that operates with both large- and medium-grain objects. The active object model is implemented with a pool of processes to reduce process creation overhead. Synchronization is managed through the pessimistic scheme and read/write-locking mechanisms. No security measures are used in Argus, and invocations are handled by the message-passing method.

Clouds[25]: A distributed system that operates with large-grain objects and employs the passive object model. Two variations of the pessimistic scheme are used, automatic and custom. Automatic implements typical read/write locks. Custom on the other hand operates with semaphores or locks. Security is maintained through the capability scheme, and requests are managed by the direct invocation method.

Eden[23]: Developed at the University of Washington in Seattle under the supervision of G. Almes, A. Black, E. Lazowska, and J. Noe. Eden supports large-grain objects using the fixed version of the active model. Security is handled through the capability scheme, and the pessimistic method of synchronization is used. Object interaction is maintained through the message-passing method.

11.4. COMPONENT SOFTWARE

According to Ref. 26,

> Component software addresses the general problem of designing systems from application elements that were constructed independently by different developers using different languages, tools, and computing platforms. The goal is to have end users and developers enjoy the same high levels of plug-and-play application interoperability that are available to consumers and manufacturers of audiovisual electronic components or commodity and custom integrated circuits.

The key technologies involved in component software include data exchange models that allow data to be uniformly exchanged through drag and drop, copy and paste (clipboard), or application program interface (API) calls; automation, which allows applications to be programmed directly, structured storage, which allows heterogeneous information to be organized and retrieved as logical units; and an interface definition language that translates one object model into another. Component software services, such as object linking and embedding 2.0 (OLE)[27] and common object request broker (CORBA)[28] are provided. The following is a partial list of features provided by OLE:

- *Automation:* Allows applications to employ command sets that operate within and across applications. For example a user can invoke a command from a word-processing program that sorts a range of cells in a spread sheet created by a different application.

- *Object Linking and Embedding:* Enables applications to be linked to data objects within other applications. For instance a spread sheet table can be linked to customized business reports, so as changes are made to this table within the spread sheet application, all report documents are automatically updated. Object embedding is the ability to embed an object within another document without maintaining a link to the object's data source. In both object linking and object embedding, applications supplying objects are called OLE servers, while applications containing objects are called OLE containers. An application can be both an OLE container and an OLE server.

- *Visual Editing:* Allows a user to create rich, compound documents easily, incorporating text, graphics, sound, video, and other diverse object types. It is unnecessary to switch between applications to create segments of the compound document: The menus and tools of the container application automatically change to the menu and tools of that object's original application, so that a user can edit an object in the context of the document, without activating and switching to another application.

- *Drag and Drop:* Enables users to drag objects from one application window to another and drop objects inside other objects.

- *Nested Object Support:* Enables objects to be nested in multiple layers within other objects and establish links to nested objects.

- *Storage-independent Links:* Enables links to be maintained between embeded objects not stored as files on disk.

- *Adaptable Links:* Maintains links between objects in many file move, copy, and rename operations.

- *Version Management:* Objects contain information about the application and version of the application that created them, which enables programmers to handle objects created by different versions of the same application.

- *Object Conversion:* Objects can be converted into different types so that different applications can be used with the same object. For example an object created with one brand of spread sheet can be converted to be interpreted by a different spread sheet application for editing.

- *Optimized Object Storage:* Objects remain on disk until needed and are not loaded into memory each time the container application is opened. The OLE has complete transacted object storage, supporting commits and rollbacks of objects to disk to ensure that data integrity is maintained as objects are stored in the file system.

11.5. PROGRAMMING ENVIRONMENTS FOR CONCURRENT ENGINEERING

It becomes more and more common for the development of large software systems to require concurrent participation of multiple team members, who in many cases are geographically separated. This requires new programming environments to support sharing software artifacts and asynchronous and/or synchronous coordination among the team members.

Several programming environments have been proposed to support concurrent engineering (e.g., Flecse[29] and PACT[30]). For example Flecse provides the following facilities:

- *RCSTool:* Allows users at different sites to access the Revision Control system (RCS) at the same time.

- *Mshell:* A multiuser command interpreter so that multiple users can interleave their commands and share responses.

- *MDebug:* A multiuser debugging tool that allows multiple users to debug a program at the same time by command interleaving and output sharing.

- *Collaborative Software Inspector (CSI):* Allows multiple users to inspect and annotate a program asynchronously. The tool then integrates annotated faults collectively and presents the integrated list to all users. This tool provides a number of multimedia supports, such as audio annotations and teleconferencing.

- *MEdit:* Allows a file to be edited by multiple users at the same time. Concurrency control is achieved by locking at multiple granularities (e.g., at function or line level).

REFERENCES

1. Rich, C., and Waters, C. R. *Programmer's apprentice* (ACM Press, 1990).
2. Waters, C. R. *IEEE Transactions on Software Engineering* **SE-11:**11, 1296–1320 (Nov. 1985).
3. Smith, D. R., Kotik, G. B., and Westfold, S. J. *IEEE Transactions on Software Engineering* **SE-11:**11, 79–103 (Nov. 1985).

4. Rubin, R. V., Golin, E. J., and Reiss, S. P. *IEEE Software* **2**:2, 73–79 (Mar. 1985).
5. Shu, N. C. *Visual programming* (Van Nostrand Reinhold, New York, 1988).
6. Ambler, A. L. "Forms: expanding the visualness of sheet languages." *Proc., 1987 Workshop on Visual Languages* (Aug. 1987), pp. 105–17.
7. Kimura, T. D., Apte, A., Sengupta, S., and Chan, J. *IEEE Computer* **28**:3, 27–35 (Mar. 1995).
8. Ambler, A. L., and Burnett, M. M. *IEEE Computer* **22**:10, 9–24 (Oct., 1987).
9. Reiss, S. P. *IEEE Transactions on Software Engineering* **SE-11**:3, 276–285 (Mar. 1985).
10. Teitelbaum, T., and Reps, T. *Communication ACM* **24**:9, 563–573 (Sept. 1981).
11. Hamilton, R., and Zeldin, S. *IEEE Transactions on Software Engineering* **SE-2**:1, 9–32 (Mar. 1976).
12. Repenning, A., and Sumner, T. *IEEE Computer* **28**:3, 17–25 (Mar. 1995).
13. Karsai, G. *IEEE Computer* **28-3**, 36–44 (Mar. 1995).
14. Roman, G. C., and Cox, K. C. "A taxonomy of program visualization systems." *IEEE Computer* **26**:12, 24 (Dec. 1993).
15. Stasko, J. T. *IEEE Computer* **23**:9, 23–29 (Sept. 1990).
16. Roman, G.-C. *et al. Journal of Visual Languages and Computing* **3-2**, 161–193 (June 1992).
17. Brown, M. H. "Zenus: a system for algorithm animation and multiView editing." *Proc. IEEE Workshop on Visual Languages.*, **4**:9 (1991).
18. Burnett, M. M., Baker, M. J., Bohus, C., Carlson, P., Yang, S., and Zee, P. "Scaling up visual programming languages." *IEEE Computer.* Vol. **28**:3, 45–54 (Mar. 1995).
19. Chin, R. S., and Chanson, S. T. *ACM Computing Surveys* **23**, 91–124 (Mar. 1991).
20. Bernstein, P. A., and Goodman, N. *ACM Computing Surveys* **13**, 185–221 (June 1981).
21. Cohen, E., and Jefferson, D. "Protection in the Hydra operating system. *Proc., 5th ACM Symposium on Operating Systems* (Nov. 1975), pp. 141–160.
22. Banino, J. S., and Fabre, J. C. "Distributed coupled actors: a CHORUS proposal for reliability." *Proc., IEEE 3d International Conference on Distributed Computing Systems* (Oct. 1982), pp. 128–34.
23. Tanenbaum, A. S., and Van Renesse, R. *ACM Computing Surveys* **17**:4, 419–470 (Dec. 1985).
24. Liskov, B. *Communications ACM* **31**:3, 300–312 (Mar. 1988).
25. Ahamad, M., and Dasgupta, P. "Fault-tolerant computing in object-based distributed computing systems." *Proc., IEEE 6th Symposium on Reliability in Distributed Software* (Mar. 1987), pp. 115–25.
26. Adler, R. M. *IEEE Computer* **28**:3, 68–77 (Mar. 1995).
27. Brockschmidt, K. *Inside OLE 2* (MicroSoft Press, Redmond, WA, 1994).
28. OMG TC document 93.12.43 (Object Management Group, Framingham, MA, Dec. 1993).
29. Dewan, P., and Riedl, J. *IEEE Computer* **26**:1, 17–27 (Jan. 1993).
30. Cutkosky, M., Engelmore, R., Fikes, R., Genesreth, M., Gruber, T., Mark, W., Tenenbaum, J., and Weber, J. *IEEE Computer* **26**:1, 28–37 (Jan. 1993).

Other Selected Topics

Chapter 12 includes some other important subjects not discussed in previous chapters; these include project management (Section 12.1), fault-tolerant system design (Section 12.2), and discrete event simulation (Section 12.3).

12.1. PROJECT MANAGEMENT

Software project management is an intricate web of specifications, resources, measurements, milestones, documentation, and management. Project inputs include specifications, resources and manpower; outputs include measurements, documentation, and the final product. The project manager obtains information necessary to produce an outline for the project team to follow, since it is easy to accomplish a task outlined in detail. This outline should also include how progress will be measured and the documentation that must be produced. However even a detailed plan can change during the development of a product. Furthermore after the project is completed, it may require maintenance or upgrading at a later date. This section outlines some steps to consider when managing a software project. The term user applies to either an outside user or an in-house requester, such as the manager of a larger project. The term team refers to the project manager's group of programmers and support personnel.

12.1.1. Manager's Role

The *Soul of a New Machine* illustrates a manager's role in real-world computer development. It describes the manager's work load as heavy while producing proposals and estimates, lighter in the middle while the project is being developed, and heavy at the end when the manager is putting out fires and trying to meet the deadline. During the middle part of the project, the manager serves as an interface to the user (or upper level management) and takes care of the nontechnical operation of the project. The manager also acts as a buffer to isolate the team from problems that do not directly concern it. This buffer allows the team to concentrate on the technical aspect of the project. The manager is ultimately responsible for successful completion of the project. The manager must control the resources needed to complete the project. If the project requires programmers, these employees must be responsible only to that project's manager.

12.1.2. Defining the Problem

Project requirements must be defined before the manager or software team does any work or further analysis. If the problem is not well-defined, a well-designed solution cannot be developed. If the problem is not formally stated in a document, the user's expectation may be misunderstood. Such a document is called the *requirements document*. The manager may have to assist the user in developing the document.

The first section of the requirements document should be an overview of the problem, since it is important to understand the application for which the software will be used. Such an overview provides information to help the manager determine if there are potential conflicts between the problem and the proposed solution. The second section should clearly state the problem so that the user and the project manager can verify that the problem is understood by both parties. Once the problem is identified, the document may outline other factors, such as required performance, budget restraints, support required from the user, documentation requirements, etc. This document should not outline methods used to solve the problem; it can however outline interfaces desired and expectations of the solution. At this point the manager decides if the project can be completed given the identified constraints, such as budget, time, and performance required. The user then reviews the document to verify that the problem identified is correct and the solution is satisfactory.

12.1.3. Proposals

The project manager must now develop a proposal to convince the user to do business with the project manager. Often the proposal is not an in depth study of the problem because for large projects, a proposal could cost a software developer considerable time and money. The depth of the proposal depends on many factors; see Ref. 1. The proposal details what is required to accomplish the project and how it should be done. The first proposal outlines tasks required and resources needed. To permit a detailed estimate, each task is divided into small manageable units; this division may use a work breakdown structure (WBS). The WBS identifies various levels of a project. The top level is the title of the project; it is designated as Level 0. Level 1 further divides the project into subsections; each subsection is further divided in a similar manner into smaller sections. This process is repeated until each task and subtask is divided into a unit small enough to assign to someone to be completed in a relatively short amount of time. It is important for the project manager to determine that the task has been completed.

The WBS may have several different implementations. For instance if the project is very large, upper management may break it down to only the project manager level; from there each project team makes its own WBS to subdivide the task. If the project is smaller, the WBS may encompass the entire project and break down all of the tasks. Once the WBS is developed, it is easier to estimate resources and time required to accomplish the project.

12.1.4. Design

The direction the manger takes to solve a problem also depends on the budget given to complete a task. The design chosen is based on the user requirements and the budget. Several design methods are available; top-level design is similar to the method used to develop the WBS: The problem is determined, then each major section is divided into a tree. This allows an abstract idea to become a detailed implementation scheme by moving down the tree. As we descends the tree, tasks become more specific components.

A bottom-up design approach is used when specifics of a situation are known and must be integrated into a working model. If existing inputs or data/software modules must be integrated, this is the best approach. A process control system is also a good candidate for this approach.

The project manager may have to update initial estimates, including the outputs expected, at this point and advise the customer. Another important point for the manager to remember is breaking down the design into small components that can be completed by a small group in a reasonable amount of time. Testing is also considered at this point: The user or project manager should create an acceptance test plan to outline tests to be applied to the system to verify that it provides the promised services.

12.1.5. Programming

During the programming phase, the project manager's role is more that of a typical manager. Hopefully during design, the problem was broken down into sufficiently small parts for the programming project leaders to manage. The project manager assures that testing is done, milestones are achieved, and documentation is completed. If there are problems completing modules on time or testing modules, the project manager may have to find personnel to assist a team or authorize overtime work. The project manager may use an assortment of CASE tools[1] to track the progress of the project (an advantage of many CASE tools is that they provide testing schemes). Since the worst people for testing a module are the ones who created it, the project manager should ensure that other teams do the testing. Quality assurance is a large part of the manager's duties during this phase, and by ensuring quality while the project is being developed, many problems can be avoided.

12.1.6. System Testing

System testing is the point in the project when all system modules are brought together. A good way of approaching testing is to bring together a few modules for testing by using some simple interface routines that simulate the rest of the system. This allows testers to verify that each module is working as expected. As more modules are added to the system and tested, problems with previously tested sections may arise. By putting the system together piece by piece, it is easier to identify which modules are creating problems. There are two general methods of assembling the final product: top down and bottom up. The choice of one method over the other is similar to the decision in design. If working from known inputs to the final results is easier, the bottom-up approach is preferred. A gee-wiz GUI may be a better candidate for top-down testing, since the whole point of a GUI is the interface.

Several CASE tools assist in testing and managing the testing process.[1] The project manager must ensure that testing is documented and on time; once again additional personnel or resources may have to be added. The manager also needs to coordinate the availability of user-furnished items required for project testing; for example if the user requires a video driver to work with a proprietary video card, the project manager has to ensure that the user makes the item available on time. Once all of the modules are working together, a final systems test is accomplished to ensure the system is performing as specified; this includes running the acceptance testing plan. Any problems found can then be corrected before the user runs the acceptance testing plan.

12.1.7. Acceptance

This is the point in the project when the project manager has to prove the product performs as promised to the user. The acceptance test plan that the user has written or approved assures that everything the two parties agreed to have been realized. This is also the time when required documentation is provided to the user. If there are problems or questions, they are taken care of, and the user may run the acceptance test again.

12.1.8. Operation

The operation phase starts with the installation of the product. Once the system is up and running, additional problems may materialize. If a warranty is provided (and it should be), the project manager may be the contact for repairs. In operation new problems may arise that were not testable, and it is in a company's best interest to fix problems they are responsible for. (The project manager should also be aware that successful completion of this project can result in more projects being awarded by the company.) Training and support for the new product may also be temporarily the project manager's responsibility. If the user has to be taught how to use a complicated system or requires only telephone support, the project manager must delegate these tasks to people who know the whole project. After the warranty, training, and support obligations (as specified in the contract) are met, the project is formally completed. New maintenance or upgrading should be handled as a new project.

12.1.9. Models

Models can facilitate managing software development even though a model cannot accurately depict the real process. However a model gives the programmer, manager, and user a common base for communication. Several popular models assist in planning and managing software projects. The simple WBS mentioned earlier may not be adequate for planning. Since it takes more time to accomplish some tasks than others, each model attempts to take time into account.

The Gantt model uses a series of lines to show start and completion times for various tasks in a project (see Figure 12.1). Unfortunately this model does not adjust for changes or delays during a project. The Critical Path method is used to

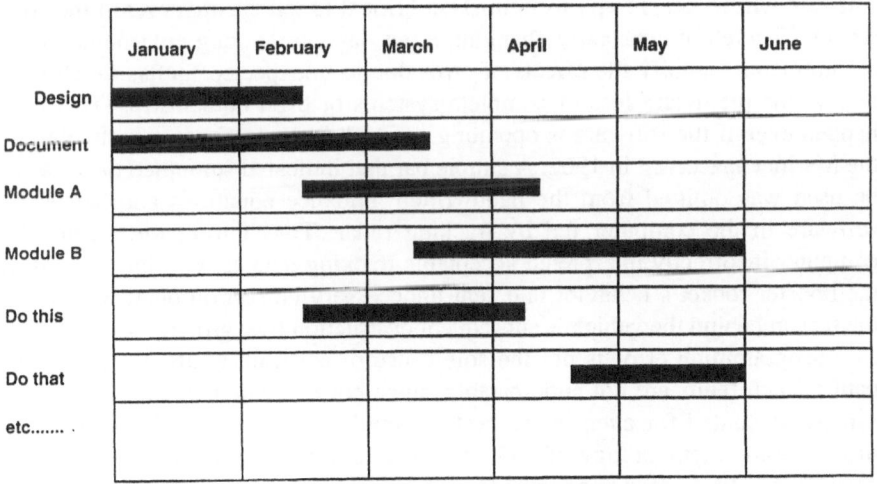

Figure 12.1. A Gantt Chart

keep track of connections between activities. It allows the manager to see the impact of one activity on another in the form of a graph. This model may have weights associated with the paths to estimate completion times. The Pert chart, related to both of the preceding models, represents an engineering process by including best and worst case estimations of completion times with critical paths. This type of chart has been used for many years in almost all engineering design disciplines. The Design Net model is a promising new model that combines Petri nets and AND/OR graphs in an attempt to model software engineering projects. It appears to take into consideration the impact of modules on one another as well as external factors.[2] Some CASE tools provide integration of Pert-type charts with design testing to assist in the whole software management process. Such tools are helpful when managing very large projects.

12.2. FAULT-TOLERANT SYSTEM DESIGN

It is commonly assumed that the software components of computing systems, unlike the more tangible hardware architecture, is immune from the effects of physical punishment, so such terms as reliability and failure rates have no meaning. While many users of personal computer software may back such an assertion, it becomes increasingly invalid in a different scenario. The past several decades have seen the emergence of real-time software applications, primarily in computer control, originally fostered by the needs of the aerospace community. A good example includes the software behind the fly-by-wire flight control systems in modern-day commercial aircraft, such as the European airbus.[3] This software is part of a broad class of increasingly large and extremely complex software whose job is to perform mission-critical functions under real-time constraints. Therefore constantly changing input data, computing environments, or requirements magnify the effects of error due to unexpected faults, which may lead to the premature loss of complete systems or even human life. (This may happen even if the software is operating correctly!) A classic case is the loss of the Mariner spacecraft in 1962: A simple bar that indicated smoothed data was to be used was omitted from the handwritten guidance equations and hence the software in the computer fed by tracking radar. Thus during the ascent, the computer incorrectly interpreted acceptable tracking data as wild fluctuations in the booster rocket's behavior and sent unnecessary correction data, which was the reason behind the vehicle's subsequent destruction by a ground safety officer.

Programming error is not the sole cause of software faults. By their very nature, such faults are not anticipatable, since not every single case (i.e., input) can be accounted for even in the best of simulators. Thus the idea behind the programming methodology of fault-tolerance is not to design software with no errors but to try to reduce errors that may arise by incorporating techniques that allow acceptable, uninterrupted service. This is accomplished by handling faults that remain in the primary software despite preventive measures. It usually helps to discuss fault tolerance with respect to the following four phases: error detection, damage assessment (the degree of system corruption), error recovery (getting the system back into an error-free state), and service continuation (ensuring against the recurrence of nontransient faults).[4] Fault-tolerant software systems generally accomplish these tasks through multiple iterations of a given functional process.[5] The two most common implementations of software fault tolerance include *N*-version programming and recovery blocks.

12.2.1. *N*-Version Programming

The *N*-version programming employs *N* functionally equivalent versions of a program created by *N* groups programming independently and using different algorithms, languages, or translators.[5] Usually $N = 3$ at least, so that all different versions can meet the same specifications; once executed majority voting logic can be used to pass on the presumably correct result to the rest of the system. A driver program (or executive segment) performs the controlling functions among the *N* versions by (1) invoking all the versions, (2) waiting for all versions to execute, and (3) comparing and acting on the *N* set of results.[6]

Some synchronization mechanism is required, usually through the use of the familiar wait and send primitives. All versions wait and do not start execution until a send is processed by the driver; then the driver waits until a send is received from all versions; at this time a voting check can be done on the results. This synchronization scheme must take into account different executions times of various versions and be able to handle the occurrence of an infinite loop generated by a fault in one of the versions. This special case highlights the use of an alternative synchronization scheme whereby a voting check is performed at a predetermined time, accommodating versions that may not be completed under the given time constraint. This allows synchronization to be controlled by the driver, and not by each version.

Each version communicates its results identically to the driver for use in a voting check. Usually the results consist of a vector of values with status flags that provide execution information. If communication traffic during the voting check becomes too large, then alternative methods, such as employing a checksum on the results, may be used.[6] Each version must also have access to identical input values. This can be done by allowing the driver to pass an input set to each version. Since this method may suffer from too much communication overhead, instead, the *N*-versions are sometimes allowed to share input from a common global data structure on a read-only basis. In this case each version retains private data in local structures, thus reducing subsequent execution time.

The central design problem in *N*-version programming concerns the voting check implemented by the driver program. In simple applications (i.e., integer calculations), an equality check can be used in the majority vote. However some applications may employ different algorithms, which results in slight discrepancies among equally tolerable results. In this case "inexact voting" is used, perhaps employing a range check.[6] A combinatorial algorithm can also be used here to analyze differences among received results so that erroneous cases can be eliminated.

Another design issue concerns the frequency of voting checks in a system[5]: If it is too low, it minimizes the inherent communications overhead but may have to account for a larger divergence of numerical variables among more program steps or to suffer from longer wait states. If the frequency is too high, it requires additional commonality among program structures to allow comparisons, which detracts from the goal of making each *N* version as independent as possible. (Damage assessment is unnecessary if each version operates atomically.) Note that the architecture of an *N*-version system follows the fault-tolerant phases mentioned earlier.

Including a voting check ensures error detection. Disregarding erroneous results shown by the check provides error recovery, and identifying minority versions and action taken to prevent similar service disruptions ensures acceptable continuous service.[6]

Systems employing *N*-version programming have been constructed and analyzed. At the heart of US Space Shuttle avionics, five identical computers run software using this fault-tolerant system approach[7]; university-based experiments have also confirmed the benefits of this approach for improving software reliability. One study in particular showed a 20-fold improvement in the probability of single-version failure using a three-version system.[6]

12.2.2. Recovery Blocks

Recovery blocks have successfully been used to ensure fault-tolerance in software systems. A primary module is first executed that satisfies the task according to specifications. Then an acceptance test is executed to determine if the system is entering a nonacceptable state (i.e., to perform error detection). If this is the case, the system returns to a restoration location, almost always before execution of the primary module. At this recovery point, an alternative module of different design and transparent to the rest of system (but compatible with the same acceptance test) is activated in hope that a similar fault will not reoccur (error recovery). Thus backward error recovery eliminates the need for damage assessment. This can be done continually, with multiple standby spares provided as such:

```
Establish recovery point
Primary module
Acceptance test
Alternate module
Acceptance test. . .
```

A more formal syntax for a recovery block scheme that also allows the nesting of multiple recovery block structures follows[6]:

```
ensure ⟨acceptance test⟩
by ⟨primary module⟩
else by ⟨alternate module 1⟩
else by ⟨alternate module 2⟩
. . .
else by ⟨alternate module n⟩
else error
```

Since real-time systems require timely as well as accurate results, a timer mechanism can also be implemented here to allow the invocation of timer-triggered interrupts if a module exceeds its predetermined time limit. This enables control to be passed to an alternative module.

In a system supporting recovery blocks, it is usually assumed that the primary module is designed for maximum efficiency—perhaps using the fastest sorting algorithms or most memory.[7] Subsequent modules need not be similar in design quality to the primary or even provide similar results! The only constraint is that these results still be acceptable to the system (as defined by the acceptance test); thus the recovery block scheme gracefully implements degrading software. The acceptance test may also be split into several separate tests, performed before as well as after execution of a module (i.e., to check input parameters passed to it). Figure 12.2 shows a typical recovery block structure employing a primary module P and a single alternative module Q under an executive program (similar to the driver mentioned earlier) as described in Ref. 5:

> The system executive in this example has a status module, a primary routine failure flag A, and an alternate routine execution counter. Prior to entering the recovery block, the status module checks flag A. If A has not been set (i.e., the primary routine has not failed), the status module formats a call to the primary routine and the recovery block proceeds normally. On entering the block, the executive formats calls to both P and Q and sets the timer for the expected maximum run time of P. Control passes to the primary call and process P is executed. After P is complete, the acceptance test is run, and if the results are acceptable and on time, control returns to the executive. The timer is reset (loaded with the appropriate interval for the next operation) and another recovery block is called (or the previous one is repeated with the new data).

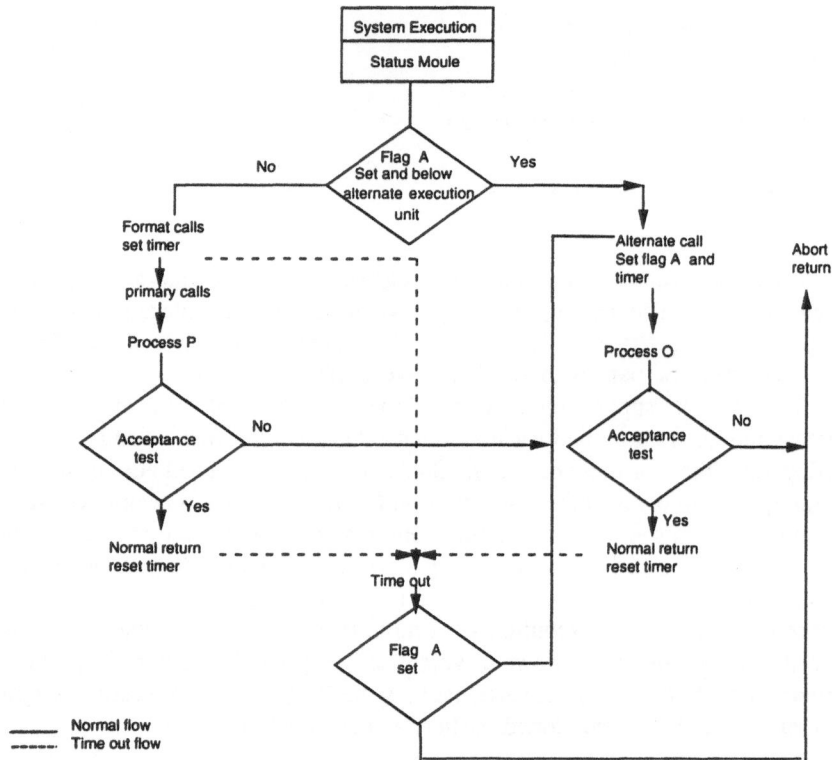

Figure 12.2. Recovery block approach. Reprinted with permission from Ref. 6. © 1986, Prentice-Hall.

If the acceptance test rejects the results of P, or if the results are not furnished within the allocated time, a transfer is made to the alternate call. The flag A is set, the timer is reset for the expected maximum duration of Q, and the process Q is executed. At the (timely) conclusion of Q, the acceptance test is once again run, and if passed, a normal return to the executive occurs and the timer is reset as described above. When the flag A has been set, a different entry into the recovery block occurs. The status module of the system executive examines the alternate routine execution counter. If this counter is below an execution limit (which may be either a system-wide fixed value or routine specific), the status module increments the counter and formats a call to the alternate routine. If, however, the alternate execution limit has been exceeded, the status module resets flag A, resets the alternate execution counter, and formats a call to the primary routine.

If the acceptance test rejects the results of Q, an abort condition exists and the program exits differently. The abort exit will also be taken if the timer runs out before a result is furnished by Q. The setting of flag A prevents execution of Q when this program does not furnish suitable results within the expected time.

It may seem that the stringent timing constraints encountered in real-time environments may prevent the use of alternative modules, but their inclusion and execution times are carefully set to provide selected stability under worst case conditions. The system is designed so that missing inputs or outputs result at most in a transient disturbance from which the system can subsequently recover.[5]

The design of the acceptance test is a final critical point. Its function is to check the acceptability of results from a module or more appropriately, the system state after execution of a module.[6] A recovery cache mechanism is usually provided (by the underlying hardware) and special instructions, such as *establish recovery point,* are accessible by the software. The cache aids development of acceptance tests by storing old values of variables that are made available through the service of a read-only prior instruction. This may be helpful in checking results of a sort operation by a module whose acceptance test can perform a checksum operation on array elements before and after execution of the algorithm.[6] The recovery cache may also store variables updated by specific modules, so that an acceptance test signals an error if it cannot access all variables it thinks a module has updated; thus a cache can help detect errors in the acceptance program itself. For example a valid design decision is usually to impose the constraint that an acceptance test may not change the state of a system during its execution, something the recovery cache itself can monitor.[6]

12.2.3. Recovery Blocks versus *N*-Version Programming

Recovery blocks differ from the *N*-version-programming scheme mentioned earlier: One program runs at a time, and error detection is provided by a test rather than comparison. Yet in the design phase each has its own strengths and weaknesses: *N*-version programming offers the advantage that each program version defines its own data structures for private data during successive program executions.[6] This allows for a greater degree of independence in the algorithms selected for each version performing a given task. Problems can arise however. One already alluded to earlier was the use of inexact voting when a range of results has to be checked. This range may be difficult to calculate, and it can change through successive executions of a version.[6] Lastly a voting check may be inappropriate for a problem with multiple or degrading (but still acceptable) results.

The recovery block scheme has been criticized for using backward error recovery. Such a requirement may be inexpensive for interacting processes or impossible with the use of nonrecoverable objects.[6] The scheme benefits from the fact that a failing module is discarded only during execution when its outputs puts the system in an erroneous state; otherwise the module can still be used in subsequent executions. Also due to its nonparallel nature, this scheme can be implemented with simpler hardware than that required by *N*-version programming.

12.2.4. Designing with Fault Trees

Though a list of all possible faults that can be encountered in a software system is impractical, it is usually possible to generalize different classes of failures in a top-down manner via software fault-tree analysis (SFTA).[8] As a tool fault trees can help identify conditions that may trigger the use of alternative modules and if necessary; fault trees can also be used as documentation in a formal design process. Specifically fault trees can aid in placing acceptance tests.

The use of SFTA was adopted from the use of fault trees in designing fault-tolerant hardware.[5] A tree is constructed by decomposing a top-level event—failure of a complete system—into distinct simpler events, such as failure of particular subsystems, which are linked by AND and OR gates. This is done continuously until it is possible to identify the failure of individual components and events with calculable probabilities. Then the probabilities of higher events are computed through the appropriate gate—AND implying multiplication of probabilities and OR, addition.

Unfortunately when it comes to software, bottom-level (primal) events do not have distinguishable failure probabilities but instead represent events whose failure can be tested in real time. A top-level event represents complete functional failure of a given module, while lower level events correspond to the module's failure to meet individual functional requirements. Tree development stops when failure can be sufficiently identified to be tested or replaced with an alternative routine or when a certain level is reached, as defined by design specifications. By examining the input/output (I/O), process requirements, and associated hierarchy of specific procedures and subroutines (via external documentation), a designer can develop the shape of the trees and determine the correct placement of an acceptance test.

Reference 4 is another work related to fault-tolerant system design; it presents a simplified approach to analyzing concurrent processes inherent in cyclic real-time systems and classifying errors. Designing and modeling hierarchically distributed fault-tolerant computer systems, where different fault-tolerant schemes can be implemented at various individual levels, are discussed in Refs. 9 and 10. Some mention must also be made of software reliability, which plays a central part in evaluating the robustness of fault-tolerant software. Reference 11 describes general probability models used to evaluate recovery block and N-version implementations. Unfortunately gauging software reliability is not a simple matter using any of the methods available.[12]

The ability to use mathematical proofs to ensure that a program follows specifications depends on which environmental aspects the designers model in their system as well as the depth of their understanding of (1) the formal language used in the specs and (2) the application itself. Formal testing on the other hand is commonly cited as having only the ability to establish the presence of errors, but not their absence. Since fault-tolerant techniques presented here cannot assure perfection either, how to rate the safety of critical systems controlled by software is an open issue. Some US government agencies, such as the Federal Aviation Administration, classify design failures as nonquantifiable errors, totally avoiding specification requirements or quantitative measurements of reliability. Reference 12 suggests limiting the role of software in high-risk applications to perform not too critical types of functions, making sure that software reliability can be demonstrated prior to system deployment. While the only remaining course may be to study the effects of design compromise between complexity and reliable operation, many vendors and users of such software systems are hesitant to release statistical information on failures due to industry competition and fear of public reaction. In any event it seems that further refinement and standardization of fault-tolerant techniques will allow software at least to perform better tasks either too laborious or impossible for human beings.

12.3. DISCRETE EVENT SIMULATION

In a discrete event simulation system, changes in the internal state of the system take place at discrete points in simulated time when an event occurs. The system can either be synchronous or asynchronous. In the first case, events are synchronized with a global clock; in an asynchronous discrete event simulation system, each process proceeds according to its own clock without global synchronization.

The following types of data structures are used in sequential simulation:

- *State Variables:* Describe the state of the system at a particular time.

- *Event List:* Shows all pending or scheduled events not yet processed in the system.

- *Global Clock:* Shows how far the simulation has progressed.

Each event in the system should contain information indicating when it is to be processed. This information is contained in a field called the *time stamp* for the event. Once an event has been processed, a new event with a higher valued time stamp (if it exists) can be scheduled for the system to process.

In a concurrent environment, each simulation process is implemented as a logical process (LP), and a set of LPs communicate through message passing. While this works well for ordinary processes, problems may arise in a concurrent simulation system. For example suppose event E1 of process LP1 has time stamp 10, and event E2 of process LP2 has time stamp 20. If LP1 schedules event E3 for process LP2 at a time stamp less than 20, then this can effect the execution of E2. The output of LP2 can be different because E3 may modify some state variables used by E2.[13] Therefore if a process depends on the outcome of event E1 to handle another event E2, then E1 must be processed before E2 or a *causality error* occurs. This is one of the most difficult problems in concurrent discrete event simulation because it is difficult to know if the event with the lowest time stamp in the event queue is indeed the next event in the process.

A concurrent discrete event simulator can be implemented in two ways: conservatively or optimistically. The consecutive approach avoids causality errors at any cost: It processes an event only if it is absolutely safe to do so. An event is considered safe only if all events it depends on have already been executed. The optimistic approach proceeds with any event, then decides if the event has caused a causality error; if it did, then the simulator recovers. This implies that each logical process must store its own history so that the process can revert to some previous state if a causality error occurs.

One popular programming language developed for simulation is MODSIM,[14] which provides constructs available in most object-oriented programming languages. Unlike these languages however, functions (or methods) are called in either of two forms. An ASK call resembles a procedural call: When executing an ASK statement, it requests an object to invoke the method; the calling code waits for the method to finish execution before proceeding further. A TELL statement is similar to an ASK except that the TELL does not wait for completion of the invoked method before proceeding.

The concept of simulation time is supported and maintained automatically in MODSIM. We are concerned only with simulation time when an event occurs that may change the state of objects in the model. Once all activities scheduled for a particular simulation time are completed, the simulation clock is advanced to the next point in simulation for which an activity is scheduled. To keep track of scheduled activities, MODSIM maintains a pending list on which the activity at hand is first. Each object also keeps its own list, thereby creating a two-dimensional structure.

There are in general two approaches to implementing discrete event simulation. One is event-oriented, in which individual routines are written to describe each discrete event in the operation of a system. This approach is fine in smaller models, but as anticipated, it becomes difficult to follow in larger models. For larger models, the process-oriented approach is better, since it allows all the behavior of an object in a model to be described in one or more TELL methods. Also once the actions of the class of objects are gathered together in an object, the simulation program can create multiple and concurrent instances of the object instance, and process objects can interact. This approach uses object-oriented programming to its full capacity to simplify the tasks at hand and handles them in a simple manner in implementing simulations. Another advantage of this method is that since its statements are expressed sequentially, it is almost analogous to the system being described.

The TELL method supports the process approach to simulation. The WAIT statement, an option of the TELL method, specifies the simulation time to elapse. When a WAIT statement is encountered, the TELL method of execution is suspended and resumes after the allocated amount of simulation time has elapsed. For synchronous activities MODSIM uses the WAIT FOR statement: One activity starts a second activity, then suspends its execution and waits for a period of simulation time for the second activity to be completed before resuming execution. A TERMINATE statement terminates a TELL method. The TERMINATE statement is recursive: It not only terminates the method that invoked it but also terminates all methods related to the terminated TELL method.

Some processes must wait for a certain condition before being executed or proceeding in a program. This need is fulfilled by the *TriggerObject* object type in conjunction with the WAIT FOR statement, which permits a pause in the method as it waits for the certain condition to occur. MODSIM also provides for an Interrupt procedure that is different from the TERMINATE method. The Interrupt procedure is used from outside an object's time-elapsing method to wake up the method before it completes the WAIT. The TERMINATE method is used from inside a process object's TELL METHOD to stop premature execution of the method.

Objects in MODSIM can also be "grouped"; i.e., a series of events can be scheduled to occur at a specific time. These events are untyped, since they can hold a variety of types. Objects can be removed from, or added to, a group. There is no limit on the number of groups an object can belong to. Another provision in MODSIM is Resource objects, which are part of the run-time library. Resource objects are very useful for acquiring and distributing resources; they are very easily modified, since they are objects. A *ResourceObj* provides an asynchronous-blocking mechanism; that is it allows simulation time to elapse while waiting for a resource. Resources are a finite pool of elements that may be acquired for some period of simulation time. Once acquired by an object, a resource is unavailable for subsequent requests until it returns to the resource pool. If resources are available, they will be assigned to the requesting object immediately; otherwise requested objects are queued; the calling method is blocked until a resource is available.

12.4. INTERNET PROGRAMMING

The World Wide Web (also known as WWW, or the Web) is a global-area hypertext information repository on the Internet, which is the physical layer of communications which connects millions of computers around the world. Based on the TCP/IP protocol, the Internet uses packet switching for data communication. The Web is an application software which sits on top of the Internet. It employs hypertext links to connect one document to other documents on the Web with *anchors* in a document. Figure 12.3 shows the concept of hypertext link.

The Web can access multiprotocol and multimedia information according to the client/server model. Since the Internet has been introduced, different kinds of services (protocols) have been proposed. Before the Web was introduced, users had to utilize different tools to access different kinds of services such as electronic mail, file transfers, news, remote connections, and so on. One of the advantages provided by the Web is that those services can be accessed with a set of protocols under a unified architecture:

- HTTP (Hypertext Transfer Protocol): the standard protocol that the Web clients and servers use to communicate with hypertexts.

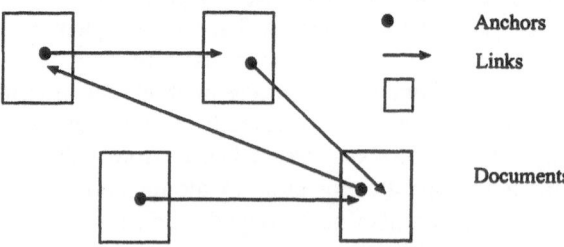

Figure 12.3. Connections of hypertexts.

- SMTP (Simple Mail Transport Protocol): a protocol for sending and receiving electronic messages.

- FTP (File Transfer Protocol): a common method of transferring files across networks.

- Gopher: a versatile menu-driven information service.

- NNTP (Network News Transfer Protocol): a common method by which articles over Usenet can be transferred.

- Telnet: a program which allows users to remotely use computers across networks.

- WAIS (Wide Area Information Services): a service that allows users to intelligently search for information among databases distributed throughout the Internet.

With hypertext links and multiprotocol communication, the diverse services offered on the Internet can now be grouped together in one place. Figure 12.4 shows the functions of the Web on the Internet.

The Uniform Resource Locator (URL) is a standard way to represent different documents, media, and network services on the World Wide Web. A URL is represented in a particular syntax to express a location of resource. The following are some examples:

- `http://www.uci.edu/WWW/library/introduction.html`: This URL refers to a Web server using the Hypertext Transfer Protocol. The name of the Web server is `www.uci.edu` and there exists a file called `introduction.html` in the `WWW/library` directory.

- `ftp://ftp.uci.edu/pub/paper.ps`: This URL refers to a host called `ftp.uci.edu` using the File Transfer Protocol (FTP). The URL refers to the `pub` directory and the `paper.ps` file within the directory.

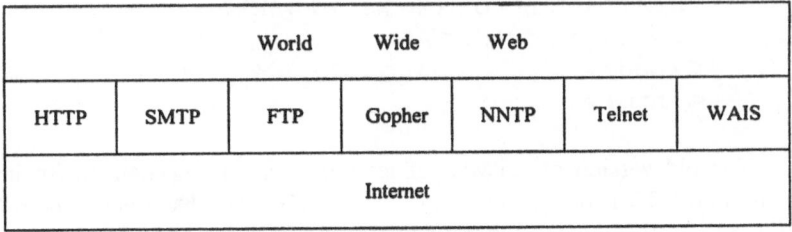

Figure 12.4. Functions of the Web.

The HyperText Mark-Up Language (HTML) is a simple markup language used to create hypertext documents on the Web. HTML is not a page-layout language. Instead, HTML gives users a way to describe the structure of a document by indicating the headings, the emphasis, and the links to other documents and so forth. HTML is defined based on the Standard Generalized Markup Language (SGML). SGML is an international standard for data encoding which is vendor-independent. By tagging data with its role and useful identifiers, SGML allows information to be readily searched and reused. An SGML document has three types of information: *data, structure,* and *format.* The data in a document may include text, graphics, images, sound, and video which can be digitized as well as some information that does not itself appear on the printed page. The tags in SGML identify the structure of a document: the headings, sub-headings, paragraphs, bullet lists, and other components. An SGML document has an associated document type definition (DTD) that specifies the structure of the document. The latest DTD for HTML can be located at *http://www.w3.org/hypertext/WWW/MarkUp/MarkUp.html.*

To denote the various elements in an HTML document, tags are used. An HTML tag consists of a left angle bracket (<), a tag name, and a right angle bracket (>). Tags are usually paired (e.g., <HTML> and </HTML>) to start and end a tag instruction. The end tag looks just like the start tag except a slash (/) precedes the text within the brackets. Some elements, such as the Line Break element, can have just one tag, <BR>. The element tags are case-insensitive. <TITLE> is equivalent to <title>. Every HTML document should contain standard HTML tags. Each document consists of the head text, the body text, and a set of tags to mark the document structure. The head contains the title, and the body contains the actual text that is made up of paragraphs, lists, and other elements. Following is a simple example:

```
<html>
<head>
<TITLE>A Simple HTML Example</TITLE>
</head>
<body>
<H1>Welcome to HTML World</H1>
<P>Hello World.</P>
</body>
</html>
```

The old version of HTML defines only a single mechanism for inserting media into HTML documents using the <IMG> tag. New versions of HTML replace the <IMG> tag with the <OBJECT> tag. A tag <OBJECT> provides a general solution for dealing with images, audio, video, applets, plug-ins, and media handlers while supporting effective compatibility with existing browsers. Using <OBJECT>, an HTML author can specify the data, and/or properties/parameters to initialize the objects to be inserted into an HTML document, as well as the code that can be used to display/manipulate the data. This specification extends HTML to support the insertion of multimedia objects including Java applets, Microsoft Component Object Model (COM) objects (e.g. ActiveX Controls and ActiveX Document embeddings), and a wide range of other media plug-ins.

VRML stands for Virtual Reality Modeling Language. It is a file format for describing 3D objects and worlds on the World Wide Web. The first version of VRML generates virtual worlds with limited interactive behaviors. These worlds can have hyper-links to other worlds, HTML documents, or other valid Multipurpose Internet Mail Extension (MIME) types. MIME provides a way for computers to exchange multimedia information using the Internet mail standards. It specifies image, audio, text, video, and other multimedia and binary file formats. A Web server uses file extensions to specify various MIME types to a Web browser. When the user selects an object with a hyper-link, the appropriate MIME viewer is launched. When the user selects a link to a VRML document from within a correctly configured WWW browser, a VRML viewer is launched, where VRML viewers are applications for navigating and visualizing the Web. More recent versions of VRML allow animations, scripting, enhanced static worlds, and prototyping.

The first version of VRML was created by Silicon Graphics, and was based on the Open Inventor file format. At the highest level of abstraction, VRML is just a way for objects to read and write objects themselves. VRML defines a set of objects useful for doing 3D graphics. These objects are called *nodes*. A node may be a cube, a sphere, a texture map, a transformation, etc. Nodes are arranged in hierarchical structures called *scene graphs*. A scene graph consists of more than one node and it defines an ordering for the nodes. A scene graph has a notion called *state* which means that the nodes that appear earlier in the world can affect nodes that appear later in the world.

Parameters are used by a node to distinguish itself from other nodes of the same type. For example, each Cube node may have a different width, and different texture map nodes may contain different images as the texture maps. These parameters are called *Fields*. A name can identify this node. Naming nodes and referring to them provides information about what is in the world. Nodes do not have to be named, but if they are named, they can have only one name. However, names do not have to be unique. An object hierarchy is implemented by allowing some nodes to contain other nodes. Parent nodes traverse their children in some order during rendering. Nodes that may have children are referred to as group nodes. Group nodes can have zero or more children. The syntax of a node definition in VRML is shown below:

```
DEF objectname objecttype { fields   children }
```

Only the object type and curly braces are required; nodes may or may not have a
name, fields, or children. For example, the following file contains a simple world
defining a view of a cylinder, lit by a directional light:

```
#VRML V1.0 ascii
Separator {
  DirectionalLight {
    direction 0 0 -1 # Light shining from viewer into
world
  }
  PerspectiveCamera {
    position  -8.6 2.1 5.6
    orientation -0.1352 -0.9831 -0.1233 1.1417
    focalDistance    10.84
  }
  Separator {  # The red cylinder
    Material {
      diffuseColor 1 0 0  # Red
    }
    Translation { translation 3 0 1 }
    Cylinder {
    radius 4
    height 3
    }
```

The Common Gateway Interface (CGI) is a means for interfacing external
applications with information servers, such as HTTP or Web servers. A plain
HTML is static, which means a text file doesn't change. A CGI program, on the
other hand, allows the server to execute external applications depending on a
client's request. CGI also makes new documents based on the client's request.
For example (Figure 12.5), a database can be used on the Web to allow clients
around the world to query it. Basically, it is necessary to create a CGI program
executed by the Web to transmit information to the database engine, and to send
the results back to the client. A CGI program is written in a programming
language such as

- Compiled languages: C, C++, FORTRAN, ADA

- Interpreted languages : PERL, TCL, UNIX shell

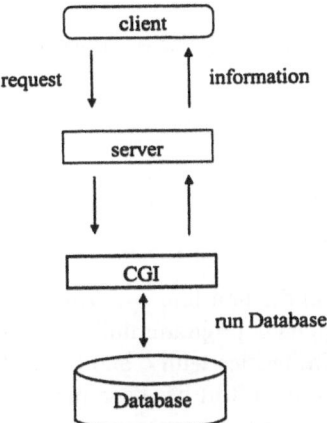

Figure 12.5. CGI.

CGI programs are activated by an anchor tag. As an example, the anchor tag to execute the CGI script `videl_page` on the server `www.uci.edu` can be:

```
<A HREF="http://www.uci.edu/cgi-bin/videl_
page">Videl_page</A>
```

When the web server processes a request to fetch a file, and if the corresponding CGI file is in the server's nominated `cgi-bin` directory, then the script will be run on the server. If the file is not executable then an error will be reported.

A CGI program usually returns an HTML page or image to be displayed as the result of its execution. When a CGI script file executes it may access environment variables to discover additional information about the process that it is to perform. The first line of the returned data must be of the form `Content-type: text/html`, which is an HTML page, or of the form `Content-type: image/gif` which is a gif image. The following is a simple CGI script on a UNIX-based system to return the name of the current system:

```
#!/bin/sh/
echo Content-type: text/html
echo
echo
echo "<HTML>"
echo "<HEAD>"
echo "</HEAD>"
```

```
echo "<BODY>"
echo "<H2> Display the name of the current sys-
tem:</H2>"
echo "<PRE>"
uname
echo "</PRE>"
echo "</BODY>"
echo "</HTML>"
```

Note that on a UNIX system the first line is *#!/bin/sh* and the file is executable.

JAVA is an object-oriented programming language developed by Sun. It shares many syntactical similarities with C and C++. But it is not based on any of those languages, neither any effort has been made to make it compatible with them. JAVA was originally created because C++ proved inadequate for certain tasks. JAVA has several features which C++ doesn't have; these include garbage collection and multi-threading; and JAVA does not include some features that C++ supports like multiple inheritance and operator overloading. JAVA was designed to allow for secure execution of code across a network. There are no pointers in JAVA. JAVA programs cannot access arbitrary addresses in memory. Furthermore JAVA was designed not only to be cross-platform in source form like C, but also in compiled binary form. Since a complied binary form is impossible across different processor architectures, JAVA is compiled to an intermediate *byte-code* which is interpreted on the fly by the JAVA interpreter. Thus in order to port JAVA programs to a new platform an interpreter and a few native code libraries are needed.

As a programming language, JAVA is simple, object-oriented, platform independent, secure, high performance, and multi-threaded:

- *Simple*: JAVA omits many features of C++ like operator overloading (although the JAVA language does have method overloading), multiple inheritance, and extensive automatic coercions. Instead, automatic garbage collection is added to simplify the task of JAVA programming. A common source of complexity in many C and C++ applications is storage management: the allocation and freeing of memory. Due to automatic garbage collection the JAVA language not only makes the programming task easier, it also dramatically cuts down bugs.

- *Object-Oriented*: Almost everything in JAVA is either a class, a method, or an object.

- *Platform Independent*: In general, a network consists of different kinds of systems with different kinds of CPUs and operating system architectures. To enable a JAVA application to execute on any platform in a network, the compiler generates an architecture-neutral object file format: the compiled code is executable on many processors, given the presence of the JAVA runtime system. JAVA programs are compiled to a byte-code format that can be read and run by interpreters on many platforms including Windows 95, Windows NT, and Solaris 2.3.

- *Secure*: JAVA is intended for use in networked/distributed environments. Therefore, JAVA code can be executed in an environment that prohibits it from introducing viruses, deleting or modifying files, or otherwise performing data destroying and computer crashing operations.

- *High Performance*: The byte-code format was designed to generate machine codes, so the actual process of generating machine code is generally simple. Efficient code is produced: the compiler does automatic register allocation and some optimization when it produces the byte-codes.

- *Multi-Threaded*: JAVA is inherently multi-threaded. A single JAVA program can have many different threads proceeding independently and continuously.

JAVA makes it possible for programs to be distributed across the networks and run on many different kinds of computers. This allows executable programs to be download from a Web server to any Web client. JAVA has a way to include inline sound and animation in a web page. JAVA also lets users interact with a web page. Instead of just reading it and perhaps filling out a form, users can now play games, calculate spreadsheets, chat in real-time, get continuously updated data, and so on. Here are just a few of the many things JAVA can do for a web page:

- Inline sounds that play in real-time whenever a user loads a page
- Music that plays in the background on a page
- Cartoon style animations
- Real-time video
- Multiplayer interactive games

Figure 12.6 shows the JAVA operations between a web server and a web client.

JAVA applets are designed to be small, fast, and transferable over network resources. JAVA applets are compiled JAVA programs that are run through a Web browser that supports JAVA. An applet can display graphics, play sound, and manipulate data. Because applets are small, they can be downloaded and executed very fast. JAVA applications are standalone programs written in JAVA and executed independently of the browser. The execution is done using the JAVA interpreter.

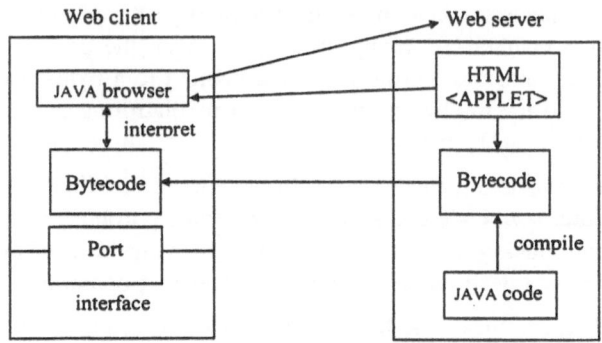

Figure 12.6. JAVA operations.

JAVASCRIPT is an easy-to-use, open, cross-platform scripting language. While JAVA is compiled, relatively complex, and distinct from HTML, JAVASCRIPT is interpreted, simple to use and compatible with HTML. JAVASCRIPT has many built-in objects that require minimal efforts for creation. Because JAVASCRIPT is interpreted, all object references are checked at runtime. JAVA applets can be called from an HTML document with the use of an <APPLET> tag where the actual complied code resides in a separate file. JAVASCRIPT can be embedded directly into the HTML code.

REFERENCES

1. Rakos, J. J. *Software project management for small-to-medium-sized projects* (Prentice-Hall, Englewood Cliffs, NJ, 1990).
2. Liu, L.-C., and Horowitz, E. *IEEE Transactions on Software Engineering* **15,** 1280–1293 (Oct. 1989).
3. Voges, U. *Software diversity in computerized control systems* (Springer-Verlag, New York, 1988), pp. 85–104.
4. Anderson, T., and Knight, J. C. *IEEE Transactions on Software Engineering* **SE-9:**5, 355–364 (May 1983).
5. Pradhan, D. K., ed. *Fault-tolerant computing: theory and techniques,* vol. 2 (Prentice-Hall, Englewood Cliffs, NJ, 1986), pp. 658–95.
6. Lee, P. A., and Anderson, T. *Fault tolerance: principles and practice* (Springer-Verlag, New York, 1990), pp. 205–41.
7. Chien, P. *Compute* **13:**8, 96 (Aug. 1991).
8. Leveson, N. G., and Stolzy, J. L. *IEEE Transactions on Reliability* **R-32:**5, 479–484 (Dec. 1983).
9. Shieh, Y.-B., Ghosal, D. Chintamaneni, P. R., and Tripathi, S. K. *IEEE Transactions on Software Engineering* **16,** 444–457 (Apr. 1990).
10. Neumann, P. G. *IEEE Transactions on Software Engineering* **SE-12,** 905–919 (Sept. 1986).
11. Scott, K. R., Gault, J. W., and McAllister, D. F. *IEEE Transactions on Software Engineering* **SE-13,** 582–592 (May 1987).

12. Littlewood, B., and Strigini, L. *Scientific American* **267**:5, 62–75 (Nov. 1992).
13. Fujimoto, R. *Communications of the ACM* **33**:10, 30–53 (Oct. 1990).
14. Belanger, R., Donovan, B., Morse, K., and Rockower, D. *MODSIM II: The language for object-oriented programming, reference manual* (CACI Products, San Diego, CA, 1990).

Index